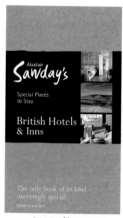

£14.99/$23.95

£12.99/$23.95

£14.99/$23.95

£14.99/$23.95

Alastair

Sawday's

Special Places to Stay

Twelfth edition
Copyright © 2007 Alastair Sawday
Publishing Co. Ltd

Published in September 2007

Alastair Sawday Publishing Co. Ltd,
The Old Farmyard, Yanley Lane,
Long Ashton, Bristol BS41 9LR, UK
Tel: +44 (0)1275 395430
Fax: +44 (0)1275 393388
Email: info@sawdays.co.uk
Web: www.sawdays.co.uk

The Globe Pequot Press,
P. O. Box 480, Guildford,
Connecticut 06437, USA
Tel: +1 203 458 4500
Fax: +1 203 458 4601
Email: info@globepequot.com
Web: www.globepequot.com

Design concept: Company X, Bristol
Maps: Maidenhead Cartographic Services
Printing: Butler & Tanner, Frome
UK distribution: Penguin UK, London

ISBN-13: 978-1-906136-02-4

A responsible business: we are committed to being a green and socially responsible
business. Here are a few things we already do: our pool cars run on recycled cooking oil
and low-emission LPG; our award-winning eco-offices are equipped with solar-heated
water, wood-pellet heating, and rainwater-fed loos and showers; we were the world's
first carbon-neutral publishing company; and we promote local and organic food via our
Fine Breakfast Scheme. Find out more at www.sawdays.co.uk

Paper and print: we have sought the lowest possible ecological 'footprint' from the
production of this book. Whenever possible, we will use paper that is either recycled
(with a high proportion of post-consumer waste) or FSC-certified, and give preference
to local companies in order to foster our local economy and reduce our carbon
footprint. Our printer is ISO 14001-registered.

Alastair Sawday's

Special Places to Stay

British
Bed & Breakfast

4 Contents

We are a small company, born in 1994 and growing slowly but surely every year – in 2007 we sold our millionth book. We have always published beautiful and immensely useful guide books, and we now also have a very successful website.

There are about 35 of us in the Company, producing the website, about 20 guide books and a growing series of environmental books under the Fragile Earth imprint. We think a lot about how we do it, how we behave, what our 'culture' is, and we are trying to be a little more than 'just a publishing company'.

Environmental & ethical policies

We have always had strong environmental policies. Our books are printed by a British company that is ISO14001 accredited, on recycled and/or FSC-certified paper, and we have been offsetting our carbon emissions since 2001. We now do so through an Indian NGO, which means that our money goes a long way. However, we are under no illusions about carbon-offsetting: it is part of a strong package of green measures including running company cars on gas or recycled cooking oil; composting or recycling waste; encouraging cycling and car-sharing; only buying organic or local food; not accepting web links with companies we consider unethical; and banking with the ethical Triodos Bank.

In 2005 we won a Business Commitment to the Environment Award and in 2006 a Queen's Award for Enterprise in the Sustainable Development category. All this has boosted our resolve to promote our green policies.

Eco offices

In January 2006 we moved into our new eco offices. With super-insulation, under-floor heating, a wood-pellet boiler, solar panels and a rainwater tank, we have a working environment kind to ourselves and to the environment. Lighting is low-energy, dark corners are lit by sun-pipes, materials are natural and one building is of green oak. Carpet tiles are from Herdwick sheep in the Lake District. The building is a delight to work in.

Ethics

We think that our role as a company is not much different from our role as the individuals within it: to play our part in the community, to reduce our ecological footprint, to be a benign influence, to foster good human relationships and to make a positive difference to the world around us.

Another phrase for the simple intentions above is Corporate Responsibility. It is a much-used buzz-phrase, but many of those adopting it as a policy are getting serious. A world-wide report by the think-tank Tomorrow's Company has revealed quite how convinced the world's major companies are that if they do not take on full responsibility for their impact, social and environmental, they will not survive.

The books – and a dilemma

So, we have created popular books and a handsome website that do good work. They promote authenticity, individuality and good local and organic food – a far cry from corporate culture. Rural economies, pubs, small farms, villages and hamlets all benefit. However, people use fossil fuel to get there. Should we aim to get our readers to offset their own carbon emissions, and the B&B and hotel owners too?

We are gradually introducing green ideas into the books: the Fine Breakfast Scheme that highlights British and Irish B&B owners who use local and organic food; celebrating those who make an extra environmental effort; gently encouraging the use of public transport, cycling and walking. We now give green and 'social' awards to pubs in our pub guide.

In 2006 we published the very successful *Green Places to Stay*, focusing on responsible travel and eco-properties around the globe. Bit by bit we will do more, and welcome ideas from all quarters. Our aim is to be a pioneering green publisher, and to be known as one. We hope one day to offer energy audits to our owners, to provide real help to those who want to 'go green'. And we will continue to champion the small-scale. We will also continue to oppose policies that encourage the growth of air traffic – however contradictory that might seem.

Our Fragile Earth series

The 'hard' side of our environmental publishing is the Fragile Earth series: *The Little Earth Book*, *The Little Food Book* and *The Little Money Book*. They consist of bite-sized essays, polemical, hard-hitting and well researched. They are a 'must have' for anyone who seeks clarity about some of the key issues of our time. We have also published *One Planet Living* with WWF.

A flagship project is the *The Big Earth Book*; it is packed with information and a stimulating and provocative read. It is being promoted, with remarkable generosity, by Yeo Valley Organic.

Lastly – what is special?

The notion of 'special' is at the heart of what we do, and highly subjective. We discuss this in the introduction to every book. We take huge pleasure in finding people and places that do their own thing – brilliantly; places that are unusual and follow no trends; places of peace and beauty; people who are kind and interesting – and genuine.

We seem to have touched a nerve with hundreds of thousands of readers; they obviously long for the independence that our books provide, for the warm human contact of Special Places, and to be able to avoid the banality and ugliness of so many other places.

A night in a Special Place can be a transforming experience.

Alastair Sawday

This is our flagship book, perhaps jointly with *French Bed and Breakfast*, so it matters greatly to us how it looks, feels, reads and works. We have entrusted the role of editor to Nicola Crosse for several years now, and her performance becomes more impressive by the book. She is a star, a veritable Dame, and this applause is the least she deserves. Her job is far more complicated than one might imagine. Readers telephone with urgent requests for "somewhere nice to go on holiday with fifteen members of my family, near the sea" or from a mobile to whisper that a dog is eating their breakfast and what should they do? Nicola is unflappable and gifted with a deep reserve of good humour. It sees her, and us, through whatever the gods can throw at us. The result is a book steeped in the best of Britain and its people.

Wendy Ogden is as calm and imperturbable as Nicola, unfailingly kind and helpful. She is the other half of the team of two, and a wonderful asset. We are very lucky to have her with us for this, her second, book. And a huge cheer for Jo Boissevain, whose hawk-eyed scrupulousness has ensured that not a word dare leave the building without her permission. She's a great copy editor.

Alastair Sawday

Thanks to: those people who did an inspection or two!

Series Editor
Alastair Sawday

Editor
Nicola Crosse

Assistant to Editor
Wendy Ogden

Editorial Director
Annie Shillito

Writing
Nicola Crosse

Accounts
Bridget Bishop, Rebecca Bebbington, Christine Buxton, Sandra Hasell, Amy Lancastle, Sally Ranahan

Editorial
Sue Bourner, Kate Ball, Jo Boissevain, Melanie Harrison, Jackie King, Florence Oldfield, Maria Serrano, Kate Shepherd, Becci Stevens, Danielle Williams

Production
Julia Richardson, Tom Germain, Rebecca Thomas, Emma Wilson

Sales & Marketing & PR
Rob Richardson, Thomas Caldwell, Sarah Bolton

Web & IT
Russell Wilkinson, Chris Banks, Isabelle Deakin, Joe Green, Brian Kimberling

Previous Editor
Laura Kinch

Inspections
Jan Adam, David Ashby, Abigail Ballinger, Neil Brown, Anne Coates, Angie Collings, Trish Dugmore, Jane Elliott, Becca Harris, Vickie MacIver, Kim Mattia, Suzie Mickleburgh, Robert & Glyn Newey, Scott Reeve, Aideen Reid, Henrietta Thewes, Bridget Truman

B&Bs have changed beyond recognition. Many are now as smart, as interesting, as beautiful and as comfortable as most hotels – and sometimes far more so. They are also, of course, terrific value. Above all, they can be fun, they can introduce you to new friends, and you know that you are putting your money into the community where you are sleeping.

In this edition of our much-loved guide there are over a hundred places new to us, some of them farmhouses in gorgeous countryside, but also more townhouses and more B&Bs purpose-built by younger folk experimenting with a change in lifestyle. You get more independence, for that is what the owners like themselves, and they are often greener, too.

The new green mood is emerging partly because it is fashionable and partly because we encourage it. We insist that all new owners sign our Fine Breakfast Scheme pledge, promising to serve only local or organic food whenever possible. It has made a difference – your breakfasts in our Special Places can almost be guaranteed to be wonderful. There are more smallholders emerging, too, living the good life with chickens, hens, pigs, etc, and B&B to help support it all. There is more vegetable growing by our owners, and there are more allotment holders among our town B&B owners. (My wife is an allotment addict, and I am in full digging support.) More owners have wildflower meadows, wildlife trails and places to birdwatch.

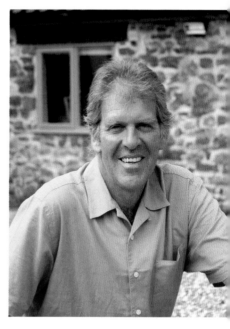

Another welcome change is that it is easier to travel to B&Bs by public transport. We have about 160 places where the owner will collect you – a Cumbrian owner recently collected me in an old Bentley – so you can leave the car at home.

I look on the world of B&B with growing affection, as things just get better and better. My only regret is that more and more visitors are demanding greater comforts and more 'gizmos'. This is a reflection, of course, of the times, but I have a soft spot for those owners who still prefer their rooms to be old-fashioned B&B rooms rather than hotel look-alikes. Bravo – especially if they do so with panache and personality.

Alastair Sawday

Photo: Tom Germain

Let's face it, office life needs all the injections of fun it can get. And here at Sawday's we don't need much of an excuse to enjoy ourselves. We celebrate birthdays, coo and marvel over the babies that are brought in by staff members, have monthly lunches together to get a chance to talk, and, on Fridays, a small delegation usually heads to the local pub for lunch. The allotment also provides a focal point for staff to meet and chat about how well the runner beans are doing, or what needs watering.

Every Thursday we have an office meeting to discuss departmental news and catch up with any notices. It takes place in our beautiful kitchen, from which we are lucky enough to look over swaying grasses, scented lavenders and tufted erigeron to the glassy pond.

From time to time, owners in the book send me heart-warming and amusing anecdotes from the battlefield that is B&B, and we like to recount these tales at the office meeting for the benefit of those members of staff who have little or no direct contact with owners. Telling these stories often gives us a merry titter or a warm glow, so we thought we'd share the best of them.

Our owners can often recommend secret beaches, gorgeous tea rooms, hidden-away pubs and lovely walks and gardens to visit

Winners of the biggest 'aaaah' factor were the stories of B&B owners' children or grandchildren attempting to help when guests arrive. One nine-year-old insists on answering the door and solemnly announcing himself 'the butler' whereupon he helps carry the bags upstairs, although declaring himself 'a little short for the role still'. Sadly, they are not all so cherubic; one boy answered the door as Spiderman and 'killed' the baffled guests. We liked the story of the ten-year-old girl who haplessly decided to come down to breakfast before getting dressed and loved the one about a four-year-old who climbed into bed with some guests and demanded a story at 6am – of course, they obliged.

Farm animals have interrupted arrivals (an owner's horse decided to foal on the front garden lawn just as guests were driving up to the door) and one farming

Photo right: Claveys Farm, entry 404
Photo left: Halftides, entry 38

couple delivered lambs in between the main course and the pudding with hardly a hiccup. One guest asked an owner on a farm if she could keep the animals quiet – the animals in question being sheep – and the owner solemnly replied that she would ask them but didn't know if they would take much notice.

A family donkey tried to rip the wing mirror off a guest's smart vintage Bentley, a mischievous parrot, meant to remain in the kitchen, shot through to the dining room and sat on the shoulder of a guest trying to have breakfast, and a runaway hamster took up residence in a guest bedroom and terrorised an elderly American lady. Dogs, as usual, have the last laugh. An owner's two dogs stealthily stole a toupee from a guest's bedroom and enjoyed a huge tug-of-war with it in the garden. The horrified owner rescued the wig, gave it a good shampoo and blow dry and popped it back in the bedroom; the guest came down to breakfast the next morning with a bouffant quiff. Not a word was said. And entire armies of Jack Russells seem to enjoy stealing tights and bras from guests' bedrooms in order to drag them through shrubberies before depositing them again. I can't imagine why they think that's fun.

Of course, sex rears its head in some of the letters. One owner was admiring the view from the bedroom window with the guests, a young husband and wife, when the husband suddenly jumped, turned to the owner and said, "Well, really!". It was only then that the family dog emerged from between his legs; he thought he had been 'goosed' by a lady 30 years his senior! I should also mention that the incidents of mistaken rooms, sudden flashes of nudity and embarrassed silences at breakfast seem to be an occupational hazard, and we do have an owner in Devon who tried to put a hot water bottle into bed while the guests were in it (she thought they were at the pub). Another owner reports finding a large torch and a packet of cashew nuts at the bottom of a retired vicar's bed – we hope he found what he was looking for…

My favourite one of all though came from a lady in London who was new to B&B and was considering offering dinner. She invited her daughter round for a test run and served her three courses perfectly at the dining room table. Just as she was clearing the table at the end and offering coffee she bent down to pick up a napkin from the floor and inadvertently emitted a little wind. "You're not fit to offer dinner to guests, Mother!" thundered her daughter.

It's not all plain sailing, the B&B life, but it does sound to us as if, mostly, everybody is having fun – both owners and guests – in these lovely, human, sometimes wacky, always special places. So thanks for sharing your funny stories with us, and livening up Thursdays no end.

Happy travelling!

Nicola Crosse

It's simple. There are no rules, no boxes to tick. We choose places that we like. We also recognise that one person's idea of special is not necessarily someone else's so there is a huge variety of places, and prices, in the book. Here you will find traditional country houses alongside converted barns brimming with contemporary art; stone cottages, weatherboard seaside homes, elegant townhouses, Edwardian and Victorian suburbia, windswept crofts in the Highlands, and a sprinkling of castles. The owners are a dazzling lot, too: you may meet farmers, actors, gardeners, potters, musicians, vintage car enthusiasts, stamp collectors, gay folk and straight folk, old duffers and young blades, hunting fans and hunt sabs, owners who will be hovering with freshly baked cake when you arrive, others who will be out in the fields or shopping for your supper and will leave the key under a stone. Mostly these are people's homes; you will encounter family life and its attendant chaos in some, and complete privacy in others. So, how to find the best place for you? Our descriptions are carefully composed to help you steer clear of places that will not suit you but lead you instead to personal paradise. So read between the lines: what we don't say is sometimes as important as what we do.

Our owners are passionate about their patch and can often recommend secret beaches, gorgeous tea rooms, hidden-away pubs and lovely walks and gardens to visit – occasionally ones that aren't normally open to the public. Some may provide maps, and even a dog, to guide you home again.

Occasionally misunderstandings occur, even with the best of intentions. So if something is awry, please don't seethe silently and write to us a week later. Say something to the owners at the time! They will be keen to put things right if they can, and it can dissolve a lot of tension if everyone is honest.

These are people's homes; you will encounter family life and its attendant chaos in some, and complete privacy in others

Inspections

We visit every place in the guide to get a feel for how both house and owner tick. We don't take a clipboard and we don't have a list of what is acceptable and what is not. Instead, we chat for an hour or so with the owner and then look round the house. It's all very informal, but it gives us an excellent idea of who would enjoy staying there. If the visit happens to be the last of the day, we sometimes stay the night. Once in the book, properties are re-inspected every three years so that we can keep things accurate.

Feedback

In between inspections we rely on feedback from our army of readers, and staff members who benefit from a familiarisation scheme and are therefore encouraged to visit properties across the series. This feedback is invaluable to us and we always follow up on comments. With your help and our own inspections we can maintain our reputation for accuracy.

The thriving relationship between us, our owners and our readers makes this the most dependable B&B guide. With regular communication, things are kept relevant and fresh. We take people in to and out of the book in response to what you and our inspectors tell us, so please stay in touch and tell us about your discoveries.

Our books celebrate human kindness, fine architecture, real food, history and landscape; we hope they are your passport to uplifting experiences. Don't forget to let us know how you got on – use the feedback form in this book or on our website at www.sawdays.co.uk.

Subscriptions

Owners pay to appear in this guide. Their fee goes towards the high cost of inspections, of producing an all-colour book and of maintaining our website. We only include places and owners that we find positively special. It is not possible for anyone to buy their way into our guides.

The thriving relationship between us, our owners and our readers makes this the most dependable B&B guide

Disclaimer

We make no claims to pure objectivity in choosing our Special Places. They are here because we like them. Our opinions and tastes are ours alone and this book is a statement of them; we hope that you will share them. We have done our utmost to get our facts right but apologise unreservedly for any mistakes that may have crept in.

You should know that we do not check such things as fire alarms, swimming pool security or any other regulation with which owners of properties receiving paying guests should comply. This is the responsibility of the owners.

Photo right: Harrowfields, entry 516
Photo left: Kennels Cottage, entry 567

Maps

The best start to planning your trip is to look at the maps at the front of the book. If you were seeking a house by the sea in Devon and you merely flicked through the Devon section, you might miss a beachside gem just over the border in Somerset or Cornwall. In cities, check individual entries for their position by postcode: www.multimap.com is a useful site.

Symbols

Below each entry in the book you will see some little black symbols. At the very back of the book is a short table explaining what each symbol means, but below is a fuller explanation of some of them. Use the symbols as a

guide, not as a statement of fact – owners occasionally bend their own rules, so it's worth asking if you may take your child or dog even if they don't have the symbol.

Children – The 👶 symbol is given to owners who accept children of any age. They are unlikely to have cots, highchairs, safety equipment or all the paraphernalia you need, so do check. If an owner welcomes children but only those above a certain age, we have put these details at the end of their write-up. These houses do not have the child symbol, but even these folk may accept your younger child if you are the only guests. Many who say no to children do so not because they don't like them but because they may have a steep stair, an unfenced pond or they find balancing the needs of mixed age groups too challenging.

Pets – The 🐕 symbol is given to places where your pet can sleep in your bedroom but not on the bed. Be realistic about your pet – if it is nervous or excitable or doesn't like the company of other dogs, people, chickens or children, then say so.

Owners' pets – The 🐈 symbol is given when the owners have their own pet on the premises. It may not be a cat! But it is there to warn you that you may be greeted by a dog or serenaded by a parrot, or indeed sat upon by a cat.

Photo: Alstonefield Manor, entry 94

Quick reference indices

At the back of the book (page 389) we list those owners:

• with houses suitable for wheelchair users
• who charge £70 or under for a room for two
• who are happy for you to stay all day
• with single rooms or who charge no single supplement
• who have wireless internet access available for guests.

A further listing refers to houses within two miles of a Sustrans National Cycle Network route (see map on page 395). Take your own bike or check if you can hire or borrow one from the owners before you travel, and enjoy a cycle ride on your break.

We only include places and owners that we find positively special. It is not possible for anyone to buy their way into our guides

Green entries

For the third time we have chosen, very subjectively, half a dozen places which are making a particular effort to be eco-friendly and have given them a full page

and an extra photo to illustrate what they're up to.

This doesn't mean other places in the guide are not taking green initiatives – many are – but we have highlighted just a few. A growing number of our B&B owners recycle, use solar heating, tend their land and animals organically, plant woodlands to encourage wildlife, cycle to post letters rather than take the car, buy natural cleaning products and renewable energy for their homes, and use eco-building methods and local building materials. The entries that had green pages in the last two editions have been given a green leaf symbol.

Types of houses

Some houses have rooms in annexes or stables, barns or garden 'wings', some of which feel part of the house, some of which don't. If you have a strong preference for being in the throng or for being apart, check those details. Consider your surroundings when you are packing: large, ancient country houses may be cooler than you are used to; city places and working farms may be noisy at times; and that peacock or cockerel we mention may disturb you.

Some owners give you a front door key so you may come and go as you please; others like to have the house empty between, say, 10am and 4pm. If you would prefer not to wander far during the day then look for the places that have the 'All day' quick reference at the back of the book (p.390).

Rooms

Bedrooms – We tell you if a room is a double, twin/double (ie. with zip and link beds), suite (with a sitting area), family or single. Most owners are flexible and can juggle beds or bedrooms; talk to them about what you need before you book. It is rare to be given your own room key in a B&B.

Bathrooms – Most bedrooms in this book have an en suite bath or shower room; we only mention bathroom details when they do not. So, you may get a separate bathroom (yours alone but not in your room) or a shared bathroom. Under certain entries we mention that two rooms share a bathroom and are 'let to same party only'. Please do not assume this means you must be a group of friends to apply; it simply means that if you book one of these rooms you will not be sharing a bathroom with strangers. If these things are important to you, please check when booking. Bath/shower means a bath with shower over; bath and shower means there is a separate shower unit.

Sitting rooms – Most B&B owners offer guests the family sitting room to share, or they provide a sitting room specially for guests. If neither option is available we generally say so, but do check. And do not assume that every bedroom or sitting room has a TV.

Meals

Unless we say otherwise, a full cooked breakfast is included. Some owners – particularly in London – will give you a good continental breakfast instead. For organic or locally sourced breakfasts, look out for the Fine Breakfast Scheme egg cup

Photo: Furzehill Farm, entry 651

symbol at the bottom of the page (see p. 385 for full details of the scheme). Some owners are fairly unbending about breakfast times, others are happy to just wait until you want it, or even bring it to you in bed.

Apart from breakfast, no meals should be expected unless you have arranged them in advance. Although we don't say so on each entry – the repetition a few hundred times would be tedious – all owners who provide packed lunch, lunch or dinner need ADVANCE NOTICE. And they want to get things right for you so, when booking, please discuss your diet and meal times. Meal prices are quoted per person, and dinner is often a social occasion shared with your hosts and other guests.

Do eat in if you can – this book is teeming with good cooks. And how much more relaxing after a day out to have to move no further than the dining room for an excellent dinner, and to eat and drink knowing there's only a flight of stairs between you and your bed. Very few of our houses are licensed, but most are happy for you to bring your own drink.

Price range and minimum stays

Each entry gives a price PER ROOM for two people. We also include prices for single rooms, and let you know if there is a supplement to pay should you choose to loll in a double bed on your own.

The price range for each B&B covers a one-night stay in the cheapest room in

low season to the most expensive in high season. Some owners charge more at certain times (during regattas or festivals, for example) and some charge less for stays of more than one night. Some owners ask for a two-night minimum stay at weekends and we mention this where possible. Most of our houses could fill many times over on peak weekends and during the summer; book early, especially if you have specific needs.

Bookings

The most popular way of booking remains the phone. That way both sides can get the feel of people and place. Do be clear about the room booked and the price for B&B and for meals. Say roughly what time you will arrive (normally after 4pm), as most hosts like to welcome you personally. Be on time if you have booked dinner; if, despite best efforts, you are delayed, phone to give warning.

Photo: The Old Farmhouse, entry 265

Requests for deposits vary; some are non-refundable, especially in our London homes, and some owners may charge you for the whole of the booked stay in advance (see below).

Payment

All our owners take cash and UK cheques with a cheque card. Few take credit cards but if they do, we have given them the appropriate symbol. Check that your particular credit card is acceptable.

Cancellations

Owners vary in their approach to cancelled bookings. Last-minute cancellations are the most irksome, even if the owners appreciate that everyone can be a victim of circumstance. Always let your host know as soon as possible and be prepared for wildly varying approaches to the money side of things. If an owner demands what may strike you as an unreasonable amount as compensation, it may be that you are the latest in a string of such cases. An owner with a more generous reaction may not often have experienced the problem. Some owners will charge you the total cost if you cancel at short notice. If an owner holds your credit card details he/she may deduct a cancellation fee from it and not contact you to discuss this.

Tipping

Owners do not expect tips. If you have been treated with extraordinary kindness, write to them, or leave a small gift. Please tell us, too – we love to hear, and we do note, all feedback.

Photo: The Devon Wine School, entry 107

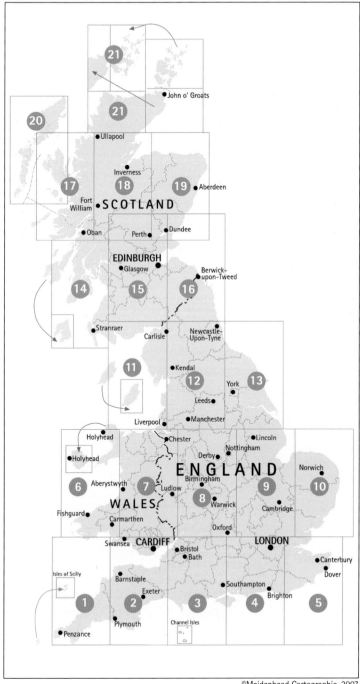

©Maidenhead Cartographic, 2007

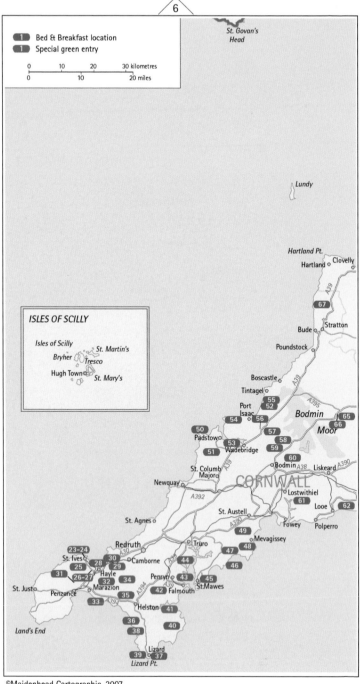

6

Bed & Breakfast location
Special green entry

0   10   20   30 kilometres
0   10   20 miles

St. Govan's Head

Lundy

Hartland Pt.
Hartland ◊   Clovelly
A39
67
Bude ◊   Stratton
Poundstock

ISLES OF SCILLY

Isles of Scilly
Bryher   St. Martin's
Tresco
Hugh Town   St. Mary's

Boscastle ◊
Tintagel ◊
Port   55
Isaac   52   Bodmin
54   56   Moor
50   57   65
Padstow ◊   58   66
53   59
51   Wadebridge   60
St. Columb   Bodmin A38   Liskeard   A390
Major ◊   CORNWALL
Newquay ◊   Lostwithiel
A392   61
St. Austell   Looe   62
Fowey   Polperro
St. Agnes ◊   49
Redruth   Mevagissey
23-24   30   Truro   47   48
St. Ives ◊   25   28   44   46
31   29   Camborne
26-27   Hayle   34   Penryn   43   45
32   Marazion   42   Falmouth   St. Mawes
St. Just   33   35
Penzance   Helston   41
36   40
38
Land's End   39   37   Lizard
Lizard Pt.

©Maidenhead Cartographic, 2007

Map 2   23

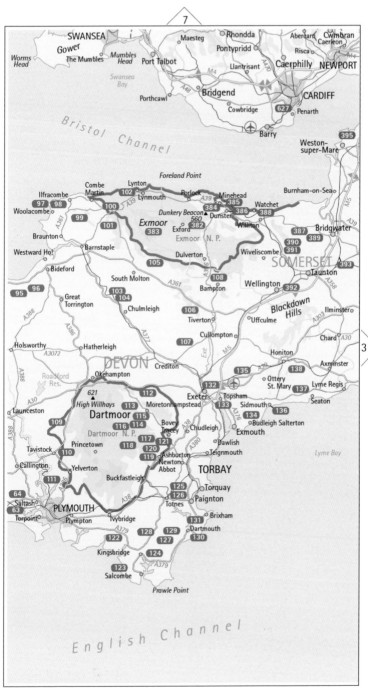

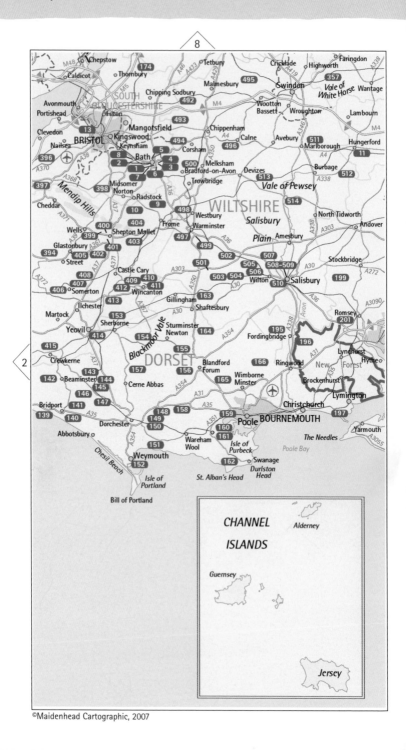

Map 4 25

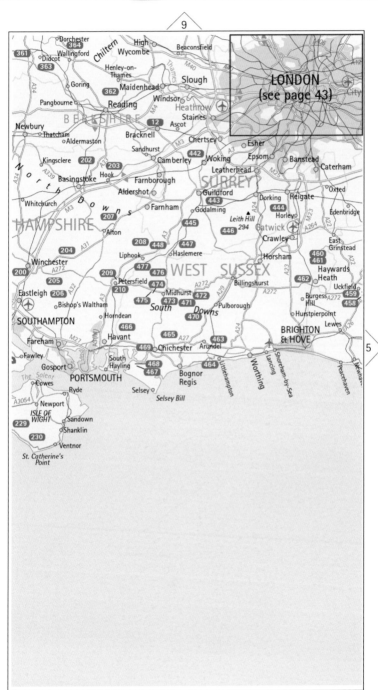

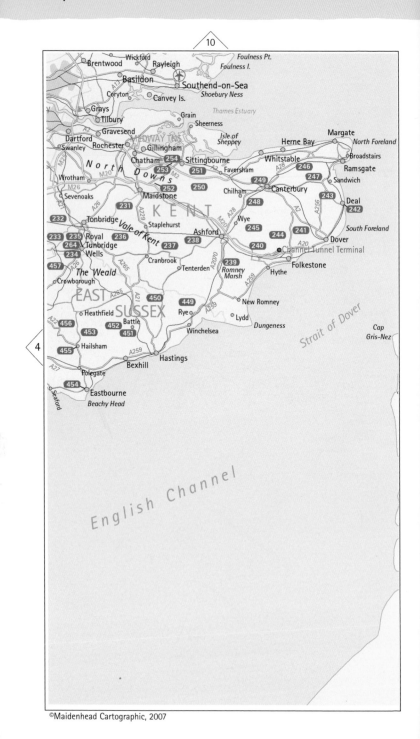

Map 6   27

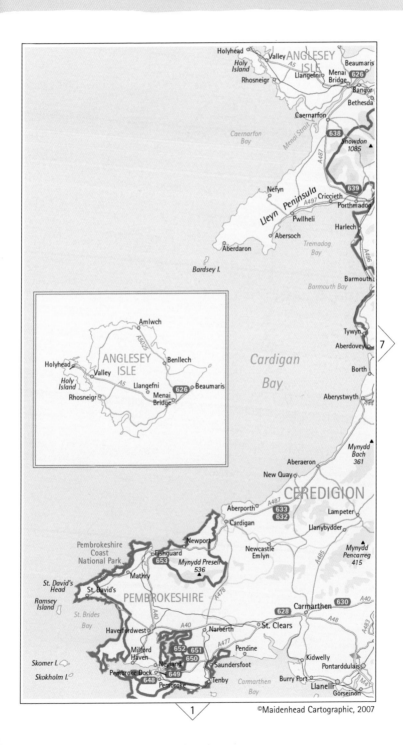

©Maidenhead Cartographic, 2007

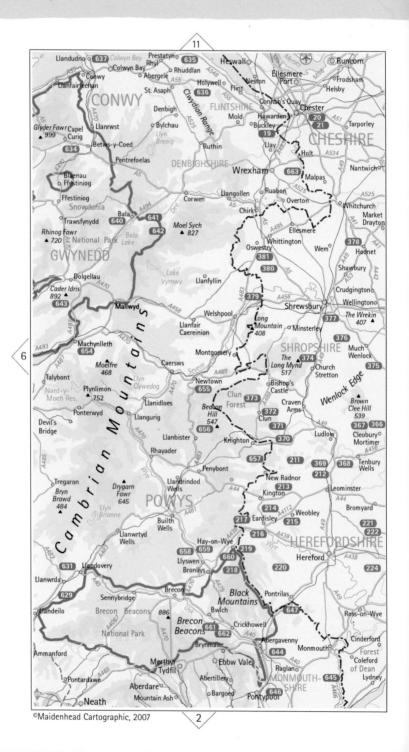

©Maidenhead Cartographic, 2007

Map 8

29

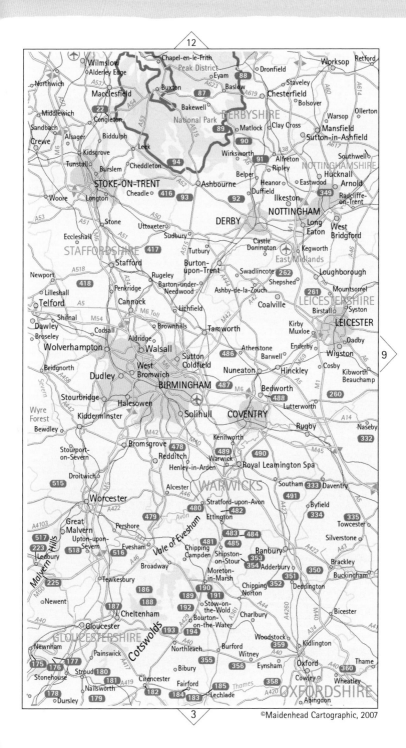

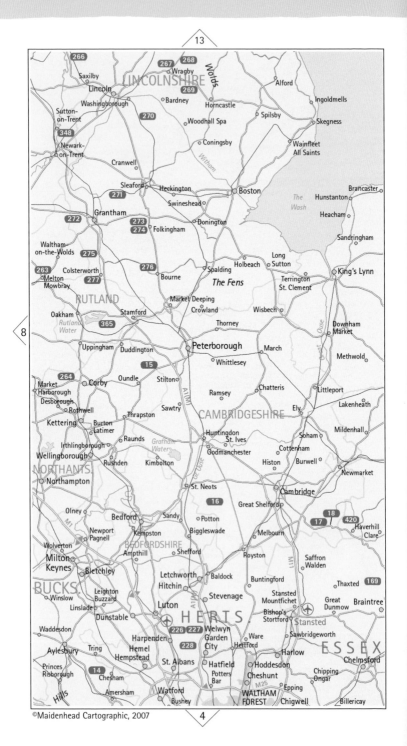

13

266 267 268
Saxilby   Wragby   Alford
LINCOLNSHIRE   Ingoldmells
Lincoln   269
Washingborough   Bardney   Horncastle
Sutton-   Skegness
on-Trent   270   Woodhall Spa   Spilsby
348   Wainfleet
Newark-   Coningsby   All Saints
on-Trent
Cranwell   Brancaster
                                          Hunstanton
Sleaford   Heckington   Boston   The   Heacham
271   Wash
                 Swineshead
Grantham   Donington   Sandringham
272   273
274 Folkingham   King's Lynn
Waltham-   Long
on-the-Wolds 275   Holbeach Sutton
263 Colsterworth   276 Spalding Terrington
Melton   Bourne   St. Clement
Mowbray   277   Wisbech
RUTLAND   Market Deeping   Downham
Oakham   Stamford Crowland   Market
Rutland 365   Thorney
Water   Methwold
Uppingham Duddington Peterborough March
264   15   Whittlesey   Littleport
Market   Stilton   Lakenheath
Harborough Corby Oundle   Chatteris Ely Mildenhall
Desborough   Ramsey
Rothwell   Sawtry   CAMBRIDGESHIRE
Kettering Burton Thrapston Grafham   Soham
Latimer   Water Huntingdon St. Ives Cottenham
Irthlingborough Raunds Godmanchester Histon Burwell
Wellingborough Rushden Kimbolton   Newmarket
NORTHANTS   St. Neots
Northampton   Great Shelford 18
Olney   Bedford   Sandy   Cambridge 17 420
Newport   Potton   Melbourn Haverhill
Pagnell Kempston Biggleswade   Clare
Wolverton Ampthill Shefford Royston Saffron
Milton   BEDFORDSHIRE   Walden
Keynes Bletchley Letchworth Baldock Buntingford Thaxted 169
Winslow Leighton Hitchin   Stansted
Linslade Buzzard   Stevenage   Mountfichet Great
Waddesdon Dunstable Luton HERTS Bishop's Dunmow Braintree
226 227   Stortford Stansted
Aylesbury Tring Harpenden Welwyn Ware Sawbridgeworth
Princes Hemel 228 Garden Hertford Harlow ESSEX
Risborough Hempstead St. Albans City Hoddesdon Chelmsford
14 Chesham Hatfield Cheshunt Chipping
Amersham Potters Epping Ongar Billericay
Watford Bar WALTHAM Chigwell
Bushey FOREST
4

©Maidenhead Cartographic, 2007

8

Map 10   31

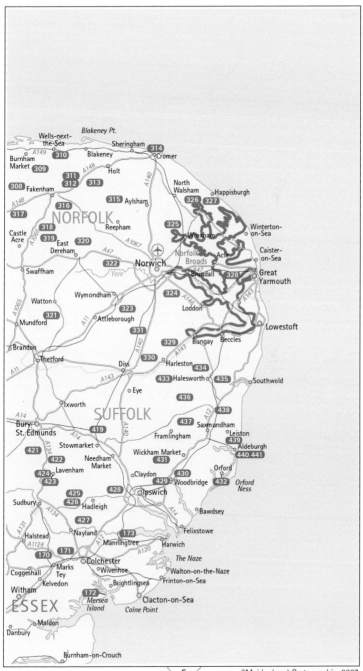

5

©Maidenhead Cartographic, 2007

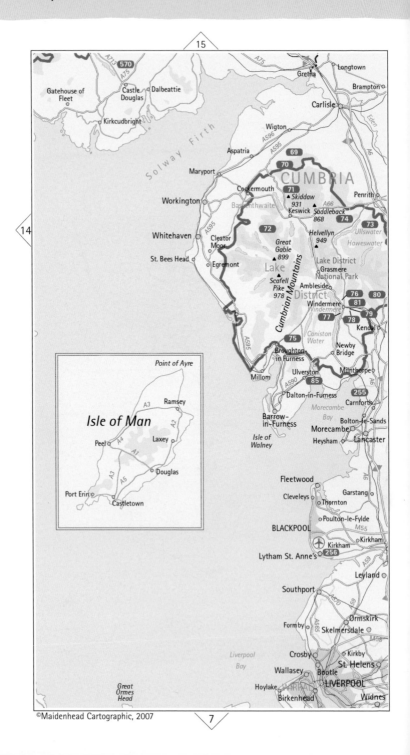

Map 12

33

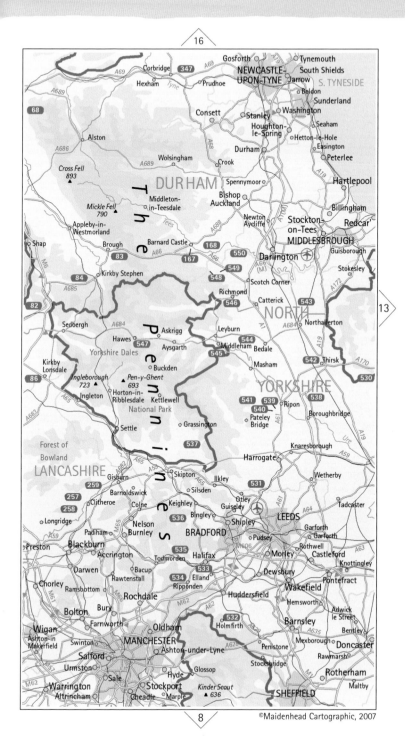

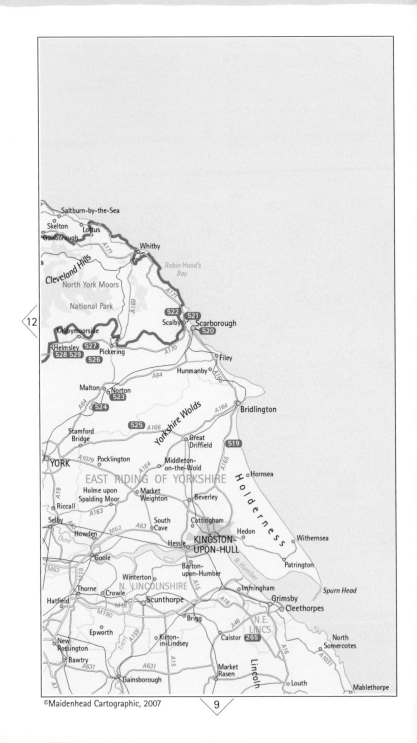

Map 14

35

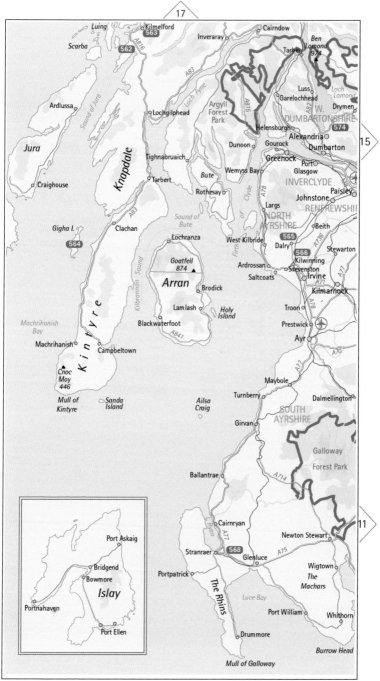

17

15

11

Luing
Scarba
Kilmelford
563
562
A816
Inveraray
Cairndow
Tarbet
Ben Lomond
974
Loch Lomond
Ardlussa
Lochgilphead
Luss
Garelochhead
Drymen
W. DUMBARTONSHIRE
Argyll Forest Park
A83
A815
Helensburgh
Alexandria
574
Jura
Craighouse
Knapdale
Tighnabruaich
Tarbert
Bute
Rothesay
Dunoon
Gourock
Greenock
Port Glasgow
Dumbarton
INVERCLYDE
Paisley
Johnstone
RENFREWSHIRE
Gigha I.
564
Clachan
A83
Sound of Jura
Lochranza
Goatfell
874
Arran
Brodick
Lamlash
Holy Island
Blackwaterfoot
A841
Sound of Bute
West Kilbride
Dalry
565
566
Wemyss Bay
Largs
Firth of Clyde
NORTH AYRSHIRE
Beith
Stewarton
Kilwinning
Stevenston
Irvine
Ardrossan
Saltcoats
Kilmarnock
Troon
A78
A77
A71
Machrihanish Bay
Machrihanish
Campbeltown
Kintyre
Kilbrannan Sound
Prestwick
Ayr
Cnoc Moy 446
Mull of Kintyre
Sanda Island
Ailsa Craig
Turnberry
Maybole
Dalmellington
A70
A77
SOUTH AYRSHIRE
Girvan
Galloway Forest Park
Ballantrae
A714
Cairnryan
A77
Newton Stewart
Stranraer
568
Glenluce
A75
Wigtown
The Machars
Portpatrick
The Rhins
Luce Bay
Port William
Whithorn
Drummore
Burrow Head
Mull of Galloway

Port Askaig
Bridgend
Bowmore
Islay
Portnahaven
Port Ellen

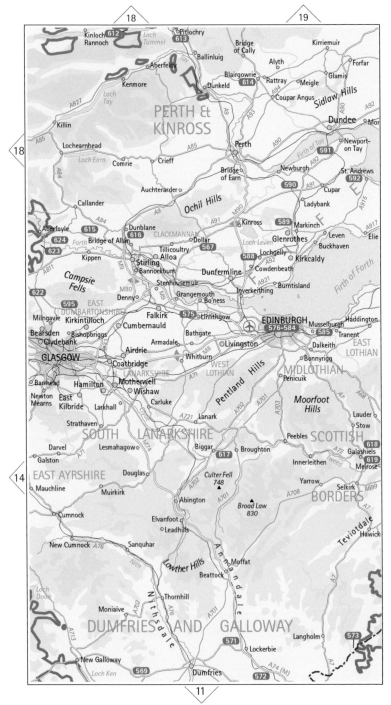

Map 16

37

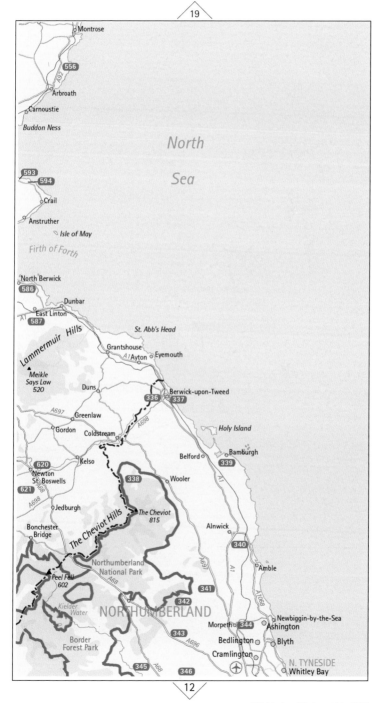

Montrose

556

Arbroath

Carnoustie

Buddon Ness

North

Sea

593 594

Crail

Anstruther

Isle of May

Firth of Forth

North Berwick

586

Dunbar

East Linton

587

Lammermuir Hills

St. Abb's Head

Grantshouse

A1 Ayton · Eyemouth

Meikle Says Law 520

Duns

Berwick-upon-Tweed

336 337

A697

Greenlaw

A698

Gordon

Coldstream

Holy Island

620

Kelso

Belford · Bamburgh

Newton St. Boswells

621

A698

Jedburgh

338

Wooler

339

A1

The Cheviot Hills

The Cheviot 815

Bonchester Bridge

Alnwick

340

Peel Fell 602

Northumberland National Park

A68

341

A697

A1

Amble

A1068

Kielder Water

NORTHUMBERLAND

342

Newbiggin-by-the-Sea

Morpeth

344

Ashington

Border Forest Park

343

A696

Bedlington

Blyth

Cramlington

345

A68

346

N. TYNESIDE

Whitley Bay

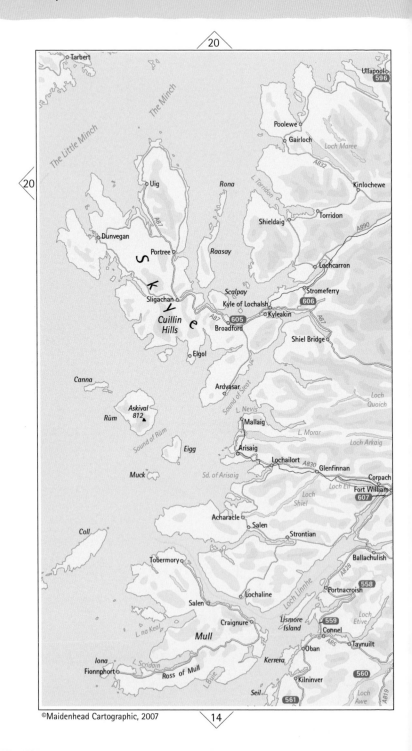

Map 18

39

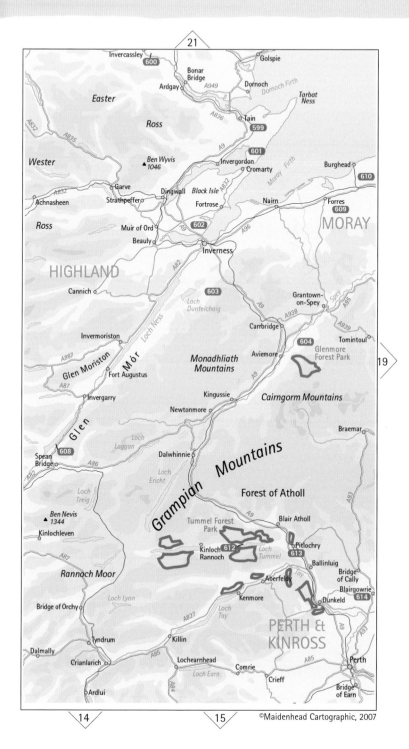

©Maidenhead Cartographic, 2007

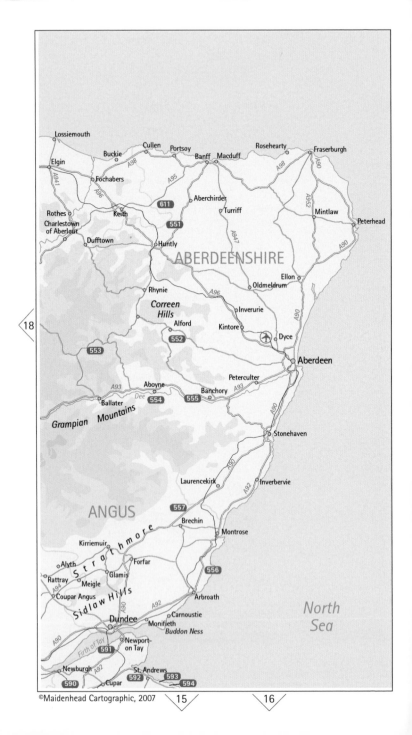

Lossiemouth
Cullen   Portsoy
Buckie   Banff Macduff   Rosehearty   Fraserburgh
Elgin
A98
Fochabers
A941   A95   A98   A90
A96
Rothes   611   Aberchirder
Keith   Turriff   Mintlaw
Charlestown   551   A952   Peterhead
of Aberlour
Dufftown   Huntly   A947
ABERDEENSHIRE
A90

Rhynie   Ellon
A96   Oldmeldrum
Correen
Hills   Inverurie
18   Alford   Kintore   A90
552   Dyce
553   Aberdeen

Aboyne   Peterculter
A93   Banchory   A93
Ballater   Dee   554   555
Grampian Mountains
A90
Stonehaven

A90
Laurencekirk   Inverbervie
A92
ANGUS   557
Brechin
Kirriemuir   Montrose
Strathmore
Alyth   Forfar
Rattray   Glamis   556
A94   Meigle
Coupar Angus   A90   A92
Sidlaw Hills   Arbroath
Dundee   Carnoustie
Monifieth
A90   Buddon Ness
591   Newport-
Firth of Tay   on Tay
Newburgh   A92   St. Andrews
590   Cupar   592   593   594

North
Sea

Map 20   41

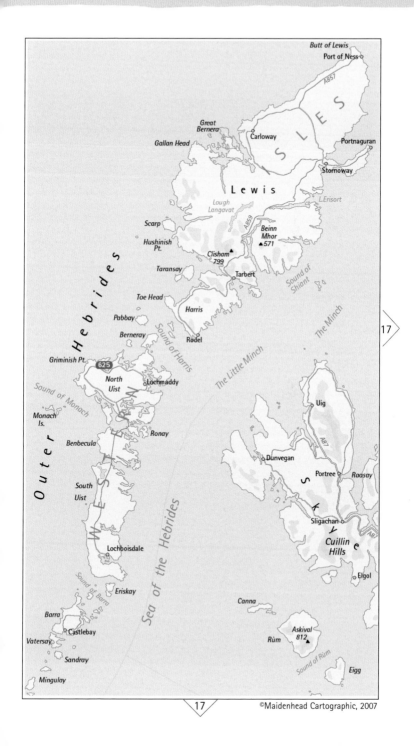

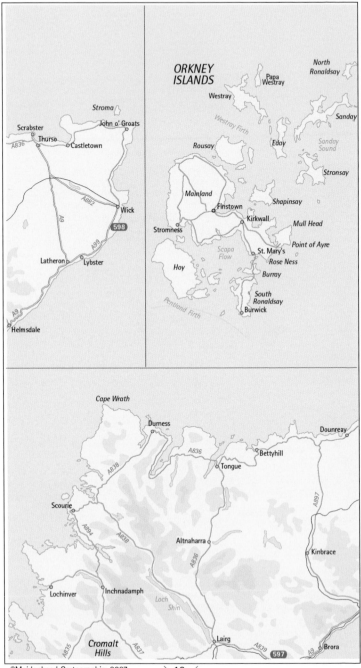

ORKNEY ISLANDS

North Ronaldsay

Papa Westray

Westray

Stroma

Sanday

Westray Firth

Scrabster

John o' Groats

Rousay

Eday

Sanday Sound

Thurso

Castletown

A836

Stronsay

Mainland

Finstown

Shapinsay

A882

Kirkwall

Mull Head

Wick

A9

Stromness

Point of Ayre

598

Scapa Flow

St. Mary's

Rose Ness

Latheron

A99

Lybster

Hoy

Burray

South Ronaldsay

A9

Pentland Firth

Burwick

Helmsdale

Cape Wrath

Durness

Dounreay

A836

Bettyhill

A838

Tongue

Scourie

A897

A894

A838

Altnaharra

Kinbrace

A838

Lochinver

Inchnadamph

Loch Shin

Cromalt Hills

A835

A837

Lairg

A839

597

A9

Brora

18

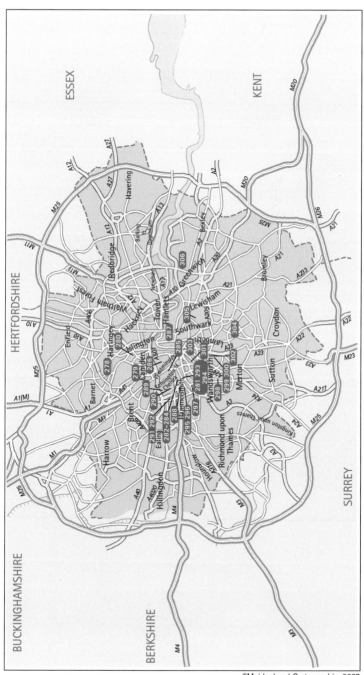

England

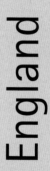

Bath & N.E. Somerset

The Grove

Up the steep hill from the centre, past elegant railings and leafy gardens around bulky villas. At the top is the large house, split in two by jealous brothers in 1805, now elegant with creams and cushions, art and artefacts, books and bucolic views. Ample bedrooms are light and comfortable with fresh flowers, thick curtains or wooden shutters and modern bathrooms. Robert, a sculptor, will chat as he rustles up your delicious, lazy breakfast in the large, bright kitchen. An oversized town garden bordering woods is yours to explore – you may even meet a deer – and the delights of Bath are a short stroll away.

Price	From £100. Singles from £80.
Rooms	3: 1 family room; 1 double with separate bathroom.
Meals	Several pubs/restaurants within a mile.
Closed	Rarely.
Directions	Approx. 1 mile south of city centre. Lyncombe Hill opposite the railway & bus stations, 0.5 miles up Lyncombe Hill into Lyncombe Vale Rd. House 300 yds down the road, end of cul-de-sac.

Mr Robert Hornyold-Strickland
The Grove,
Lyncombe Vale Road, Bath,
Bath & N.E. Somerset BA2 4LR

Tel	01225 484282
Fax	01225 444549
Email	rhstower@aol.com
Web	www.bathbandb.com

Map 3   Entry 1

Bath & N.E. Somerset

14 Raby Place

A listed Regency house within walking distance of the city centre, blessed with contemporary art and organic food: a treat. Muriel's is no run-of-the-mill B&B but part of a classic Bath stone five-storey terrace built in 1824 and filled with eclectic modern art – one of her passions. Her second is living by organic principles and everything tastes delicious: yogurt, fruits, cereals, cooked breakfasts, coffee, tea. Some traffic hum is discernible but you are in one of England's finest cities and the beautifully proportioned bedrooms and spotless bathrooms hold all you need. *Free parking permit for road outside.*

Price	£65-£70. Singles £35.
Rooms	5: 2 doubles, 1 double/twin; 1 twin with separate shower; 1 single with separate bath.
Meals	Restaurants 8-minute walk.
Closed	Rarely.
Directions	Bathwick Hill is a turning off the A36 towards Bristol; look for signs to university at top of hill. No. 14 on left-hand side as you go uphill, before left turn into Raby Mews.

Muriel Guy
14 Raby Place,
Bathwick Hill,
Bath,
Bath & N.E. Somerset BA2 4EH

Tel	01225 465120

Map 3   Entry 2

47 Sydney Buildings

Simone has a natural sense of hospitality and spoils you with Franco-Caribbean colour: breakfasts of fruit, yogurt and cereals (much organic) are served on beautiful Limoges china, as well as full English. Bedrooms have a touch of 18th-century boudoir with their embroidered sheets, antique brass beds, frou-frou easy chairs and sumptuous drapes; views sail over the charming garden – all box parterre, lavender and rambling roses in summer – to the floodlit Abbey. Simone is wonderfully attentive and the delights of Bath, with its Thermae Spa, are a short walk down the hill. *Minimum stay 2 nights at weekends*

Price	From £80. Singles £65.
Rooms	2: 1 double; 1 twin/double with separate shower & wc.
Meals	Pubs/restaurants 10-minute walk.
Closed	Christmas.
Directions	From Bath centre, signs to American Museum. At A36/r'about 1st exit onto Bathwick Hill. Sydney Buildings 1st road on right, house 300 yards on right. All-day parking.

Mrs Simone Johnson
47 Sydney Buildings,
Bathwick Hill, Bath,
Bath & N.E. Somerset BA2 6DB
Tel   01225 463033
Fax   01225 461054
Email   sydneybuildings@bigfoot.com
Web   www.alexishousebath.co.uk

✗ 🚂 ⚗

Map 3   Entry 3

Tolley Cottage

Breakfast on the patio and watch the barges pass the bottom of the garden; raise your eyes to Bath Abbey on the skyline. This Victorian house is a ten-minute walk from the city centre and its heritage glories. Sunny and bright, rooms are a comfortable mix of contemporary and classical; books, art and interesting glass pieces catch the eye. Bedrooms are calming and charming with toile de Jouy and elegant furniture; white bathrooms sparkle. Judy cooks special breakfasts; James, Master of Wine, can arrange tastings. Both are warm and relaxed, and love sharing their home.

Price	£80. Singles £70.
Rooms	2: 1 double, 1 twin.
Meals	Pubs/restaurants 10-minute walk.
Closed	Christmas.
Directions	Follow signs for American Museum & University up Bathwick Hill. Take first turn right to Sydney Buildings. House 200 yds on right.

Judy John
Tolley Cottage,
23 Sydney Buildings, Bath,
Bath & N.E. Somerset BA2 6BZ
Tel   01225 463365
Fax   01225 333275
Email   jj@judyj.plus.com
Web   www.tolleycottage.co.uk

✗ ⚗

Map 3   Entry 4

Bath & N.E. Somerset

77 Great Pulteney Street

Tea and cakes await down the elegant stone steps to a garden flat in this broad street of immaculate Georgian houses. Inside all is pale wood, modern art, bergère chairs and palms; the sitting room is light and airy; walls sport modern art and there's a view over the rugby pitch. Downstairs is a comfortable bedroom with loads of books and its own door to a small but delightfully well-designed garden. Breakfast here in summer at your own pace; Ian is a fanatic foodie and dinner will also be special. Henry may play the Northumbrian pipes for you if you ask nicely; the shops are a hop away.

Bath & N.E. Somerset

Grey Lodge

In a conservation area, yet only a short drive from the centre of Bath, the views are breathtaking from wherever you stand. The steep valley rolls out ahead of you from most of the rooms, and from the garden comes a confusion and a profusion of scents and colours – a glory in its own right. The friendly and likeable Sticklands are conservationists as well as gardeners and have a Green Certificate to prove it. Breakfasts are a feast: bacon and eggs, cereals, home-grown jam, smoked fish and much more. Jane will tell you all about wonderful local gardens to visit.

Price	£75–£90. Singles from £55.
Rooms	1 double.
Meals	Dinner from £20.
	Packed lunch from £5.
Closed	Rarely.
Directions	A4 into centre of Bath.
	Last house before Laura Place on
	south side of Great Pulteney St.
	Parking by arrangement;
	7-minute walk from station.

Price	£75–£85. Singles £45–£50.
Rooms	3: 2 twins/doubles, 1 family room.
Meals	Pub/restaurant 2 miles.
Closed	Rarely.
Directions	From A36, 3 miles out of Bath on
	Warminster road, take uphill road
	by lights & Viaduct Inn. 1st left,
	100 yds, signed Monkton Combe.
	After village, house 1st on left;
	0.5 miles on.

	Ian Critchley & Henry Ford
	77 Great Pulteney Street,
	Bath,
	Bath & N.E. Somerset BA2 4DL
Tel	01225 466659
Email	ianhenry@77pulteneyst.co.uk
Web	www.77pulteneyst.co.uk

	Jane & Anthony Stickland
	Grey Lodge,
	Summer Lane, Combe Down, Bath,
	Bath & N.E. Somerset BA2 7EU
Tel	01225 832069
Fax	01225 830161
Email	greylodge@freenet.co.uk
Web	www.greylodge.co.uk

Map 3   Entry 5

Map 3   Entry 6

Bath & N.E. Somerset

Manor Farm Barn

Duchy of Cornwall farmland stretches as far as the eye can see; the views from this converted barn – with light open-plan spaces – are splendid by any standards, but remarkable considering you are so close to Bath. There's much wildlife, too: sparrowhawks nest in the gable end, buzzards circle above the valley, and deer may gaze at you eating your breakfast. Giles, who pots, and Sue, who paints, are gentle and easygoing hosts; spruce guest rooms have built-in wardrobes, houseplants and excellent beds. For those in search of birdsong and country peace after a day on the hoof in Bath.

Bath & N.E. Somerset

Corston Fields Farm

In rolling agricultural land, a short hop from Bath and its new spa, the Addicotts have given over swathes of their farm to natural habitat for indigenous wildlife – and have a Gold Award under the Duke of Cornwall's Habitat Award scheme to boot. Gerald, a keen rugby supporter, and Rosaline are utterly committed to the environment, and flax from the vibrant blue linseed crops is used to heat their sturdy, stone-mullioned and listed house. The large rooms – the best in the house – have all the mod cons. Come for the setting, the far-reaching views and the wonderful hosts. *Min. stay two nights at weekends.*

Price	£60-£70. Singles £40-£42.50.
Rooms	2: 1 twin/double; 1 double with separate shower.
Meals	Pubs/restaurants 2.5 miles.
Closed	Christmas & New Year.
Directions	From Bath, A367 (Wells Rd). At Red Lion r'bout right (Bristol A4). Straight on, pass Culverhay School on left. After 100 yds left to Englishcombe. There, right after postbox to church, fork right, follow road; last on right.

Price	From £74. Singles £50.
Rooms	4: 1 double; 1 double, 1 twin sharing bath (2nd room let to same party only). Annexe: 1 double.
Meals	Pub 300 yds.
Closed	Christmas & New Year.
Directions	From A4 west of Bath, A39 through Corston. 1 mile on, just before Wheatsheaf Pub (on right), right. Signed 200 yds along lane on right.

Sue & Giles Barber
Manor Farm Barn,
Englishcombe, Bath,
Bath & N.E. Somerset BA2 9DU

Tel 01225 424195
Mobile 07966 501016
Email info@manorfarmbarn.com
Web www.manorfarmbarn.com

Gerald & Rosaline Addicott
Corston Fields Farm,
Corston, Bath,
Bath & N.E. Somerset BA2 9EZ

Tel 01225 873305
Fax 01225 874421
Email corston.fields@btinternet.com
Web www.corstonfields.com

Map 3   Entry 7

Map 3   Entry 8

Hollytree Cottage

Meandering lanes lead to this 17th-century cottage, with roses round the door, a grandfather clock in the hall and an air of genteel tranquillity. The cottage charm has been updated with Regency mahogany and sumptuous sofas. There's even a four-poster bed and the bedrooms have long views over farmland and undulating countryside. Behind is a sloping, south-facing garden with a pond and some rare trees and shrubs. A place to come for absolute peace and quiet, birdsong and walks and the joys of elegant Bath 20 minutes away. Julia knows the city well so can help you plan trips.

Melon Cottage Vineyard

Interesting, child-friendly hosts who are entirely natural and unbusinesslike make this place special; it's excellent value, too. The large Mendip-style 'long cottage' with mullioned windows and beams made of ships' timbers, fronted by a small vineyard, is temptingly close to dinner at Babington House, the treasures of Bath and Wells, the gardens and concerts at Stourhead, and Gregorian chant in Downside Abbey. Rooms are very simple, the jams are homemade and the hosts the kindest you may meet. No sitting room, but tea in the walled garden is rich compensation. *Children over five welcome.*

Price	£70-£80. Singles £40.
Rooms	4: 2 doubles, 1 twin, 1 four-poster.
Meals	Pub/restaurant 0.5 miles.
Closed	Rarely.
Directions	From Bath, A36 to Wolverton. Just past Red Lion, turn for Laverton. 1 mile to x-roads; towards Faukland; downhill for 80 yds. On left, just above farm entrance on right.

Price	£45-£55. Singles £25.
Rooms	3: 1 family room (zip-link beds & divan); 1 double, 1 single, sharing bath.
Meals	Pubs 2 miles.
Closed	Rarely.
Directions	From Bath A367, Wells road, through Radstock. After 3 miles, at large r'bout, B3139 for Trowbridge. After 1.1 miles, and dip in road, right up drive. House at top, visible from road.

	Mrs Julia Naismith
	Hollytree Cottage,
	Laverton, Bath,
	Bath & N.E. Somerset BA2 7QZ
Tel	01373 830786
Fax	01373 830786
Email	julia@naismith.fsbusiness.co.uk
Web	www.hollytreecottagebath.co.uk

	Virginia & Hugh Pountney
	Melon Cottage Vineyard,
	Charlton,
	Radstock, Bath,
	Bath & N.E. Somerset BA3 5TN
Tel	01761 435090
Email	v.pountney@virgin.net
Web	www.meloncottage.co.uk

Map 3   Entry 9

Map 3   Entry 10

Berkshire

Wilton House

With its handsome Queen Anne frontage, "the most ambitious house in Hungerford" (Pevsner) conceals medieval origins. A classic townhouse in a charming market town, its interior is a panelled, soft-painted delight. Light floods through sash windows onto paintings and prints, books and antiques and wide, inviting sofas; bedrooms are understatedly elegant and relaxing; bathrooms are grand. So is breakfast in the 18th-century dining room: the Welfares look after you perfectly. All this, antique shops to the front and a walled garden with cordon-trained fruit trees behind. *Children over eight welcome.*

Price	From £70. Singles from £50.
Rooms	2: 1 double, 1 twin/double.
Meals	Packed lunch £5. Pub 100 yds.
Closed	Christmas.
Directions	M4 exit 14; A338 to A4; right for Marlborough, turning at Bear Hotel onto Salisbury road (A338). Over canal bridge into High St. House 200 yds past Town Hall on right.

Deborah & Jonathan Welfare
Wilton House,
33 High Street, Hungerford,
Berkshire RG17 0NF

Tel	01488 684228
Fax	01488 685037
Email	welfares@hotmail.com
Web	www.wiltonhouse-hungerford.co.uk

✕ 🚉 🍷 🐾 ♿

Map 3   Entry 11

Berkshire

Whitehouse Farm Cottage

Once you get past the housing estates of Bracknell, this is a fabulous find. A 17th-century farmhouse with a delightful garden, and two charmingly converted barns with their own entrances. Garden Cottage has a beamed drawing room downstairs and a gallery bedroom with creamy walls and a cast-iron bed. The Old Forge has the blacksmith's fireplace and lovely views onto the courtyard garden and its pebble mosaics. The single is in the house with its own comfortable sitting room. Locally sourced breakfasts with fresh bread are served in the house by friendly Louise – she and her husband are film prop makers.

Price	£75-£90. Singles £65.
Rooms	3: 1 single & sitting room. Old Forge: 1 double. Cottage: 1 double & sitting room.
Meals	Picnics by arrangement. Pubs/restaurants within 1 mile.
Closed	Christmas & occasionally.
Directions	From A329, take B3408 to Binfield. Left at r'bout, left at traffic lights, into St Marks Road. Then 2nd left Foxley Lane, 1st left Murrell Hill Lane. House is 1st on right.

Louise Lusby
Whitehouse Farm Cottage,
Murrell Hill Lane,
Binfield,
Berkshire RG42 4BY

Tel	01344 423688
Mobile	07711 948889
Email	garden.cottages@ntlworld.com

✕ 🚉 🍷 🐾

Map 4   Entry 12

Bristol

Park House

It was the first house to be built in Clifton Park in 1797 – and is surprisingly peaceful. Fight your way past an engaging muddle – books, pictures, shells, fossils and pre-war sports gear – to plain, old-fashioned bedrooms. The upstairs one has views over one of the walled gardens where white Call ducks potter; the downstairs twin is next to a library stuffed with books. Breakfast is in a light sitting room at a large table. Delia is wise, friendly and kind and you are within strolling distance of Georgian Clifton's shops, bars, restaurants, bridge and hills. The University is strolling distance. *Children over 12 welcome.*

Price	£75. Singles £55.
Rooms	2: 1 double, 1 twin.
Meals	Restaurants an easy walk.
Closed	24 December–2 January; 1 week over Easter.
Directions	Directions given when booking. From Temple Meads station, take 8 or 9 bus to Student Union, Queens Road, Clifton.

Mrs Delia Macdonald
Park House,
19 Richmond Hill,
Clifton,
Bristol BS8 1BA
Tel   0117 9736331

Map 3   Entry 13

Buckinghamshire

Field Cottage

Sue, relaxed and friendly, is the consummate professional: the fitted bedrooms are immaculate, chintzy and filled with treats, and the bathrooms pristine. She has also created a horticultural haven amid open fields (old-fashioned roses, a willow tunnel, colourful clematis). The peachy guest sitting room is neat and comfortable – doors swing open onto the garden and a patio suntrap – and you tuck into homemade muffins at breakfast surrounded by peaceful pastoral views. It's walking distance across fields to the pub and to the Ridgeway National Trail, Britain's oldest road. *Children over 12 welcome.*

Price	£65–£70. Singles £40–£45.
Rooms	3: 1 double; 1 twin with separate shower; 1 single with separate bath/shower.
Meals	Pub 0.5 miles.
Closed	Christmas & New Year.
Directions	South on A413 from Wendover. Pass Jet station, left to Kings Ash; 2 miles on, left at x-roads, past pub; 0.5 miles on, sharp left onto bridlepath; 2nd gate along.

Mike & Sue Jepson
Field Cottage,
St Leonards, Tring,
Buckinghamshire HP23 6NS
Tel   01494 837602
Fax   01494 837137
Email   michael.jepson@lineone.net
Web   www.fieldcottagebandb.co.uk

Map 9   Entry 14

Cambridgeshire

Bridge Cottage

Watch the cattle drinking peacefully at the river as you tuck into scrumptious breakfast. It was the setting that won Judy and Rod over and they've transformed a no-nonsense bungalow into a cottage full of light, sloping ceilings and unexpected character. A small, pretty garden borders the Willowbrook, with a decked terrace at the water's edge – just the spot to sit with a glass of wine or a cup of tea. Kingfishers flash by and you will probably see a red kite; your charming hosts have binoculars to borrow. Judy has only just begun B&B but does it with natural brilliance and loves every minute.

Price	From £70. Singles £38.
Rooms	3: 1 double, 1 twin; 1 double with separate bath.
Meals	Pub/restaurant 2 miles.
Closed	Rarely.
Directions	A1 to Peterborough junction. Take A605 signed Oundle & Northampton for 4 miles. At 1st r'bout right through Fotheringhay, then Woodnewton. House is first on left on bridge.

Judy Colebrook
Bridge Cottage, Oundle Road,
Woodnewton, Peterborough,
Cambridgeshire PE8 5EG
Tel: 01780 470779
Mobile: 07979 644864
Email: enquiries@bridgecottage.net
Web: www.bridgecottage.net

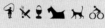

Map 9   Entry 15

Cambridgeshire

Model Farm

This is country-quiet, close to Cambridge and suitable for independent souls. Two of the bedrooms are in a separate wing with their own entrance, one up a circular metal staircase, one on the ground floor – not swish but spotless, with good walk-in showers and views. There's no guest sitting room, but the bedrooms are a decent size and the beds comfortable. You may wander outside round the garden and farm buildings; though this is a busy arable farm, sheep still graze the land. There's homemade jam for breakfast and honey from the hives, served in a nice little breakfast room.

Price	£55. Singles £33.
Rooms	3 doubles.
Meals	Pub/restaurant 3 miles.
Closed	Rarely.
Directions	From A1198 at Longstowe onto B1046. House on right after 3 miles, before Little Gransden.

Sue Barlow
Model Farm,
Little Gransden,
Cambridgeshire SG19 3EA
Tel: 01767 677361
Email: suebarlow@modelfarm.org.uk
Web: www.modelfarm.org.uk

Map 9   Entry 16

Cambridgeshire

Springfield House

A fine mix of town and country: you are in a rural village yet wonderfully close to Cambridge. The former school house hugs the bend of a river, its French windows opening to rambling, delightful gardens. The conservatory, draped with a huge mimosa, is an exceptional spot for summer breakfasts. Beds and bedrooms are large and comfortable, with thick curtains, books, flowers and garden views. This is an old-fashionedly elegant home; there's Charlie the flat-coated retriever, a family bustle in the holidays, and Judith, a quietly nurturing hostess. Good value.

Price	£55-£65. Singles £45.
Rooms	2 doubles.
Meals	Pubs 150 yds.
Closed	Rarely.
Directions	A1307 from Cambridge, left into High St. 1st right after The Crown (on left) into Horn Lane. House on right next to chapel, before ford.

Judith Rossiter
Springfield House,
14-16 Horn Lane,
Linton,
Cambridgeshire CB21 4HT

Tel	01223 891383
Fax	01223 890335
Web	www.springfieldhouse.org

Map 9 Entry 17

Cambridgeshire

The Old Chapel

Tardis-like, this 1823 converted chapel opens out to a series of lovely light rooms and a gorgeous garden with cows peeping over the fence. You have a large drawing room with a wood-burner, a dining room with a grand piano, a verdant conservatory, a fabulous library, even a sauna. Bedrooms are beautifully dressed with cream bedspreads, pale carpets, fine antiques and heaps of cushions; bathrooms have gleaming tiles and fresh flowers. Alex and Ian are both keen cooks and love entertaining; the vast kitchen, with arched chapel windows, has a huge table and food is sourced as locally as possible. Good fun.

Price	£65-£70. Singles £40-£45.
Rooms	2: 1 double; 1 single with separate bath.
Meals	Dinner £25. Pubs easy walking distance. Restaurants 7 miles.
Closed	Rarely.
Directions	A1307 dir. Haverhill. Thro' Linton; after dual carriageway, left slip road into village. Left at sign of horse on green towards West Wickham. House on left, past brick council houses.

Alexandra & Ian Jennison-Rose
The Old Chapel,
West Wickham Road,
Horseheath,
Cambridgeshire CB21 4QA

Tel	01223 894027
Email	alexchapel@btinternet.com

Map 9 Entry 18

Cheshire

The Mount

Britain at its best: rare trees planted in 1860, bountiful flowers, a pond, a vegetable garden and Rachel – delightful, warm and friendly. The Victorian house, built for a Chester corn merchant and furnished in a traditional style, has garden views from every light-filled window. You get an airy drawing room, a high-ceilinged dining room and comfortable, spacious, country-house bedrooms with attractive paintings and soft furnishings. A haven for garden buffs and walkers – and there's a tennis court too. Chester, North Wales and two airports are conveniently close. *Arrivals after 5pm.*

Price	£60. Singles from £37.
Rooms	4: 2 doubles, 2 twins/doubles.
Meals	Pub/restaurant 0.5 miles.
Closed	Christmas & New Year.
Directions	From A55, A5104 south; 2nd r'bout left towards Pennyfordd; left off A5104 (Lester's Lane) for Higher Kinnerton. House 0.75 miles on right, sharp bend.

Jonathan & Rachel Major
The Mount,
Higher Kinnerton, Chester,
Cheshire CH4 9BQ

Tel 01244 660275
Fax 01244 660275
Email themount@higherkinnerton.com
Web www.bandbchester.com

Map 7 Entry 19

Cheshire

Cotton Farm

Only a four-mile hop from Roman Chester and its 900-year-old cathedral is this sprawling, red-brick farmhouse. Elegant chickens peck in hedges, ponies graze, lambs frisk and cats doze. The farm, run by conservationists Nigel and Clare, is under the Countryside Stewardship Scheme – there are wildflower meadows, summer swallows and 250 acres to roam. Bedrooms are large, stylish farmhouse with lovely fabrics and touches of luxury (bath towels are huge), but best of all is the relaxed family atmosphere. And breakfasts, delicious and beautifully presented. *Stabling available. Children over ten welcome.*

Price	£65. Singles £45.
Rooms	3: 2 doubles, 1 twin.
Meals	Pub 1.5 miles.
Closed	Rarely.
Directions	A51 Chester-Nantwich. 1.5 miles from outskirts, after golf course on left, right, down Cotton Lane, signed Cotton Edmunds; 1.5 miles, left on sharp right-hand bend; 2nd drive on right.

Clare & Nigel Hill
Cotton Farm,
Cotton Edmunds, Chester,
Cheshire CH3 7PG

Tel 01244 336616
Mobile 07840 682042
Email info@cottonfarm.co.uk
Web www.cottonfarm.co.uk

Map 7 Entry 20

Cheshire

Greenlooms Cottage

This pretty cottage was where the estate's chief hedger and ditcher lived. The smallholding has gone but the walnuts, quinces and garden pump remain – and the views still reach to the Peckforton Hills. Now it is a stylishly simple and fun place to stay, thanks to Deborah – traveller, ex-potter, fabulous cook – and Peter, furniture-maker and restorer. Follow your nose to the Aga-cosy kitchen where the best black pudding and bacon are waiting to fuel you for a day on the Cheshire cycle route. Return to two sweet bedrooms, one up one down: crisp white duvets, Floris soaps, ethnic touches.

Price	£60. Singles from £40.
Rooms	2: 1 double, 1 twin.
Meals	Dinner, £25 with wine. Pub 3 miles.
Closed	Never.
Directions	A41 Whitchurch; south from Chester. After petrol station, 2nd left at antiques shop. On for 1.5 miles thro' village, right into Martins Lane; 1 mile on right.

Deborah Newman
Greenlooms Cottage,
Martins Lane,
Hargrave, Chester, Cheshire
CH3 7RX
Tel   01829 781475
Email   dnewman@greenlooms.com
Web   www.greenlooms.com

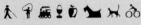

Map 7   Entry 21

Cheshire

Lower Key Green Farm

Aga-cooked breakfasts with home-baked bread, home-laid eggs and sausages, Staffordshire oatcakes: just the thing to set you up for a day's walking in the Peak District. A solid, unpretentious farmhouse – David's family have farmed here for generations – whose flagged floors, beamed ceilings, scrubbed tables and throws create an easy comfort. Janet and David are open and down to earth – talented too; their artwork is on display. The bedroom has a cottagey simplicity; a Victorian washstand and a slipper bath add delight, as do homemade biscuits and sherry. There are good food pubs with pretty views nearby.

Price	£70. Singles £40.
Rooms	1 twin/double.
Meals	Pub 10-minute drive.
Closed	Rarely.
Directions	From A54, A523 towards Leek. Thro' Bosley village, turn right; after 40mph and Queen's Arms sign, onto Tunstall Rd; 2nd farm on left after 0.5 miles.

Janet Heath
Lower Key Green Farm,
Bosley, Macclesfield,
Cheshire SK11 0PB
Tel   01260 223278
Fax   01260 223278
Email   lowerkeygreen@hotmail.com
Web   www.lowerkeygreen.co.uk

Map 8   Entry 22

Cornwall

Organic Panda B&B & Gallery

A five-minute walk from busy St Ives, with a panoramic view of the bay: boutique B&B in perfect harmony with this artistic spot. Come for a bold scattering of modern art, a ten-seater rustic table and spacious contemporary bedrooms whose chunky beds, white walls and raw-silk cushions reveal a laid-back style. Shower rooms are small but perfectly formed. Andrea is an artist and theatre designer, Peter a photographer and organic chef; the food sounds delicious and they bake their own bread. And the most beautiful coastal road in all England leads to St Just. *Min. three nights: July/August, Easter & Christmas.*

Price	£75–£120.
Rooms	3: 2 doubles, 1 twin.
Meals	Packed lunch £10. Restaurants 10-minute walk.
Closed	Rarely.
Directions	A3074 to St Ives. Signs to leisure centre; house behind 3rd sign, on left-hand bend.

Peter Williams & Andrea Carr
Organic Panda B&B & Gallery,
1 Pednolver Terrace, St Ives,
Cornwall TR26 2EL
Tel   01736 793890
Fax   01736 793890
Email   info@organicpanda.co.uk
Web   www.organicpanda.co.uk

Map 1   Entry 23

Cornwall

11 Sea View Terrace

In a smart row of Edwardian villas, with views over harbour, island and sea, is a delectable retreat. Sleek, softy coloured interiors are light and gentle on the eye – an Italian circular glass table here, a painted seascape there – creating a deeply civilised feel. Bedrooms are perfect with crisp linen, vistas of whirling gulls, your own terrace; bathrooms are state-of-the-art. Rejoice in softly boiled eggs with anchovy and chive-butter soldiers for breakfast – or continental in bed if you prefer. Grahame looks after you impeccably and design aficionados will be happy. *Free admission to Tate Gallery & Barbara Hepworth Museum.*

Price	£95–£115. Singles from £70.
Rooms	3 suites.
Meals	Dinner, with wine, from £25 (groups only). Packed lunch £10. Pubs/restaurants 5-minute walk.
Closed	Rarely.
Directions	At Porthminster Hotel, signs for Tate; down Albert Rd, right just before Longships Hotel. Limited parking.

Grahame Wheelband
11 Sea View Terrace,
St Ives,
Cornwall TR26 2DH
Tel   01736 798440
Email   elevenseaviewterrace@btinternet.com
Web   www.11stives.co.uk

Map 1   Entry 24

Cornwall

Jamies

Breathe in the sweeping ocean views from this stylish 1920s villa. Airy bedrooms are hotel-smart with white bed linen, striped or checked curtains and fresh new bathrooms; all rooms have a great feeling of space and two have sitting areas. Crisp linen and silver at the dining table create an elegant mood at breakfast – enjoy a delicious fruit salad while taking in the views, or admire some of artist Felicity's inspiring work. Generous Felicity and Jamie are ex-hoteliers with a great sense of fun, and can tell you about all the local restaurants, galleries and coastal walks. *Children over 12 welcome.*

Price	£100. Singles £80.
Rooms	4: 3 twins/doubles, 1 suite.
Meals	Pub 5-minute walk. Restaurants 25 minute-drive.
Closed	Rarely.
Directions	A30, then A3074 for St Ives. At Carbis Bay, Marshalls estate agents & Methodist church on left. Next right down Pannier Lane; 2nd right is Wheal Whidden; 1st house on left.

Felicity & Jamie Robertson
Jamies,
Wheal Whidden,
Carbis Bay, St Ives,
Cornwall TR26 2QX

Tel	01736 794718
Email	info@jamiesstives.co.uk
Web	www.jamiesstives.co.uk

Map 1   Entry 25

Cornwall

The Old Vicarage

Artists will be inspired, not just with the proximity to St Ives but with Jackie's dazzling collection of her own and other artists' work. This is a light, airy, welcoming house whose big sash windows overlook a subtropical garden; wander at will after a grand breakfast of fresh fruit and local bacon and sausages. Bedrooms have soft coloured walls, deeply comfortable beds, period furniture and more lovely artwork adding spots of colour; bathrooms are gleaming and fresh. There's a sandy beach 20-minutes' walk away and you can join the coastal path just up the road. Wonderful house, lovely owner.

Price	£65-£75. Singles £35-£40.
Rooms	3: 1 twin; 1 double with separate bath, 1 single sharing bath (same party only).
Meals	Pubs 5-8 minute walk. Restaurants in St Ives 2.5 miles.
Closed	1 November-15 March.
Directions	A30 dir. Penzance. At 2nd Hayle r'bout, A3074 St Ives. After Wyvale Garden Centre, over mini r'bout; right at next one & into Lelant. Brush End is lane on left after sign for Elm Farm. House at end.

Jackie & Howard Hollingsbee
The Old Vicarage,
Brush End,
Lelant, St Ives,
Cornwall TR26 3EF

Tel	01736 753324
Email	bookings@oldvicaragelelant.co.uk
Web	www.oldvicaragelelant.co.uk

Map 1   Entry 26

Cornwall

The Old Courthouse

Built in 1574 on the main route to St Ives, this history-laden house in the village of Lelant has been most sympathetically revived. The attention to detail is superb as solid old flagged floors combine with pure white walls and contemporary art rubs up to aged stone and wood. Bedrooms – one facing the road – are light, calming and comfortable. Fresh flowers and herbs abound, bathrooms have natural soaps and snowy white towels. Linda, a qualified aromatherapist, is an attentive host, bakes her own bread, uses masses of local produce and serves it all most stylishly in her pretty, low-ceilinged dining room.

Price	From £65. Singles £45.
Rooms	3: 2 doubles; 1 double with separate shower.
Meals	Pub 0.25 miles.
Closed	Rarely.
Directions	A30 for St Ives. 2nd exit at Penzance R'bout onto A3074. Pass garden centre. Over 1st mini r'bout, right at 2nd r'bout. House on left in dip before hill.

Linda Elphick
The Old Courthouse,
Lelant, St Ives,
Cornwall TR26 3EB

Tel	01736 751798
Mobile	07949 292006
Email	lindaelphick@onetel.com
Web	www.oldcourthousecornwall.co.uk

Map 1   Entry 27

Cornwall

Treglisson

This is minutes from St Ives, the glorious bay and some nifty surfing beaches. Inside the old farmhouse, all is calm and peaceful. Stephen and Heather are thoughtful, fun, easy-going and filled with enthusiasm for looking after you: large light bedrooms in soft colours, generous beds with lovely linen, modern white bathrooms, good art on the walls, a beautiful antique-marble hall floor. Cornish Aga-cooked breakfasts can be relished late if you prefer; in the evening, take a sundowner to the pretty conservatory or curl up with a book in the guest sitting room. There's a heated indoor pool too. Great value.

Price	£50–£70. Singles from £30.
Rooms	4: 1 double, 1 twin, 2 family rooms.
Meals	Pubs/restaurants 2-5 miles.
Closed	Christmas & New Year.
Directions	A30 to Hayle; 4th exit on r'bout into Hayle. Left at mini r'bout into Guildford Rd; up hill for 1 mile. Turn left at green sign into lane.

Stephen & Heather Reeves
Treglisson,
Wheal Alfred Road,
Hayle,
Cornwall TR27 5JT

Tel	01736 753141
Email	steve@treglisson.co.uk
Web	www.treglisson.co.uk

Map 1   Entry 28

Cornwall

House at Gwinear

An island of calm – it sits, as it has for 500 years, in its own bird-trilled acres a short drive from St Ives. The mood is now artistic, for the Halls are devoted to the encouragement of the arts and crafts which is reflected in their lifestyle. There's no stuffiness – just fresh flowers on the breakfast table, a piano in the corner, rugs on polished floors and masses of books. In a separate wing you have a cosy bedroom and sitting room and a fine view of the church from the bath. The big, lawn-filled gardens are there for bare-footed solace, and your interesting hosts couldn't be nicer.

Price	From £65.
Rooms	1 twin/double & sitting room.
Meals	Occasional dinner. Pub 1.5 miles.
Closed	Rarely.
Directions	From A30 exit Hayle (Loggans Moor r'bout); 100 yds left at mini-r'bout; 400 yds left for Gwinear; 1.5 miles, top of hill, driveway on right, just before 30mph Gwinear sign.

Charles & Diana Hall
House at Gwinear,
Gwinear,
St Ives,
Cornwall TR27 5JZ

Tel	01736 850444
Fax	01736 850444
Email	charleshall@btinternet.com

Map 1   Entry 29

Cornwall

Calize Country House

Beneath wheeling gulls and close to blond beaches, the big square 1870 house has amazing views of skies and sea. Virginia Woolf's lighthouse is in the bay and winter seals cavort at the colony nearby. A fresh, uncomplicated décor brings the tang of the sea to every room. Artworks recall a world of surf; deckchair stripes clothe the dining table and dress the window; traditional sofas call for quiet times with a book. Upstairs, patterned or pale walls, practical bath or shower rooms, perhaps a sea view. Jilly and Nigel are testament to the benefits of sea air and look after you beautifully.

Price	£80–£90. Singles £50.
Rooms	4: 2 doubles, 1 twin, 1 single.
Meals	Packed lunch £5. Pub 350 yds.
Closed	Rarely.
Directions	Exit A30 at Cambourne (West) A3047. Left, then right at r'bout. Right on entering Conner Downs, then on for 2 miles. House on right after sign for Gwithian.

Jilly Whitaker
Calize Country House,
Gwithian, Hayle,
Cornwall TR27 5BW

Tel	01736 753268
Fax	01736 753268
Email	jilly@calize.co.uk
Web	www.calize.co.uk

Map 1   Entry 30

Cornwall

Trezelah Farmhouse

You'll feel high here, on the moor between Penzance and St Ives. The humble manor farmhouse with solid stone walls and huge chimney breast at one end has a light and fresh interior of waxed floors, limed walls, Indian scatter rugs, books, a wood-burner and soft white sofas. Small bedrooms with fine antiques and gentle lighting will calm you, as will the unusually pretty bathrooms – and the lovely Caro who painted many of the pictures here. Stride out round the north coastal path, then take a breather at the Tinners Arms in Zennor and go all Lawrencian; this is a wonderful part of Cornwall.

Price	£70.
Rooms	3: 2 doubles;
	1 twin with separate bath.
Meals	Pub 3 miles.
Closed	Rarely.
Directions	After Tesco r'bout heading into Penzance on A30, B3311 towards St Ives. Through Gulval, left at Badgers Cross towards Chysauster; left to Trezelah.

Caro Woods
Trezelah Farmhouse,
Trezelah, Badgers Cross,
Penzance,
Cornwall TR20 8XD
Tel   01736 874388
Email   info@trezelah.co.uk
Web   www.trezelah.co.uk

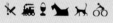

Map 1   Entry 31

Cornwall

Ennys

Prepare to be spoiled. A fire smoulders in the sumptuous sitting room, tea is laid out in the Aga-warm kitchen, and bedrooms are luxurious: a king-size bed or an elegant modern four-poster, powerful showers and crisp white linen. The stylishness continues into the suites and everywhere there are fascinating artefacts from Gill's travels, designer fabrics and original art. The road ends at Ennys, so it is utterly peaceful; walk down to the river and along the old towpath to St Ives Bay. Or stay put: play tennis (on grass!) and swim in the heated pool sunk deep into the tropical gardens.

Price	£80–£115. Singles from £65.
Rooms	5: 2 doubles, 1 twin/double. Barn: 2 family suites.
Meals	Pub 3 miles.
Closed	8 November–20 December. 3 January–15 March.
Directions	2 miles east of Marazion on B3280, look for sign & turn left leading down Trewhella Lane between St Hilary & Relubbus. On to Ennys.

Gill Charlton
Ennys,
St Hilary, Penzance,
Cornwall TR20 9BZ
Tel   01736 740262
Fax   01736 740055
Email   ennys@ennys.co.uk
Web   www.ennys.co.uk

Map 1   Entry 32

Cornwall

Ednovean Farm

There's a terrace for each immaculate bedroom – one truly private – with views to the wild blue yonder and St Michael's Mount Bay: an enchanting outlook that changes with the passage of the day. Come for peace, space and the best of 'boutique B&B': eclectic fabrics and colours, pretty lamps, gleaming copper, fluffy bathrobes and handmade soaps. The beamed, open-plan sitting/dining area is an absorbing mix of exotic, rustic and elegant; have full breakfast here or continental in your room. A footpath through the field leads to the village; walk to glorious Prussia Cove and Cudden Point, too.

Price	£80–£90. Singles £70–£80.
Rooms	3: 2 doubles, 1 four-poster.
Meals	Pub 5-minute walk.
Closed	Christmas.
Directions	From A30 after Crowlas r'bout, A394 to Helston. 0.25 miles after next r'bout, 1st right for Perranuthnoe. Farm drive on left, signed.

Christine & Charles Taylor
Ednovean Farm,
Perranuthnoe,
Penzance,
Cornwall TR20 9LZ
Tel   01736 711883
Email   info@ednoveanfarm.co.uk
Web   www.ednoveanfarm.co.uk

Map 1   Entry 33

Cornwall

Drym Farm

Rural, but not too deeply: the Tate at St Ives is a 15-minute drive. The 1705 farmhouse, beautifully revived, is surrounded by ancient barns, a dairy and a forge, fascinating to Cornish historians. Jan arrived in 2002, with an enthusiasm for authenticity and simple, stylish good taste. French limestone floors in the hall, striking art on the walls, a roll top bath, a *bateau lit*, an antique brass bed. Paintwork is fresh cream and taupe. There are old fruit trees and young camellias, a TV-free sitting room with two plump sofas and organic treats at breakfast. Charming and utterly peaceful.

Price	£70–£90. Singles from £55.
Rooms	3: 2 doubles each with separate bath; 1 twin sharing bath.
Meals	Pubs/restaurants within 4 miles.
Closed	Rarely.
Directions	From A30 to Hayle; through Hayle to r'bout, left to Helston. At Leedstown, left towards Drym. Follow road until right turn to Drym. Farm fourth on lane, on right after Drym House.

Jan Bright
Drym Farm,
Drym, Praze-an-Beeble,
Camborne,
Cornwall TR14 0NU
Tel   01209 831039
Email   drymfarm@hotmail.co.uk
Web   www.drymfarm.co.uk

Map 1   Entry 34

Cornwall

The Gardens

Two old miners' cottages combine to create this small, modest, well-tended home. Irish Moira, a retired midwife, adores flowers and her posies brighten every corner; Goff, a potter, tends the vegetables. Both are charming and kind. Sweet snug bedrooms have patchwork quilts, cotton sheets, antique linen runners and plenty of books. One is on the ground floor overlooking the pretty cottage garden, two are up a narrow stair. Aga-cooked breakfasts and homemade jams are brought to the sun-streamed conservatory; in the sitting room a woodburner belts out the heat. Great value.

Price	£60–£68. Singles £30–£34.
Rooms	3: 2 doubles;
	1 twin/double with separate bath.
Meals	Packed lunch from £7.50.
	Pubs & restaurants 10-minute drive.
Closed	Christmas & New Year.
Directions	A394 Helston to Penzance, 2nd right after Ashton Post Office for Tresowes Green. After 0.25 miles, sign for house on right.

Moira & Goff Cattell
The Gardens,
Tresowes,
Ashton,
Helston,
Cornwall TR13 9SY
Tel   01736 763299

🚶 ✘ 🚆 ♟

Map 1   Entry 35

Cornwall

Chydane

All that separates you from the sand and sea is the coastal path. At the far end of the spectacular, three-mile beach is Porthleven; beyond, West Penwith stretches magically into the distance. All this, and lighthouses, basking sharks, dolphins. One elegant double room, with gorgeous linen, a superb bed and a chesterfield, opens onto a French balcony overlooking the waves. The bathrooms, too, are warm and you get thick white bathrobes, lovely candles, big showers. Up steep stairs to the attic is a second room with a porthole window and a new bathroom. Walk to an excellent pub for dinner. *Children over 12 welcome.*

Price	£120. Singles £75.
Rooms	2: 1 double;
	1 double with separate bathroom.
Meals	Pub/restaurant 0.5 miles.
Closed	Christmas.
Directions	From Helston A3083 to the Lizard. After 2 miles right to Gunwalloe. Right before Halzephron Inn. Chydane on right above beach.

Carla & John Caslin
Chydane,
Gunwalloe Fishing Cove,
Helston,
Cornwall TR12 7QB
Tel   01326 241232
Email   carla.caslin@btinternet.com

✘ ♟

Map 1   Entry 36

Cornwall

Landewednack House

The view to the sea is heart-stopping; house and garden are bathed in a magical, ever-changing light. Spirits will soar as soon as you arrive and it's Susan's aim to cosset you in her immaculate house. Antony the chef keeps the wheels oiled and the food coming – try his green crab soup or succulent lobster. Erik is a real gourmand and has a covetable cellar of over 2,000 bottles of wine. Toile, chintz and fresh linen in the bedrooms add to the luxury, and bathrooms sparkle. Swim in the serene sheltered pool, laze in the pavilion or walk the three minutes to the sea. *Minimum two-night stay during July & August.*

Price	From £126. Singles £63–£75.
Rooms	3: 2 doubles, 1 twin.
Meals	Dinner, 4 courses, £33–£38.
Closed	Open all year.
Directions	From Helston, A3083 south. Just before Lizard, left to Church Cove. Follow signs for about 0.75 miles. House on left behind blue gates.

	Susan Thorbek
	Landewednack House,
	Church Cove, The Lizard,
	Cornwall TR12 7PQ
Tel	01326 290877
Fax	01326 290192
Email	luxurybandb@landewednackhouse.com
Web	www.landewednackhouse.com

Map 1   Entry 37

Cornwall

Halftides

Hugely enjoyable and special, surrounded by three acres with a private path down to the beach. Light-filled bedrooms are upbeat and fun with gorgeous fabrics, unusual wallpapers, crisp linen, dreamy views; bathrooms are sleek in glass and chrome. Susie is an artist and a chef and will give you a delicious organic breakfast, and a dinner of seasonal food – perhaps a barbecue in the garden in summer. Take the coastal path north or south, visit the working harbour in the village – or snaffle a packed lunch from Susie and head for the beach. This is the perfect place to relax and unwind.

Price	£75–£90. Singles £55–£60.
Rooms	3: 1 double; 1 double, 1 single sharing separate bath.
Meals	Dinner £20–£25. Packed lunch £10.
Closed	February.
Directions	A3083 to Lizard, right to Cury, 5 miles; pass Poldhu beach & enter Mullion. Right into Laflouder Lane, follow lane to very end, past sign 'Private Road'. House is 1st on right.

	Charles & Susie Holdsworth Hunt
	Halftides,
	Laflouder Lane,
	Mullion, Helston,
	Cornwall TR12 7HU
Tel	01326 241935
Email	halftides@btinternet.com
Web	www.halftides.co.uk

Map 1   Entry 38

Cornwall

Carmelin

The setting is sensational: you are perched on the last strip of land before the Atlantic which swirls around the Lizard at England's most southerly point. Breakfasts – hearty, continental, delicious – have to fight for your attention, so all-encompassing are the views. The bedroom has them too, from two big windows; they overlook your own patio and the sea beyond... waking is sheer delight. Attic rooms are ideal for children aged over seven. John and Jane are gentle, relaxed people who enjoy their guests; walk the coastal path and return to a lovely home-cooked meal. *French, Italian & Afrikaans spoken.*

Price	From £72. Singles by arrangement.
Rooms	1 double with separate bath/shower.
Meals	Continental breakfast. Dinner from £16. BYO. Pub within walking distance.
Closed	Rarely.
Directions	From Helston to the Lizard; at Lizard Green, right, opp. Regent Café (head for Smugglers Fish & Chips); immed. right, pass wc on left. Road unmade; on for 500 yds; double bend; 2nd on right.

Jane & John Grierson
Carmelin,
Pentreath Lane,
The Lizard, Helston,
Cornwall TR12 7NY

Tel	01326 290677
Email	pjcarmelin@btinternet.com
Web	www.bedandbreakfastcornwall.co.uk

Map 1   Entry 39

Cornwall

Treleague

Surrounded by the unspoilt coves and fishing villages of the Lizard, this simply converted 17th-century barn is home to swallows, who sometimes swoop in looking for their old nesting spot. The original barn doors on the top floor open onto a Spanish parador feel and a huge dining/sitting hall with wood-burner, handsome pine furniture and a large oil painting by Bart O'Farrel. Bedrooms are uncluttered and light with beams, iron beds and smart TVs; two are reached over a little footbridge. Mark and Carrie are warmly enthusiastic and give you good coffee, delicious fruit salad, and eggs from their hens.

Price	£64–£74. Singles £45–£55.
Rooms	3 doubles.
Meals	Pubs within walking distance.
Closed	Never.
Directions	A3083 Helston-Lizard. Pass HMS Culdrose airbase on left; at mini r'bout, left onto B3293 St Keverne; through Laddenvean; sharp bend towards Porthhallow; 250 yds on left, house signed.

Mark & Carrie Hayes
Treleague,
St Keverne, Helston,
Cornwall TR12 6PQ

Tel	01326 281500
Mobile	07790 716388
Email	mark@treleague.co.uk
Web	www.treleague.co.uk

Map 1   Entry 40

Cornwall

The Hen House

Greenies will explode with delight: Sandy and Gary are passionately committed to sustainability. Unless you're interested in recycling, a greeting talk with maps, loads of local tips and all things green, this isn't for you. More enlightened souls will adore the spacious, colourful rooms, the bright fabrics, the wildflower meadow with inviting sun loungers, the pond, the tai chi, the fairy-lit courtyard at night, the scrumptious local food, the birdsong. There's even a sanctuary room for reiki and reflexology set deep into the earth. Join in or flounder. *Minimum stay two nights. Children over 12 welcome.*

Low energy light bulbs, composting and recycling are just the starting point here: rainwater is harvested in containers from both roofs, and guests are given information on sustainability and encouraged to buy local: everything from your breakfast egg to the plate it sizzles on is from Cornwall. Sandy and Gary have made a deliberate choice to adopt a less materialistic lifestyle and a simpler existence; they have recently constructed a paper and bamboo palace on the sands at Looe Bar as part of a community project.

Price	£65-£75. Singles £60.
Rooms	2 doubles.
Meals	Pub/restaurant 1 mile.
Closed	Rarely.
Directions	Off B3293 to St Keverne from Helston, left to Newtown-in-St Martin. After 2 miles right at T-junc. Follow road for 2-3 miles then left fork. Round 7 bends then right at triangulation stone for Tregarne.

Sandy & Gary Pulfrey
The Hen House, Tregarne,
Manaccan, Helston,
Cornwall TR12 6EW

Tel	01326 280236
Mobile	07809 229958
Email	henhouseuk@aol.com
Web	www.thehenhouse-cornwall.co.uk

SPECIAL
GREEN ENTRY
see page 17

Map 1 Entry 41

Cornwall

Bosvathick

A huge old Cornish house that has been in Kate's family since 1760 along with all the pictures, books, heavy furniture, Indian rugs, ornate plasterwork, pianos and even a harp. Historians and garden lovers will be in their element: pass three Celtic crosses dating from the 7th century before the long drive finds the imposing house (all granite gate posts and lions) and a magnificent garden with grotto, lake, pasture and woodland. Bedrooms are traditional, full of books, antiques and lovely views; bathrooms are plain, functional and clean. Come then to experience a 'time warp' and Kate's good breakfasts.

Price	£60. Singles £45.
Rooms	2: 1 twin with separate bath; 1 twin with shared bath.
Meals	Packed lunch £4. Pubs 2 miles.
Closed	Easter, Christmas & New Year.
Directions	From Constantine, signs to Falmouth. 2.5 miles, pass Bosvathick Riding Stables, next entrance on left. Drive thro' gate posts & green gate. A map can be sent to visitors.

Kate & Stephen Tyrrell
Bosvathick,
Constantine,
Falmouth,
Cornwall TR11 5RD

Tel	01326 340103, 01326 340153
Email	kate@forgottenhouses.co.uk
Web	www.pasticcio.co.uk/bosvathick

Map 1   Entry 42

Cornwall

Tregew Vean

Once the home of a packet skipper, this pretty Georgian slate-hung house stands in a sunny spot above Flushing. From the garden with its palms, agapanthus, olive and fig trees, you glimpse the Fal estuary. The house is fresh and elegant, with tenderly cared-for antiques and an entertaining straw hat collection in the hall; Sandra and Rodney – both chatty and charming – give you comfortable bedrooms in your own part of the house. Flushing is a ten-minute walk and in the village there are two pubs that do food and a fish restaurant on the quay. There's plenty to do and you can catch the passenger ferry to Falmouth.

Price	From £80. Singles £45.
Rooms	2: 1 double, 1 double sharing bath (same party only).
Meals	Pubs/restaurants 0.25 miles.
Closed	Christmas.
Directions	From Penryn towards Mylor. After 1 mile right to Flushing. Entrance 1 mile down road on right, 30 yds before T-junction.

Sandra & Rodney Myers
Tregew Vean,
Flushing, Falmouth,
Cornwall TR11 5TF

Tel	01326 379462
Mobile	07770 663774
Email	tregewvean@aol.com
Web	www.tregewvean.co.uk

Map 1   Entry 43

Cornwall

Trevilla House

The sea and peninsula wrap around you – an enviable position – and the King Harry ferry gives you an easy reach into the glorious Roseland peninsula. Frog stencils add a humorous touch to the bathroom, and the freshly decorated bedrooms are old-fashioned and comfortable, the twin with garden views and a sofa, the double with sea views. Jinty is warm and welcoming and rustles up delicious breakfasts in the sunny conservatory that looks south over the sea. Trelissick Gardens and the Copeland China Collection are just next door, and the Maritime Museum, cycling, watersports and coastal walks close by.

Price	From £70. Singles by arrangement.
Rooms	3: 1 twin; 1 double with separate bath/shower & sitting room. Extra single for same party.
Meals	Restaurants/pubs 1-2 miles.
Closed	Christmas & New Year.
Directions	A390 to Truro; A39 to Falmouth. At double r'bout with garage, left off 2nd r'bout (B3289); pass pub on left; at x-roads, left (B3289); 200 yds on, fork right to Feock. On to T-junc., then left; 1st on right.

	Jinty & Peter Copeland
	Trevilla House,
	Feock, Truro,
	Cornwall TR3 6QG
Tel	01872 862369
Mobile	07791 977621
Email	jinty@trevilla.com
Web	www.trevilla.com

Map 1 Entry 44

Cornwall

Pelyn

Sheep on the hillside driveway remain curiously unmoved by the view that sweeps so lushly down to the creek. Set in its own green acres, minutes from golden beaches, this modern house built around an 11th century dwelling, is a peaceful, and contemporary hideaway. Smugglers from a nearby cove once visited; nowadays a tap at the door brings a lobster instead. Fresh flowers are some of the personal touches in light, airy bedrooms (one cosy with sofa) and charming country bathrooms. Tuck into home eggs and local bacon in the conservatory in summer as you gaze out on rabbits and birds.

Price	£75. Singles £50.
Rooms	2: 1 twin/double; 1 double with separate bathroom.
Meals	Lobster & wine dinner £30, by arrangement. Packed lunch £7.50. Pubs 5-minute drive.
Closed	Rarely.
Directions	To Gerrans & Portscatho. Thro' Gerrans, road to St Anthony Head. Just after Percuil, turning next drive right at 150 yds in dip in road & sharp bend. Signed.

	Graham & Bridget Reid
	Pelyn,
	Gerrans,
	Portscatho, Truro,
	Cornwall TR2 5ET
Tel	01872 580837
Email	pelyncreek@aol.com
Web	www.pelyncreek.com

Map 1 Entry 45

Cornwall

Pine Cottage

The Cornish sea laps the steep quay of this narrow inlet's port, its blue horizon just visible from the window of the elegant bedroom high up on the coveside. A perfect spot to wake on a summer's morn. The house is as sunny as its owner, the guest bedroom charmingly informal with its hand-painted violet-strewn wallpaper, super big bed and shelves brimming with books. A handful of small open-top fishing boats slips out at dawn to bring back catches of crab and lobster. Clare will give you a splendid breakfast of warm fruit salad, local bacon and eggs and home-grown tomatoes.

Price	£85.
Rooms	1 double.
Meals	Pub 100 yds.
	Restaurants within 5 miles.
Closed	Rarely.
Directions	From Tregony, A3078 to St Mawes. After 2 miles, at garage, left to Portloe. Thro' village to Ship Inn. Right fork after pub car park. Cottage immed. on left between white gateposts up drive.

Clare Holdsworth
Pine Cottage,
Portloe,
Truro,
Cornwall TR2 5RB

Tel	01872 501385
Web	www.pine-cottage.net

Map 1 Entry 46

Cornwall

Hay Barton

The giant windows overlook many acres of farmland, well-stocked with South Devon cows and their calves. Jill and Blair give you locally sourced breakfast in the smart dining room with its giant flagstones and family antiques; later, retire to the guest sitting room with log fire. Bedrooms are pretty with fresh garden flowers, soft white linen, floral green walls and stripped floors. Gloriously large panelled bathrooms have roll top baths and are painted in soft, earthy colours. Guests are welcome to chuck a ball or two around the tennis court; there are good gardens to explore and restaurants nearby.

Price	£80. Singles £50.
Rooms	2 twins/doubles.
Meals	Pubs 1-2 miles.
Closed	Rarely.
Directions	A3078 from Tregony village towards St Mawes. After 1 mile, house on left, 100 yds down lane.

Jill & Blair Jobson
Hay Barton,
Tregony, Truro,
Cornwall TR2 5TF

Tel	01872 530288
Mobile	07813 643028
Email	jill@haybarton.com
Web	www.haybarton.com

Map 1 Entry 47

Cornwall

Bodrugan Barton

Everything's just right – the setting, the windy lanes, the gentle activity of the farm, the delightful hosts who look after you with such enthusiasm. What's more, there are freshly decorated bedrooms, good bathrooms, family antiques and the promise of a fine breakfast. The dining room is huge: even with sofas and a wood-burner, you could turn a cartwheel. An ancient lane leads to Colona Bay: small, secluded and full of rock pools. There's an indoor pool and sauna, too, and Heligan and the Eden Project nearby. Blissful. *Children over 12 welcome. Guided walks by arrangement.*

Price	£80. Singles £45.
Rooms	3: 1 double; 1 double, 1 twin, each with separate bath/shower.
Meals	Pub 0.5 miles.
Closed	Christmas & New Year.
Directions	St Austell B3273 for Mevagissey. At x-roads on hill, right to Heligan, avoiding Mevagissey. Through Gorran, bend left to Portmellon. After 1.5 miles, right at grass triangle into farm, before hill.

Sally & Tim Kendall
Bodrugan Barton,
Mevagissey,
Cornwall PL26 6PT
Tel   01726 842094
Email   stay@bodrugan.co.uk
Web   www.bodrugan.co.uk

Map 1   Entry 48

Cornwall

Bosillion

A special set up. Beautiful rooms in your part of the house lead onto a pretty, tiered garden – take your breakfast out here and relax in the sun. Come for cool calm colours, elegant antiques, a big bedroom and a real sense of privacy. The farmhouse has been in the family since the 1600s and Annabel and Jonathon have renovated thoughtfully and with flair. Your delightful bathroom has everything you need and your fridge is filled with summer fruits, walnut bread, and local produce ready for your breakfast – continental only. You are close to Heligan, the Eden Project and the beaches of the Roseland peninsular. Wonderful.

Price	£80.
Rooms	1 suite for 2.
Meals	Restaurants nearby.
Closed	Christmas & New Year.
Directions	From Truro, A390 for St Austell. 6 miles on, through Grampound; on leaving village, at top of hill, right at speed limit sign into Bosillion Lane. House 150 yds on left.

Jonathon & Annabel Croggon
Bosillion,
Bosillion Lane,
Grampound, Truro,
Cornwall TR2 4QY
Tel   01726 883327
Email   jcroggon@tiscali.co.uk

Map 1   Entry 49

Cornwall

Mother Ivey Cottage

So close to the sea that there are salt splashes on the windows! Exceptionally lovely hosts here and a simple refuge (once a fish cellar for processing catches) from crashing surf and Atlantic winds. Look out of the window to the big blue below, swim to the lifeboat launch, barbecue on the beach. The coastal path is stunning and you can walk to surfing beaches or just drop down to the quiet bay beneath your window. Cultured, kind hosts and a relaxed atmosphere, but bedrooms and bathrooms are basic so not for those who like their B&Bs stylish or sparkling. Families love it.

Price	From £60. Singles by arrangement.
Rooms	2 twins. Extra single bed.
Meals	Dinner from £20. Packed lunch from £5.
Closed	Rarely.
Directions	From St Merryn, right for Trevose Head. Over sleeping policemen. After tollgate ticket machine, right thro' 2nd farm gate. On towards sea; cottage gate at end of track, on right.

Phyllida & Antony Woosnam-Mills
Mother Ivey Cottage,
Trevose Head,
Padstow,
Cornwall PL28 8SL
Tel   01841 520329
Email antony@trevosehead.co.uk

Map 1   Entry 50

Cornwall

Ballaminers House

Slate slabs, planked floors and deep sash windows with field views in this welcoming old farmhouse five minutes from Padstow. Generous, artistic Amanda serves delicious breakfasts in a heritage green room elegant with family heirlooms and small chandelier – or outdoors in summer. The cosy, light bedrooms are spotless and charming, with Designers Guild fabrics, soft colours, Balinese touches. Thoughtful extras include magazines, fruit basket, bath oils and Indonesian dressing gowns; one bathroom has a roll top tub that fits two! In the garden a series of hedged 'rooms' provide flowers for the house. *Children over ten welcome.*

Price	£70-£85. Singles £55-£85.
Rooms	3: 2 doubles, 1 twin, sharing 2 bathrooms.
Meals	Pubs/restaurants 5-minute drive.
Closed	Never.
Directions	A39 after Wadebridge, signed A389 Padstow. Reach Little Petherick; over hump bridge to whitewashed cottage at corner of unmarked lane; left up lane bearing right; on right, opp. pink house.

Amanda Fearon
Ballaminers House,
Little Petherick, Padstow,
Cornwall PL27 7QT
Tel   01841 540933
Mobile 07903 270199
Email   pandafearon@aol.com
Web   www.ballaminershouse.co.uk

Map 1   Entry 51

Cornwall

Caradoc of Tregardock

Crashing breakers, wheeling gulls, carpets of wild flowers in the spring; a dream for artists and a tonic for everyone. Walk down to the secluded tidal beach with two miles of sand, rock pools, caves and some tricky surfing. The sympathetically restored listed buildings are set around a grassy courtyard within 300 acres of farmland. You can B&B or self cater – all is perfect for large or small groups and there's a studio for art and yoga. Bedrooms are light and airy with white walls and uninterrupted Atlantic views. There are large, safe lawns and a summerhouse and deck for glorious sunsets. *Cream teas.*

Price	£90–£140. Singles £45–£70. Under 5s free. Self-catering £500–£2,500 p.w.
Rooms	4 + 1: 4 twins/doubles. Cottage for 4 (1 double, 1 twin).
Meals	Dinner £35. Pubs/restaurants 2 miles. Private chef special occasions.
Closed	Rarely.
Directions	South from Delabole; 2 miles right to Treligga; 2nd farm road, signed.

	Janet Cant Caradoc of Tregardock, Treligga, Cornwall PL33 9ED
Tel	01840 213300
Fax	01840 213300
Email	info@tregardock.com
Web	www.tregardock.com

Map 1 Entry 52

Cornwall

Roskear

Rosina modestly refers to her home as offering "simple cottage B&B" but this is just perfect as a rural retreat and for families, with all the attractions ten minutes by car. A large sitting room with log fire, a warm and smiling hostess, estuary views, happy dogs, clucking hens – this is countryside at its most charming. There's a sunny spot in the garden for summer breakfasts served on blue china, 30 acres of woodland and 40 of grassland to explore – and dining in one of the famous restaurants in Padstow. The Camel cycle trail is nearby and you can hire bikes locally. Uncomplicated, good value.

Price	From £60. Singles £30.
Rooms	2: 1 double with separate bath; 1 double sharing bath (let to same party only).
Meals	Pubs/restaurants 0.5–6 miles.
Closed	Rarely.
Directions	Bypass Wadebridge on A39 for Redruth. Over bridge, pass Esso garage on left; then first right to Edmonton. By modern houses turn immed. right to Roskear over cattle grid.

	Rosina Messer–Bennetts Roskear, St Breock, Wadebridge, Cornwall PL27 7HU
Tel	01208 812805
Mobile	07748 432013
Email	rosina@roskear.com
Web	www.roskear.com

Map 1 Entry 53

Cornwall

Porteath Barn

What a spot! This upside-down house is elegantly uncluttered and cool with seagrass flooring and a wood-burner in the sitting room. Bedrooms – not vast – have fresh flowers, quilted bedspreads and there's an Italian marble shower room; the feel is private with your own doors to the lovely, large garden. Walks from here down a path with ponds will take you to Epphaven Cove and the beach at the bottom of the valley or to a good pub for supper if you're feeling hearty. The Bloors have perfected the art of B&B-ing, being kind and helpful without being intrusive. *Children over 12 or by arrangement.*

Price	From £75. Singles by arrangement.
Rooms	3: 2 twins/doubles, each with separate bath or shower; 1 double let to same party only.
Meals	Pub 1.5 miles.
Closed	Rarely.
Directions	A39 to Wadebridge. At r'bout follow signs to Polzeath, then to Porteath Bee Centre. Through Bee Centre shop car park, down farm track; house signed on right after 150 yds.

Jo & Michael Bloor
Porteath Barn,
St Minver,
Wadebridge,
Cornwall PL27 6RA
Tel   01208 863605
Fax   01208 863954
Email   mbloor@ukonline.co.uk

Map 1   Entry 54

Cornwall

Upton Farm

A restored farmhouse set back from the rugged coastline with unrivalled views, from Tintagel to Port Isaac and beyond… sunsets are sublime. Bedrooms are traditional and smart, there's a games room and safe storage for surfers. Slate slabs in the hall, gentle colours throughout; from the depths of the sea-green sofa in your drawing room, breathe in those AONB views. Such seclusion! Yet ten minutes across fields is the coastal path and, nearby, serious surfing, great pub, restaurant and more. Kick-start your day with Ricardo's signature muesli. *Minimum stay two nights July & Aug. Children over eight welcome.*

Price	£85-£95. Singles from £60.
Rooms	3: 2 doubles, 1 twin.
Meals	Pub/restaurant 1 mile.
Closed	Rarely.
Directions	South through Delabole, near end of village right into Treligga Downs Rd; 0.5 miles to T-junc; turn right. 1 mile on, pass Trecarne Farm on left; 100 yds, house on right.

Elizabeth & Ricardo Dorich
Upton Farm,
Trebarwith, Delabole,
Cornwall PL33 9DG
Tel   01840 770225
Fax   01840 770377
Email   ricardo@dorich.co.uk
Web   www.upton-farm.co.uk

Map 1   Entry 55

Cornwall

Tremoren

Views stretch sleepily over the Cornish countryside. You might feel inclined to do nothing more than snooze over your book on the terrace, but the surfing beaches, the Camel Trail and the Eden Project are all close by. The stone and slate former farmhouse has been smartly updated with a light and airy ground-floor bedroom – all soft colours, pretty china and crisp bed linen – and a swish, power-shower bathroom. Your red-walled sitting room, full of books and interesting maps, leads out onto the flower-filled terrace: perfect for that evening drink. Lanie is bubbly and engaging, and food is her passion.

Price	£80.
Rooms	1 double & sitting room.
Meals	Dinner, 4 courses, £25. Inn 0.5 miles.
Closed	Rarely.
Directions	A39 to St Kew Highway through village; left at Red Lion. Down lane, 1st left round sharp right-hand bend. 2nd drive on right; signed.

Philip & Lanie Calvert
Tremoren,
St Kew, Bodmin,
Cornwall PL30 3HA
Tel 01208 841790
Fax 01208 841031
Email la.calvert@btopenworld.com
Web www.sunsell.com/clients/tremoren

Map 1 Entry 56

Cornwall

Polrode Mill Cottage

A lovely, solid, beamy, 17th-century cottage in a birdsung valley. Inside, flagged floors, Chesterfields, a wood-burner and a light open feel. Your friendly young hosts live next door; they are working hard on the informal flower and vegetable garden, much of the produce is used in David's delicious homemade dinners, there's pumpkin marmalade and eggs from the hens. Bedrooms are cottage-cosy with stripped floors, comfy wrought-iron beds and silver cast-iron radiators; fresh bathrooms have double-ended roll top baths. A slight hum of traffic outside but no matter, inside it is blissfully peaceful.

Price	£75–£90. Singles £55.
Rooms	3 doubles.
Meals	Dinner, 3 courses, £27.
Closed	Rarely.
Directions	From A395 take A39 towards Camelford. Through Camelford; continue on A39 to Knightsmill. From there, 1.8 miles up on left-hand side.

Deborah Hilborne & David Edwards
Polrode Mill Cottage,
Allen Valley, St Tudy,
Bodmin,
Cornwall PL30 3NS
Tel 01208 850203
Email polrode@tesco.net
Web www.polrodemillcottage.co.uk

Map 1 Entry 57

Cornwall

Higher Lank Farm

Families rejoice: you can only come if you have a child under five! Celtic crosses in the garden and original panelling hint at the house's 500-year history; one bedroom is resplendent with oak, the other two more traditional. Nursery teas begin at 5pm, grown-up suppers are later and Lucy will cheerfully babysit while the rest of you slink off to the pub. Farm-themed playgrounds are covered in safety matting and grass, there are piglets and chicks, a pony to ride, eggs to collect, a nursery rhyme trail, a sand barn for little ones and cream teas in the garden. Oh, and real nappies are provided!

Price	From £85. Singles by arrangement.
Rooms	3 family rooms.
Meals	Supper £16.25. Nursery tea £4.75. Packed lunch £7. Pub 1.5 miles.
Closed	November-Easter.
Directions	From Launceston, A395, then A39 thro' Camelford. Left onto B3266 to Bodmin. After 4 miles, left signed Wenfordbridge Pottery; over bridge, past pottery & on brow of hill, left into lane; house at top.

Lucy Finnemore
Higher Lank Farm,
St Breward,
Bodmin,
Cornwall PL30 4NB
Tel 01208 850716
Email higherlankfarm@waitrose.com
Web www.higherlankfarm.co.uk

Map 1 Entry 58

Cornwall

Lavethan

A glorious house in the most glorious of settings: views sail down to the valley. It rambles on many levels and is part 15th-century: walls are stone, floors are flagged, stairs are oak. The bedrooms in the house are lovely; one, part of the old chapel, has stone lintels that cross it, all are sunny, with proper bathrooms and lovely old baths for wallowing in. Catherine is a warm hostess and has decorated lavishly in country style; the guest sitting room is hugely welcoming with books, flowers and piano. All this and acres of ancient woods, Celtic crosses and a heated pool in the old walled garden. *Children over ten welcome.*

Price	£70-£90. Singles £40-£50.
Rooms	4: 2 twins/doubles; 2 doubles, each with separate bath.
Meals	Occasional dinner £25. Pub 0.25 miles.
Closed	Rarely.
Directions	From A30, turn for Blisland. There, past church on left & pub on right. Take lane at bottom left of village green. 0.25 miles on, drive on left (granite pillars & cattle grid).

Christopher & Catherine Hartley
Lavethan,
Blisland, Bodmin,
Cornwall PL30 4QG
Tel 01208 850487
Fax 01208 851387
Email chrishartley@btconnect.com
Web www.lavethan.com

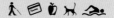

Map 1 Entry 59

Cornwall

Cabilla Manor

Rich, exotic rugs, cushions and artefacts from around the world, and Louella's sumptuous hand-stencilled fabrics and furniture. There's a treasure round every corner of this fine manor on the edge of Bodmin Moor, and an opera house in one of the barns. Huge beds, coir carpets and garden flowers in your rooms, a dining room crammed floor to ceiling with books, many of them Robin's (a writer and explorer). A lofty conservatory for meals overlooks elegant lawns, garden and tennis court; the views are heavenly, the hosts wonderful and the final mile thrillingly wild.

Cornwall

Collon Barton

Come for the lofty position on a grassy hillside, the phenomenal views over unspoiled countryside and the pretty creekside village of Lerryn. This 18th-century farmhouse is approached up a pretty, stone lane; it's a working sheep farm and an artistic household (sculptures galore) with traditional, peaceful bedrooms on the second floor and an elegant drawing room for guests. Anne sells huge dried hydrangeas and, on sunny days, welcomes you with tea in the summer house. Guided walks, canoeing and biking from the village and the Eden Project 20 minutes away. *Children & pets by arrangement.*

Price	£80. Singles £40.
Rooms	4: 1 double; 2 doubles, 1 twin, sharing 2 baths.
Meals	Dinner, 3 courses, £30. Pub 4 miles. Restaurant 8-10 miles.
Closed	Christmas & New Year.
Directions	6 miles after Jamaica Inn on A30, left for Cardinham. Through Millpool & straight on, ignoring further signs to Cardinham. After 2.5 miles, left to Manor 0.75 miles; on right down drive.

Robin & Louella Hanbury-Tenison
Cabilla Manor,
Mount, Bodmin,
Cornwall PL30 4DW
Tel   01208 821224
Fax   01208 821267
Email   louella@cabilla.co.uk
Web   www.cabilla.co.uk

Map 1   Entry 60

Price	£75-£80. Singles £45-£50.
Rooms	2: 1 twin/double, 1 twin.
Meals	Pub 10-minute walk.
Closed	Christmas.
Directions	A390 to Lostwithiel. Take 1st left down Grenville Road, signed Lerryn, 400 yds left at x-roads to Lerryn and St Winnow. In village, before bridge, left to Couch's Mill and Liskeard. 70 yds bear left into cul-de-sac and take farm lane 500 yds to top.

Anne & Iain Mackie
Collon Barton,
Lerryn, Lostwithiel,
Cornwall PL22 0NX
Tel   01208 872908
Fax   01208 873812
Mobile   07721 090186
Email   i.mackie@btconnect.com

Map 1   Entry 61

Cornwall

Sheviock Barton

This is Cornwall's 'Forgotten Corner' set in an Area of Outanding Natural Beauty. The house is opposite the church, rooted in time and space, its massive walls echoing their 400 years of history. All is fresh and delightful within, immaculate yet inviting. You breakfast in a perfect farmhouse kitchen: rugs on slate, Welsh dresser, comfy blue sofas and Aga to match. Heavy calico curtains and deep red walls in the guests' sitting room, bar billiards and table tennis in the games room, a charming simplicity in the warm bedrooms. Your hosts are the nicest people.

Price	From £70. Singles £40.
Rooms	3: 2 doubles, 1 family/twin for 3-4.
Meals	Pub/restaurant 0.5 miles.
Closed	Christmas & Boxing Day.
Directions	To Sheviock on A374. House opposite church.

Carol & Tony Johnson
Sheviock Barton,
Sheviock, Torpoint,
Cornwall PL11 3EH
Tel 01503 230793
Mobile 07775 688403
Email thebarton@sheviock.freeserve.co.uk
Web www.sheviockbarton.co.uk

Map 1   Entry 62

Cornwall

Buttervilla Farm

Gill and Robert are so good at growing vegetables (organically) they supply the local restaurants; all is cut and delivered within three hours. They're pretty good at looking after you too, in a totally relaxed fashion, with breakfasts of superb rare-breed bacon and modern Cornish suppers; fish and Red Ruby steak are specialities. No sitting room but bedrooms are big, colourful, comfortable and cared for; bathrooms are smart with solar-powered showers. Explore these 15 beautiful eco acres, stride the coastal path or head for the surf. Young and fun – with soul.
Minimum stay three nights July & August.

Price	£75–£85. From £55.
Rooms	3 doubles.
Meals	Dinner, 3 courses, £25. Restaurants 5-7 miles.
Closed	Rarely.
Directions	Turn by Halfway House at Polbathic for Downderry. House 400 yds up hill from inn, on left; signed before lane.

Gill & Robert Hocking
Buttervilla Farm,
Polbathic,
St Germans, Torpoint,
Cornwall PL11 3EY
Tel 01503 230315
Email info@buttervilla.com
Web www.buttervilla.com

Map 2   Entry 63

Cornwall

Lantallack Farm

Life and art exist in happy communion: Nicky loves playing the piano and runs courses in landscape painting and sculpture. This is a heart-warming place — hens in the orchard, fine breakfasts in the walled garden, a super outdoor pool, a straw-yellow sitting room with a log fire... and bedrooms with delicious beds and books galore. The gorgeous old Georgian farmhouse has breathtaking views over countryside, streams and wooded valleys. Set off to discover the Walkers' leat-side trail, and make a fuss of Polly, the Gloucester Old Spot pig, on the way. You will be inspired.

Price	From £80. Singles by arrangement.
Rooms	2 doubles.
Meals	Pubs/restaurants 1 mile.
Closed	Rarely.
Directions	A38 through Saltash & on for 3 miles. At Landrake 2nd right at West Lane. After 1 mile, left at white cottage for Tideford. House 150 yds on, on right.

Nicky Walker
Lantallack Farm,
Landrake, Saltash,
Cornwall PL12 5AE
Tel   01752 851281
Fax   01752 851281
Email   nickywalker44@tiscali.co.uk
Web   www.lantallack.co.uk

Map 2   Entry 64

Cornwall

Hornacott

The garden, in its lovely valley setting, has seats in little corners poised to catch the evening sun — perfect for a pre-dinner drink. The peaceful house is named after the hill and you have a private entrance to your wonderfully fresh and airy suite: a room with twin beds plus a large, square, high sitting room with windows that look down onto the wooded valley. With CD player, music, chocolates and magazines you'll feel beautifully self-contained. Jos, a kitchen designer, and Mary-Anne clearly enjoy having guests, and give you fresh local produce and free-range eggs for breakfast.

Price	From £76. Singles £45.
Rooms	1 suite. Single room for child available.
Meals	Dinner, 3 courses, £18. BYO.
Closed	Christmas.
Directions	B3254 Launceston-Liskeard. Through South Petherwin, down steep hill, last left before little bridge. House 1st on left.

Jos & Mary-Anne Otway-Ruthven
Hornacott,
South Petherwin, Launceston,
Cornwall PL15 7LH
Tel   01566 782461
Fax   01566 782461
Email   stay@hornacott.co.uk
Web   www.hornacott.co.uk

Map 1   Entry 65

Cornwall

Trevadlock Manor

No wonder Mickey has a twinkling smile and Carey is relaxed and chatty – they're London escapees! And have landed here, in a house that dates from 1530 with a Celtic Cross and mullion windows. Light pours into the long drawing room with open fire, comfy sofas with bright throws, well-thumbed books and good pictures. Bedrooms (delightfully private in the west wing) are light, fresh and simple, with sleigh beds, hand-painted French furniture and glorious views; warm bathrooms have soft towels. A sizzling full English is all you need for tackling the moor – or a potter outside to meet the goats.

Price	£50-£70.
Rooms	3: 1 double; 2 twins sharing bath.
Meals	Light suppers available.
Closed	End July to end August & Christmas.
Directions	A30 to Cornwall. 6 miles beyond Launceston exit left to Callington on B3257. Through Plusha turn right to Trevadlock, North Hill. Follow lane for 0.75 miles, house on right signed.

Mickey & Carey Bruton
Trevadlock Manor,
Lewannick, Launceston,
Cornwall PL15 7PW

Tel	01566 782227
Mobile	07879 403835
Email	manor@trevadlock.wanadoo.co.uk
Web	www.trevadlockmanor.co.uk

Map 1 Entry 66

Cornwall

The Old Vicarage

The first sight of quirky chimneys – the spires of former owner Reverend Hawker's parish churches – sets the scene for a house of theatricality. Jill, Richard and their home burst with knowledge on the eccentric vicar, local history and Victoriana. Rooms are casually grand, dotted with *objets* – brass gramophone, magic lantern, policemen's helmets. Browse books in the study, play the drawing room grand piano, sip brandy over billiards. Bedrooms are country-house pretty, bathrooms clean if cheerfully dated. Views reach to the sea. Walk off breakfast along the cliffs. Mobiles don't work. Bliss.

Price	£80. Singles £40.
Rooms	3: 1 double, 1 twin, 1 single.
Meals	Occasional dinner. Pub 10 minute walk.
Closed	December-January.
Directions	From A39 at Morwenstow, follow signs towards church. Small turning on right, just before church, marked 'public footpath'. Drive down to house.

Jill & Richard Wellby
The Old Vicarage,
Morwenstow,
Cornwall EX23 9SR

Tel	01288 331369
Fax	01288 356077
Email	jillwellby@hotmail.com
Web	www.rshawker.co.uk

Map 1 Entry 67

Cumbria

Sirelands

Sirelands, once a gardener's cottage, stands among rhododendrons and spreading trees on a sunny slope, a stream trickling gently by. The Carrs have lived here for many years and the house has a reassuringly lived-in feel. Enjoy home-grown produce over dinner at a polished country table, then retire to the sitting room, delightful with log basket and honesty bar. Sash windows overlook the lightly wooded garden, visited by roe deer and a variety of birds. Bedrooms and bathrooms are pleasant, carpeted and peaceful. Angela loves cooking and treats you to tea and homemade cake on arrival.

Price	£80.
Rooms	2: 1 twin; 1 double with separate bath/shower.
Meals	Dinner, 2-3 courses, £21–£26. Pubs 1.5 miles.
Closed	Rarely.
Directions	M6 north to junc. 43; A69 Newcastle; 3 miles to traffic lights. Right, on to Heads Nook; house 2 miles after village.

Angela Carr
Sirelands,
Heads Nook,
Brampton, Carlisle,
Cumbria CA8 9BT
Tel   01228 670389
Mobile   07748 101513
Email   carr_sirelands@btconnect.com

Map 12   Entry 68

Cumbria

The Old Rectory

The setting of this lovely old house could hardly be more pastoral. Many of its rooms face south and have superb views, with mountains and fells beyond. History has created an intriguing house full of unexpected corners; the old rectory dates from around 1360 but bedrooms are freshly contemporary and have super big beds. Gill cooks in imaginative 'bistro' style, David knows his wines and you eat by candlelight in a 16th-century room. They're relaxed and charming and, when the place is full, create a fabulous house-party feel. Outside, red squirrels and well-fed rabbits, a croquet lawn and stunning Skiddaw.

Price	From £90. Singles from £45.
Rooms	3: 1 double, 1 twin/double; 1 double with separate bath.
Meals	Dinner, 3 courses, £29. Pub 10-minute drive.
Closed	Christmas & New Year.
Directions	B5305 to Wigton; at A595, left. After 5 miles, left to Boltongate. Left at T-junc.; in village, signs for Ireby; down hill, last driveway on left.

Gill & David Taylor
The Old Rectory,
Boltongate, Ireby,
Cumbria CA7 1DA
Tel   01697 371647
Mobile   07801 900316
Email   boltongate@talk21.com
Web   www.boltongateoldrectory.com

Map 11   Entry 69

Cumbria

High Houses

The hilltop views will take your breath away – as will the drive to get up here! The wonderful old yeoman's house is surrounded by farmland and fell, fitting backdrop to an interior that brims with stylish simplicity. Be charmed by bare walls, stone slabs, vast rugs, planked floors, roaring fires, old Knole sofa, painted four-poster, wagging Jack Russells and... a thrilling stairway to the loft where the chickens roosted, now a bolthole for kids. Electricity is supplied by generator; breakfast – homemade sausages, eggs from the hens – is by the Aga, masterminded by Jill who just couldn't be nicer.

Price	£80. Singles £50.
Rooms	3: 1 double; 1 four-poster with separate shower, 1 twin/double, with cockloft for children, sharing shower.
Meals	Lunch £10-£15. Dinner, 2-4 courses, £25. Supper £15. Packed lunch £5. Pub/restaurant 2 miles.
Closed	Rarely.
Directions	On A591, 2 miles from Castle Inn Hotel, right for Ireby. After 2 miles, steep hill; right over cattle grid for Snittlegarth, bear right after 2nd grid; 0.5 miles up lane, past barn.

	Miss Jill Green High Houses, Snittlegarth, Ireby, Wigton, Cumbria CA7 1HE
Tel	01697 371549
Mobile	07929 397273
Email	enquiries@highhouses.co.uk
Web	www.highhouses.co.uk

Map 11   Entry 70

Cumbria

Willow Cottage

Gaze across rooftops through tiny windows towards the towering mass of Skiddaw, the Lakes' third highest mountain. Here is a miniature cottage garden with sweet peas, herbs, vegetables and flowers... all suitably rambling. Lovely Roy and Chris have kept most of the old barn's features: wooden floorboards, wonderful beams. Dried flowers, pretty china, antique linen, glowing lamps and patchwork quilts, a collection of christening gowns... dear little bedrooms have panelled bathrooms and old pine furniture. TV is delightfully absent, classical music plays and you are in the heart of a farming village.

Price	£60-£65. Singles £40-£45.
Rooms	2: 1 double, 1 twin.
Meals	Packed lunch £3.50. Pub 300 yds.
Closed	December-January.
Directions	From Keswick A591 to Carlisle (6.5 miles) right for Bassenthwaite village (0.5 miles). Straight on at village green, house on right.

	Roy & Chris Beaty Willow Cottage, Bassenthwaite, Keswick, Cumbria CA12 4QP
Tel	01768 776440
Email	chrisbeaty@amserve.com
Web	www.willowbarncottage.co.uk

Map 11   Entry 71

Cumbria

New House Farm

The large, comfortable beds, the linen, the fabrics, the pillows – comfort par excellence. You'll be impressed by the renovation, too – the plasterwork stops here and there to reveal old beam, slate or stone. A trio of the bedrooms are named after the mountain each faces; Swinside brings the 1650s house its own spring water. The breakfast room has a wood-burner, hunting prints and polished tables for Hazel's breakfasts which will fuel your adventures, the sitting room sports fireplaces and brocade sofas, and walkers will fall gratefully into the hot spring spa. *Children over six welcome.*

Price	£148. Singles £74-£115.
Rooms	5: 2 doubles, 1 twin/double. Stables: 2 four-posters.
Meals	Lunch from £6 (April-November), Dinner, 3-5 courses, £23-£31. Pubs 2.5 miles.
Closed	Never.
Directions	A66 to Cockermouth, then B5289 for Buttermere. Signed left 2.5 miles south of Lorton.

Hazel Thompson
New House Farm,
Lorton, Cockermouth,
Cumbria CA13 9UU

Tel	01900 85404
Fax	01900 85478
Email	hazel@newhouse-farm.co.uk
Web	www.newhouse-farm.co.uk

Map 11   Entry 72

Cumbria

Whitbysteads

Swing into the yard of a gentleman's farmhouse at the end of a drive lined with gorse, stone walls and sheep. It's a working farm, so lots going on with four-wheel drives, dogs and bustle. Victoria does styles and periods well: warm rugs, flowery sofas with plain linen armchairs, modern family paintings. The main bedroom is sumptuous and stylish with grand views over fells, the smaller room simpler; bathrooms are old-fashioned and big. A touch of London in the country with native sheep and busy hens outside the front door – and great hosts! Dress up in the evening for dinner at Sharrow Bay. *Garden open for NGS.*

Price	£80-£100.
Rooms	2: 1 double; 1 twin with separate bath.
Meals	Children's tea available. Pub 0.5 miles.
Closed	Rarely.
Directions	Exit 39 M6. A6 north, thro' Askham village past shop on right, thro' open gate, over 3 cattle grids. House on right after long drive.

Mrs Victoria Lowther
Whitbysteads,
Askham, Penrith,
Cumbria CA10 2PG

Tel	01931 712284
Fax	01931 712211
Email	info@gnap.fsnet.co.uk
Web	www.whitbysteads.org

Map 11   Entry 73

Cumbria

Greenah

Tucked into the hillside off a narrow lane, this 1750s smallholding is surrounded by fells, so is perfect for walkers. Absolute privacy for four friends or family with your own entrance to a beamed and stone-flagged sitting room with woodburning stove, creamy walls and cheery floral curtains. Warm bedrooms have original paintings, good beds, hot water bottles, bathrobes and a sparkling bathroom – which has a loo with a remarkable view. Malcolm is a climber; Marjorie is totally committed to organic food so you get a fabulous breakfast and good advice about the local area. Fell walking is not compulsory!

Price	£72-£80. Singles £44.
Rooms	2: 1 double, 1 twin sharing shower (let to same party only).
Meals	Packed lunch £6. Pubs/restaurants 3 miles.
Closed	Rarely.
Directions	M6 junc. 40 follow A66 west. Left for Matterdale; after 1.5 miles, left for Dacre. Up the hill, right fork to Lowthwaite, house 100 yds on right.

Marjorie & Malcolm Emery
Greenah,
Mattterdale,
Penrith,
Cumbria CA11 0SA
Tel   01768 483387
Email   enquiries@greenah.co.uk
Web   www.greenah.co.uk

Map 11   Entry 74

Cumbria

Cockenskell Farm

Sara loves her hill-farm garden, with its wild rhododendrons and fruitful orchards. Inside are beamed bathrooms and faded lemon quilts, old pine and patterned walls, idiosyncratic touches of colour and dashes of eccentricity. Relax with a book in the conservatory, stroll through the magical garden or tackle a bit of the Cumbrian Way which meanders through the fields to the back: hop over the dry-stone wall. Sara, a delightful, energetic presence, gives you home-grown fruits in season, sometimes walnuts. History seeps from every pore, the place glows with loving care and to stay here is a treat.

Price	£70. Singles from £35.
Rooms	3: 1 twin; 1 twin with separate bath; 1 single sharing bath.
Meals	Lunch £10. Packed lunch £5. Pubs 2 miles.
Closed	Mid-November to end of February.
Directions	In Blawith, opp. church up narrow lane, through farmyard. Right after cattle grid, over fell, right at fork through gates & up drive.

Sara Keegan
Cockenskell Farm,
Blawith, Ulverston,
Cumbria LA12 8EL
Tel   01229 885217
Mobile   07909 885086
Email   keegan@cockenskell.co.uk
Web   www.cockenskell.co.uk

Map 11   Entry 75

Cumbria

Fellside Studios

Two perfect studios in the tranquil Troutbeck valley: come for seclusion, stylishness and breathtaking views. Make your own sandwiches – or candlelit dinners – and get up when the mood takes you; come and go as you please. The flowerbeds spill with heathers and there's a secluded terrace for continental breakfast in the sun – delivered the night before for early risers; your hospitable hosts live in the attached house. Expect oak floors, slate shower rooms, immaculate kitchenettes with designer touches, DVD players, comfortable chairs and luxurious towels. Wonderful. *Minimum stay two nights.*

Price	£70–£90. Singles from £45.
Rooms	2 studios: each with 1 double, 1 twin/double & kitchen.
Meals	Pub/restaurant 0.5 miles.
Closed	Open all year.
Directions	From Windermere, A592 north for 3 miles; after bridge, immed. before church, left signed Troutbeck; 300 yds, 1st house on right.

Monica & Brian Liddell
Fellside Studios,
Troutbeck,
Cumbria LA23 1PE
Tel   01539 434000
Email   enquiry@fellsidestudios.co.uk
Web   www.fellsidestudios.co.uk

Map 11   Entry 76

Cumbria

Low Fell

Louise and Stephen are warm, fun, helpful, and their well-orchestrated house full of maps, lists, books and guides. Bedrooms are bright, sunny, pretty, with elegant patterned or checked fabrics, heavenly big beds, plump pillows and warm towels; the suite up in the loft is a super hideaway and you overlook trees animated with tuneful birds. Enjoy warm homemade bread and Aga pancakes at breakfast, warm your toes by the fire in winter, relax in the secluded garden with a glass of wine in summer. The house is a five-minute stroll from the lake and bustling Bowness. *Children over ten welcome.*

Price	£70–£90. Half-price for children.
Rooms	3: 1 double, 1 family suite (1 double, 1 twin).
Meals	Pubs/restaurants 200 yds.
Closed	Christmas.
Directions	From Kendal, A591 to Windermere; signs to Bowness. Bear left at bottom of hill & 1st left opp. church. Follow road past Burneside Hotel on right; house 50 yds, on right.

Louise & Stephen Broughton
Low Fell,
Ferney Green,
Bowness-on-Windermere,
Windermere, Cumbria LA23 3ES
Tel   01539 445612
Email   louisebroughton@btinternet.com
Web   www.low-fell.co.uk

Map 11   Entry 77

Cumbria

Low House

A mile from Windermere bustle, 17th-century Low House is a hidden gem. Generosity is key here: immense fires, capacious dressers, grand beds piled with duvets, coverlets and pillows. The bathrooms, too – hugely thick towels and opulent mirrors. Breakfast? Wonderful, in bed or downstairs. Curl up by the fire in the snug or the drawing room, dip into a book, take tea, pour yourself a sherry. Set off on sunny days on walks from the door. Best of all, you may 'hire' Johnnie to take you on the lake in his 1930s sailing boat, or on a grand tour in his classic Bentley. What a treat!

Price	£80–£120. Singles £50–£70.
Rooms	3: 2 doubles, 1 twin/double.
Meals	Dinner £30 (min. 6). Pubs/restaurants 1 mile.
Closed	Christmas.
Directions	M6 exit 36; A590/591, past Kendal; 1st left at r'bout onto B5284 to Crook; 5 miles (past Windermere golf course); right signed Heathwaite; 100 yds on right.

Johnnie & Heather Curwen
Low House,
Windermere,
Cumbria LA23 3NA

Tel	01539 443156
Mobile	07711 840842
Email	info@lowhouse.co.uk
Web	www.lowhouse.co.uk

Map 11   Entry 78

Cumbria

Gillthwaite Rigg

All is calm and ordered in this light, airy and tranquil Arts and Crafts house. Come for nature and to be surrounded by countryside – you may spot a badger or deer. Find panelled window seats, gleaming oak floors, leaded windows, wooden latched doors and motifs moulded into white plaster. Bedrooms, reached via a spiral staircase, have an uncluttered simplicity and mountain and lake views. Banks of books, a woodburner for cold nights and kind, affable hosts add cheer. Rhoda and Tony are passionate about conservation and wildlife in their 14 acres. *Babies & children over six welcome.*

Price	£70–£80. Singles £45.
Rooms	2: 1 double, 1 twin/double.
Meals	Pubs/restaurants 1 mile.
Closed	Christmas & New Year.
Directions	M6 junc. 36; A590 & A591 to r'bout; B5284 (signed 'Hawkshead via ferry') for 6 miles. After golf club, right for Heathwaite. Bear right up hill past nursery. Next drive on right; central part of manor.

Rhoda M & Tony Graham
Gillthwaite Rigg,
Heathwaite Manor,
Lickbarrow Road, Windermere,
Cumbria LA23 2NQ

Tel	01539 446212
Fax	01539 446212
Email	tony_rhodagraham@hotmail.com

Map 11   Entry 79

Cumbria

Low Jock Scar

A good breakfast, a drive off to the high Cumbria hills, the prospect of a slap-up dinner (fresh, local, great value) and a bed in a comfy room. As Low Jock Scar is folded into the leafy valley, so you are wrapped in the warmth of Philip and Alison's welcome. The 70s-built stone house is a homely haven for guests, with its cosy lounge and pretty conservatory for convivial meals. Floral bedrooms, one in the annexe, have garden views — and the gardens, six acres of woodland and burbling beck, are the Midwinters' pride and joy. They are the soul of kindness and run a tight and happy ship.

Price	£58–£70. Singles from £39.
Rooms	4: 2 doubles, 1 twin; 1 twin/double with separate bath.
Meals	Dinner, 5 courses, £23. Packed lunch £4.
Closed	November–March.
Directions	From Kendal, A6 to Penrith. After 5 miles, Plough Inn on left. After 1 mile turn into lane on left.

Alison & Philip Midwinter
Low Jock Scar,
Selside,
Kendal,
Cumbria LA8 9LE
Tel   01539 823259
Fax   01539 823259
Email   ljs@avmail.co.uk

Map 11   Entry 80

Cumbria

Middle Reston

A proper Edwardian summer house in the heart of the Lakes (Windermere is the nearest) set high and with mature rhododendrons. Inside is crammed with beautiful dark furniture, Turkish rugs, gorgeous paintings, oak overmantles and fires in every room. Two traditional bedrooms have claret walls and dark carpets; the yellow attic room is more modern; all are a good size and entirely quiet. Make yourselves at home in two huge drawing rooms. Ginny and Simon are great fun and give you a stylish breakfast; then explore the magic outside — especially in spring, with curtseying daffodils and bobbing lambs.

Price	£70–£90.
Rooms	3: 1 double; 2 twins sharing bath.
Meals	Pub 2 miles.
Closed	Christmas & occasionally.
Directions	A591 Kendal-Windermere; 500 yds past 2nd Staveley turning, turn right by small blue bicycle sign, then immediately hard left up drive.

Simon & Ginny Johnson
Middle Reston,
Staveley, Kendal,
Cumbria LA8 9PT
Tel   01539 821246
Fax   01539 821809
Email   simonhj@btinternet.com
Web   www.lake-district-accomodation.com

Map 11   Entry 81

Cumbria

Howestone Barn

In the back of most-beautiful-beyond and reached down narrow lanes, this converted barn is a gorgeous retreat for two or four. Rick and Gillian give you privacy and an upstairs sitting room with log stove, comfy sofa, exposed beams and a balcony to take in the views. Bedrooms are plain and elegantly rustic with sweeping beams and modern, stone-tiled bathrooms. Breakfast is delivered: sausages and bacon from their Saddlebacks, eggs from their hens, homemade organic bread. Stroll along lowland tracks, watch curlews and lapwings, puff to the top of Whinfell. Windermere, Ambleside and Beatrix Potter's house are near.

Price	£50–£90. Singles from £35.
Rooms	Barn with 2 twins/doubles & sitting room.
Meals	Packed lunch £5. Pub/restaurant 3.5 miles.
Closed	Rarely.
Directions	A685 Kendal-Appleby. 500 yds after Morrison's petrol, left signed Mealbank; over long hill after Mealbank, after 2nd bridge at Patton, take middle road of 3. After Borrans Farm, left fork; 0.25 miles on left.

Rick & Gillian Rodriguez
Howestone Barn,
Whinfell, Kendal,
Cumbria LA8 9EQ
Tel	01539 824373
Mobile	07901 732379
Email	stay@lapwingsbarn.co.uk
Web	www.lapwingsbarn.co.uk

Map 12   Entry 82

Cumbria

Augill Castle

Huge and surprising – most people arrive unprepared for the scale of it. The 1841 Victorian folly comes with turreted rooms, soaring fairy-tale castle windows and vaulted ceilings. Grand, yes, but intimate too: you should feel comfortably at home in the drawing room with its tumbling curtains, well-loved antiques, old rugs on polished floors and African touches. Bedrooms, too, are historic but homely. No uniforms, no rules, just Wendy, Simon and their staff who ply you with delicious food, scented hot water bottles, big pillows and massive tubs. Fancy getting married here? You can.

Price	£140. Singles £100.
Rooms	10: 4 doubles, 4 twins/doubles, 2 four-posters.
Meals	Dinner £35 (Fri/Sat only). Can cater for groups. Pub/restaurant 1 mile.
Closed	Never.
Directions	M6 junc. 38; A685 through Kirkby Stephen. Just before Brough, right for South Stainmore; signed on left after 1 mile.

Simon & Wendy Bennett
Augill Castle,
Brough, Kirkby Stephen,
Cumbria CA17 4DE
Tel	01768 341937
Fax	01768 342287
Email	enquiries@stayinacastle.com
Web	www.stayinacastle.com

Map 12   Entry 83

Cumbria

Coldbeck House

An old mill leat runs through the garden — elegant with trees, populated by woodpeckers and red squirrels. Belle's forte is her cooking and Richard assists with walks; both are natural hosts. The dignified 1820s house with Victorian additions has sanded and polished floors, antiques and splendid stained glass, a guest sitting room with a log-burning stove and a country-house feel. Bedrooms are delightful: expect fresh flowers, homemade biscuits, and towels to match colourful walls. It's peaceful here, on the edge of a village with a green, and you are in unsurpassed walking country.

Price	£80–£90. Singles £45–£50.
Rooms	3: 2 doubles, 1 twin.
Meals	Dinner, 2-4 courses, £18.50–£30. Pubs within 5-minute walk.
Closed	Christmas.
Directions	M6 exit 38; A685 to Kirkby Stephen; 6 miles, then right to Ravenstonedale. 1st left opp. Kings Head pub; drive imme. on left.

Belle Hepworth
Coldbeck House,
Ravenstonedale, Kirkby Stephen,
Cumbria CA17 4LW
Tel   01539 623407
Mobile   07966 799171
Email   belle@coldbeckhouse.co.uk
Web   www.coldbeckhouse.co.uk

Map 12   Entry 84

Cumbria

Courtyard Cottage

South Lakeland's friendliest, and quirkiest, market town. Specialist shops, festivals, cobbled streets and, down a back alley, a brightly-potted courtyard, smiling Linda and homemade cake. Both bedrooms have a contemporary feel with brushed metal beds, crisp linen, modern art; bathrooms are a heady mix of fluffy towels, gleaming chrome and heavenly scents from little bottles. There's a guest sitting room too, with DVDs and a leather sofa. If you can still move after Linda's famous breakfast (try her black pudding cake) the Cumbria Way starts here and you can take a packed lunch for later. Perfect.

Price	£70–£76.
Rooms	2: 1 double; 1 double with separate bath.
Meals	Packed lunch available. Pubs/restaurants 100 yds.
Closed	Rarely.
Directions	Signs into town centre. Keep on one-way system to NatWest bank. House directly opposite bank's car park, in a courtyard. Parking nearby.

Steven & Linda Weathers
Courtyard Cottage,
9a Queen Street,
Ulverston,
Cumbria LA12 7AF
Tel   01229 581662
Email   lin@courtyardcottage.com
Web   www.courtyardcottage.com

Map 11   Entry 85

Cumbria

Lavender House

An 1850s house – the local vet's for many years – a comfortable stroll away from the centre of the bustling little market town with its interesting shops and pubs; John can collect you if you come by train. Tea and homemade cake are served in the yellow sitting room – admire Diana's lovely paintings on the walls – with comfy chairs and a fire on chilly days. Bedrooms are bright, with vibrant cushions and antique furniture; bathrooms have big mirrors, thick towels and plenty of soaps and bubbles. On sunny mornings try a Manx kipper on the roof terrace with its 'Mary Poppins' views and smart potted plants.

Price	£60–£70. Singles from £35.
Rooms	2: 1 double; 1 twin/double with separate bath.
Meals	Packed lunch £6. Pub/restaurant 150 yds.
Closed	Rarely.
Directions	M6 junc. 36; A65 Kirkby Lonsdale. After 6.5 miles, left at roundabout. Pass Booth's supermarket. Right at junction. House 50 yds on left; park in drive.

John & Diana Craven
Lavender House,
17 New Road, Kirkby Lonsdale,
Cumbria LA6 2AB

Tel	01524 272086
Mobile	07775 564157
Email	info@lavenderhousebnb.co.uk
Web	www.lavenderhousebnb.co.uk

Map 12   Entry 86

Derbyshire

The Hollow

Wake in sunny, south-facing bedrooms to the sound of birds, feast on Elisabeth's own fruits at breakfast and step across the enchanting garden into footpaths and fields. Warm and interested people, the family are bird-lovers and guest-lovers in equal measure. Elisabeth also bakes bread, buys "best local" and has generally made this charming village house a treat to visit. Bedrooms and bathrooms are wonderfully old-fashioned – burr maple suites, chintz curtains, silk flowers – and have gentle hill views to the Peaks. Inspirational walking country and Chatsworth a ten-minute drive.

Price	£65. Singles £45.
Rooms	2: 1 double with separate bath/shower; 1 twin with separate shower.
Meals	Pubs/restaurants 200 yds.
Closed	Christmas & New Year.
Directions	On A6, 1.5 miles from Bakewell, right to Ashford-in-the-Water. Immed. left; right to Monsal Head & right at Monsal Head Hotel into Little Longstone. Pass Pack Horse pub on left. House almost opp.

Elisabeth Chadwick
The Hollow,
Little Longstone,
Bakewell,
Derbyshire DE45 1NN

Tel	01629 640746

Map 8   Entry 87

Derbyshire

Horsleygate Hall

Hens and guinea fowl animate the charming old stable yard, and the gardens are vibrant and fascinating, with stone terraces and streams, hidden patios, modern sculptures and seats in every corner... the Fords, attentive and kind, encourage you to explore. Inside the 1783 house, Margaret has created yet more charm. There is a warm, timeless, harmonious feel, with worn kilims on pine boards, striped and floral wallpapers, deep sofas and pools of light. Breakfast is served round a big table in the old schoolroom – homemade jams and oatcakes, garden fruit, eggs from the hens. Special. *Children over five welcome.*

Price	£65-£75. Singles from £40.
Rooms	3: 1 double; 1 family room, 1 twin sharing bath.
Meals	Pub 1 mile.
Closed	23 December-4 January.
Directions	M1 exit 29; A617 to Chesterfield; B6051 to Millthorpe; Horsleygate Lane 1 mile on, on right.

Robert & Margaret Ford
Horsleygate Hall,
Horsleygate Lane,
Holmesfield,
Derbyshire S18 7WD

Tel	0114 289 0333
Fax	0114 289 0333

⚔ ⚲ ⊷

Map 8   Entry 88

Derbyshire

The Dower House

The very lovely double-fronted dower house sits at the top of a prosperous street of Georgian houses. Inside, all is as you would hope: deep sofas, spacious beds, fine fabrics, warm colours, brightness and light. After a day visiting Bakewell and Chatsworth, how comforting to return to a pretty guest sitting room with an honesty bar and a real fire. Big warm traditional bedrooms have curtain-tie comfort and pictures galore, bathrooms a William Morris theme. There's a walled garden and a treasure of a village, and Marsha and John will furnish you with details on walks in the National Park, and local events.

Price	£95. Singles £70.
Rooms	3: 1 double; 1 double, 1 twin, each with separate bath.
Meals	Packed lunch £4. Pub/restaurant 300 yds.
Closed	Christmas & New Year.
Directions	3 miles from Matlock on A6 for Bakewell. Left on B5057 signed Winster for 3 miles. House at end of Main Street.

John & Marsha Biggin
The Dower House,
Main Street, Winster,
Derbyshire DE4 2DH

Tel	01629 650931
Fax	01629 650932
Email	fosterbig@aol.com
Web	www.thedowerhousewinster.com

⚔ ⚲ ⊿ ⊷ ⚙

Map 8   Entry 89

Derbyshire

Manor Farm

Between two small dales, close to great houses (Chatsworth), lies this cluster of ancient farms and church. Once the home of Anthony Babington, friend of Mary Queen of Scots, Manor Farm seems rooted in time. Simon and Gilly, warm and delightful, are sorting out their romantic new home, and Gilly raises prize pigs. The stunning arched kitchen is where guests are served breakfast (scrumptious, organic); the sitting room has less antiquity. Bedrooms have a simple country comfort, the beamy double is charming, shower rooms modernised, a pretty garden swoops to fields and distant river. *Children over six welcome.*

Price	£60-£70. Singles £40-£50.
Rooms	3: 1 double, 1 twin/double; 1 double with shared bath.
Meals	Pubs 5-10 minute drive.
Closed	Christmas & New Year.
Directions	From M1 exit 28. A38 then A615 following Matlock signs all the way. Left 3 miles before Matlock, signed Dethick Lane. Down lane 1 mile.

Simon & Gilly Groom
Manor Farm,
Dethick, Matlock,
Derbyshire DE4 5GG

Tel	01629 534302
Fax	01629 534008
Email	gillygroom@ntlworld.com
Web	www.manorfarmdethick.co.uk

Map 8   Entry 90

Derbyshire

Mount Tabor House

On a steep hillside between the Peaks and the Dales, a chapel with a peaceful aura and great views. Inside, the look is contemporary: exposed stone walls, colourful church windows, original touches, a metalwork chandelier. After a mouthwatering dinner (with produce mostly local and organic), retire to a luxurious bed; your room is as inviting as can be and bathrooms are a treat. This is a relaxed and easy place to stay and breakfasts can be as carnivorous or as herbivorous as you wish, served on the balcony in summer. Fay is a delight and committed to her guests' comfort.

Price	£80. Singles from £60.
Rooms	2: 1 double, 1 twin/double.
Meals	Occasional dinner. Pubs 2 miles.
Closed	Christmas.
Directions	M1 exit 26; A610 towards Ripley. At Sawmills, right under r'way bridge, signed Crich. Right at marketplace onto Bowns Hill. Chapel 200 yds on right. Can collect from local stations.

Fay Whitehead
Mount Tabor House,
Bowns Hill, Crich, Matlock,
Derbyshire DE4 5DG

Tel	01773 857008
Mobile	07813 007478
Email	mountabor@msn.com
Web	www.mountabor.co.uk

Map 8   Entry 91

Derbyshire

Park View Farm

An amazing farm stay, run by hospitable hosts. Daringly decadent, every inch of this plush Victorian farmhouse brims with flowers, sparkling trinkets, polished brass, plump cushions and swathes of chintz. The rooms dance in swirls of colour, frills, gleaming wood, lustrous glass, buttons and bows – it is an extravagant refuge after a long journey. New-laid eggs from the hens for breakfast, fresh fruits and homemade breads accompany the grand performance. The solid brick farmhouse sits in 370 organic acres and Kedleston Hall Park provides a stunning backdrop. *Children over eight welcome.*

Price	£80–£90. Singles £50–£60.
Rooms	3: 2 doubles; 1 double with separate bath.
Meals	Pub/restaurant 1 mile.
Closed	Christmas.
Directions	From A52/A38 r'bout west of Derby, A38 north, 1st left for Kedleston Hall. House 1.5 miles past park on x-roads in Weston Underwood.

Linda & Michael Adams
Park View Farm,
Weston Underwood, Ashbourne,
Derbyshire DE6 4PA
Tel   01335 360352
Fax   01335 360352
Email   enquiries@parkviewfarm.co.uk
Web   www.parkviewfarm.co.uk

Map 8   Entry 92

Derbyshire

Rose Cottage

Peaceful Rose Cottage lies up a tiny country lane – brighter and airier than 'cottage' would suggest. The hall sets the tone: Indian rugs on a tiled floor, a grandfather clock and ancestral paintings (there's one of Lord Byron!). Bedrooms are traditional and you may gaze on dreamy views across the Dove valley and the Dales. Although elegant, the house is nevertheless a home and guests are treated as friends. No off-limits: a small book-lined sitting room for guests and a big informal garden. Cynthia (Australian) and Peter are the most delightful couple for whom nothing is too much trouble.

Price	£64–£68. Singles £45.
Rooms	2: 1 double; 1 twin with separate bath.
Meals	Pub 2 miles.
Closed	Christmas.
Directions	From Ashbourne, A515 Lichfield road. After 4 miles, right onto B5033. After 1 mile, 2nd lane on right; 0.5 miles on, on right.

Peter & Cynthia Moore
Rose Cottage,
Snelston,
Ashbourne,
Derbyshire DE6 2DL
Tel   01335 324230
Fax   01335 324651
Email   pjmoore@beeb.net

Map 8   Entry 93

Derbyshire

Alstonefield Manor

Country manor house definitely, but delightfully understated and cleverly designed to look natural. Local girl Jo spoils you with warm, homemade scones and tea when you arrive, on the lawns overlooking the rolling hills, or in the elegant drawing room with its soft pale tones and warming fire. The bedroom soothes the soul with a painted wooden floor, antique iron bed, vintage linen, huge fluffy towels and a cool, quirky bathroom. Wake to birdsong – and a candlelit breakfast with local bacon and Staffordshire oatcakes. After a game or two of badminton or croquet, take supper at The George in the village. A joy.

Price	£80. Singles £50.
Rooms	1 double with separate bath.
Meals	Pub 100 yds.
Closed	Christmas & occasionally.
Directions	A515 north out of Ashbourne; 6 miles, left into Alstonefield. Over the bridge (river Dove) and up hill. Take 1st left on entering village, go towards the church. House on right.

Robert & Jo Wood
Alstonefield Manor,
Alstonefield, Ashbourne,
Derbyshire DE6 2FX
Tel   01335 310393
Mobile   07968 143964
Email   stay@alstonefieldmanor.com
Web   www.alstonefieldmanor.com

Map 8   Entry 94

Devon

The Stables

Biscuits, flowers and a glowing log-burner on arrival, breakfast whenever you want it, wellies and waxed jackets on tap. Rupert and Kim are busy farmers and artist/designers (ask to see their beautiful garden trugs) who choose to give guests what they would most like themselves. So… you have the whole of the stables, tranquil, beautifully restored and with field and sky views. Downstairs is open-plan plus kitchen; upstairs, sloping ceilings, warm wood floors, big bed, soft towels. It's cosy yet spacious, stylish yet homely, and the Atlantic coast is the shortest drive.

Price	£75. Singles £50.
Rooms	Barn for 2: 1 double, sitting room & kitchen.
Meals	Pub 3 miles.
Closed	Never.
Directions	A39 to Woolfardisworthy. At T-junc. in village, left. 0.5 miles left to Stibb X. Over bridge bear right, then left. Uphill, right towards Leworthy & Mill; 0.5 miles; on left.

Rupert & Kim Ashmore
The Stables,
Leworthy Barton,
Woolsery,
Bideford,
Devon EX39 5PY
Tel   01237 431140
Email   kim@westcountrylife.co.uk

Map 2   Entry 95

Devon

Beara Farmhouse

The moment you arrive at the whitewashed farmhouse you feel the affection your hosts have for the place. Richard is a lover of wood and a fine craftsman – every room echoes his talent; he also created the pond that's home to mallards and geese. Ann has laid brick paths, stencilled, stitched and painted, all with an eye for colour; bedrooms and guest sitting room are delectable and snug. Open farmland all around, sheep, pigs and hens in the yard, the Tarka Trail on your doorstep and hosts happy to give you 6.30am breakfast should you plan a day on Lundy Island. Readers love this place. *Min. two nights June-Sept.*

Price	£65. Singles by arrangement.
Rooms	2: 1 double, 1 twin.
Meals	Pub 1.5 miles.
Closed	20 December–5 January.
Directions	From A39, left into Bideford, round quay, past old bridge on left. Signs to Torrington; 1.5 miles, right for Buckland Brewer; 2.5 miles, left; 0.5 miles, right over cattle grid & down track.

Ann & Richard Dorsett
Beara Farmhouse,
Buckland Brewer,
Bideford,
Devon EX39 5EH

Tel   01237 451666
Web   www.bearafarmhouse.co.uk

Map 2   Entry 96

Devon

Victoria House

Beachcombers, surfers and walkers will be in their element in this Edwardian seaside villa where all of the bedrooms have magnificent views. Choose between two in the main house with state-of-the-art bathrooms and one in the annexe with a beach-hut feel and a private deck. Heather is lively and fun, she and David are ex-RAF and clearly enjoy looking after you; breakfast is a main meal of nuts, fresh fruits, yogurts, eggs benedict, smoked salmon or The Full Monty. You are on the coastal road to Woolacombe for International Surf and Kite Surfing competitions; Lundy is always in view. Bucket and spade bliss.

Price	£70-£120.
Rooms	3: 2 doubles, 1 family room.
Meals	Occasional dinner. Packed lunch £8. Pubs 200 yds.
Closed	Never.
Directions	From B3343, right for Mortehoe. Through village & past the old chapel. Down steep hill, with the bay ahead; house 3rd on left.

Heather & David Burke
Victoria House,
Chapel Hill, Mortehoe,
Woolacombe, Devon EX34 7DZ

Tel   01271 871302
Fax   01271 871302
Email   heatherburke59@fsmail.net
Web   www.victoriahousebandb.co.uk

Map 2   Entry 97

Devon

Southcliffe Hall

An Argentinian chandelier, antique French radiators, a rediscovered Victorian garden; we love this gorgeous, grandly idiosyncratic house overlooking the sea. Eccentric owners have left their mark on what was originally the Manor House. Kate and Barry are young and enthusiastic. Vast bedrooms have rich carpets, big beds, antique flourishes. Bathrooms are fabulous one-offs – roll top baths to porcelain loos. Tea in the drawing room or the terraces, dinner in the panelled dining room; at breakfast, local produce. Spot deer in the woodland, walk to the beach, hike along the coast. Great fun.

Price	£100. Singles by arrangement.
Rooms	2 twins/doubles.
Meals	Dinner, 3 courses, £25. Pub 5-minute walk.
Closed	Rarely.
Directions	From A361, B3343 towards Woolacombe. Turn right, thro' Lincombe, into Lee. Long drive to house is on left, between village hall and Fuschia Tearoom.

Kate Seekings & Barry Jenkinson
Southcliffe Hall,
Lee,
Devon EX34 8LW

Tel	01271 867068
Mobile	07910 473725
Email	stay@southcliffehall.co.uk
Web	www.southcliffehall.co.uk

✗ ♀ ⚕ 🐾

Map 2   Entry 98

Devon

Hewish Barton

The second you arrive you're 'away from it all'. In the majestic Georgian house framed by green hills and a garden bouncing with birds, Maggi gives you delicious homemade cake for tea. You get a kitchen, too, and a lovely log-fired sitting room full of artefacts and books. Bedrooms have big sash windows, generous wardrobes and amazing views; baths encourage long soaks. Come for home comforts, home cooking, breakfasts by the Aga, woodland paths… and Woolacombe and Ilfracombe (the next Padstow?) down the road. Good value, great for couples *and* house parties, and the loveliest hosts.

Price	From £65. Singles from £37.50.
Rooms	3 doubles. Guest kitchen.
Meals	Dinner, 3 courses, from £20 (min. 6). BYO. Pub 2 miles.
Closed	Rarely.
Directions	A361 to Barnstaple. Follow A39 past hospital, left onto B3230 to Ifracombe. Thro' Muddiford; 1 mile, quarry on left, right into drive.

Maggi & Keith Wase
Hewish Barton,
Muddiford,
Barnstaple,
Devon EX31 4HH

Tel	01271 850245
Email	hewish_barton@mwase.freeserve.co.uk
Web	www.hewish-barton.co.uk

🚶 ✗ ♀ ⚕

Map 2   Entry 99

Devon

Beachborough Country House

A gracious 18th-century rectory with stone-flagged floors, lofty windows, wooden shutters, charming gardens. Viviane is vivacious and she spoils you with seemingly effortless food straight from the Aga, either in the kitchen or in the elegant dining room with twinkling fire. Chickens cluck, horses whinny but otherwise the peace is deep; this is perfect walking or cycling country. Ease any aches and pains in a steaming roll top; bathrooms are awash with fluffy towels, large bedrooms are fresh as a daisy with great views – admire them from the window seats. Combe Martin is a short hop for a grand beach day.

Price	From £60. Singles £40.
Rooms	3: 1 twin/double, 2 doubles.
Meals	Dinner, 2-3 courses, from £16.
Closed	Rarely.
Directions	From A361 take A399 for 12 miles. At Blackmoor Gate, left onto A39. House 1.5 miles on right.

Viviane Clout
Beachborough Country House,
Kentisbury, Barnstaple,
Devon EX31 4NH

Tel	01271 882487
Mobile	07732 947755
Email	viviane@beachborough.freeserve.co.uk
Web	www.beachboroughcountryhouse.co.uk

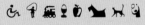

Map 2   Entry 100

Devon

Bratton Mill

Absolute privacy down the long track to a thickly wooded and beautifully secluded valley: watch for dragonflies, red deer, buzzards and the flash of the kingfisher. To the backdrop of a rushing stream is the house, painted traditional white and filled with treasure – including Marilyn who spoils you with elegant china, fresh flowers, warm bathrooms, crisp linen and a comforting decanter of port. Breakfast is locally sourced and superb; in summer, eat by the stream to almost deafening birdsong. There are simple strolls or robust hikes straight from the door. Wonderful. *Self-catering cottage & folly available.*

Price	£75-£95. Singles from £45.
Rooms	2: 1 double/twin, 1 four-poster. Children's rooms available.
Meals	Dinner/supper available. Pub close walking distance.
Closed	Rarely.
Directions	From Bratton Fleming High Street turn into Mill Lane. Down road for 0.5 miles thro' railway cutting; turn right.

Marilyn Holloway
Bratton Mill,
Bratton Fleming,
Barnstaple,
Devon EX31 4RU

Tel	01598 710026
Email	contact@brattonmill.co.uk
Web	www.brattonmill.co.uk

Map 2   Entry 101

Devon

Sea View Villa

The sea-captain's house gazes down from its wooded perch on beautiful Lynmouth below. There's a short, steep path up... then the pampering begins. Chris cooks, Steve does (sparkling) front of house. Bedrooms are warm and vibrant in black and silver, ochre and cream, and dinner is a full blown performance with theatrical touches: perfumed candles, soft music, maybe local lamb then "flambé Jamaican bananas". Rise early for a glorious Exmoor safari (spot the red deer) then ease away your aches and pains with an in-house holistic massage. The attention to detail here is fabulous.

Devon

Lower Hummacott

Bright clear colours, antique furniture, charming decorative touches. There are fresh fruit and flowers in the bedrooms (one with a king-size bed) and two guest sitting rooms. Delicious, organic and traditionally reared meat, veg and eggs, fresh fish, homemade cakes... As if that were not enough, the Georgian farmhouse has a stunning formal garden created from scratch – spring-fed pools, lime walk, pergola, arches, herbaceous beds and a new gazebo. Liz, a weaver, and Tony, an award-winning artist (he has a gallery in the house) are charming and friendly and look after you beautifully.

Price	£90-£110. Singles £40.	Price	£66.
Rooms	4: 2 doubles; 2 twins sharing bath.	Rooms	2 doubles.
Meals	Dinner, 5 courses, £30.	Meals	Dinner £27 (Sunday & Monday only). Pub/restaurant 1.5 miles.
Closed	January-mid-February.	Closed	Rarely.
Directions	From M5 exit 23; A39 for Minehead; on to Porlock along coast to Lynmouth. Sea View Villa off Watersmeet Road, up path, directly opp. church.	Directions	0.5 miles east of Kings Nympton village is Beara Cross; go straight over marked to Romansleigh for 0.75 miles; Hummacott is 1st entrance on left by the iron wheel.

Steve Williams & Chris Bissex
Sea View Villa,
6 Summerhouse Path, Lynmouth,
Devon EX35 6ES
Tel   01598 753460
Fax   01598 753496
Email   reservations@seaviewvilla.co.uk
Web   www.seaviewvilla.co.uk

Tony & Liz Williams
Lower Hummacott,
Kings Nympton,
Umberleigh,
Devon EX37 9TU
Tel   01769 581177
Fax   01769 581177

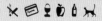

Map 2   Entry 102

Map 2   Entry 103

Devon

Hillbrow House

You could be forgiven for thinking this 'house on the hill' is genuine Georgian – but it's mostly new, with a deep veranda and glorious views over the golf course (and, on a clear day, to distant Dartmoor). The light, uncluttered rooms are neat as a pin with coordinated colours, thick fabrics, antiques and your own upstairs studio sitting room; bedrooms have feather pillows, proper blankets and luxurious bathrooms. Golfers and walkers will be in paradise, surfers can reach Croyde easily and a plethora of gentler beaches lie in the other direction. Stoke up on delicious homemade granola for breakfast.

Price	From £80. Singles £45.
Rooms	2: 1 double; 1 double with separate bath.
Meals	Dinner, 3 courses, £25. Pubs/restaurants within walking distance.
Closed	Christmas.
Directions	Take B3226 from South Molton for 5 miles. Turn right for Chittlehamholt, left at T-junc, then through village. House is last on right.

	Clarissa Roe
	Hillbrow House,
	Chittlehamholt,
	Devon EX37 9NS
Tel	01769 540214
Email	clarissaroe@btinternet.com
Web	www.hillbrowhouse.com

Map 2   Entry 104

Devon

Sannacott

On the southern fringes of Exmoor you're in huntin' and shootin' country. This is a stud farm – the Trickeys breed national hunt racehorses – and there's a riding stables close by. Downstairs is a happy mix of casual countryside living, antiques, open fires and family pictures. Bedrooms are traditional, clean and comfortable, all have lovely long views across rolling hills and trees, and you can come and go as you please. Clare bakes her own bread, most produce is organic or local and there's a pretty cottagey garden to wander through. Great for walkers, riders, birdwatchers and nature lovers.

Price	£60–£70.
Rooms	3: 1 double; 1 twin/double sharing bath. Annexe: 1 twin with separate bath/shower.
Meals	Occasional dinner, 3 courses, £20. Pub 5 miles.
Closed	Rarely.
Directions	M5 J27; A361 for Barnstaple, past Tiverton, 15.5 miles; right at r'bout (small sign Whitechapel). 1.5 miles to junc., right towards Twitchen & N. Molton; 1.5m to 3rd on left, black gates.

	Mrs E C Trickey
	Sannacott,
	North Molton,
	Devon EX36 3JS
Tel	01598 740203
Fax	01598 740513
Email	mctrickey@hotmail.com
Web	www.sannacott.co.uk

Map 2   Entry 105

Devon

West Bradley

Total immersion in beauty – doves in the farmyard, hens in the orchard, fields on either side of the long drive. Privacy, too, in your 18th-century upside-down barn on the side of the owners' Devon longhouse – and views. A handmade oak staircase, oak floors, two freshly furnished bedrooms (one up, one down), a good big sitting room with a gas-fired wood-burner and a kitchen you would be happy to use. Phillida can bring breakfast to you here, or you can tuck into full English in the farmhouse dining room. There will be homemade something on arrival and a good choice of local pubs.

Price	£80. Singles £50.
Rooms	2: 1 twin/double; 1 twin with separate shower. Guest kitchen.
Meals	Pubs within 5 miles.
Closed	Rarely.
Directions	B3137 Tiverton-Witheridge; on towards Rackenford & Calverleigh. After pink thatched cottage (2 miles), fork left to Templeton; West Bradley 2 miles; on left before village hall.

Martin & Phillida Strong
West Bradley,
Templeton,
Tiverton,
Devon EX16 8BJ

Tel	01884 253220
Mobile	07779 241048
Email	martinstrong@westbradley.eclipse.co.uk

Map 2   Entry 106

Devon

The Devon Wine School

Alastair and Carol run their wine school from this delightfully rural spot – and look after you to perfection. Chill out in an open-plan sitting/dining room with wooden floors, smart chesterfields, Xian terracotta warriors, claret walls and rolling views. Bedrooms are light, unfussy and elegant, bathrooms are swish, food is taken seriously and sourced locally (an organic beef farmer lives next door). The atmosphere is relaxed and friendly; the wine, obviously, is a joy – and reasonably priced! There's a hard tennis court for working up an appetite and no light pollution; star-gazers will be happy.

Price	£70. Singles £50.
Rooms	2: 1 twin/double, 1 double with child's room (no extra charge).
Meals	Dinner, 3 courses, from £20. Occasional lunch. Pub 1 mile.
Closed	Rarely.
Directions	From Cadeleigh, 1.5 miles to Postbox Cross, turn left to Cheriton Fitzpaine. Follow road to Redyeates Cross x-roads, then right, house is 150 yds on left down track.

Alastair & Carol Peebles
The Devon Wine School,
Redyeates Farm, Cheriton Fitzpaine,
Crediton, Devon EX17 4HG

Tel	01363 866742
Fax	01363 860100
Email	alastair@devonwineschool.co.uk
Web	www.devonwineschool.co.uk

Map 2   Entry 107

Devon

Staghound Cottages

Brilliant for walkers and cyclists: the cottage is a mile from Exmoor, near the Bristol to Padstow cycle route, and Penny – a potter whose work fills the house – has space for bikes and wet clothes. *And* there's a bus stop outside. Built as an inn several centuries ago (there's a still-functioning pub next door), it overlooks meadows and rolling hills. The interior is not luxurious but simple, calm and appealing; bedrooms, big and small, have wonky floors and beds with fresh cotton. No guest sitting room but you'll be out exploring all day and Penny will start you off with a great breakfast.

Price	£45-£55. Singles £25.
Rooms	3: 1 double; 1 twin/double, 1 single sharing bath/shower.
Meals	Packed lunch £4. Restaurants 2 miles.
Closed	Christmas.
Directions	M5 exit 27 for Tiverton; 7 miles, right at r'bout for Dulverton; left at next r'bout. At Black Cat junc. take middle road to Dulverton; in Exbridge, left at round house; 300 yds on left.

Penny Richards
Staghound Cottages,
Exebridge, Dulverton,
Devon TA22 9AZ

Tel	01398 324453
Mobile	07796 883938
Email	penny@staghound.co.uk
Web	www.staghound.co.uk

Map 2 Entry 108

Devon

Burnville House

Granite gateposts, Georgian house, rhododendrons, beechwoods and rolling fields of sheep: that's the setting. But there's more. Beautifully proportioned rooms reveal subtle colours, elegant antiques, squishy sofas and bucolic views, stylish bathrooms are sprinkled with candles, there are sumptuous dinners and pancakes at breakfast. Your hosts left busy jobs in London to settle here, and their place breathes life – space, smiles, energy. Swim, play tennis, walk to Dartmoor from the door, take a trip to Eden or the sea. Or... just gaze at the moors and the church on the Tor and listen to the silence, and the sheep.

Price	From £70. Singles £45.
Rooms	2 doubles.
Meals	Dinner from £15. Pub 2 miles.
Closed	Rarely.
Directions	A30 Exeter-Okehampton; A386 dir. Tavistock. Right for Lydford opp. Dartmoor Inn; after 4 miles (thro' Lydford), Burnville Farm on left (convex traffic mirror on right).

Victoria Cunningham
Burnville House,
Brentor, Tavistock,
Devon PL19 0NE

Tel	01822 820443
Fax	01822 820443
Email	burnvillef@aol.com
Web	www.burnville.co.uk

Map 2 Entry 109

Devon

Mount Tavy Cottage

Rural bliss – but just a short walk to Tavistock (best market town 2005). One guest wrote: "There's no better place to recover from stress." Everything is geared to your comfort – pretty rooms, four-poster and half-tester beds, deep, free-standing baths. Joanna and Graham, a lovely Devon couple, have worked hard to restore this former gardener's bothy, Graham making much of the furniture himself. Two new bedrooms have been created in the potting shed across the courtyard: bed and breakfast in glorious seclusion. Outside are ponds – one with a breezy pagoda for summer suppers – and a walled Victorian garden.

Price	From £60. Singles from £30.
Rooms	3: 2 twins/doubles, 1 four-poster, each with separate bath.
Meals	Dinner, 3 courses, £20. Pub 2 miles.
Closed	Rarely.
Directions	From Tavistock B3357 towards Princetown; 0.25 miles on, after Mount House School, left. Drive past lake to house.

Mr & Mrs G H Moule
Mount Tavy Cottage,
Tavistock,
Devon PL19 9JL
Tel 01822 614253
Mobile 07776 181576
Email graham@mounttavy.fsnet.co.uk
Web www.mounttavy.freeserve.co.uk

Map 2 Entry 110

Devon

South Hooe Mine

Quirky and delightful! Pretty bedrooms have fresh wildflowers, beautiful linen, a quiet elegance. The lovely Trish makes fresh bread and Martha the donkey helps her win the battle with nature but often has her front feet in the kitchen. Tartan curtains, polished antiques and paintings in the dining room, and a terrace with soaring views. On summer nights sleep peacefully next to the magical Tamar in your own yurt. Short breaks available in a secluded, separate cottage even nearer the river. Sail in, through the AONB, to the jetty, or join a writing course. *Babes in arms & children over eight welcome.*

Price	From £70-£85. Singles from £35.
Rooms	2 twins/doubles, one with extra single/dressing room.
Meals	Supper rarely. Pub 3 miles.
Closed	Rarely.
Directions	Into Bere Alston on B3257, left for Weir Quay. Over x-roads. Follow Hole's Hole sign, right for Hooe. Fork left for South Hooe Farm; 300 yds on, turn sharply back to your left & down track.

Trish Dugmore
South Hooe Mine,
Hole's Hole,
Bere Alston,
Yelverton,
Devon PL20 7BW
Tel 01822 840329
Email southhooe@aol.com

Map 2 Entry 111

Devon

Higher Eggbeer Farm

Over 900 years old and still humming with life: pigs, cows, ponies, rabbits, and chickens share the rambling gardens. Sally Anne and William are artistic, fun, slightly wacky and eccentric. It's an adventure to stay, so keep an open mind: the house is a historic gem and undeniably rustic. Huge inglenook fireplaces, interesting art, books, piano, wellies, muddle and charm. Your lovely hosts will take children to feed animals and collect eggs, and will babysit. Be wrapped in peace in your own half of the house (with beautiful drawing room), immersed in a magnificent panorama of forest, hills and fields of waving wheat.

Price	£55-£70. Singles £40.
Rooms	3: 2 twins/doubles sharing bath (2nd room let to same party); 1 double in main house sharing bath.
Meals	Restaurants in village, 5-minute walk.
Closed	Rarely.
Directions	A30 to Okehampton. After 10 miles left exit into Cheriton Bishop; 1st left after Old Thatch pub, signed Woodbrooke. Down & up hill; road turns sharp left but you don't. Turn right down private lane.

Sally Anne & William Selwyn
Higher Eggbeer Farm,
Cheriton Bishop,
Exeter,
Devon EX6 6JQ
Tel   01647 24427

Map 2   Entry 112

Devon

Cyprian's Cot

A charming terraced cottage of 16th-century nooks and crannies and beams worth ducking. The setting is exquisite: the garden leads into fields of sheep, the Dartmoor Way goes through the town and the Two Moors Way skirts it. Shelagh, a lovely lady, gives guests their own sitting room with a fire, lit on cool nights; breakfasts, served in the cosy dining room, are fresh, free-range and tasty. Up the narrow stairs and into simple bedrooms – a small double and a tiny twin. A perfect house and hostess, and a perfect little town to discover, with its pubs, fine restaurant and delicatessen, organic shop and tearoom.

Price	£55. Singles fom £30.
Rooms	2: 1 twin; 1 double with separate bath.
Meals	Pubs/restaurants in village.
Closed	Rarely.
Directions	In Chagford pass church on left; 1st right beyond Globe Inn opposite. House 150 yds on right.

Shelagh Weeden
Cyprian's Cot,
47 New Street,
Chagford,
Devon TQ13 8BB
Tel   01647 432256
Email   shelagh-weeden@lineone.net
Web   www.cyprianscot.co.uk

Map 2   Entry 113

Devon

Easdon Cottage

Replenish your soul in this light and beautifully proportioned cottage; if the charming big double in the house is taken, you may stay in the nearby Barn. Both have tranquillity and delightful moor views. The interiors are an enchanting mix of good pictures, oriental rugs, books, plants and some handsome Victorian finds. You are in a classic Devon valley yet the wilderness of Dartmoor lies just beyond the door, and the sweet cottage garden is filled with birds. Liza and Hugh's veggie and vegan breakfasts are imaginative and delicious. *Children & pets by arrangement.*

Price	From £60. Singles from £30.
Rooms	1 twin/double.
Meals	Supper £10-£20. Packed lunch £5. Pub/restaurant 3 miles.
Closed	Rarely.
Directions	A38 from Exeter; A382 for Bovey Tracey. There, left at 2nd r'bout for Manaton; 2 miles beyond Manaton, right at x-roads for M'hampstead. 0.5 miles on, right, signed Easdon. On left up track.

	Liza & Hugh Dagnall
	Easdon Cottage,
	Long Lane,
	Manaton,
	Devon TQ13 9XB
Tel	01647 221389
Fax	01647 221389
Email	easdondown@btopenworld.com

Map 2   Entry 114

Devon

The Gate House

A dear house in a dear village, grander inside than you might think. The medieval longhouse (1460) has all the low beams and wonky walls you could hope for, and is properly looked after. Rose-print curtains and spruce quilts in the bedrooms, a wood-burner and flowers in the sitting room – and robes, good soaps and soft towels... such care is taken you can't help but feel spoiled. John and Sheila are delightful attentive hosts who serve you delicious Aga-side meals on white linen with candles. A small pool in the gardens overlooks beautiful woodland and moors; you may not want to leave.

Price	£72-£78. Singles £50.
Rooms	3: 2 twins/doubles; 1 double with separate bath/shower.
Meals	Supper trays £12.50. BYO. Packed lunch available. Pub/restaurant 50 yds.
Closed	Rarely.
Directions	From Moretonhampstead via Pound St to North Bovey (1.5 miles). House 25 yds off village green, down Lower Hill past inn on left.

	John & Sheila Williams
	The Gate House,
	North Bovey,
	Devon TQ13 8RB
Tel	01647 440479
Fax	01647 440479
Email	srw.gatehouse@virgin.net
Web	www.gatehouseondartmoor.co.uk

Map 2   Entry 115

Devon

Vogwell Cottage

Utter stillness pervades the valley. All you hear when you open your window are birdsong and brook – and the occasional chug-chug of the tractor. John and Christina have extended the old gamekeeper's cottage to create this cosy, unpretentious, woodland retreat. Your bedroom is old-fashioned and cottagey, light and airy with its own tiny wainscotted bathroom, the shared sitting room has books, board games (no TV here!) and open fire, and there's a sun room to loll around in. Come for the setting, delightful birdsong, great walking, delicious country cooking, the friendly dogs and the much-loved hens.

Price	£60. Singles £30.
Rooms	1 twin/double.
Meals	Dinner, 4 courses, £25. Supper £15. Packed lunch £5. Full-board available. Pubs 4 miles.
Closed	Christmas.
Directions	From Bovey Tracey signs to Manaton & Becky Falls; straight on past Kestor Inn in Manaton for 3.3 miles, following signs to Moretonhampstead. On left down lane.

John & Christina Everett
Vogwell Cottage,
Manaton,
Devon TQ13 9XD
Tel   01647 221302
Web   www.vogwellcottage.co.uk

Map 2   Entry 116

Devon

Bagtor House

What a setting! A ten-minute walk and you're on the moor. Enfolded by garden, green fields and sheep, the 15th-century house with the Georgian façade is the last remaining manor in the parish. Find ancient beauty in granite flagstones, oak-panelled walls, great fireplaces glowing with logs and country dressers brimming with china. Sue looks after hens, geese, labradors, guests, grows everything and makes her own bread. She offers you a large and elegant double room with an antique brass bed and, steeply up the stairs, a big attic-cosy suite perfect for families. Warm, homely, spacious, civilised.

Price	From £64. Singles by arrangement.
Rooms	2: 1 double, 1 family room, each with separate bath/shower.
Meals	Restaurants/pubs 1 mile.
Closed	Christmas.
Directions	From A38 to Plymouth, A382 turn off at r'bout, 3rd exit to Ilsington; up through village, 2nd left after hotel (to Bickington),1st crossroads right to Bagtor, 0.5 miles on, right next to Farm.

Sue Cookson
Bagtor House,
Ilsington, Dartmoor,
Devon TQ13 9RT
Tel   01364 661538
Fax   01364 661538
Email   sawreysue@hotmail.com
Web   www.bagtormanor.co.uk

Map 2   Entry 117

Devon

Corndonford Farm

An ancient Devon longhouse and an engagingly chaotic haven run by warm and friendly Ann and Will, along with their Shire horses and Dartmoor ponies. Steep, stone circular stairs lead to bedrooms; bright lemon walls, a four poster with lacy curtains, gorgeous views over the cottage garden and a bathroom with a beam to duck. A place for those who want to get into the spirit of it all – maybe help catch an escaped foal, chatter to the farm workers around the table; not for fussy types or Mr and Mrs Tickety Boo. Good for walkers too – the Two Moors Way footpath is on the doorstep. *Children over ten by arrangement.*

Price	£56. Singles £33.
Rooms	2: 1 twin, 1 four-poster sharing bath.
Meals	Pub 2 miles.
Closed	Christmas.
Directions	From A38 2nd Ashburton turn for Dartmeet & Princetown. In Poundsgate pass pub on left; 3rd right on bad bend signed Corndon. Straight over x-roads, 0.5 miles, farm on left.

Ann & Will Williams
Corndonford Farm,
Poundsgate,
Newton Abbot,
Devon TQ13 7PP
Tel 01364 631595
Email corndonford@btinternet.com

�

Map 2   Entry 118

Devon

Tudor House

A merchant's townhouse now happily given over to rooms for the Agaric Restaurant. Sophie and Nick are young, fun and very clever: in these mostly large, individually styled rooms, fabrics are plush, colours innovative and bathrooms have roll tops or a wet room style shower. A breakfast room is cool with leather and palms; full English or anything else you want is delivered here. Don't come without booking into the restaurant for fabulous modern British cooking – then stagger two steps down the street to your well-earned bed. Ashburton bustles with good food shops, antiques and books.

Price	£75–£125. Singles £50.
Rooms	5: 2 doubles, 1 family, 1 single; 1 double with separate bath.
Meals	Owner's restaurant next door. Packed lunch from £10 for 2.
Closed	Rarely.
Directions	From A38 follow signs to Ashburton. North Street is the main street, house is on the right after the Town Hall.

Sophie & Nick Coiley
Tudor House,
36 North Street, Ashburton,
Devon TQ13 7QD
Tel 01364 654478
Email eat@agaricrestaurant.co.uk
Web www.agaricrestaurant.co.uk

Map 2   Entry 119

Devon

Penpark

Clough Williams-Ellis of Portmeirion fame did more than design an elegant house; he made sure it communed with nature. Light pours in from every window, and the enchanting woodland garden and farmland views lift the spirits. The big double has apricot walls, a comfy sofa and its own balcony; the private suite has arched French doors to the garden and an extra room for young children. Antiques and heirlooms, African carvings, silk and fresh flowers – it is deeply traditional and comforting. Your generous hosts have been doing B&B for years and look after you so well.

Price	From £70. Singles by arrangement.
Rooms	3: 1 family suite; 1 twin/double with separate bath; 1 double with separate shower.
Meals	Pub 1 mile.
Closed	Rarely.
Directions	A38 west to Plymouth; A382 turn off; 3rd turning off r'bout, signed Bickington. There, right at junc. (to Plymouth), right again (to Sigford & Widecombe). Over top of A38; 1st entrance on right.

Madeleine & Michael Gregson
Penpark,
Bickington,
Newton Abbot,
Devon TQ12 6LH
Tel   01626 821314
Email   maddy@penpark.co.uk
Web   www.penpark.co.uk

Map 2   Entry 120

Devon

Hooks Cottage

The hideaway miner's cottage may have few original features but the setting is special. At the end of a long bumpy track is a lush oasis carved out of woodland. Mary, gently spoken, and Dick have a finely judged sense of humour, and labrador Archie will charm you. It is simple, rural, close to the Moors, with river and birdsong to unwind stressed souls. Carpeted bedrooms have a faded floral charm and pretty stream views; bathrooms are plain. Enjoy local sausages and Mary's marmalade for breakfast, the garden with horses, bluebells in spring, a swimming pool and 12 acres to explore.

Price	£50-£60. Singles from £30.
Rooms	2: 1 double, 1 twin.
Meals	Occasional supper, £15. Pub/restaurant 2 miles.
Closed	Rarely.
Directions	From A38, A382 at Drumbridges for Newton Abbot; 3rd left at r'bout for Bickington. Down hill, right for Haytor. Under bridge, 1st left & down long, bumpy track, past thatched cottage to house.

Mary & Dick Lloyd-Williams
Hooks Cottage,
Bickington,
Ashburton,
Devon TQ12 6JS
Tel   01626 821312
Email   hookscottage@yahoo.com

Map 2   Entry 121

Devon

Orchard Cottage

Tucked into a quiet village corner, this is the last cottage in a row of three. Walk through the pretty garden, past seats that (sometimes!) bask in the sun and down to your own entrance and terrace... you may come and go as you please. Your bedroom is L-shaped and large, with a comfortable brass bed and a super en suite shower; it is spotless yet rustic. The Ewens are friendly and fun, their two spaniels equally so and you are brilliantly sited for Dartmoor, Plymouth, the sand and the sea. Breakfasts in the beamed dining room are generous and delicious; this is excellent value B&B.

Price	£50. Singles £35.
Rooms	1 double.
Meals	Pubs 300 yds.
Closed	Christmas.
Directions	A379 from Plymouth for Modbury. On reaching Church St at top of hill, before Modbury, fork left at Palm Cross, then 1st right by school into Back St. Cottage 3rd on left, past village hall.

Maureen Ewen
Orchard Cottage,
Back Street, Palm Cross Green,
Modbury, Devon PL21 0QZ

Tel	01548 830633
Fax	01548 830633
Mobile	07979 558568
Email	moewen@talktalk.net

Map 2 Entry 122

Devon

Rafters Barn

A delightful and peaceful 300-year-old barn along the narrowest of lanes and with soaring views down a valley to the sea. This is big sailing country but mostly agricultural so you will avoid the madding crowds. You have a comfy guest sitting room with big sofas and a wood-burner that belts out the heat, neat bedrooms in bright colours with pretty touches, tiled bathrooms that gleam and a great big breakfast in the open hallway. Elizabeth is thoughtful and smiley and will point you to the best beaches and places to eat in Salcombe. Or let her cook for you – on produce fresh from farmers' markets.

Price	£65. Singles £40.
Rooms	3: 1 double, 1 twin; 1 single with separate bath.
Meals	Dinner £15. Pubs/restaurants 4 miles.
Closed	Christmas & New Year.
Directions	A381 dir. Salcombe. Just before Hope Cove sign, right to Bagton & S. Huish. Follow lane for 1 mile; 30 yds past saw mill, right up farm lane; at bottom on left.

Elizabeth Hanson
Rafters Barn,
Holwell Farm, South Huish,
Kingsbridge, Devon TQ7 3EQ

Tel	01548 560460
Mobile	07971 293288
Email	raftersdevon@yahoo.co.uk
Web	www.raftersdevon.co.uk

Map 2 Entry 123

Devon

Washbrook Barn

Hard not to feel happy here – even the blue-painted windows on rosy stone walls make you want to smile. Inside is equally sunny. The barn – decrepit until Penny bought it four years ago – rests at the bottom of a quiet valley. She has transformed it into a series of big, light-filled rooms with polished wooden floors, pale beams and richly coloured walls lined with fabulous watercolours: the effect is one of gaiety and panache. No sitting room as such, but armchairs in big, impeccable bedrooms from which one can admire the view. The beds are divinely comfortable and the fresh bathrooms sparkle.

Price	£70-£75. Singles £50.
Rooms	3: 1 double; 1 double, 1 twin, each with separate bath/shower.
Meals	Dinner occasionally available in winter. Pubs/restaurants 10-min walk.
Closed	Christmas & New Year.
Directions	From Kingsbridge quay to top of Fore St; right into Duncombe St; on to T-junc; left to Church St. Right into Belle Cross Rd; 150 yds, right into Washbrook Lane; 100 yds left; at bottom on right.

Penny Cadogan
Washbrook Barn,
Washbrook Lane, Kingsbridge,
Devon TQ7 1NN
Tel   01548 856901
Mobile   07989 502194
Email   penny.cadogan@homecall.co.uk
Web   www.washbrookbarn.co.uk

Map 2   Entry 124

Devon

Manor Farm

Capable Sarah is a fanatical gardener, and produces vegetables that will find their way into your (excellent) dinner, and raspberries for your muesli. She keeps bees and hens too, so there's honey and eggs for breakfast, served in a smart red dining room. The farmhouse twists and turns around unexpected corners thanks to ancient origins, and the good-sized bedrooms, one with its own bathroom, both painted light yellow, are reached via two separate stairs – nicely private. The lovely village is surrounded by apple orchards and has two good pubs for eating out.

Price	£70. Singles £35.
Rooms	2: 1 double; 1 twin with separate bath/shower.
Meals	Dinner £15-£21. Packed lunch £4-£5. Pubs 500 yds.
Closed	Rarely.
Directions	From Newton Abbot, A381 for Totnes. After approx. 2.5 miles, right for Broadhempston. Past village sign, down hill & 2nd left. Pass pub on right & left 170 yds on into courtyard.

Sarah Clapp
Manor Farm,
Broadhempston,
Totnes,
Devon TQ9 6BD
Tel   01803 813260
Fax   01803 813260
Email   mandsclapp@btinternet.com

Map 2   Entry 125

Devon

Parliament House

The ancient rambling house (where William of Orange held his first Parliament) is on the road at the bottom of the valley, and has been beautifully restored by two designers. This is a fresh, stylish and charming cottage where wallpapers, napkins and toile de Jouy are to Carole's own design. White walls and serene colours form a lovely backdrop for pretty touches. Breakfasts are feasts — creamy mushrooms on a toasted muffin, three sorts of bread — and bedrooms are low-ceilinged and cosy with cast-iron fireplaces and hand-stencilled paper. There's a sitting room and a library with a piano — and the garden is a joy.

Price	From £75.
Rooms	2: 1 double; 1 twin/double with separate bath/shower.
Meals	Pubs/restaurants within 2 miles.
Closed	Rarely.
Directions	From Totnes, A385 Paignton road; 2 miles on, right at Riviera Sports Cars. House 1st on right. Just past house to parking area on right.

Carole & Harry Grimley
Parliament House,
Longcombe,
Totnes,
Devon TQ9 6PR
Tel   01803 840288
Email   parliamenthouse@btopenworld.com

✗ 🚂 ♟ 🐈 ⋊

Map 2   Entry 126

Devon

Lower Norton Farmhouse

Hard to believe the downstairs bedroom was a calving pen and its smart bathroom the dairy. Now it has a seagrass floor and a French walnut bed. All Glynis's rooms are freshly decorated, and she and Peter are the most amenable hosts, genuinely happy for you to potter around all day should you wish to do so. For the more active, a yacht on the Dart and a cream Bentley are to hand, with Peter as navigator and chauffeur — rare treats. Return to gardens, paddocks, peaceful views, super dinners and a big log fire. Off the beaten track, a tremendous find. *Children over ten welcome.*

Price	From £70. Singles from £55.
Rooms	3: 2 doubles, 1 twin.
Meals	Dinner, 2 courses, £20. Lunch £7.50. Packed lunch £6. Pub/restaurant 1.5 miles.
Closed	Rarely.
Directions	From A381 at Halwell, 3rd left signed Slapton; 4th right after 2.3 miles signed Valley Springs Fishery at Wallaton Cross. House down 3rd drive on left.

Peter & Glynis Bidwell
Lower Norton Farmhouse,
Coles Cross, East Allington,
Totnes, Devon TQ9 7RL
Tel   01548 521246
Mobile   07790 288772
Email   peter@lowernortonfarmhouse.co.uk
Web   www.lowernortonfarmhouse.co.uk

✗ ♟ 🦴 🐈 ⋊

Map 2   Entry 127

Devon

Riverside House

The loveliest 17th-century cottage with wisteria and honeysuckle growing up its walls and the tidal river estuary bobbing past with boats and birds; in summer you can dip your toes in the water while sitting in the garden. Felicity, an artist, and Roger, a passionate sailor, give you beautiful bedrooms, fresh flowers, thick towels and pretty china. No need to stir from your fine linen-and-down nest to use the binoculars: bedrooms have long views over the water and wide windows. Wander up to the pub for dinner – in fine weather they have quayside barbecues and live music. *Minimum stay two nights at weekends.*

Price	From £70. Singles from £60.
Rooms	2: 1 double; 1 double with separate shower.
Meals	Packed lunch £6. Pubs 300 yds.
Closed	Rarely.
Directions	In Tuckenhay, pass Maltsters Arms on left to 2nd thatched house on left, at right angle to road. Drive past, turn at bridge and return to slip lane.

Felicity & Roger Jobson
Riverside House,
Tuckenhay, Totnes,
Devon TQ9 7EQ

Tel	01803 732837
Mobile	07710 510007
Email	felicity.jobson@riverside-house.co.uk
Web	www.riverside-house.co.uk

Map 2 Entry 128

Devon

Woodside Cottage

From a narrow decorative window, a charming vignette of Devon: a winding lane edged by fat hedgerows, a cow-dotted hillside. The 18th-century former gamekeeper's cottage is folded into Devon's gentle green softness. Bedrooms are fresh and charming, the drawing and dining rooms formal and immaculate. Tim and Sally welcome you with tea and homemade cake; breakfast on homemade bread and muesli, with eggs from neighbouring hens. An excellent gastropub, the sea and moors are all near; at night see the beam from Start Point lighthouse. *Minimum stay two nights (except November-March).*

Price	From £75. Singles by arrangement.
Rooms	3: 2 doubles, 1 twin/double.
Meals	Packed lunch £5. Half-board option with dinner & wine at village pub.
Closed	Christmas.
Directions	A381 from Totnes to Halwell, A3122 for Dartmouth. After Dartmouth Golf Club, right at sign to house & Blackawton; 0.3 miles before Blackawton, cottage on right.

Tim & Sally Adams
Woodside Cottage,
Blackawton, Dartmouth,
Devon TQ9 7BL

Tel	01803 898164
Fax	07075 020769
Email	sawdays@woodsidedartmouth.co.uk
Web	www.woodsidedartmouth.co.uk

Map 2 Entry 129

Devon

Nonsuch House

The photo says it all! You are in your own crow's nest, perched above the flotillas of yachts zipping in and out of the estuary mouth: stunning. Kit and Penny are great fun and look after you well; Kit is an ex-hotelier, smokes his own fish fresh from the quay and knocks out brilliant dinners. Further pleasures lie across the water: a five-minute walk brings you to the ferry that transports you and your car to the other side. Breakfasts in the conservatory are a delight, bedrooms are big and comfortable and fresh bathrooms sparkle. *Children over ten welcome. Minimum stay two nights at weekends.*

Price	£95-£125. Singles £70-£100.
Rooms	4: 3 twins/doubles, 1 double.
Meals	Dinner, 3 courses, £27.50. (Not Tues/Wed/Sat.) Pub/restaurant 5-minute walk & short boat trip.
Closed	Rarely.
Directions	2 miles before Brixham on A3022, A379. After r'bout, fork left (B3205) downhill, through woods, left up Higher Contour Rd, down Ridley Hill. At hairpin bend.

Kit & Penny Noble
Nonsuch House,
Church Hill, Kingswear,
Dartmouth, Devon TQ6 0BX
Tel   01803 752829
Fax   01803 752357
Email   enquiries@nonsuch-house.co.uk
Web   www.nonsuch-house.co.uk

♿ ✗ 🖂 ☕ 🐾 🐕

Map 2   Entry 130

Devon

The White House

A great little place in a peaceful corner; gaze on the sparkling Dart estuary from the comfort of your deep bed. A maritime theme plays throughout this relaxing, book-filled home, and there's classical music at breakfast. Fresh and cheerful bedrooms have tea, coffee, sherry, chocolates, bathrobes and views; more panoramas from the wide garden terrace by the river. In winter the guest sitting/breakfast room is cosy with open fire, comfortable chairs, masses of books. A ferry transports you to Dartmouth and on to Totnes, and Hugh and Jill are gracious and generous hosts. *Children by arrangement.*

Price	£80. Singles £55.
Rooms	2 doubles.
Meals	Pubs a short walk.
Closed	Christmas.
Directions	Downhill into Dittisham, sharp right immed. before Red Lion. Along The Level, up narrow hill & house entrance opp. at junc. of Manor St & Rectory Lane.

Hugh & Jill Treseder
The White House,
Manor Street,
Dittisham,
Devon TQ6 0EX
Tel   01803 722355
Fax   01803 722355

✗ 🚂 ☕

Map 2   Entry 131

Devon

The Garden House

Refulgent! An extraordinary restoration of a 1930s house, carried out with passion and joy. Bedrooms are sumptuous and filled with all you might need; beds plump with cushions, fabrics smooth, colours vibrant, scents divine. The exuberance reaches the garden; Jane's energy among the pots, quirky topiary and tulips is almost palpable. A huge collection of books are stacked hither and thither, the chandeliers sparkle, candles flicker and there's a vast choice of breakfasts, beautifully served. It may not be minimalist but it is deeply comfortable, good-humoured and an easy walk into the city.

Price	£75–£80. Singles £40.
Rooms	3: 1 double; 1 twin, 1 single sharing bath.
Meals	Pubs/restaurants nearby.
Closed	Rarely.
Directions	M5 junc. 30 for city centre & university. Behind Debenhams, Longbrook St into Pennsylvania Rd. Through lights, 2nd left into Hoopern Ave; house at end on left.

David Woolcock
The Garden House,
4 Hoopern Avenue, Pennsylvania,
Exeter, Devon EX4 6DN

Tel	01392 256255
Fax	01392 256255
Email	david.woolcock1@virgin.net
Web	www.exeterbedandbreakfast.co.uk

Map 2   Entry 132

Devon

Beach House

Lapping at the riverside garden is the Exe estuary, wide and serene. Birds and boats, the soft hills beyond, a gorgeous Georgian house on the river and kind hosts who have been here for years. The garden is beautiful, full of topiary, old apple trees and box hedging; you may breakfast in the conservatory or in the dining room – enjoy raspberries and blackberries in season. No guest sitting room but comfy chairs in the bedrooms, which are soft and chintzy, with antique white bedspreads, charmingly old-fashioned bathrooms and estuary views. Cycle into Exeter, for culture and Cathedral.

Price	£80. Singles £45.
Rooms	2: 1 twin, 1 double.
Meals	Pubs/restaurants 8-minute walk.
Closed	Christmas & New Year; January-March.
Directions	M5 exit 30; signs to Exmouth. Right at George & Dragon. After 1 mile, immed. left after level crossing. At mini r'bout, left down The Strand. House last on left by beach.

Trevor & Jane Coleman
Beach House,
The Strand, Topsham,
Exeter,
Devon EX3 0BB

Tel	01392 876456
Fax	01392 873159
Email	janecoleman45@hotmail.com

Map 2   Entry 133

Devon

Simcoe House

A gem of a setting, this gracious 1790 house built for General John Simcoe is within strolling distance of the beach and town. There are stunning views from wide windows in the lovely guest sitting room, so find a book and settle in a comfy chair while the sun streams in. Jane gives you breakfast in the pretty conservatory or the dining room. Bedrooms are sunny and charming with fresh flowers and fabulous vistas. Laze on the terrace, look up the house history in the local museum or relish the Jurassic coast. A unique house with a beachy feel and delightful owners. *Children over ten welcome.*

Price	£70-£80. Singles £50.
Rooms	2: 1 double, 1 twin.
Meals	Pubs/restaurants 5 minute walk.
Closed	Christmas.
Directions	M5 junc. 30 onto A376. Then B3179 to Budleigh Salterton (approx. 8 miles). Into town centre then left opposite The Creamery, onto Fore Street Hill. 300 yds on right.

Jane Crosse
Simcoe House,
8 Fore Street Hill,
Budleigh Salterton,
Devon EX9 6PE
Tel   01395 446013
Mobile   07747 633060

Map 2   Entry 134

Devon

Larkbeare Grange

Expectations rise as you follow the tree-lined drive to the immaculate Georgian house... and are met, the second you enter this elegant, calm and characterful home. The upkeep is perfect, the feel is chic and the whole place exudes well-being. Sparkling sash windows fill big rooms with light, floors shine and the old grandfather clock ticks away the hours. Expect the best: goose down duvets on king-size beds, contemporary luxury in fabric and fitting, flexible breakfasts and lovely long views from the bedroom at the front. Charlie, Savoy-trained, and Julia are charming and fun: you are in perfect hands.

Price	£85-£105. Singles from £70.
Rooms	3: 2 doubles, 1 twin/double.
Meals	Supper from £18.50. BYO. Pub 1.5 miles.
Closed	Rarely.
Directions	From A30 Exmouth & Ottery St Mary junc. At r'bouts follow Whimple signs. 0.25 miles, right; 0.5 miles, left signed Larkbeare. House 1 mile on left.

Charlie & Julia Hutchings
Larkbeare Grange,
Larkbeare, Talaton, Exeter,
Devon EX5 2RY
Tel   01404 822069
Fax   01404 823746
Email   stay@larkbeare.net
Web   www.larkbeare.net

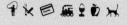

Map 2   Entry 135

Devon

Rose Cottage

Step back in time to seaside fun and bracing walks. Tucked down a quiet street in sleepy Sidmouth, this is a quick hop to the beach – why not rent the family's beach hut? – or onto the coastal path. With stripped pine floorboards, stained-glass features and pretty cushions, Jackie has created a friendly, homely place. Bedrooms are small but jolly with quilted covers and sunny walls, two have tiny showers, another has a slipper bath. There's homemade muesli and organic bacon for breakfast in a room with a seaside teashop feel; no sitting room but a large garden with a slide and swing for children.

Price	From £70. Singles from £55.
Rooms	4: 2 doubles, 1 twin; 1 double with separate bath.
Meals	Packed lunch £5. Pubs/restaurants 300 yds.
Closed	Christmas, New Year & occasionally.
Directions	From Exeter A3052 to Sidmouth. Over r'bout at Woodlands Hotel. House is 100 yards on left just before zebra crossing.

Jacalyn & Neil Cole
Rose Cottage,
Coburg Road, Sidmouth,
Devon EX10 8NF

Tel	01395 577179
Mobile	07708 063820
Email	neilsurf@tesco.net
Web	www.rosecottage-sidmouth.co.uk

Map 2 Entry 136

Devon

Glebe House

Set on a hillside with fabulous views over the Coly valley, this late-Georgian vicarage has become a heart-warming B&B. The views will entice you, the hosts will delight you and the house is filled with interesting things. Chuck and Emma spent many years at sea – he a Master Mariner, she a chef – and have filled these big light rooms with cushions, kilims and treasured family pieces. There's a sitting room for guests, a sweet conservatory with a vintage vine, peaceful bedrooms with blissful views and bathrooms that sparkle. All this, three goats, wildlife beyond the ha-ha and the fabulous coast a hike away.

Price	From £60. Singles £40.
Rooms	3: 1 double, 1 twin/double, 1 family.
Meals	Pubs/restaurants 2.5 miles.
Closed	Christmas & New Year.
Directions	A375 from Honiton; left opposite Hare & Hounds on B3174 to Seaton. 2nd left to Southleigh, 1.5 miles. In village 1st left to Northleigh; 600 yds, drive on left.

Emma & Chuck Guest
Glebe House,
Southleigh, Colyton,
Devon EX24 6SD

Tel	01404 871276
Fax	01404 871276
Email	emma_guest@talktalk.net
Web	www.guestsatglebe.com

Map 2 Entry 137

Devon

West Colwell Farm

Devon lanes, pheasants, bluebell walks *and* sparkling B&B. The Hayes clearly love what they do; ex-TV producers, they have converted this 18th-century farmhouse and barns into a cosy, warm and stylish place to stay. Be charmed by original beams and pine doors, heritage colours and clean lines. Bedrooms feel self-contained, two have terraces overlooking the wooded valley and the largest is tucked under the roof. Linen is luxurious, showers are huge and breakfasts (Frank's pancakes, lovely bacon, eggs from next door) are totally flexible. A pretty garden in front, beaches nearby, peace all around. Bliss.

Price	From £70. Singles £50.
Rooms	3 doubles.
Meals	Restaurants in Honiton.
Closed	Christmas.
Directions	3 miles from Honiton; Offwell signed off A35 Honiton-Axminster road. In centre of village, at church, down hill. Farm 0.5 miles on.

Frank & Carol Hayes
West Colwell Farm,
Offwell, Honiton,
Devon EX14 9SL

Tel	01404 831130
Fax	01404 831769
Email	stay@westcolwell.co.uk
Web	www.westcolwell.co.uk

Map 2   Entry 138

Dorset

Seahill House

Spectacular views! Catch them from the bedrooms and the sweeping gardens. This handsome house stands up and away from the summer crowds above the World Heritage Jurassic coast, next to National Trust land – great walking country. Jane and Adrian, good company and well-travelled, have created a hugely comfortable home and B&B: antique furniture and books in the main rooms, bedrooms with pretty colours and good fabrics. You are in an Area of Outstanding Natural Beauty and a five-minute amble down to Seatown beach and the old Anchor Inn, great for a pint and a crab sandwich. *Children over 12 welcome.*

Price	From £70. Singles by arrangement.
Rooms	2: 1 twin/double; 1 double with separate bathroom.
Meals	Pub 5-minute walk. Restaurants in Chideock.
Closed	Christmas & New Year.
Directions	Into Chideock on A35, turn south into Duck Street, signed to Seatown, then right fork. At top of hill take access road on right-hand side. Signed on right.

Jane & Adrian Tamone
Seahill House,
Seahill Lane, Seatown, Chideock,
Dorset DT6 6JT

Tel	01297 489801
Mobile	07989 940793
Email	jane@seahill.co.uk
Web	www.seahill.co.uk

Map 3   Entry 139

Dorset

Innsacre Farmhouse

Alone in its 22 acres of orchard, valley and wooded hills, this beautiful farmhouse is wrapped in peace. Inside, 17th-century stone walls, low beams and a warm Gallic flair – most special at night when logs glow and prettily dressed tables shimmer. Charming bedrooms – none of which are big – have Provençal beds and good colours, the lightest and biggest fitting a small sofa; bathrooms have touches of glamour. You are two miles from the Jurassic Coast, a World Heritage Site – walk for miles, then dine like kings. Food and wine are Sydney and Jayne's passion; enjoy their bounty. *Arrival after 4pm.*

Price	£85–£105.
Rooms	4: 3 doubles, 1 twin.
Meals	Supper for late arrivals, £17.50. Dinner, 3 courses, £21.50. Picnic £10. Pub 2 miles.
Closed	October, Christmas & New Year.
Directions	From Dorchester A35 for Bridport. After 13 miles 2nd road signed left to Shipton Gorge & Burton Bradstock; 1st left up long drive to farmhouse.

Sydney & Jayne Davies
Innsacre Farmhouse,
Shipton Gorge,
Dorset DT6 4LJ
Tel 01308 456137
Email innsacre.farmhouse@btinternet.com
Web www.innsacre.com

Map 3 Entry 140

Dorset

Orchard Barn

Immerse yourself in huge chalk cliffs, fabulous sea scapes and secret villages hiding in green folds. This is 'River Cottage' country and you will eat like kings – from the dazzling breakfast menu (try Jersey cream on your porridge) to delicious light suppers, all as local and organic as possible. Inside your own barn-like sitting room a fire burns brightly all day, bedrooms are nurturing and fresh, bathrooms awash with perfumed oils and fluffy towels. Nigel and Margaret are old hands at making everything very relaxing indeed. Sit on the terrace in summer and admire the lovely garden.

Price	£95–£110. Singles from £55.
Rooms	2 twins/doubles.
Meals	Light supper £4.75–£15.50. Pubs/restaurants within 3 miles.
Closed	Rarely.
Directions	From A35 east of Bridport within 30mph limit, left into Lee Lane (with 6' 6" width restriction) & follow to bottom. Over bridge, round bend & into Dead End Lane. On right.

Nigel & Margaret Corbett
Orchard Barn,
Bradpole, Bridport,
Dorset DT6 4AR
Tel 01308 455655
Fax 01308 455655
Email corbett@lodgeatorchardbarn.co.uk
Web www.lodgeatorchardbarn.co.uk

Map 3 Entry 141

Dorset

Crosskeys House

A pub, cobbler's shop, blacksmith's, this handsome stone house, right on the village crossroads, has settled with ease into its new role. Robin and Liz, no strangers to running a B&B, are relaxed and efficient and help guests with the best pubs, walks and day-trip ideas. Rooms are softly traditional – plump sofas, family antiques – while portraits of Robin's ancestors keep a watchful eye. Crisply furnished bedrooms, not large, are indulgent with king-size beds, thick towels and interesting books. The house is near the road but there's a courtyard garden for breakfast and water fresh from the well.

Price	£80. Singles from £52.50.
Rooms	2 doubles/twins.
Meals	Packed lunch £5. Pub 200 yds.
Closed	Rarely.
Directions	A35 to Bridport then A3066 to Beaminster. B3163 to Broadwindsor. House is on the one-way system.

Robin & Liz Adeney
Crosskeys House,
High Street, Broadwindsor,
Beaminster, Dorset DT8 3QP
Tel   01308 868063
Fax   01308 868063
Email   robin.adeney@care4free.net
Web   www.crosskeyshouse.com

Map 3   Entry 142

Dorset

Woodwalls House

Quiet seclusion among birds, badgers and wildflowers. The 1806 keeper's cottage sits in its own 12 acres where lovely walks lead in all directions. It is all thoroughly comforting and welcoming: heated towel rails and padded hangers, wonderful antiques and bits of china, lacy bedspreads, countryside views and a charming terrace for tea – nothing is too much trouble for Sally. Your kind, wildlife-loving hosts rustle up fine breakfasts of 'Beaminster bangers' and honey from their bees. There's great walking and you can try your hand at croquet or tennis. Perfect. *Minimum stay two nights at weekends.*

Price	£70-£80. Singles from £50.
Rooms	2: 1 double; 1 twin with separate bath/shower.
Meals	Pub 500 yds.
Closed	Christmas.
Directions	Leave Yeovil on A37 to Dorchester. After 1 mile, right for Corscombe; 6 miles to Corscombe; left after village sign down Norwood Lane; 300 yds, 1st white gate on right.

Sally & Tony Valdes-Scott
Woodwalls House,
Corscombe,
Dorchester,
Dorset DT2 0NT
Tel   01935 891477
Fax   01935 891477
Web   www.woodwallshouse.co.uk

Map 3   Entry 143

Dorset

Higher Holway Farm

Heaven to walk here rather than drive. Hop over the cattle grid and amble down the quilted valley to find a listed, deliciously renovated farmhouse with a distinct 'designer-style' interior. Downstairs has chunky beams, soft colours, fresh flowers and a light, airy sitting room; ample bedrooms are deeply smart with the best linen, floaty goose down and restful views. Food is taken seriously; try a Beaminster banger for breakfast (on the elegant terrace in summer) or one of Sarah's Cordon Bleu dinners. The MacMillan Way is on the doorstep; for walkers who demand solace, this is perfect.

Price	£85. Singles £50.
Rooms	2: 1 twin, 1 twin/double.
Meals	Dinner with wine, £25. Pubs/restaurants 5-10 minute drive.
Closed	Christmas.
Directions	A37 Yeovil-Dorchester. Turn right to Evershot, left towards Cattistock. Left at x-roads to Cattistock. 1.5 miles; where telegraph poles finish on right, farm is on left.

Nigel & Sarah Hadden-Paton
Higher Holway Farm,
Cattistock, Dorchester,
Dorset DT2 0HH

Tel	01935 83822
Fax	01935 83820
Email	bumble@hadden-paton.com
Web	www.higherholwayfarm.co.uk

Map 3   Entry 144

Dorset

Fullers Earth

Such an English feel: the village with pub, post office and stores, the walled garden with fruit trees beyond (source of perfect compotes and breakfast jams), the gentle church view. This listed house – its late-Georgian face added in 1820 – was where the Cattistock huntsmen lived; the unusual thatched stables alongside housed their steeds. Guests share a large and lovely sitting room in sand, cream and dove-blue; carpeted bedrooms have a lofty feel; the resplendent coastline – at times dramatic, at other times softly serene – is yours to discover, and Wendy and Ian will always plan your walks with you.

Price	£75-£85. Singles from £55.
Rooms	2 doubles.
Meals	Pub 500 yds.
Closed	Christmas.
Directions	From A37 take Cattistock turning downhill to T-junc. Left through village. Pub on left. After 90 degree right-hand bend, 5th house on right.

Wendy Gregory
Fullers Earth,
Cattistock, Dorchester,
Dorset DT2 0JL

Tel	01300 320190
Mobile	07968 325698
Email	stay@fullersearth.co.uk
Web	www.fullersearth.co.uk

Map 3   Entry 145

Dorset

Gray's Farmhouse

The views from the ramparts of Eggardon hill fort are superb: from here you can gaze down on the soft stone farmhouse and the sleepy flower-decked lanes. This former shooting lodge has huge flagstones, stripped floors, chunky pine doors and Rosie's collectible paintings on the walls. Excellent breakfasts are served looking across the grounds to a stream, then Powerstock Common and footpaths through ancient wildflower meadows and woodland rich in wildlife. Rosie and Roger will advise on exploring the secret valleys of Hardy country and the spectacular World Heritage coast. *Minimum stay two nights.*

Price	£70–£75. Singles from £60.
Rooms	3: 1 double, 1 double/family, 1 twin/double across courtyard.
Meals	Pub 3 miles.
Closed	Rarely.
Directions	On A37, A356 from D'chester, left at 1st sign for T. Porcorum. Through, & up hill 1 mile. At x-roads, right for Powerstock, under bridge. Track 0.5 miles on left, opp. white post. At end, on left.

	Rosie & Roger Britton
	Gray's Farmhouse,
	Toller Porcorum,
	Dorchester,
	Dorset DT2 0EJ
Tel	01308 485574
Email	rosieroger@farmhousebnb.co.uk
Web	www.farmhousebnb.co.uk

Map 3   Entry 146

Dorset

Frampton House

A grand Grade II*-listed house in parkland landscaped by Capability Brown… and two labradors, Potter and Dodger, to greet you as you scrunch up the gravel. Beyond the Georgian façade lies a delicious mix of English and Gallic styles. Bedrooms combine comfort with outstanding views, a magnificent four-poster in one, everywhere fine linen and plump pillows. Georgina is a portrait painter and a food and arts writer. Breakfasts, served in the conservatory, are true-blue English, with spectacular bangers. Log fires in the drawing room in winter, tea on the terrace in summer, dinners accompanied by French wines.

Price	£65–£85.
Rooms	2: 1 double/twin, 1 four-poster.
Meals	Dinner, 3 courses with wine, £22.50. Pubs 2 miles.
Closed	Rarely.
Directions	A37 Dorchester-Yeovil; A356 for Crewkerne/Maiden Newton. In Frampton, left at green; over white bridge; left, opp. Frampton Roses. 'Private' track to house, signed 3rd on left.

	Georgina & Nicholas Maynard
	Frampton House,
	Frampton, Dorchester,
	Dorset DT2 9NH
Tel	01300 320308
Fax	08454 580531
Email	maynardryder@btconnect.com
Web	www.frampton-house.co.uk

Map 3   Entry 147

Dorset

The White Cottage

Strolling distance from magnificent Athelhampton House and its stunning gardens is this thatched cottage which Lindsay and Mark, escapees from London, have been renovating madly. It's a bright and sunny house with gorgeous bedrooms, super linen, fresh flowers, plump pillows, chocolates; generous bathrooms have thick white towels and lovely bottles of lotions. The suite has its own entrance, large sitting room, comfortable sofas and soft pink and cream bedroom. The river Piddle runs through the garden – fish for brown trout but put them back! You will be well fed – Lindsay's passion is cooking.

Price	£70–£120.
Rooms	3: 1 double, 1 suite for 2-4 (with sofabed); 1 twin with separate bath.
Meals	Dinner £16–£18. Pub 1 mile.
Closed	Open all year.
Directions	A35 exit Puddletown & Athelhampton; signs for Athelhampton House. Left at lights in Puddletown; house 200 yds on right, after Athelhampton House.

Lindsay & Mark Piper
The White Cottage,
Athelhampton, Dorchester,
Dorset DT2 7LG

Tel	01305 848622
Mobile	0777 8987906
Email	markjamespiper@aol.com
Web	www.white-cottage-bandb.co.uk

Map 3 Entry 148

Dorset

The Old Manor

Few B&Bs are as stately as this – Pevsner described the magnificent manor as being "refined to a point of perfection". Gaze over the lake through mullioned windows, sleep in a hand-carved four-poster, warm yourself in front of a Jacobean fireplace. There are beautiful rugs on stone and wooden floors, lavish period fabrics and a stair tower made from just one oak tree. This is the perfect place to return to after a hearty walk straight from the door in rolling Hardy countryside and Andrew and Mulu pamper you; Mulu can even give you a beauty treatment in the salon. *Children by arrangement.*

Price	£100–£120. Singles £65–£75.
Rooms	3: 1 double, 1 twin, 1 four-poster.
Meals	Restaurant within walking distance.
Closed	Mid-December to mid-January.
Directions	At r'bout on A35, 1 mile NE of Dorchester, follow sign to Kingston Maurward gardens & animal park. In grounds, follow estate road, keep straight ahead past Kingston Maurward House.

Andrew & Mulu Thomson
The Old Manor,
Kingston Maurward, Dorchester,
Dorset DT2 8PX

Tel	01305 261110
Mobile	07799 097219
Email	thomson@kingston-maurward.co.uk
Web	www.kingston-maurward.co.uk

Map 3 Entry 149

Dorset

Higher Came Farmhouse

A listed farmhouse of two halves, the front 100 years younger than the back. Inside, winding corridors, sloping floors and the odd wonky wall. Bedrooms are a good size, particularly the cream triple, which has its own dressing room and views of the garden. All are comfortable with good mattresses, bottles of mineral water, thick bathrobes and a melée of patterns on walls, drapes, sofas and bed covers. Lisa and Tim, B&B pros, are terrific with guests and deliver great breakfasts. The place hums with birdsong, the garden is lovely and Dorchester is a five-minute drive.

Price	£60–£70. Singles £38.
Rooms	3: 1 triple; 1 twin/double, 1 triple, each with separate bath.
Meals	Packed lunch £3.50. Pub/restaurant 2.5 miles.
Closed	Rarely.
Directions	From Dorchester bypass A354 to Weymouth. 1st left to Winterbourne Herringston; at T-junc. right, on for 1 mile; look out for golf course, next left to house.

Lisa Bowden
Higher Came Farmhouse,
Higher Came, Dorchester,
Dorset DT2 8AP
Tel 01305 268908
Mobile 0797 0498773
Email enquiries@highercame.co.uk
Web www.highercame.co.uk

Map 3 Entry 150

Dorset

Marren

On the Dorset coastal path, with spectacular views of Portland, a blissfully tranquil and bird-rich spot. Designers Peter and Wendy have transformed their 1920s house and the interiors sing with good taste; antique pine floors softened with kilims, colours contemporary. From six acres of terraced and wooded garden, step into your airy room, perfect with its own entrance, deep-mattressed bed, crisp sheets and luxurious bathroom. Breakfasts of farm produce and homemade bread will set you up for clifftop hikes – leave the low-slung Morgan at home: the track here is adventurously steep!

Price	£80.
Rooms	2 doubles.
Meals	Pub 1 mile.
Closed	Rarely.
Directions	On A353 after Poxwell, left at Ringstead sign; up hill (not to Ringstead), over cattle grid into NT car park; cross & drive through gate 'No Cars'; 2 more gates; 100 yds after 3rd gate, sharp right down steep track.

Peter Cartwright
Marren,
Holworth, Dorchester,
Dorset DT2 8NJ
Tel 01305 851503
Mobile 07957 886399
Email marren@lineone.net
Web www.marren.info

Map 3 Entry 151

Dorset

Glenthorne

A Victorian former rectory with turn-of-the-century tiles and staircase, vibrant colours, stuffed foxes, elephant tusks and ornate mahogany; character, too, in the drawing room with log fire and the roomy bedrooms. There are boat-spotted sea views all the way to Portland and Chesil, an informal garden where you may trip over a fossil or two, a heated pool, and a path to a secret sandy beach. Bring your boat or use your hosts' – they both paint and their work hangs on the walls here. Weymouth is bustling with restaurants, shops, kite and jazz festivals and has the best sunshine record on the south coast.

Price	£60–£100. Singles from £40.
Rooms	3: 1 twin, 1 family; 1 family with separate bath/shower.
Meals	Pub 500 yds. Restaurants 10-min walk.
Closed	Rarely.
Directions	A354 Weymouth to Portland, 0.5 miles to top of hill. As road bears right, turn left into Old Castle Road. Follow signs to house.

Mrs Olivia Nurrish
Glenthorne,
15 Old Castle Road, Weymouth,
Dorset DT4 8QB
Tel 01305 777281
Mobile 07831 751526
Email info@glenthorne-holidays.co.uk
Web www.glenthorne-holidays.co.uk

Map 3 Entry 152

Dorset

Windrush Farm

Fun to breakfast in the farmhouse kitchen with its polished oak table and rag-rolled dresser full of colourful plates. Upstairs, too, is delightful – creaky carpeted floors, sloping ceilings, a maze of corridors and cubby holes. Well-furnished bedrooms are in soft yellows and blues, pinks and creams; paintings, prints and books catch your eye. On colder evenings, your charming hosts will light a fire for you in the sitting room, traditional and snug, while for summer there's a scented, rambler-strewn garden and a terrace with the loveliest views. Bustling Sherborne is a ten-minute drive.

Price	From £75. Singles from £45.
Rooms	2: 1 double with separate bath; 1 twin sharing bath (2nd room let to same party only).
Meals	Dinner £20. Pub/restaurant 2 miles.
Closed	Christmas.
Directions	A357 Wincanton-Templecombe; 2nd turn Stowell, on right opp. entrance to Horsington House. Down hill past church for 0.5 miles; on left after phone box.

Richard & Jenny Gold
Windrush Farm,
Stowell,
Sherborne,
Dorset DT9 4PD
Tel 01963 370799
Email jennygold@hotmail.co.uk

Map 3 Entry 153

Dorset

Golden Hill Cottage

Deep in the countryside lies Stourton Caundle and this charming thatched cottage. All yours are a carpeted twin room with pleasant village view and a shower, and a downstairs sitting room cosy with antiques, paintings on the walls and a fire. In the morning Anna, courteous and kind, brings you splendid platefuls of local bacon and sausage, homemade jams and Dorset honey; nothing is too much trouble for these owners. There are glorious walks from the village, a good pub that serves real ales, and Sherborne, Montacute and Stourhead for landscape, culture and history. *Babes in arms welcome.*

Price	From £60. Singles from £30.
Rooms	1 twin & sitting room.
Meals	Pubs/restaurants within 3 miles.
Closed	Rarely.
Directions	From Sherborne, A352 to Dorchester; after 1 mile, left onto A3030; on to far end of Bishops Caundle, left to Stourton Caundle; after sharp left into village street, house 200 yds on right.

Anna & Andrew Oliver
Golden Hill Cottage,
Stourton Caundle,
Sturminster Newton,
Dorset DT10 2JW

Tel	01963 362109
Email	anna@goldenhillcottage.co.uk
Web	www.goldenhillcottage.co.uk

✗ ♀ ♿

Map 3   Entry 154

Dorset

Manor Barn

What was once an L-shaped cow shed is now a rather smart self-contained barn – attached to the main house and with views to an Iron Age hill. Relax in a roomy and beamed sitting room with squashy sofas, white walls, a woodburning stove; down a corridor are two restful bedrooms with delightful linen and huge fluffy pillows. It is all very rustic-contemporary. A huge breakfast is brought to you, and kind Carolyn will cook a delicious, locally sourced supper if you want a night in with a DVD. Perfect for friends or families and you have complete independence. *Children over eight welcome.*

Price	£85. Singles £50.
Rooms	2 twins/doubles.
Meals	Dinner £15-£20. Light supper £10. Pub in village & more within 3 miles.
Closed	Rarely.
Directions	South on A350 from Shaftesbury; right at sign 'Child Okeford 3 miles'. Just before village, drive is on left, opposite 30 ft high hedge.

Carolyn Sorby
Manor Barn,
Upper Street, Child Okeford,
Blandford, Dorset DT11 8EF

Tel	01258 860638
Mobile	07973 595344
Email	carisorby@btinternet.com
Web	www.manorbarnbedandbreakfast.co.uk

♿ ✗ 📖 ♀ ⚲ 🐈

Map 3   Entry 155

Dorset

Stickland Farmhouse

An encapsulation of much that is charming about Dorset... a soft, delightful thatched cottage in an enviably rural setting. Sandy and Paul have poured love into this listed farmhouse and garden, the latter bursting with lupins, poppies, foxgloves, clematis, delphiniums. Sandy, so welcoming, serves guests delicious breakfast in an Aga-warmed kitchen. Cottagey bedrooms have comfy mattresses and good pictures on the walls and one room opens to the garden. You are in a village with its own pub, and Cranbourne Chase, rich in barrows and hill forts, is close by. *Children over ten welcome.*

Price	£65. Singles £45.
Rooms	3: 2 doubles, 1 twin.
Meals	Pub 15-minute drive.
Closed	Christmas & New Year.
Directions	Leave Blandford for SW, cross river Stour. Hard right after Bryanston school for W. Stickland (4.5 miles). Down North St, right signed W. Houghton. House 150 yds on left with 5-bar gate.

Sandy & Paul Crofton-Atkins
Stickland Farmhouse,
Winterborne Stickland,
Blandford Forum, Dorset DT11 0NT

Tel	01258 880119
Mobile	07932 897774
Email	sticklandfarmhouse@sticklanddorset.fsnet.co.uk
Web	mysite.freeserve.com/stickland

Map 3   Entry 156

Dorset

Holyleas House

Breakfast by a log fire in the elegant dining room in winter – a feast of free-range eggs, homemade jams and marmalades. All the rooms are stylish and well decorated, with lovely prints, many lamps and stunning views; bedrooms are full of light. After a day out or a good walk, hunker down by the fire in the drawing room with a good book. This is a fabulous house, comfortable and easy. Its walled half-acre garden with herbaceous borders is Tia's passion. She is genuinely welcoming – as are her two friendly dogs – and is happy to babysit. *Minimum stay two nights in high season & at weekends.*

Price	£75-£80. Singles £40.
Rooms	3: 1 double, 1 twin/double; 1 single with separate bath.
Meals	Supper tray £8 on first night. Pub a short walk.
Closed	Christmas & New Year.
Directions	From Dorchester, B3143 into Buckland Newton over x-roads; Holyleas on right opp. village cricket pitch.

Tia Bunkall
Holyleas House,
Buckland Newton, Dorchester,
Dorset DT2 7DP

Tel	01300 345214
Mobile	07968 341887
Email	tiabunkall@holyleas.fsnet.co.uk
Web	www.holyleashouse.co.uk

Map 3   Entry 157

Dorset

Honeycombe Cottage

As dreamy as its name, the 16th-century cottage in the village, with deep walls, open fireplaces and flagged floors houses two dogs, one cat and gentle, generous Heather. Now her children have flown the nest, she gives you a garden that blooms as wonderfully as the house and, up under the eaves, soft curtains, soothing colours, aromatic oils and a delicious bed. Have breakfast (pancakes with maple syrup, bacon from up the road) in the homely kitchen, or outside on fine days, where lawns and borders drift effortlessly into orchard, fields and hills. An all-year-round delight. *Children over five welcome.*

Price	From £70.
Rooms	2 twin/doubles.
Meals	Pubs/restaurant 5-minute walk.
Closed	Rarely.
Directions	From A31 to Bere Regis on West Street. At end of village, left down 'No Through Road', over bridge. Thatched wall on left, cottage at end.

Heather Loxton
Honeycombe Cottage,
Shitterton, Bere Regis,
Dorset BH20 7HU

Tel	01929 471660
Mobile	07746 497171
Email	heather.loxton@virgin.net
Web	www.honeycombecottage.com

Map 3   Entry 158

Dorset

Bering House

At the end of a quiet cul-de-sac, an immaculate retreat. Pretty little sofas, golden taps, coordinating drapes – Renate is justly proud. Gaze from the balcony of your sumptuous suite on sparkling Poole harbour, biscuits and sherry to hand. The garden room, too, has every little extra – dressing gowns, sweets, fruit, videos, bathroom treats. Summer breakfasts are served among the birds, the flowers and the breezes on blue and white Spode china, or in the dining room off a darkly wooden table. Fresh fruit, Parma ham, smoked salmon, kedgeree: the choice is superb. Amazing harbourside B&B.

Price	£65–£80. Singles by arrangement.
Rooms	2: 1 twin/double; 1 twin/double suite & kitchenette.
Meals	Pub 400 yds.
Closed	Rarely.
Directions	From A35/A350 Upton, take Blandford road B3068 south for Hamworthy & Rockley Park; 1.5 miles on right at Red Lion into Lake Rd; under bridge past Yachtsman Pub; 2nd left down Branksea Ave; last on left.

Renate & John Wadham
Bering House,
53 Branksea Avenue,
Poole,
Dorset BH15 4DP

Tel	01202 673419
Fax	01202 667260
Email	johnandrenate@tiscali.co.uk

Map 3   Entry 159

Dorset

North Mill

It's the setting that does it. The river Piddle rushes past this pretty 16th-century listed mill house on the edge of the Saxon town of Wareham. The guest bedrooms (large double, smaller twin) overlook garden, river and water meadows, the guests' sitting/dining room has a wood-burner for chilly evenings and the house is furnished with lovely paintings and antiques. Breakfast includes fresh eggs from Sally's hens and homemade bread, marmalade and jams. Dorchester is close by and the World Heritage coastline and the beaches and hills of Purbeck beckon.

Price	From £70. Singles £45.
Rooms	2: 1 double; 1 twin with separate bath/shower.
Meals	Dinner, 3 courses with wine, £20. Pubs/restaurants 5-minute walk.
Closed	Rarely.
Directions	On entering Wareham, right up Shatters Hill just after garage. Right down footpath opposite Mill Lane.

Sally Dubuis
North Mill,
Wareham,
Dorset BH20 4QW
Tel   01929 555142
Mobile   07976 273385
Web   www.northmill.org.uk

Map 3   Entry 160

Dorset

Gold Court House

Anthea and Michael have created a mood of restrained luxury and uncluttered, often beautiful, good taste in their Georgian townhouse. Bedrooms are restful in cream with mahogany furniture, sloping ceilings, beams, armchairs and radios. There's a large drawing room and good paintings. Your hosts are delightful – "they do everything to perfection," says a reader; both house and garden are a refuge. Views are soft and lush yet you are in the small square of this attractive town; the house was rebuilt in 1762 after a great fire, and the Hipwells added their creative spin seven years ago. *Children over ten welcome.*

Price	£70-£75. Singles £45.
Rooms	3: 1 twin/double; 2 twins/doubles, each with separate bath.
Meals	Dinner £17.50, available in winter. Restaurants 50 yds.
Closed	Rarely.
Directions	From A35, A351 to Wareham. Follow signs to town centre. In North St, over lights into South St. 1st left into St John's Hill; house on far right-hand corner of square.

Anthea & Michael Hipwell
Gold Court House,
St John's Hill, Wareham,
Dorset BH20 4LZ
Tel   01929 553320
Fax   01929 553320
Email   info@goldcourthouse.co.uk
Web   www.goldcourthouse.co.uk

Map 3   Entry 161

Dorset

Lower Lynch House

On the glorious Isle of Purbeck, where the wind blows the trees sideways, this wisteria-strewn house sits in a tranquil fold. At the end of a long woodland track: warm, clean and comfortable B&B. Your gentle hosts give you Aga-cooked breakfast at tables overlooking courtyard and garden; small, old-fashioned bedrooms with pale colours and florals are as peaceful as can be. No sitting room, but a small sofa in the double. You are minutes from the coastal path, so this is the perfect spot for walkers, birdwatchers, shell-seekers and anybody who relishes being away from the city.

Price	From £60. Singles by arrangement.
Rooms	2: 1 twin; 1 double with separate bath.
Meals	Inn 0.75 miles.
Closed	Christmas & New Year.
Directions	A351 from Wareham to Corfe Castle. At end of village fork right on B3069 for Kingston. Left 0.5 miles down track (sign on roadside).

Bron & Nick Burt
Lower Lynch House,
Kingston Hill,
Corfe Castle,
Dorset BH20 5LG
Tel   01929 480089
Email   bronburt@tiscali.co.uk

Map 3   Entry 162

Dorset

Century Cottage

Folded away where three counties meet is this creamy yellow, 19th-century cottage in the lee of a village church. Intimate and unstuffy, its English and Dutch antiques, ceramics and tiled floors reflect Jutta and Richard's eclectic style and global wanderings. Chat to your sociable hosts in the cosy book-lined sitting room or wander into the terraced garden with its pink hollyhocks, tumbling roses and country views. Snuggle into a soft bed crowned with charming floral cornucopia. And before you leave this peaceful place, peek at the enchanting seashells in the smallest room! Brilliant value.

Price	£60. Singles £35.
Rooms	1 double with separate bath.
Meals	Dinner £15. Pub 200 yds.
Closed	Rarely.
Directions	A303 onto A350 towards Shaftesbury. Signs to Semley. Past pub, bear right. Past school and phone box, yellow cottage on right.

Mr & Mrs R P Carless
Century Cottage,
Semley,
Shaftesbury,
Dorset SP7 9AU
Tel   01747 830432
Email   jmcarless@tiscali.co.uk
Web   www.century-cottage.co.uk

Map 3   Entry 163

Dorset

The Old Forge, Fanners Yard

Tim and Lucy are tangibly happy in this beautifully restored forge. It was built in the 1700s; the wheelwright and carriage-builder from the local estate used to work here. Tim has beautifully restored the cosy gypsy caravan which has super views and a picnic table outside. The attic bedrooms are snug, with Lucy's quilts, country antiques and sparkling bathrooms. Delicious Aga-cooked breakfasts include eggs from their own free-strutting hens, organic sausages and bacon, home-grown jams, apple juice straight from the orchard. The Downs beckon walkers; warm corners invite readers. Utterly genuine.

Price	From £65.
Rooms	3: 1 double, 1 family; 1 double in gypsy caravan with separate shower & wc (20 yds away).
Meals	Pub/restaurant 1 mile.
Closed	Rarely.
Directions	From Shaftesbury, A350 to Compton Abbas. House 1st on left before Compton Abbas sign. Left; entrance on left.

	Tim & Lucy Kerridge
	The Old Forge, Fanners Yard,
	Compton Abbas, Shaftesbury,
	Dorset SP7 0NQ
Tel	01747 811881
Fax	01747 811881
Email	theoldforge@hotmail.com
Web	www.theoldforgedorset.co.uk

Map 3   Entry 164

Dorset

Crawford House

Below, the river Stour winds through the valley and under the medieval, nine-arched bridge. Above, an Iron Age hill fort; between is Crawford House. It's an elegant Georgian house in an acre of walled garden, soft and pretty inside with an easy, relaxed atmosphere. Carpeted bedrooms are homely and warm, with long curtains; one room has four-poster twin beds with chintz drapes. The sun streams through the floor-to-ceiling windows of the downstairs rooms, and charming 18th- and 19th-century oil paintings hang in the pale green dining room. Visit the Isle of Purbeck coastline – a World Heritage Site.

Price	From £60. Singles £30.
Rooms	3: 1 twin/double; 1 twin with separate bath; 1 twin with separate shower.
Meals	Pub in village 0.5 miles.
Closed	Mid-October-mid-April.
Directions	A350 north; after entering Spetisbury, 1st gateway immed. on left after crossroads (B3075).

	Andrea Lea
	Crawford House,
	Spetisbury,
	Blandford,
	Dorset DT11 9DP
Tel	01258 857338
Fax	01258 858152
Email	andrea@lea8.wanadoo.co.uk

Map 3   Entry 165

Dorset

Thornhill

Here is a pretty Thirties' thatched house, with peaceful views from every window... of fields, woods and two landscaped acres. Sara and John encourage the wildlife on their patch; you may spot a deer on the lawn. Inside are patterned fabrics and old-fashioned candlewick covers, pastel walls and polished antiques. All is neat, tidy, spacious and spotless, and Sara pays attention to detail: a toothbrush for the forgetful, fruit and chocolates in the rooms, a choice of teas. Walkers can stride out straight from the door, gardeners will be happy here – and bridge players, if they come on a Thursday!

Price	From £56. Singles from £28.
Rooms	3: 1 double, 1 twin, 1 single, all sharing 2 baths. Possible use of separate bath.
Meals	Pub/restaurant 400 yds.
Closed	Rarely.
Directions	From Wimborne B3078 towards Cranborne. Right to Holt. After 2 miles Thornhill on right, 200 yds beyond Old Inn.

John & Sara Turnbull
Thornhill,
Holt,
Wimborne,
Dorset BH21 7DJ
Tel 01202 889434
Email scturnbull@lineone.net

Map 3 Entry 166

Durham

34 The Bank

In this impressive Georgian townhouse live Eva, Ian, an eccentric Hungarian vizsla and Georgina. Georgina is the resident ghost whose manners are unfailingly polite; Eva and Ian merely run the place. Ian cooks the breakfasts and Eva arranges them artistically because that's her thing. They love their guests and provide beautiful rooms – white quilts, bold walls, easy chairs – and much comfort in the sitting room with open fire. Sally forth to see the rest of bonny Barney on the Tees: the castle, the antique shops and the restaurant next door where Cromwell really stayed. Marvellous.

Price	From £55. Singles from £40.
Rooms	3: 1 double, 1 twin, 1 four-poster.
Meals	Pubs/restaurants 50 yds.
Closed	Rarely.
Directions	At A1 Scotch Corner, A66 west for 14 miles. Then 1st dual carriageway; right for Barnard Castle. At lights right over bridge, left at T-junc. to Butter Market. Left down bank, house on left.

Ian & Eva Reid
34 The Bank,
Barnard Castle,
Durham DL12 8PN
Tel 01833 631304
Email evasreid@aol.com
Web www.number34.com

Map 12 Entry 167

Durham

The Coach House

There's so much to gladden your heart – the cobbled courtyard that evokes memories of its days as a coaching inn, the river running through the estate, the drawing room's log fire, the delicious breakfasts, the blackberry crumbles with cream... and Peter and Mary, your kind, unstuffy, dog-adoring hosts (they have three well-behaved ones). Every creature comfort has been attended to in this small, perfect, English country house: lined chintz, starched linen, cushioned window seats, cut flowers, heated towel rails. Friendly, delightful, and the perfect stepping stone to Scotland or the south.

Price	£80. Singles £50.
Rooms	2: 1 twin/double; 1 twin/double with separate bath.
Meals	Dinner, 3 courses, £25. Pub/restaurants within 3 miles.
Closed	Rarely.
Directions	A1(M) to Scotch Corner. A66 west for 8 miles until Greta Bridge turn-off. House on left just before bridge.

Peter & Mary Gilbertson
The Coach House,
Greta Bridge, Barnard Castle,
Durham DL12 9SD

Tel	01833 627201
Fax	01833 627201
Email	info@coachhousegreta.co.uk
Web	www.coachhousegreta.co.uk

Map 12   Entry 168

Essex

Brook Farm

Lovely large Georgian windows fill the house with light, unpretentious family pieces warm the friendly bedrooms and the low carved crossbeam in the family room is late medieval. Anne, country lover and B&B-er, has farmed here for over 30 years and her sheep and horses roam these 100 acres. You breakfast (well) at a long table on antique benches, and nod off, after a pub supper, on a comfy sofa. Logs fill the copper, hunting prints line the walls and there are magazines and books to delve into. The handsome bright farmhouse is full of country charm – yet 30 minutes from Stansted.

Price	£60-£70. Singles £35-£45.
Rooms	3: 1 twin; 1 double, 1 family room, both with separate bath.
Meals	Packed lunch £3-£5. Pubs 1.5 miles.
Closed	Rarely.
Directions	House on B1053, 500 yds south of Wethersfield.

Mrs Anne Butler
Brook Farm,
Wethersfield,
Braintree,
Essex CM7 4BX

Tel	01371 850284
Fax	01371 850284
Email	abutlerbrookfarm@aol.com

Map 9   Entry 169

Essex

Caterpillar Cottage

Traditional bricks, clapboard dormer windows, tall chimneys – this looks like the real thing. But the 'converted farm building' in the grounds of Patricia's former grand house is brand new! Filled with fine furniture, family photographs and *objets* from far-flung travels, it invites relaxation. The double-height, vaulted sitting room brims with sofas and books, and logs crackle on chilly nights. Bedrooms are simple and comfortable with decent-sized bathrooms. Patricia, a lively grandmother, adores children while her big garden promises home-grown fruit and tranquillity.

Price	From £60. Singles from £30.
Rooms	2: 1 triple;
	1 double with separate bath/shower.
Meals	Packed lunch available.
	Pubs 50 yds.
Closed	Rarely.
Directions	A12 to A1124. In Fordstreet,
	cottage through shared gateway,
	opposite pub.

Patricia Mitchell
Caterpillar Cottage,
Fordstreet,
Aldham,
Colchester,
Essex CO6 3PH
Tel 01206 240456
Fax 01206 240456

Map 10　Entry 170

Essex

The Old Rectory

Scrunch up to this Georgian-fronted, wisteria-wrapped family house. Six children are variously away or busying about tending all sorts of fowl and four-legged folk; Bella, gracious and easy, makes it all look a doddle. Come for lovely walks through an ancient woodland cleared to free bluebells and your own private 'studio' bolthole with duckpond deck. There are tall windows, a long sofa, free-range flowers, yards of books and beckoning beds, a kitchen (make your own organic breakfast and just taste those eggs) and a classy bathroom. Just ten minutes from Colchester.

Price	From £90. Singles £45–£50.
Rooms	1 twin.
Meals	Pubs/restaurants nearby.
Closed	Christmas.
Directions	A12, take A1124 towards Halstead.
	After 1st r'bout, right at Brick &
	Tile pub, into Spring Lane then
	right on Argent's Lane; left uphill at
	T-junc., then 1st left Cooks Hall
	Road; blue gates at first bend.

Bella Huddart
The Old Rectory,
West Bergholt,
Colchester,
Essex CO6 3EX
Tel 01206 241637
Mobile 07768 511755
Email bella_huddart@hotmail.co.uk

Map 10　Entry 171

Essex

Bromans Farm

The island of Mersea is surprisingly secluded, and Bromans Farm is in the most tranquil corner; the sea murmurs across the Saltings where the Brent geese wheel and the great Constable skies stretch. The house began in 1343 – nearly as old as the exquisite church. The Georgians added their bit, but the venerable beams and uneven old construction shine through. It is a sunny, comfortable house, with good bedrooms and warm bathrooms, a snug book-filled sitting room, a beautiful Welsh oak dresser in the breakfast room, and a conservatory gazing over the large garden. Wild walks beckon.
Min. stay two nights at weekends.

Price	£70–£80. Singles £40.
Rooms	2: 1 double, 1 twin, each with separate bath.
Meals	Pub 0.5 miles.
Closed	Rarely.
Directions	From Colchester B1025, over causeway, bear left. After 3 miles, pass Dog & Pheasant pub; 3rd right into Bromans Lane. House 1st on left.

Mrs Ruth Dence
Bromans Farm,
East Mersea,
Essex CO5 8UE
Tel   01206 383235
Fax   01206 383235
Email   bromansfarm@btopenworld.com
Web   www.bromansfarm.co.uk

Map 10   Entry 172

Essex

Emsworth House

Unexpectedly tranquil, this 1937 vicarage – with wide views over the Stour and some wonderful light for painting – will both energise and calm you. Penny, an artist, is a generous host and looks after you well. This is Constable country so great for walking, you are near to Frinton beach and good golf, sailing and riding. Return to comfy sofas and chairs, open fires and good books, fairly basic bedrooms with a country feel and the odd African throw or splash of colour, lots of lovely paintings and a garden filled with birds. Perfect for families too – Penny has camp beds and a can-do attitude.

Price	From £55. Singles from £45.
Rooms	3: 1 double, 1 twin; 1 double with separate bath.
Meals	Pub/restaurant 0.5 miles.
Closed	Rarely.
Directions	A12-A120 (to Harwich) & left to B1035; right at TV mast to Bradfield, 2 miles; house on right.

Penny Linton
Emsworth House,
Ship Hill, Station Road,
Bradfield, Maningtree,
Essex CO11 2UP
Tel   01255 870860
Email   emsworthhouse@hotmail.com
Web   www.emsworthhouse.co.uk

Map 10   Entry 173

Boyts Farm

A magnolia rambles around the wooden mullioned windows and an old oak door admits you to the 16th-century farmhouse. Stone flags, Georgian panelling and polished wooden stairs are softened by pale fabrics, comfortable sofas, books and flowers. The effect is simple, uncluttered, pleasing. The bedrooms are delightful too, one with an original Thirties' bathroom. John and Sally are inspired gardeners in their Italianate two acres: orchards, ponds, ha-has, paddocks and canal. Breakfast on orchard stewed fruits and homemade jams. The house is handsome, the setting wonderful, the peace a balm.

Grove Farm

Boards creak and you duck, in a farmhouse of the best kind: simple, small-roomed, stone-flagged, beamed, delightful. The walls are white, the furniture is good and there are pictures everywhere. In spite of great age (16th-century), it's light, with lots of windows. You'll be fed well, too; the 400 acres are farmed organically and Penny makes a grand breakfast – continental at busy times. Stupendous views across the Severn estuary to the Cotswolds, the Forest of Dean on the doorstep and woodland walks, carpeted with spring flowers. And there is simply no noise – unless the guinea fowl are in voice.

Price	£80. Singles £35-£40.
Rooms	2: 1 double, 1 twin.
Meals	Pub/restaurant 3-minute walk.
Closed	21 December-2 January.
Directions	M5 junc. 16; A38 for Gloucester. After 6 miles, turn for Tytherington. From north, M5 junc. 14; A38 for Bristol. Turn for Tytherington after 3 miles.

Price	£60-£70. Singles £30.
Rooms	2: 1 double; 1 twin/double with separate bath.
Meals	Packed lunch £4. Pub 2 miles.
Closed	Rarely.
Directions	2 miles south of Newnham on A48, opp. turn for Bullo Pill, large 'pull-in' with phone box on right; turn here; follow farm track to end.

Sally Eyre
Boyts Farm,
Tytherington,
Wotton-under-Edge,
Gloucestershire GL12 8UG
Tel   01454 412220
Email jve@talktalk.net

Penny & David Hill
Grove Farm,
Bullo Pill, Newnham,
Gloucestershire GL14 1DZ
Tel   01594 516304
Fax   01594 516304
Email davidandpennyhill@btopenworld.com
Web   www.grovefarm-uk.com

Map 3   Entry 174

Map 8   Entry 175

Gloucestershire

Frampton Court

Deep authenticity in this magnificent Grade I-listed house. The manor of Frampton-on-Severn has been in the family since the 11th century and although Rollo and Janie look after the estate, it is Gillian who greets you on behalf of the family and looks after you (very well). Exquisite examples of decorative woodwork and, in the hall, a cheerful log fire; perch on the mouseman fire seat. Bedrooms are traditional with antiques, panelling and long views. Beds have fine linen, bathrooms are delectably antiquated. Stroll around the ornamental canal, soak up the old-master views. An architectural masterpiece.

Price	£110. Singles £85 (week only).
Rooms	3: 1 twin/double, 1 double, 1 four-poster.
Meals	Dinner £24.50. Pub across the green. Restaurant 3 miles.
Closed	Rarely.
Directions	From M5 junc. 13 west, then B4071. Left down village green, 400 yds, then look to left! 2nd turning left, between two chestnut trees & thro' ornamental gates in wall.

Rollo & Janie Clifford
Frampton Court,
Frampton-on-Severn,
Gloucestershire GL2 7EQ

Tel	01452 740267
Mobile	07795 116086
Email	framptoncourt@framptoncourtestate.co.uk
Web	www.framptoncourtestate.co.uk

Map 8   Entry 176

Gloucestershire

The Old School House

The perfect English scene: a late 18th century house tucked down a lane off the country's longest village green; a garden alive with colourful posies; walks by the canal. Bedrooms are large with fluffy towels, crisp linen, muted yellows and rich velvety plums. It's a wonderful house that feels freshly decorated and Carol wants you to treat it as home. When we visited, there was a jigsaw puzzle that invited a challenge, dogs and cats happily co-existed and the visitors' book was inscribed: "We'll be back" (and return they do). At breakfast, fresh eggs, elegant china, pots of homemade jam. *Children over ten welcome.*

Price	£70. Singles £40.
Rooms	2: 1 twin/double, 1 twin.
Meals	Pub 0.5 miles. Restaurant 5 miles.
Closed	Christmas & New Year.
Directions	A38 for Bristol, west onto B4071; 1st left & drive length of village green; 300 yds after end, right into Whittles Lane. House last on right. 3 miles from junc. 13 on M5.

Carol & William Alexander
The Old School House,
Whittles Lane,
Frampton-on-Severn,
Gloucestershire GL2 7EB

Tel	01452 740457
Email	theoldies@the-oldschoolhouse.co.u
Web	www.the-oldschoolhouse.co.uk

Map 8   Entry 177

Gloucestershire

Drakestone House

A treat by anyone's reckoning. Utterly delightful people with wide-ranging interests (ex British Council and college lecturing; arts, travel, gardening) in a manor-type house full of beautiful furniture. The house was born of the Arts and Crafts movement: wooden panels painted green, a log-fired drawing room for guests, handsome old furniture, comfortable proportions, good beds with proper blankets. The garden's massive clipped hedges, Monterey Pines and smooth, great lawn are impressive, as is the whole place – and the views stretch to the Severn Estuary and Wales.

Price	£76. Singles £48.
Rooms	3: 1 twin/double, 1 double, 1 twin, each with separate bath/shower.
Meals	Dinner £25. BYO. Pub/restaurant under 1 mile.
Closed	December-January.
Directions	B4060 from Stinchcombe to Wotton-under-Edge. 0.25 miles out of Stinchcombe village. Driveway on left marked, before long bend.

Hugh & Crystal Mildmay
Drakestone House,
Stinchcombe,
Dursley,
Gloucestershire GL11 6AS
Tel 01453 542140
Fax 01453 542140

Map 8   Entry 178

Gloucestershire

Lodge Farm

A plum Cotswolds position, a striking garden, stylish décor, exceptional linen – there are plenty of reasons to stay here. Then there are your flexible hosts, who can help wedding groups, give you supper en famille next to the Aga or something smarter round the dining-room table with crystal and silver: perfect for a house party. The sitting room has flowers, family photographs and lots of magazines; throughout are flagstones, Bath stone and wood. Home-produced (Hebridean) lamb for dinner, maybe, and excellent coffee at breakfast. The Salmons breed thoroughbreds and can stable your horse.

Price	£55-£70. Singles from £45. Family room £75.
Rooms	4: 2 twins/doubles; 1 twin/double, 1 family room sharing bath.
Meals	Dinner, 3 courses, £20. Packed lunch £8.50. Pub/bistro 2.5 miles.
Closed	Rarely.
Directions	From Cirencester A433 to Tetbury, right B4014 to Avening. After 250 yds, left onto Chavenage Lane. Lodge Farm 1.3 miles on right; left of barn.

Mrs Nicola Salmon
Lodge Farm,
Chavenage, Tetbury,
Gloucestershire GL8 8XW
Tel 01666 505339
Mobile 07836 221457
Email rsalmon@lodgefarm.vianw.co.uk
Web www.lodgefarm.co.uk

Map 8   Entry 179

Gloucestershire

Nation House

Three cottages were knocked together to create this house, now listed and wisteria-clad. Beams are exposed, walls are pale and hung with prints, floors are close-carpeted in pinky beige, the sitting room is formally cosy and quiet. Bedrooms show off a cottage garden theme with fat quilts, low beams and lattice windows; the bathroom is spotless and the shower room compact. In summer, breakfast in the conservatory on still-warm homemade bread, local bacon and sausages, Brenda's preserves. The village is a Cotswold treasure, with two good eating places and with many walks from the door.

Price	£60–£75. Singles £40.
Rooms	3: 1 suite; 2 doubles sharing bath.
Meals	Pubs 50 yds.
Closed	Rarely.
Directions	From Cirencester A419 for Stroud. After 7 miles right to Bisley. Left at village shop. House 50 yds on right.

Brenda & Mike Hammond
Nation House,
George Street,
Bisley,
Gloucestershire GL6 7BB
Tel   01452 770197
Email   nation.house@homecall.co.uk

Map 8   Entry 180

Gloucestershire

Well Farm

Perhaps it's the gentle, unstuffy attitude of Kate and Edward. Or the great position of the house with its glorious views across the valley. Whatever, you'll feel comforted and invigorated by your stay here. It's a real family home and guests have a fresh, pretty bedroom that feels very private, and the use of a comfortable, book-filled sitting room that opens to a courtyard – Kate is an inspired gardener. Sleep soundly on crisp linen with the softest of pillows, wake to the deep peace of the countryside and tuck in to eggs from their own hens, local sausages, good bacon. The area teems with great walks.

Price	£75–£80.
Rooms	1 twin/double & sitting room.
Meals	Dinner from £20. Pubs nearby.
Closed	Rarely.
Directions	Directions on booking.

Kate & Edward Gordon Lennox
Well Farm,
Frampton Mansell, Stroud,
Gloucestershire GL6 8JB
Tel   01285 760651
Email   kategl@btinternet.com.
Web   www.well-farm.co.uk

Map 8   Entry 181

Gloucestershire

107 Gloucester Street

Slip through gates into a narrow courtyard of potted shrubs and honey-coloured Cotswold stone. This modest Georgian merchant's house is three minutes from the charming town centre yet blissfully quiet. Inside: buttery colours, well-loved antiques, soft uncluttered spaces. Restful, understated bedrooms are small, chic and spotless. Kitchen breakfasts overlook the sheltered garden – a verdant spot for relaxing in summer. For evenings, a creamy first-floor sitting room with a small log fire. Ethne and her ex-army husband are full of fun and good humour – very special. *Children over ten welcome.*

Gloucestershire

The Old Rectory

English to the core – and to the bottom of its lovely garden, with a new woodland walk and plenty of quiet places to sit. You sweep into the circular driveway to a yellow labrador welcome. The house, despite its magnificent age, throbs with family energy and warmth – Caroline is calmly competent and amiable, with a talent for understated interior décor. The two large, airy bedrooms are furnished with antiques, very good beds, a chaise longue or an easy chair, even a bottle opener and wine glasses. Elsewhere, old furniture and creaky floorboards complete the sense of well-being in a very special place.

Price	£70. Singles £50.
Rooms	2: 1 double, 1 twin.
Meals	Hotel 300 yds & restaurants 8-minute walk.
Closed	Easter & Christmas.
Directions	Directions on booking.

Price	£80. Singles £50.
Rooms	2: 1 double, 1 twin.
Meals	Pub 200 yds.
Closed	December–January.
Directions	South through village from A417. Right after Masons Arms. House 200 yds on left, through stone pillars.

Ethne McGuinness
107 Gloucester Street,
Cirencester,
Gloucestershire GL7 2DW

Tel   01285 657861
Fax   01285 657861
Email   ethne@mcguinness78.freeserve.co.uk

Roger & Caroline Carne
The Old Rectory,
Meysey Hampton, Cirencester,
Gloucestershire GL7 5JX

Tel   01285 851200
Fax   01285 850452
Email   carolinecarne@cotswoldwireless.co.uk

Map 8   Entry 182

Map 8   Entry 183

Gloucestershire

Kempsford Manor

On the edge of the Cotswolds, this 17th-century village house is surrounded by large hedges and mature trees. Crunch up the gravelled drive to find floor-to-ceiling bay windows, dark pine floors with patterned rugs, wood panelling and built-in bookcases. Bedrooms vary hugely – one has a Chinese theme – but all are a good size and have super garden views; bathrooms are functional and old-fashioned. Two acres of beautifully tended gardens (snowdrops are special here) lead to an orchard and a canal walk; stoke up on Zehra's homemade muesli and come back for dinner – vegetables are homegrown.

Price	£65. Singles £35.
Rooms	3: 1 double; 1 double, 1 single, each with separate bath.
Meals	Dinner available. Pub 200 yds.
Closed	Open all year.
Directions	A419 Cirencester-Swindon; Kempsford is signed with Fairford. Right into village, past small village green; on right, through stone columns. Glass front door, by a fountain.

Mrs Zehra I Williamson
Kempsford Manor,
High Street,
Fairford,
Gloucestershire GL7 4EQ
Tel   01285 810131
Email   ipek@kempsfordmanor.co.uk
Web   www.kempsfordmanor.co.uk

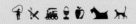

Map 8   Entry 184

Gloucestershire

Lady Lamb Farm

Light pours into perfectly proportioned rooms through windows hung with velvet and chintz; soft sofas entice; china sits in alcoves on both sides of the fireplace. Jeanie and James, farmers, inventors, built the honey-stone house years ago and have kept their Cotswold dream ship-shape. You can play tennis and swim in the pool, bedrooms are a good size and have dreamy views, Aga breakfasts are scrumptious; locally cured bacon and eggs from the chickens that strut on the manicured lawn. Fishing, cycling and golf can all be organised for you and Kelmscott Manor (the country home of William Morris) is close.

Price	From £65. Singles £45.
Rooms	2: 1 twin; 1 twin/double with separate bath.
Meals	Pubs/restaurants 1-4 miles.
Closed	Christmas & New Year.
Directions	From Fairford on A417. After 0.5 miles look for sign for Waitenhill and Cherry Tree House. Entrance directly opposite on left.

Jeanie Keyser
Lady Lamb Farm,
Meysey Hampton, Cirencester,
Gloucestershire GL7 5LH
Tel   01285 712206
Fax   01285 712206
Mobile 0787 6418966
Email   jeanie@jameskeyser.co.uk

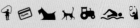

Map 8   Entry 185

Gloucestershire

Isbourne Manor House

The part-Tudor, part Georgian house is named after the river flowing through its garden. Sudeley Castle is next door — just nip through the kissing gate into the glorious grounds. David, an organic grain merchant, and Felicity are gentle-mannered and easy, and treat you to breakfasts of homemade and local produce. One bedroom has an ornately carved, comfortable four-poster; the twin, under the eaves, has its own sun terrace. In the drawing room: oils on walls, antiques, an honesty bar and open fire. Winchcombe is a satisfying little town, with useful shops, buzzing inns and a real sense of community.

Price	£75-£100. Singles from £60.
Rooms	3: 1 double, 1 four-poster; 1 twin with separate shower.
Meals	Pubs/restaurants 2-5 minute walk.
Closed	Christmas & possibly Easter.
Directions	On B4632 between Cheltenham & Broadway. Turn into Castle St by White Hart in village centre. On left at bottom of steep hill.

Felicity & David King
Isbourne Manor House,
Castle Street, Winchcombe,
Gloucestershire GL54 5JA

Tel	01242 602281
Mobile	07818 290109
Email	felicity@isbourne-manor.co.uk
Web	www.isbourne-manor.co.uk

Map 8   Entry 186

Gloucestershire

5 Ewlyn Road

In a bustling suburb of Cheltenham, Barbara's red-brick villa reveals fixtures and fittings rarely seen — and its changeless character gives it an unusually restful feel. Lifelong hostess, Barbara looks after her guests with old-fashioned, effortless ease. The bedroom is peaceful, the bathroom clean and purposeful, the front room perfect for cosy contemplation and good conversation. With her restaurant background Barbara treats you to the best Gloucester Old Spot bacon and free-range eggs — whenever you wish, and outside the sunny back door in summer. Authentic, great value B&B.

Price	£50. Singles £25.
Rooms	1 twin sharing bath.
Meals	Pubs/restaurants a 5-minute walk.
Closed	Rarely.
Directions	From A40, signs to Stroud then Cheltenham College. Up Bath Road past shops; at x-roads, veg shop on left. Left signed Emmanuel Church; 2nd on right; front door to side.

Barbara Jameson
5 Ewlyn Road,
Cheltenham,
Gloucestershire GL53 7PB

Tel	01242 261243

Map 8   Entry 187

Gloucestershire

Westward, Sudeley Lodge

Susie and Jim are highly organised and efficient, juggling teenage children, horses and B&B. She's also a great cook (Leith trained). The grand, but cosy, house sits above Sudeley Castle surrounded by its own 600 acres; all bedrooms look west to long views. Colours, fabrics and furniture are in perfect harmony, beds and linen are inviting, and the easy mix of elegant living and family bustle is delightful. There's tea on the terrace in summer and by a log fire in winter... your hosts delight in sharing this very English home. Wonderful walks on your doorstep and all those honey-hued Cotswold villages just beyond.

Price	From £80. Singles £55.
Rooms	3: 1 double, 2 twins/doubles.
Meals	Pubs/restaurants 1 mile.
Closed	December-January.
Directions	From Abbey Sq., Winchcombe, go north; after 50 yds, right into Castle St. Follow for 1 mile; after farm buildings, right for Sudeley Lodge; follow for 600 yds. House on right; first oak door.

Susie & Jim Wilson
Westward, Sudeley Lodge,
Winchcombe, Cheltenham,
Gloucestershire GL54 5JB

Tel	01242 604372
Fax	01242 609198
Email	jimw@haldon.co.uk
Web	www.westward-sudeley.co.uk

Map 8   Entry 188

Gloucestershire

Windy Ridge House

Astonishing! Find mullioned windows, gables, roofs of stone slate and thatch, winding staircases and unexpected corners. The bonhomie starts on arrival: Nick and Jennifer are the second generation to own this family home and they are delighted to throw open house, arboretum and prize-winning gardens to guests. All is polished to perfection, there's a grand country-house feel; bedrooms are warm, carpeted and cosy. Take a book to the pine-panelled drawing room, help yourself from the honesty bar, or fling yourself into tennis, croquet and a swim in the summer heated pool. Sumptuous, generous, great fun.

Price	From £80. Singles from £60.
Rooms	3: 1 double; 1 double, 1 twin, both with separate bath.
Meals	Pub 100 yds.
Closed	Rarely.
Directions	From Stow, north for Broadway on A424 for 2 miles to Coach & Horses pub on left. Opposite, turn right by post box & 30mph signs down single-track lane. Entrance 100 yds down on left, bear left up drive.

Nick & Jennifer Williams
Windy Ridge House,
Longborough, Moreton-in-Marsh,
Gloucestershire GL56 0QY

Tel	01451 830465
Fax	01451 831489
Email	nick@windy-ridge.co.uk
Web	www.windy-ridge.co.uk

Map 8   Entry 189

Gloucestershire

Wren House

Barely two miles from Stow on the Wold, peaceful Wren House oozes style and charm. The pretty stone house was built before the English Civil War and Kiloran spent two years renovating it. The results are a joy. Downstairs, light-filled, elegant rooms with glowing rugs on pale Cotswold stone; upstairs, delicious bedrooms, spotless bathrooms and a doorway to duck. Breakfasts include cream from the Jersey cows in the fields over the wall, and the well-planted garden, in which you are encouraged to sit, has far-reaching rural views. Explore rolling valleys and glorious gardens. Perfect. *Children over ten welcome.*

Price	£90–£100. Singles from £60.
Rooms	2: 1 twin/double; 1 twin/double with separate bath/shower.
Meals	Pubs/restaurants 2 miles.
Closed	Occasionally.
Directions	A429 between Stow & Moreton; turn to Donnington; 400 yds, bear left uphill; 100 yds, sign on right in wall and entrance before it, set back from lane by an evergreen hedge.

Kiloran McGrigor
Wren House,
Donnington, Moreton-in-Marsh,
Gloucestershire GL56 0XZ

Tel	01451 831 787
Mobile	07802 676673
Email	enquiries@wrenhouse.net
Web	www.wrenhouse.net

Map 8   Entry 190

Gloucestershire

Lower Farm House

Once the Home Farm of the Leigh estate, the house has a perfect Georgian feel – an enormous hallway, high ceilings, sash windows, elegantly proportioned rooms – and, although graciously furnished, is not dauntingly formal. The pale-carpeted bedrooms are a good size, softly serene and with restful views over the garden; a joy to wander through or sit out in. Nicholas and Zelie are charming, articulate and love entertaining. Meals – everything as organic and locally sourced as possible – sound superb: cooking and gardening are Zelie's passions. Bustling little Stow-on-the-Wold is a hop and a skip away.

Price	£90–£96. Singles £55.
Rooms	2: 1 double, 1 twin.
Meals	Dinner £30. Pubs/restaurants 1.5 miles.
Closed	Rarely.
Directions	A436 from Stow; after 3 miles, left to Adlestrop; right at T-junc; after double bend, drive 50 yds on right; sign at end of drive.

Nicholas & Zelie Mason
Lower Farm House,
Adlestrop, Moreton-in-Marsh,
Gloucestershire GL56 0YR

Tel	01608 658756
Fax	01608 659458
Email	zelie.mason@talk21.com
Web	www.adlestrop-lowerfarm.com

Map 8   Entry 191

Gloucestershire

Rectory Farmhouse

Once a monastery, now a farmhouse with style. Passing a development of converted farm buildings to reach the Rectory's warm Cotswold stones makes the discovery doubly exciting. More glory within: Sybil, a talented designer, has created something immaculate, fresh and uplifting. A wood-burner glows in the sitting room, bed linen is white, walls cream; beds are superb, bathrooms sport cast-iron slipper baths and power showers and views are to the church. Sybil used to own a restaurant and her breakfasts – by the Aga or in the conservatory under a rampant vine – are a further treat.

Price	From £87. Singles £60.
Rooms	2 doubles.
Meals	Pubs/restaurants 1 mile.
Closed	Christmas & New Year.
Directions	B4068 from Stow to Lower Swell, left just before Golden Ball Inn. Far end of gravel drive on right.

Sybil Gisby
Rectory Farmhouse,
Lower Swell,
Stow-on-the-Wold,
Gloucestershire GL54 1LH
Tel 01451 832351
Email rectory.farmhouse@cw-warwick.co.uk

Map 8 Entry 192

Gloucestershire

Grove Farm House

Masses of charm and style here – the 1789 Cotswold farmhouse is much loved and is a restful place to stay. Outbuildings, courtyards and granary are in the same warm stone as the house, and your hosts are friendly, fun and terrific cooks. Angela is Cordon Bleu trained. Breakfasts and occasional dinners are served in the dining room, where lovely oils complement the oak beams and flagged floors. Country bedrooms are stylish with curtains in Colefax florals and there are robes in the bathrooms. Walking and riding all around, a good village pub and a pool for summer swims.

Price	£85–£90. Singles £55.
Rooms	3: 1 double, 1 twin; 1 double with extra single bed.
Meals	Occasional dinner £25. Pub 50 yds.
Closed	Christmas.
Directions	In middle of village, pass Plough Inn on left; look for gates on right.

Angela Storey
Grove Farm House,
Cold Aston, Cheltenham,
Gloucestershire GL54 3BJ
Tel 01451 821801
Fax 01451 821108
Email angela@cotswoldbedandbreakfast.com
Web www.cotswoldbedandbreakfast.com

Map 8 Entry 193

Gloucestershire

Clapton Manor

Karin and James's 16th-century manor is as all homes should be: loved and lived-in. And, with three-foot-thick walls, flagstoned floors, sit-in fireplaces and stone-mullioned windows, it's a gorgeous and impressive pile. The enclosed garden, full of birdsong and roses, wraps itself around the house. One bedroom has a secret door that leads to a fuchsia-pink bathroom; the other room, smaller, is painted deep green and has wonderful garden views. Wellies, dogs, barbours, log fires... and breakfast by a vast Tudor fireplace on homemade bread and jams and eggs from the hens. A happy, charming family home.

Price	From £90. Singles £80.
Rooms	2: 1 double, 1 twin/double.
Meals	Pub/restaurants within 15-minute drive.
Closed	Christmas & New Year.
Directions	A429 Cirencester-Stow. Right signed Sherborne & Clapton. In village, pass grassy area to left, postbox in one corner; house straight ahead on left on corner.

Karin & James Bolton
Clapton Manor, Clapton-on-the-Hill,
Bourton on the Water,
Gloucestershire GL54 2LG
Tel 01451 810202
Mobile 07967 144416
Email bandb@claptonmanor.co.uk
Web www.claptonmanor.co.uk

Map 8 Entry 194

Hampshire

Common Farm Cottage

Two perfect garden hideaways for lovers, poets and dreamers in deeply rural Hampshire. Inside is pure doll's house – Cath Kidston meets Milly Molly Mandy – with vintage quilts, old pine, soft blue walls, sisal carpets and heart-shaped biscuits – even a sprig of lavender for your pillow. Laze in bed with breakfast – fresh croissants, homemade jam, eggs from Elaine's hens – or take it onto the deck and spot heron, ducks and moorhens on the trout lakes. You're on the edge of the New Forest so walkers will be happy; let beauty therapist Elaine massage away any aches and pains, then take a swing in the hammock.

Price	£75-£80. Singles £50.
Rooms	2 studios, each with 1 double.
Meals	Full English tea £10. Cream tea £3. Pub 1 mile.
Closed	Rarely.
Directions	Fordingbridge for Sandleheath, then Damerham. Compass Inn on left, over small bridge; next left towards South End. Then turn onto the common; 2nd on left.

Elaine Avery
Common Farm Cottage,
The Common,
Damerham, Fordingbridge,
Hampshire SP6 3HR
Tel 01725 518870
Email info@hideawaybedandbreakfast.co.uk
Web www.hideawaybedandbreakfast.co.uk

Map 3 Entry 195

Hampshire

Sandy Corner

Stride straight onto open moorland from this smallholding on the edge of the New Forest – a great spot for anyone who loves walking, cycling, riding, wildlife and outdoor space. And there's plenty of room for wet clothes and muddy boots. Cattle graze within ten feet of the window, you may hear the call of a nightjar in June, Dartford warblers nest nearby, happy hens cluck around the yard. Sue also keeps a horse, two cats, a few sheep. You have a little guest sitting room, lovely fresh bedrooms, good home cooking and a marvellous, away-from-it-all feel. You can walk to one pub; others are nearby.

Price	From £68. Singles from £42.
Rooms	2 doubles.
Meals	Packed lunch £6.
	Restaurant 2.5 miles.
Closed	Christmas & New Year.
Directions	On A338, 1 mile S of Fordingbridge, at small x-roads, turn for Hyde & Hungerford. Up hill & right at school for Ogdens; left at next x-roads for Ogdens North; on right at bottom of hill.

	Sue Browne
	Sandy Corner,
	Ogdens North,
	Fordingbridge,
	Hampshire SP6 2QD
Tel	01425 657295

Map 3   Entry 196

Hampshire

Bay Trees

Step in from the village street and you find yourself in a striking hall where the guest book perches on the music stand! Comfortable bedrooms have just been refurbished, the double with French windows opening to a lush suntrap of a garden – a wonderful surprise – full of arbours and weeping willow and a brook at the end with a seat for two. Breakfasts are gourmet here, served in the conservatory overlooking the magnolia. Robert, humorous and down-to-earth, makes you feel at ease the moment you arrive. The shingle beach with views to the Isle of Wight is a sprint away. *Minimum stay two nights at weekends.*

Price	£75–£115. Singles from £45.
Rooms	3: 1 double, 1 four-poster; 1 triple, 1 single sharing bath (2nd room let to same party only).
Meals	Restaurants/pubs 100 yds.
Closed	Rarely.
Directions	From Lymington follow signs for Milford-on-Sea (B3058). On left, just past village green.

	Robert Fry
	Bay Trees,
	8 High Street,
	Milford-on-Sea, Lymington,
	Hampshire SO41 0QD
Tel	01590 642186
Email	rp.fry@virgin.net
Web	www.baytreebedandbreakfast.co.uk

Map 3   Entry 197

Hampshire

Old Fullerton Station

Yes, it was a station – built in 1865 and serving the 'Sprat and Winkle' line from Andover to Southampton. Stroll along the platform, admire the original fretwork, enter the old waiting room where a marble fire-surround installed for a visit by Queen Victoria is still a striking feature. The whole of this sunny, delightful, very comfortable house is full of such talking points. Terance is a photographer and designer, Jane is charming and likeable and will tell you all you want to know about the area. She can organise fishing – Fullerton is in the lovely Test valley – and even provide a hamper. *Children over eight welcome.*

Price	£70. Singles £45.
Rooms	2: 1 double, 1 twin.
Meals	Pub 500 yds.
Closed	Rarely.

Stop Press
No longer doing B&B

Map 3   Entry 198

Hampshire

Yew Tree House

The views, the house and the villagers are said to have inspired Charles Dickens, who escaped London, wisely, for the peace of this valley. The warm red brick was there 200 years before him; the rare dovecote (to which you may have the key) at the end of the herbaceous border 300 years before that. Delightful artistic hosts, generous with their time, have created a house of understated elegance: a yellow-ochre bedroom with Descamps bed linen, cashmere/silk curtains designed by their son, a view onto an enchanting garden, a profusion of flowers. The village is as tranquil as the house.

Price	£60. Singles by arrangement.
Rooms	2: 1 twin;
	1 double with separate bath.
Meals	Pub in village.
Closed	Rarely.
Directions	From A30 west of Stockbridge for 1.5 miles, left at minor x-roads. After 2 miles left at T-junc. House on left at next junction opp. Greyhound.

Philip & Janet Mutton
Yew Tree House,
Broughton,
Stockbridge,
Hampshire SO20 8AA

Tel	01794 301227
Email	pandjmutton@onetel.com

Map 3   Entry 199

Hampshire

Brymer House

Complete privacy in a B&B is rare. Here you have it, a 12-minute walk from town, cathedral and water meadows. Relax in your own half of a Victorian townhouse immaculately furnished and decorated and with a garden to match – all roses and lilac in the spring. Fizzy serves sumptuous breakfasts, there's a log fire in the guests' sitting room and fresh flowers abound – guests have been delighted. You are also left with an 'honesty box' so you may help yourselves to drinks. Bedrooms are small and elegant, with antique mirrors, furniture and bedspreads; bathrooms are first class. *Children over seven welcome.*

Price	£65–£75. Singles £50–£54.
Rooms	2: 1 double, 1 twin.
Meals	Pubs/restaurants nearby.
Closed	Christmas.
Directions	M3 junc. 9; A272 Winchester exit, then signs for Winchester Park & Ride. Under m'way, straight on at r'bout signed St Cross. Left at T-junc. St Faith's Rd veers off 100 yds ahead to the left on reaching bend.

Guy & Fizzy Warren
Brymer House,
29/30 St Faith's Road, St Cross,
Winchester, Hampshire SO23 9QD

Tel	01962 867428
Mobile	07762 201076
Web	www.brymerhouse.co.uk

Map 4   Entry 200

Hampshire

Ranvilles Farm House

The herringbone brickwork is just one of the features that grants this unusual house Grade II* listing. It dates from the 13th century – Richard de Ranville sailed here from Normandy with his family. A large bed in a big room overlooks a courtyard of old barns, and two further rooms are in the newer courtyard wing: modern and with level access, perfect for the less mobile. Delicious breakfasts are served in the palest grey dining room, grand with long table and huge paintings. There are five acres of garden, a paddock, lots of books and an easy atmosphere. Bill and Anthea are dynamic and fun.

Price	£55–£70. Singles from £35.
Rooms	3 twins/doubles (one could be a family room).
Meals	Pub/restaurant 1 mile.
Closed	Rarely.
Directions	Exit M27 junc. 2; A3090 for Romsey. Climb hill; Gardener's Lane on left; on 100 yds, on south side of dual carriageway; house marked by flagpole. Crossing marked with 2 white posts.

Bill & Anthea Hughes
Ranvilles Farm House,
Romsey, Hampshire SO51 6AA

Tel	02380 814481
Fax	02380 814481
Email	info@ranvilles.com
Web	www.ranvilles.com

Map 3   Entry 201

Hampshire

Manor House

Outside is a courtyard with a dovecote: pretty for breakfasts in the sun. This remarkable manor house was built in 1546 with timber from the forest that supplied the wood for the *Mary Rose*. The place is full of intriguing and fascinating features: dark beams, diamond-leaded windows and witches' marks on the fireplace to ward off evil. But this is no museum – kind, friendly Wren and Rhydian make you comfortably at home aided by their well-mannered spaniel. The rooms have a warm, peaceful elegance and much of the impeccable upholstery has been fashioned by Wren.

Price	£80. Singles from £45.
Rooms	2: 1 double; 1 single sharing bath.
Meals	Pubs/restaurants 2 miles.
Closed	Christmas & New Year.
Directions	M4 junc 11; A33 to Bramley, 14 miles. House at western end of village in Vyne Road, close to junc. with The Street.

Wren & Rhydian Vaughan
Manor House,
Bramley, Tadley, Basingstoke,
Hampshire RG26 5DW

Tel	01256 881141
Fax	01256 881141
Email	info@manorhouse.biz
Web	www.manorhousebramley.co.uk

Map 4   Entry 202

Hampshire

Little Cottage

Just 45 minutes from Heathrow but the peace is deep, the views are long and the wildlife thrives – watch fox and deer, hear the rare nightjar. Chris and Therese grow many of their own vegetables and fruit, source meat locally and give you superb home cooking; guests have a lovely sitting room with an eclectic mix of modern and antique furniture, and a pretty terrace overlooks the garden. Bedrooms are all ground-floor, fresh and light, the double has distant views; perfect for walkers and those who seek solace from urban life but don't want to go too far. *Minimum stay two nights at weekends. Children over 12 welcome.*

Price	£65-£75. Singles £45.
Rooms	3: 1 twin/double, 1 double, 1 single.
Meals	Dinner from £12.50. Pub 1.5 miles.
Closed	Between Christmas & New Year & occasionally.
Directions	B3011 from A30 in Hartley Wintney for 1.5 miles. Cottage just before the continuous double white line down the middle of road becomes a single line.

Chris & Therese Abbott
Little Cottage,
Hazeley Heath, Hook,
Hampshire RG27 8LY

Tel	01252 845050
Mobile	07721 462214
Email	info@little-cottage.co.uk
Web	www.little-cottage.co.uk

Map 4   Entry 203

Hampshire

Mulberry House

Deep into Jane Austen country, among ancient apple trees and rosebushes in Hampshire parkland, is Mulberry House – the red-brick stable block of Old Alresford House. Peter and Sue's charm permeates their lovely home and B&B. Private, quietly elegant guest rooms share a sitting room and kitchenette; the one in the eaves overlooks a pretty courtyard where a fountain plays. When the weather is fine, breakfast beneath the wisteria and vine-hung pergola on home-laid eggs and homemade jams. Suppers promise lively conversation, delicious food, fresh flowers. Comfortably English.

Price	£70. Singles £40.
Rooms	2: 1 double, 1 twin/double.
Meals	Supper from £20. Packed lunch £8. Pubs/restaurants within 10-minute walk.
Closed	Never.
Directions	M3 exit 9, signs to Alresford. In town centre, left onto B3046 to church on right. Then right into Colden Lane. House is 3rd on right through field gate.

Sue & Peter Paice
Mulberry House,
Colden Lane, Old Alresford,
Hampshire SO24 9DY
Tel 01962 735518
Fax 01962 736155
Email suepaice@btinternet.com
Web www.mulberryhousebnb.com

Map 4 Entry 204

Hampshire

The Old School House

A galleried landing connects the addition to the Victorian flint-and-brick schoolhouse and you can't see the join! Susie is a natural, easy, courteous host and a welcoming atmosphere surrounds you. There is a delightful guest sitting room with an open fire in winter, comfy seats, magazines and piles of books. The double room – smart in pinks and creams – has three windows facing south to the garden, the twin too, so both feel light and airy. Sleep deeply, draw in the rural quiet, then breakfast on locally smoked, handcut bacon with eggs from their own hens and homemade marmalades and jams. *Children over eight welcome.*

Price	From £70. Singles £50.
Rooms	2: 1 double; 1 twin/double with separate bath.
Meals	Pubs within 5 miles.
Closed	Christmas.
Directions	M3 exit 9; A272 to Petersfield. After 2 miles, fork right to Warnford & Preshaw, over x-roads; 300 yds; house 2nd on left, just past turning to right.

Susie Lintott
The Old School House,
Lane End,
Owslebury, Winchester,
Hampshire SO21 1JZ
Tel 01962 777248
Fax 01962 777744
Email susie.lintott@btinternet.com

Map 4 Entry 205

Hampshire

Hampshire

Little Ashton Farm

Part 18th-century farm cottage, part extended Victorian extension, this is a laid-back, friendly house and Felicity loves having guests. She's a keen cook with a burgeoning kitchen garden: plums, peaches, figs for bottling and jamming. You eat in the dining room or conservatory; delicious "everything's local" breakfasts and dinners that are hard to resist. Separate staircases lead to the large triple under the rafters and the smaller cottage double; both have garden views, good linen and furniture, books and paintings, cosy Guatamalan throws. Country walks from the doorstep, yet close to the M27, M3 and Winchester.

The Manor House

Gracious yet informal, a crisp Regency house in this little corner of Hampshire where Jane Austen wrote most of her books. Clare will spoil you, even collect you from the station if you come without a car. Bedrooms are airy and light with space for chairs, knick-knacks and family pictures; bathrooms are smart. Eat a delicious home-cooked breakfast in the elegant dining room whose French windows overlook glorious lawns, impressive herbaceous borders and mature trees. Clare has a good knowledge of places to visit locally – especially gardens; she even organises garden tours to Normandy.

Price	£70. Singles £40.
Rooms	2: 1 double, 1 triple.
Meals	Lunch £10. Dinner, 3 courses, £20. Packed lunch £5. Pubs/restaurants nearby.
Closed	Mid-December-28 March.
Directions	B2177 Winchester to Portsmouth. Just after 40mph sign into Bishop's Waltham, left into Ashton Lane. 0.75 miles up on left, black wrought-iron gates into drive.

Price	£75. Singles £45.
Rooms	2: 1 double; 1 twin with separate bath.
Meals	Pub 0.5 miles.
Closed	Never.
Directions	A31 north of Alton, signed for Alton, Bordon & Holybourne. Over railway; 1st right into Holybourne. After 300 yds road dips, proceed up hill and at top turn left into Church Lane; 100 yds on left up gravel drive without gate.

Felicity & David Webb-Carter
Little Ashton Farm,
Ashton Lane, Bishop's Waltham,
Hampshire SO32 1FR

Tel	01489 894055
Mobile	07760 221785
Email	flossywebb@hotmail.com
Web	www.littleashtonfarm.20m.com

Clare Whately
The Manor House,
Holybourne, Alton,
Hampshire GU34 4HD

Tel	01420 541321
Fax	01420 83175
Mobile	07711 655450
Email	clare@whately.net

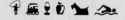

Map 4   Entry 206

Map 4   Entry 207

Hampshire

Land of Nod

A 1939 house of character with hosts to match and one of the greatest gardens in the book… seven tended acres within 100 acres of woodland. There are azaleas and camellias, specimen trees, croquet, tennis and wildlife. Breakfast in the chinoiserie dining room, designed by Jeremy – the allegorical tableau is charming. Both bedrooms have garden views; one has a fireplace with Beatrix Potter tiles, the other a fine collection of flower prints on the walls. Original baths have vast taps. Flexible breakfasts are locally sourced and seasonal fruit and preserves come from the garden. *Children over ten welcome.*

Price	From £80. Singles from £50.
Rooms	2: 1 twin; 1 twin with separate bath.
Meals	Restaurants 5-minute drive.
Closed	Rarely.
Directions	South on A3 to lights at Hindhead. Straight across & after 400 yds, right onto B3002. On for 3 miles. Entrance (signed) on right in a wood.

Jeremy & Philippa Whitaker
Land of Nod,
Headley,
Bordon,
Hampshire GU35 8SJ
Tel 01428 713609
Fax 01428 717698

Map 4   Entry 208

Hampshire

Little Shackles

Gaze upon the pretty Arts and Craft house from the comfort of the hammock or solar-heated pool: this is a charming place to stay. Rosemary advises on local gardens to visit (her own two acres are also special) and is the loveliest of hosts. Your bedroom has an elegant country air - firm beds, gingham and fine florals – and spring-like bathroom with fluffy bathrobe and views to fresh green fields. Breakfast looking out on the lush garden, i plentiful; dinner, at the lovely old drover' pub down the sleepy lane, is a simpl treat; and the walks on the South Down are marvellous.

Price	£64. Singles £20-£35.
Rooms	2: 1 twin/double, 1 single sharing bath (2nd room let to same party only).
Meals	Packed lunch £5. Pub 0.5 miles.
Closed	Rarely.
Directions	From London, A3/A272 junc. Petersfield; right at r'bout, over level crossing; first left into Tilmore Rd leading to Harrow Lane. House 2nd driveway on right.

Rosemary Griffiths
Little Shackles,
Harrow Lane,
Petersfield,
Hampshire GU32 2BZ
Tel 01730 263464
Fax 01730 263464
Email martgriff@freenet.co.uk

Map 4   Entry 209

Hampshire

Mizzards Farm

Wow! The central hall is three storeys high, its vaulted roof open to the rafters. This is the oldest part of this rambling, mostly 16th-century farmhouse: kilims and fine antiques look splendid with the ancient flagstones. There's a drawing room for musical evenings and an upstairs conservatory from which you can see the garden with its lake, swimming pool, outdoor chess and sculptures. The four-poster is extraordinarily kitsch with electric curtains, the other bedrooms traditional and fresh. Come in the summer for mini Glyndebourne on the lawn. *Children over eight welcome. Min. stay two nights.*

Price	£70–£85. Singles by arrangement.
Rooms	3: 1 double, 1 twin, 1 four-poster.
Meals	Pubs 0.5 miles.
Closed	Christmas & New Year.
Directions	From A272 at Rogate, turn for Harting & Nyewood. Cross humpback bridge; drive signed to right after 300 yds.

Harriet & Julian Francis
Mizzards Farm,
Rogate,
Petersfield,
Hampshire GU31 5HS
Tel 01730 821656
Fax 01730 821655
Email francis@mizzards.co.uk

Map 4   Entry 210

Herefordshire

Pear Tree Farm

A delightful old farmhouse in a quiet spot close to Wigmore Castle and Ludlow; Steve and Jill will spoil you rotten. Dinner is a sumptuous affair with much homegrown produce and a lively menu – it's licensed too, if you fancy a drink. Much panache in the décor, with delightful drapes and medieval-style chairs, tan leather sofas and polished boards, a Mexican hammock in the garden and space to chill. The upstairs bedrooms are fresh and lovely with seductive candlelit bathrooms and the downstairs is spacious and stylish with solid oak floors and a woodburning stove. *Children over ten welcome.*

Price	From £90.
Rooms	3: 1 twin, 1 double; 1 double with separate bath.
Meals	Dinner £27.50. Restaurants 10-minute drive. Pub 5 minutes walk.
Closed	Rarely.
Directions	A4110 north to Wigmore. At 'Welcome' sign on for 150 yds, then right. Drive 1st on left.

Steve Dawson & Jill Fieldhouse
Pear Tree Farm,
Wigmore,
Herefordshire HR6 9UR
Tel 01568 770140
Fax 01568 770140
Email info@peartree-farm.co.uk
Web www.peartree-farm.co.uk

Map 7   Entry 211

Herefordshire

Bunns Croft

The timbers of the medieval house, and there are many, are probably 1,000 years old. Little of the structure has ever been altered and it is an absolute delight: stone floors, rich colours, a piano, books and cosy chairs. Cruck-beamed bedrooms are snugly small, the stair to the family rooms is steep – this was a yeoman's house – and the twin's bathroom has its own sweet fireplace. The countryside is 'pure', too, with 1,500 acres of National Trust land five miles away. Anita is charming, loves her garden and her guests, grows her own fruit and veg and makes fabulous dinners. Just mind your head.

Price	£60-£68. Singles £30.
Rooms	4: 1 double, 2 singles, sharing bath (let to same party only); 1 twin.
Meals	Dinner, 3 courses, £20. Pub 3 miles.
Closed	Rarely.
Directions	From Leominster, A49 towards Ludlow; 4 miles to village of Ashton, then left. House on right behind postbox after 1 mile.

	Mrs Anita Syers-Gibson
	Bunns Croft,
	Moreton Eye,
	Leominster,
	Herefordshire HR6 0DP
Tel	01568 615836

✗ ♀ ☕ ✗

Map 7   Entry 212

Herefordshire

Staunton House

The Georgian rectory's well-proportioned rooms, painstakingly restored, brim with beautiful furnishings and fine furniture. The original oak staircase leads to peaceful bedrooms with comfortable, well-dressed beds; the blue room looks onto garden and pond. It's a house that matches its owners – quiet, traditional and country-loving. Wander through the lovely garden, drive to Hay or Ludlow, stride some ravishing countryside, play golf near Offa's Dyke; return to Rosie and Richard's delicious dinner in the elegant dining room or in the new kitchen if you prefer. You will be well tended here.

Price	From £70. Singles £40.
Rooms	2: 1 double, 1 twin/double.
Meals	Dinner, 2-4 courses, £15-£25. Pub/restaurant 2.5 miles.
Closed	Rarely.
Directions	A44 Leominster-Pembridge; right to Shobdon. After 0.5 miles, left to Staunton-on-Arrow; at x-roads, over into village. House opp. church with black wrought-iron gates.

	Rosie & Richard Bowen
	Staunton House,
	Staunton-on-Arrow, Pembridge,
	Leominster, Herefordshire HR6 9HR
Tel	01544 388313
Mobile	07780 961994
Email	rosbown@aol.com
Web	www.stauntonhouse.co.uk

✗ ☕ ✗ 🏊 ♟

Map 7   Entry 213

Herefordshire

Bollingham House

The views alone might earn the house a place in this book. But there's more... a beautifully furnished interior and an interesting four-acre garden with a perfumed rose walk. Stephanie and John, working unobtrusively to make your stay enjoyable, are natural hosts. Bedrooms are large, bright and comfortable, and Stephanie has cleverly brought vibrant colours, fine furniture and paintings together with a dash of elegance. Gaze from your windows across the Wye Valley to the Malvern Hills, or west to the Black Mountains. Stephanie's cooking is worth a detour.

Price	From £75. Singles from £40.
Rooms	2: 1 twin; 1 double with separate bath.
Meals	Dinner from £20. Packed lunch £5. Pub 2 miles.
Closed	Occasionally.
Directions	A438 Hereford to Brecon road, towards Kington on A4111; through Eardisley; house 2 miles up hill on left, behind long line of conifers.

Stephanie & John Grant
Bollingham House,
Eardisley,
Herefordshire HR5 3LE
Tel   01544 327326
Email   grant@bollinghamhouse.com
Web   www.bollinghamhouse.com

Map 7   Entry 214

Herefordshire

Garnstone House

Come for peace and quiet in the Welsh Marches, good food and lovely, humorous, down-to-earth hosts. The atmosphere is easy, and the furniture a lifetime's accumulation of eclectic pieces and pictures and prints of horses, hounds and country scenes. After dinner and good conversation, climb the picture-lined stairs to comfortingly carpeted bedrooms with brass beds and dressing tables and a bathroom that is properly old-fashioned. Delicious breakfasts and a stunning garden to explore — the variety and colour of the springtime flowers are astonishing and the clematis is a glory.

Price	From £70. Singles from £35.
Rooms	2: 1 double, 1 twin sharing bath.
Meals	Dinner from £20. Pub/restaurant 1 mile.
Closed	Rarely.
Directions	A480 from Hereford; after 10 miles, right onto B4230 for Weobley. After 1.75 miles, right onto private road; 2nd on left over cattle grid.

Dawn & Michael MacLeod
Garnstone House,
Weobley,
Herefordshire HR4 8QP
Tel   01544 318943
Email   macleod@garnstonehouse.co.uk
Web   www.garnstonehouse.co.uk

Map 7   Entry 215

Herefordshire

Winforton Court

Dating from 1500, the Court is dignified in its old age — undulating floors, great oak beams, thick walls. It is a dramatic, colourful home with exceptional timber-framed bedrooms; one room has an Indian-style bathroom and huge roll top bath, the suite a sitting area with two sofas. You also have a roomy guest sitting room and a small library for restful evenings. Your hosts are delightful and spoil you with decanters of sherry and bedside chocolates; a long room has been converted to seat 35 — great for family functions. Visit Hay, walk down to the Wye or relax in the splendid garden. *Fishing can be arranged.*

Price	£72-£90. Singles from £60.
Rooms	3: 1 double, 1 four-poster, 1 four-poster suite.
Meals	Pub/restaurant 2-minute walk.
Closed	Christmas.
Directions	From Hereford, A438 into village. House on left with a green sign & iron gates.

Jackie Kingdon
Winforton Court,
Winforton,
Herefordshire HR3 6EA
Tel   01544 328498
Fax   01544 328498
Web   www.winfortoncourt.co.uk

Map 7   Entry 216

Herefordshire

Hall's Mill House

Remote lanes bring you, finally, to this most idyllic spot — a stone cottage tucked into a wooded valley. The sitting room is snug with wood-burner and sofas but the kitchen is the hub of the place — delicious breakfasts and dinners are cooked on the Aga. Grace, chatty and easy-going, obviously enjoys living in her modernised mill house. Rooms are small, fresh, with exposed beams and slate sills; only the old mill interrupts the far-reaching, all-green views. Drift off to sleep to the sound of the Arrow burbling by — a blissful tonic for city-dwellers. Great value, too. *Children over four welcome.*

Price	£40-£55. Singles £20-£27.50.
Rooms	3: 1 double; 1 double, 1 twin, sharing bath.
Meals	Dinner from £15. Pub/restaurant 3 miles.
Closed	Christmas.
Directions	A438 from Hereford. After Winforton, Whitney-on-Wye & toll bridge, sharp right for Brilley. Left fork to Huntington, over x-roads & next right to Huntington. Next right into no through road, then 1st right.

Grace Watson
Hall's Mill House,
Huntington,
Kington,
Herefordshire HR5 3QA
Tel   01497 831409

Map 7   Entry 217

Ty-mynydd

Six miles over open heathland from Hay-on-Wye, it is a bumpy, precipitous approach up the mountainside to Ty-Mynydd, but this renovated, stone-flagged farmhouse is worth every jolt. Sheep graze the hillside, the views are simply the best and the garden is colourful, informal, delightful. Turn on the taps and taste water straight from your hosts' own mountain stream; awake to bacon and eggs produced in the fields around you (this is a working organic farm). The lovely young family give you two sweetly restful rooms on the ground floor, one with 'that view', and a simple country bathroom. The sunsets are magical.

Nicky and John and their cows, pigs and sheep live the good, slow life on these 130 acres of ancient organic pastureland, criss-crossed with John's dry stone walls. They are part of an environmental management scheme – Tir Gofal: the Better Woodlands for Wales Scheme. They recycle and compost 90% of their waste, all their products are chemical-free and they use organic bed linen, bath oils and toiletries. The hens are more 'all over the place' than free range; the egg yolks are a deep orange and delicious.

Price	From £70. Singles £50.
Rooms	2 doubles sharing bath (2nd room let to same party only).
Meals	Pubs 6-8 miles.
Closed	December-February.
Directions	From Hay on A438, 1st left after Swan Hotel; 6 miles uphill to open heath under Hay Bluff; 1st right signed Capel Y Ffin; 1 mile, signed.

Miss N Spenceley
Ty-mynydd,
Llanigon, Hay-on-Wye,
Herefordshire HR3 5RJ
Tel   01497 821593
Email   nikibarber@tiscali.co.uk
Web   www.tymynydd.co.uk

SPECIAL
GREEN ENTRY
see page 17

Map 7 Entry 218

Herefordshire

Lower House

I was in the equatorial forest, surely. The view reached over a pattern of tree tops to a distant hill, whose mist hovered as it awaited the day's heat. The house, itself a forest of old timber, is almost lost within the beautiful garden. It is old, but restored with affection. Stairs twist and creak, the unexpected awaits you. Bedrooms are panelled or timber-clad, bathrooms are neat, there is a handsome room where you eat a superb breakfast, read or play the piano. Nicky and Pete are unpretentious and easy, steeped in good taste and this exquisite project, next to Offa's Dyke path and on the Welsh border. *Minimum stay two nights.*

Price	From £70.
Rooms	2: 1 double; 1 double with separate bath.
Meals	Pubs/restaurants 1 mile.
Closed	Rarely.
Directions	East through Hay on B4348 for Bredwardine. On the edge of Hay, right into Cusop Dingle; 0.75 miles, old mill house on left; drive on right, across stone bridge over stream.

Nicky & Peter Daw
Lower House,
Cusop Dingle,
Hay-on-Wye,
Herefordshire HR3 5RQ
Tel   01497 820773
Email   nicky.daw@btinternet.com
Web   www.lowerhousegardenhay.co.uk

Map 7   Entry 219

Herefordshire

Ladywell House

Snuggling in the Golden Valley, wrapped by ancient oaks and a deep peacefulness, you will breathe a sigh of happiness as you step inside. The whitewashed, Edwardian dower house is welcoming and informal with understated good taste: soft colours, family paintings, antiques. The four-poster bedroom is regal, the twin is fresh in blues and creams, and bathrooms are stylish and spoiling. Breakfast in the light conservatory, take drinks to the garden, dine well by candlelight at a rustic oak table. Sarah and Charles are warm and generous – this is very much 'open house'.

Price	£55-£70. Singles from £45.
Rooms	2: 1 four-poster; 1 twin with separate bath.
Meals	Dinner, 3 courses, from £20. Pub 10-minute drive.
Closed	Rarely.
Directions	From A465 Hereford-Abergavenny, B4348 towards Hay-on-Wye. In Vowchurch, left towards Michaelchurch. Through hamlet of Turnastone, house 0.5 miles on right.

Charles & Sarah Drury
Ladywell House,
Turnastone, Vowchurch,
Herefordshire HR2 0RE
Tel   +44 (0)1981 550 235
Mobile   +44 (0)7970 510 110
Email   sarah@lamontarnie.com
Web   www.ladywellhouse.com

Map 7   Entry 220

Herefordshire

Dovecote Barn

Super people – natural hosts – and an easy atmosphere. This is an exceptional B&B and there's much of architectural interest as well: a copse of 17th-century oak beams and timbers above and masses of light. Judy (an artist) created the conversion then decorated with style. Bedrooms are simple and charming, with fresh flowers beautifully arranged, good soaps, books, and electric blankets to ensure the deepest sleep. Breakfasts are lavish and include homemade bread and jams. There's the freshest food for dinner, and you can also eat at the local pub – kind Judy or Roger will ferry you.

Herefordshire

Moor Court Farm

The buildings, about 500 years old, ramble and enfold both gardens and guests. This is an honest, authentic farmhouse in a deeply rural position. Elizabeth, a busy farmer's wife, manages it all efficiently with husband Peter; they were lambing when we were there. They also dry their own hops and in September you can watch the lovely old oast house (with resident owls and bats) at work. Elizabeth is an excellent, traditional cook – make the most of the home-produced meat, preserves and vegetables. Cottagey bedrooms have plump pillows and goose down duvets; one has views to the Malvern hills.

Price	£70. Singles £45.
Rooms	3: 1 double; 1 twin/double with separate bath & shower; 1 double with travel cot & toddler bed (let to same party only).
Meals	Dinner, 3 courses, £27. BYO. Pub 1 mile.
Closed	Rarely.
Directions	At Burley Gate r'bout on A417, A465 for Bromyard. At Stoke Lacy church, on right; right again; then 2nd right to entrance.

Price	From £60. Singles £30.
Rooms	3: 1 double, 2 twins.
Meals	Dinner, 3 courses, from £19.
Closed	Rarely.
Directions	From Hereford, east on A438. A417 into Stretton Grandison; 1st right past village sign, through Holmend Park. Bear left past phone box. House on left.

Roger & Judy Young
Dovecote Barn,
Stoke Lacy,
Herefordshire HR7 4HJ

Tel | 01432 820968
Mobile | 07775 916372
Email | dovecotebarn@mail.com
Web | www.dovecotebarn.co.uk

Elizabeth & Peter Godsall
Moor Court Farm,
Stretton Grandison,
Ledbury,
Herefordshire HR8 2TP

Tel | 01531 670408
Fax | 01531 670408
Web | www.moorcourtfarm.co.uk

Map 7   Entry 221

Map 7   Entry 222

Herefordshire

The Barn House

You are right on the main street but there's an acre of garden (take tea out here or an evening drink in summer) and it's very peaceful. Inside: beams, Chippendale panels in the staircase, a long table for delicious breakfasts and an upstairs sitting room. The bright yellow bedroom is the largest, with comfortable chairs and art from around the world. The other double is smaller and the twin, with toe-to-toe beds, is best for friends sharing. All are newly carpeted and have fluffy white robes for the quick flit to the vast bathroom with huge antique bath. More of a quiet hotel feel than a traditional B&B.

Price	£75-£85. Singles £60.
Rooms	3: 1 double; 1 double, 1 twin sharing bath .
Meals	Pubs/restaurants 50 yds.
Closed	Christmas & New Year.
Directions	From Ledbury bypass, A449 for Worcester & town centre. House on left just past Somerfield but before central town x-roads.

Judi Holland
The Barn House,
New Street,
Ledbury,
Herefordshire HR8 2DX
Tel   01531 632825
Email barnhouseledbury@btconnect.com
Web   www.thebarnhouse.net

Map 8   Entry 223

Herefordshire

Hall End House

Classic English elegance on these 500 farmed acres — and a string of polo ponies. The Jeffersons have devoted enormous care to the restoration of Hall End and welcome you kindly. You have two drawing rooms to choose from and a conservatory, then up the spiral stairs to a new, very private bedroom, available in the summer only. A handsome staircase leads to wide landings and the other rooms; an elegant twin with fine linen and a super bathroom, and the delightful four-poster. Lamb and beef from this well-managed farm are served on delicate Spode china. *Children over 12 welcome. Minimum stay two nights May-September.*

Price	£90-£99.
Rooms	3: 1 double, 1 twin, 1 four-poster.
Meals	Dinner, 4 courses, £27.50 (winter only). BYO. Supper, 2 courses, coffee & chocolates, £17.50. Pub 2.5 miles.
Closed	Christmas & New Year.
Directions	From Ledbury A449 Ross-on-Wye road to Much Marcle. Right between garage & stores. Right after 300 yds for Rushall & Kynaston. After 2.5 miles, drive on left.

Angela & Hugh Jefferson
Hall End House,
Kynaston, Ledbury,
Herefordshire HR8 2PD
Tel   01531 670225
Fax   01531 670747
Email khjefferson@hallend91.freeserve.co.uk
Web   www.hallendhouse.com

Map 7   Entry 224

Herefordshire

The Grove House

Pimms and pomp in 13 acres of gardens and pastures. This house is cosseting, beams and furniture gleam richly in winter firelight and the guests' drawing room is large, elegant and generously furnished with plump sofas. You sleep either in the house's heart, among 14th-century timbers, or in the garden house with its more modern style. Dinner is a smart affair or a buffet for a large party, cooked deliciously by Ellen. It is delightfully chic, a tad shabby in parts, and you can have fun poking your head round the French windows trilling "anyone for tennis?" The court is yours, and a swimming pool next door.

Price	£80-£85. Singles £57.
Rooms	3: 1 twin/double, 2 four-posters.
Meals	Dinner £32 (min. 4).
	Pubs/restaurants in Ledbury, 3 miles.
Closed	Christmas.
Directions	M50 exit 2, for Ledbury; 1st left to Bromsberrow Heath; right by post office, up hill, house on right.

Michael & Ellen Ross
The Grove House,
Bromsberrow Heath, Ledbury,
Herefordshire HR8 1PE
Tel   01531 650584
Mobile   07960 166903
Email   ross@the-grovehouse.co.uk
Web   www.the-grovehouse.com

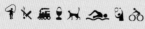

Map 8   Entry 225

Hertfordshire

West Lodge

With Luton Airport a short drive, it is an unexpected treat to find somewhere so tranquil. At the end of country lanes, behind a sweep of gravel drive, the imposing red-brick edifice is new, well-designed and sits in an acre of garden; fields and woodland are visible beyond the lawns. Inside, an abundance of windows and light and a smart and luxurious décor. Rooms range from a voluptuous double to a more functional single; colourful bathrooms gleam. Downstairs, traditional sofas, chintz and some good antiques – all very swish. Best of all, Jean-Christophe Novelli's restaurant is a 15-minute drive!

Price	£70-£85. Singles from £45.
Rooms	3: 1 twin; 1 double with separate bath/shower;
	1 single with separate shower.
Meals	Pub in village.
Closed	Rarely.
Directions	A1 exit 4 take B653. At Wheathampstead, B651 towards Kimpton. Just before village, left on single track road to Porters End & house.

Pauline & Graeme Tarbox
West Lodge,
Porters End,
Kimpton, Hitchin,
Hertfordshire SG4 8ER
Tel   01438 832633
Fax   01438 832633
Email   westlodgebb@yahoo.co.uk

Map 9   Entry 226

Homewood

Lutyens built this wonderful 1901 house for his mother-in-law, Lady Lytton. It is set down a long drive in six acres of gardens and fields, and architectural peculiarities abound. Samantha has applied her considerable artistic skills to the interior; new is the double bedroom's pretty stencilled floor. The reception rooms are particularly elegant and formal: unusual colour schemes offset magnificent antiques, tapestries and chinoiserie. Your hosts give you an excellent breakfast, can converse in a clutch of languages, will book tables and taxis if required. And their pets are happy to welcome yours.

Price	£80. Singles £50. Suite £80–£120.
Rooms	3: 1 double, 1 family suite for 4. 1 double with separate shower also available.
Meals	Pub 15-minute drive. Occasional dinner, including wine, £30 (min. 4).
Closed	20 December–3 January.
Directions	Into Knebworth B197, into Station Rd (becomes Park Lane); 300 yds after m'way bridge, left into public footpath; 300 yds; bear left through gates; house at end.

Samantha Pollock-Hill
Homewood,
Old Knebworth,
Hertfordshire SG3 6PP
Tel   01438 812105
Email   sami@homewood-bb.co.uk
Web   www.homewood-bb.co.uk

Map 9   Entry 227

The Old Rectory

A happy spirit pervades the Grade II*-listed rectory, thanks to the likeable, relaxed and very spoiling Dunns. Warm, light, candy-striped rooms lie across a cobbled courtyard and bathrooms are equally inviting. Enjoy a very delicious breakfast on the sunny terrace overlooking gardens in summer; finish the day with a nightcap in the inglenook-cosy, deep-red walled dining room. The conservation village trumpets George Bernard Shaw's house and a gem of an inn, there are concerts at Knebworth, green walks aplenty and you're just 35 minutes from London. *Children by arrangement.*

Price	£90. Singles by arrangement.
Rooms	3 twins/doubles.
Meals	Meals by arrangement. Pub 2-minute walk.
Closed	Christmas.
Directions	Exit A1 junc. 4. Follow signs to B653, towards Wheathampstead. At r'bout on to B653; 1st right for Codicote & Ayot St Lawrence. Left up Bride Hall Lane, signed Shaws Corner. Right into drive before red phone box in village.

Helen & Dick Dunn
The Old Rectory,
Ayot St Lawrence,
Welwyn,
Hertfordshire AL6 9BT
Tel   01438 820429
Fax   01438 821844
Email   ayotbandb@aol.com

Map 9   Entry 228

Isle of Wight

North Court

The Harrisons bought this glorious Jacobean house for its matchless grounds: 15 acres of pathed terraced gardens, exotica and subtropical flowers. The house, too, is magnificent, with 80 rooms, its big, comfortable guest bedrooms in two wings. The library houses a full-size snooker table (yes, you may use it) and the vast music room a grand piano (yours to play). The dining room has separate tables and delightful Nina Campbell wallpaper. Step back in time – in a quiet, untouristy village in lovely downland, this large house is very much a family home, and the perfect base for walkers and garden lovers.

Price	£60-£90. Singles £40-£50.
Rooms	6 twins/doubles.
Meals	Occasional light meals. Pub 3-minute walk through gardens.
Closed	Rarely.
Directions	From Newport, drive into Shorwell; down a steep hill, under a rustic bridge & right opp. thatched cottage. Signed.

John & Christine Harrison
North Court,
Shorwell,
Isle of Wight PO30 3JG
Tel   01983 740415
Mobile   07955 174699
Email   christine@northcourt.info
Web   www.northcourt.info

Map 4   Entry 229

Isle of Wight

Gotten Manor

Such character, such style – miles from the beaten track, bordered by beautiful stone barns. There's a refreshing simplicity to this unique Saxon house where living space was above, downstairs was for storage. Romantic bedrooms, one hidden up a steep open stair, have limewashed walls, wooden floors, A-frame beams, sofas. You sleep on a French rosewood bed, you bathe in a roll top tub in the room! Wallow by candlelight with a glass of wine. The garden bursts with magnificent fruit trees; Caroline's breakfasts include smoked salmon and smoothies. Rustic perfection, ancient peace. *Min. stay two nights at weekends.*

Price	£70-£90. Singles by arrangement.
Rooms	2 doubles.
Meals	Pub 1.5 miles.
Closed	Rarely.
Directions	0.5 miles south of Chale Green on B3399. After village, left at Gotten Lane. House at end of lane.

Caroline Gurney-Champion
Gotten Manor,
Gotten Lane, Chale,
Isle of Wight PO38 2HQ
Tel   01983 551368
Mobile   07746 453398
Email   as@gottenmanor.co.uk
Web   www.gottenmanor.co.uk

Map 4   Entry 230

Kent

Reason Hill

Brian and Antonia's 200-acre fruit farm is perched on the edge of the Weald of Kent, with stunning views over orchards and oast houses. The farmhouse has 17th-century origins (low ceilings, wonky floors, stone flags) and there's a new conservatory; colours are soft, antiques gleam and the mood is relaxed. The roomy double has a bay window and armchairs, the pretty twin looks over the garden. Come in spring for the blossom, summer for the fresh fruit and anytime for a break — the Greensand Way runs along the bottom of the farm, you are close to Sissinghurst Castle and 45 minutes from the Channel tunnel.

Price	£70.
Rooms	3: 1 double; 1 twin with separate shower, 1 single sharing shower (let to same party only).
Meals	Pubs within 3 miles.
Closed	Christmas & New Year.
Directions	From Maidstone A229 towards Hastings. After 4.5 miles, right at lights on B2163. In Coxheath, left up Westerhill Road, 0.2 miles then right into private road. Leave large white house on left, follow road through fruit trees to Reason Hill.

Brian & Antonia Allfrey
Reason Hill,
Linton, Maidstone,
Kent ME17 4BT
Tel   01622 743679
Mobile   07775 745580
Email   antonia@allfrey.net

Map 5   Entry 231

Kent

Charcott Farmhouse

The 1750 tile-hung brick farmhouse is very much a home — and to a charming family. You share a sitting room in the old bakehouse with the original bread oven and a TV, while ample bedrooms are simple but fresh, with country views; one has a forest of oak beams, another its own stair. Nicholas and Ginny enjoy the buzz of company, but understand your need for privacy. Make the most of their knowledge of the historic houses and gardens of Kent, many of which are a 20-minute drive. Breakfast is a happy affair with heaps of homemade bread and marmalade and free-range eggs. Best of all, you may come and go as you please.

Price	£55–£60. Singles £40–£45.
Rooms	3: 2 twins; 1 twin with separate bath.
Meals	Pub 5-minute walk.
Closed	Christmas Day & very occasionally.
Directions	B2027 0.5 miles north of Chiddingstone Causeway. Equidistant between Tonbridge, Sevenoaks & Edenbridge.

Nicholas & Ginny Morris
Charcott Farmhouse,
Charcott, Leigh,
Tonbridge,
Kent TN11 8LG
Tel   01892 870024
Email   charcottfarmhouse@btinternet.com

Map 5   Entry 232

Kent

Hoath House

Mervyn and Jane are fun. They live in a fascinating house which creaks under its own history, and takes you on a journey through medieval, Tudor and Edwardian times. Breakfast in what was a medieval hall, all heavy panelling, low ceilings and small, leaded windows; wander through 23 acres of formal and informal gardens. Ancestors, and a new charcoal drawing of Mervyn, gaze from the walls, dark staircases wind up to roomy, traditional bedrooms with super views, bathrooms are 1930s with chunky taps. Not for shallow style-seekers, but imaginative souls will adore it. *Minimum stay two nights at weekends.*

Price	£60-£70. Singles £30-£35.
Rooms	3: 1 double with separate bath; 2 twins sharing bath.
Meals	Supper/dinner £12.50-£20. Pubs 2.5 miles.
Closed	Christmas & New Year.
Directions	From A21, signs to Penshurst Place; go past vineyard up Grove Road; right at T-junc. for Edenbridge; through village, bearing left, for Edenbridge. House 0.5 miles on left.

Mr & Mrs Mervyn Streatfeild
Hoath House,
Chiddingstone Hoath,
Edenbridge,
Kent TN8 7DB

Tel 01342 850362
Email jstreatfeild@hoath-house.freeserve.co.uk

Map 5   Entry 233

Kent

40 York Road

A smart Regency townhouse, slap bang in the centre of Royal Tunbridge Wells and a five-minute walk from the delightfully preserved Pantiles. Patricia will enjoy cooking for you – in another life she served up delights for hungry skiers coming off the French mountains. She is a gentle presence and leaves you to come and go as you please; guests have a comfortable sitting room and bright, spotless bedrooms that are quieter than you may think. In the summer you may breakfast outside in the pretty courtyard garden before wandering into town for the cluster of great little shops and restaurants. *Children over 12 welcome.*

Price	From £65. Singles from £38.
Rooms	2 twins/doubles.
Meals	Dinner, 4 courses with wine, £20. Picnic available. Pub/restaurant nearby.
Closed	23 December-2 January.
Directions	From M25 junc. 5 onto A21, then A26 through Southborough to Tunbridge Wells. Take sign for Lewes, incline left taking 4th road left. Halfway along, on left. Car parks nearby, from £3.50 per 24 hours.

Patricia Lobo
40 York Road,
Tunbridge Wells, Kent TN1 1JY

Tel 01892 531342
Fax 01892 531342
Email yorkroad@tiscali.co.uk
Web www.yorkroad.co.uk

Map 5   Entry 234

Kent

Swan Cottage

A delightful Georgian townhouse in Tunbridge Wells, just near the Pantiles with its covered walkways between shops, coffee houses and spas. Your genial host is an artist, his studio can be seen through the glass wall in the open-plan dining room and his engaging pen and ink drawings dot every wall. Bedrooms have plenty of space, are comfortable and contemporary with big sash windows and fresh flowers; bathrooms are roomy, light and white, one with rooftop views. In summer there's a little patio for local sausages and eggs at a pink table under the magnolia tree. And the High Street is at the bottom of the road.

Price	£75. Singles £50.
Rooms	2: 1 twin/double; 1 single with separate bath.
Meals	Pubs/restaurants 200 yds.
Closed	Rarely.
Directions	From railway station follow High Street for 300 yds, left up Little Mt Sion. House faces you at top of hill. Parking to left of house.

David Gurdon
Swan Cottage,
17 Warwick Road,
Tunbridge Wells,
Kent TN1 1YL
Tel   01892 525910
Email   swancot@btinternet.com
Web   www.swancottage.co.uk

Map 5   Entry 235

Kent

West Winchet

Annie goes the extra mile: homemade compotes and jams with croissants and brioches on the breakfast table, treats in your room. The house is spotless but infectiously informal, the Parkers are great company and Annie is a treasure. Light, bright, ground-floor bedrooms are in the post-Edwardian wing, one with French windows which open on to the gardens; all is polished, nothing looks out of place: traditional fabrics, soft carpeting, fresh flowers and towels changed every day. Breakfast in the splendid drawing room with garden views – or in bed. *Children over five welcome.*

Price	From £70. Singles from £50.
Rooms	2: 1 double, 1 twin.
Meals	Pubs 2 miles.
Closed	Christmas & New Year.
Directions	A262 to Goudhurst. There, B2079 to Marden. House 2.5 miles from village, on left.

Annie Parker
West Winchet,
Winchet Hill, Goudhurst,
Cranbrook,
Kent TN17 1JX
Tel   01580 212024
Fax   01580 212250
Email   annieparker@jpa-ltd.co.uk

Map 5   Entry 236

Barclay Farmhouse

Breakfast on fresh fruits, warm croissants, banana bread, eggs en cocotte; Lynn's good food welcomes you. The weatherboarded guest barn has a solid, been-here-for-ever feel and is in perfect trim. A cosy, oak-floored dining room, a patio for summer, views onto a big peaceful garden and a bird-happy pond. Gleaming bedrooms have brocade bedspreads, French oak furniture, lotions, potions and flat-screen TVs; shower rooms are spot-on. Couples, honeymooners, garden lovers – many would love it here (though not children: the pond is deep). Immaculate, warm-hearted B&B – and glorious Sissinghurst nearby.

The Old Stables

They created the lovely garden from scratch and it's worth a wander for the tree house alone: it's fabulous. Penny and John are the nicest people – interesting, fun and Penny a great cook and home-baker. The windows were made to open upwards to stop the horses catching draughts, and they open upwards still – hard to believe the sitting room was once a stable. So relaxing... a dog to stroke, a piano to play, a garden with views. Bedrooms are peaceful, light and airy – comfy beds, fresh garden flowers, ducks by the bath – and superb breakfasts worth getting up for. Come to joyfully unwind.

Price	£70. Singles from £55.		Price	£55–£65. Singles from £40.
Rooms	3 doubles.		Rooms	3: 1 double;
Meals	Pubs/restaurants 1 mile.			1 double, 1 twin sharing bath.
Closed	Rarely.		Meals	Dinner, 2 courses, from £17.50.
Directions	From Biddenden centre, south on A262: Tenterden road. 0.7 miles, bear right (signed Par3 Golf, Vineyard & Benenden). Immed. on right.			BYO. Pub/restaurant 3 miles.
			Closed	Rarely.
			Directions	A28 Bethersden; opp. cricket pitch, follow sign into village. Left at school into Wissenden Lane; 1.5 miles, bear left at next junc.; 5th house on right.

Lynn Ruse
Barclay Farmhouse,
Woolpack Corner, Biddenden,
Kent TN27 8BQ
Tel   01580 292626
Fax   01580 292288
Email   info@barclayfarmhouse.co.uk
Web   www.barclayfarmhouse.co.uk

Penny & John Gillespie
The Old Stables,
Wissenden, Bethersden,
Kent TN26 3EL
Tel   01233 820597
Fax   01233 820199
Email   pennygillespie@theoldstables.co.uk
Web   www.theoldstables.co.uk

Map 5   Entry 237

Map 5   Entry 238

The Old Rectory

On a really good day (about once every five years) you can see France. But you'll be more than happy to settle for the superb views over Romney Marsh, the Channel in the distance. The big, friendly house, built in 1850, has impeccable, elegant bedrooms and good bathrooms; the large, many-windowed sitting room is full of books, pictures and flowers from the south-facing garden. Marion and David are both charming and can organise transport to Ashford International for you. It's remarkably peaceful – perfect for walking (right on the Saxon Shore path), cycling and birdwatching. *Children over ten welcome.*

Stowting Hill House

A classic Georgian manor house in an idyllic and peaceful setting with lovely gardens, close to the North Downs Way. This warm, civilised home mixes Tudor with Georgian styles and the friendly owners welcome you with tea and flowers from the garden. There's a conservatory full of blooms and greenery, a comfortable guest sitting room with sofas, log fire and fine views, and Aga-cooked breakfasts and dinner if required. Comfortable bedrooms are traditional and attractively furnished. You are ten minutes from the Chunnel but this is worth more than one night. *Children over ten welcome.*

Price	£65–£75. Singles £45.
Rooms	2: 1 twin; 1 twin with separate bath/shower.
Meals	Pubs within 4 miles.
Closed	Christmas & New Year.
Directions	M20, exit 10 for Brenzett/Hastings on A2070. After 6 miles, right for Hamstreet; immed. left; in Hamstreet, left B2067. After 1.5 miles, left (Ash Hill); 700 yds on right.

Price	From £80. Singles £50.
Rooms	2: 1 twin/double, 1 twin.
Meals	Dinner from £25. Pub 1 mile.
Closed	Christmas & New Year.
Directions	From M20 junc. 11, B2068 north. After 4.6 miles, left opp. Jet garage. House at bottom of hill on left, after 1.7 miles. Left into drive.

Marion & David Hanbury
The Old Rectory,
Ruckinge,
Ashford,
Kent TN26 2PE
Tel   01233 732328
Email   oldrectory@hotmail.com
Web   www.oldrectoryruckinge.co.uk

Richard & Virginia Latham
Stowting Hill House,
Stowting, Ashford,
Kent TN25 6BE
Tel   01303 862881
Fax   01303 863433
Mobile   07803 157987
Email   vjlatham@hotmail.com

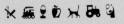

Map 5   Entry 239

Map 5   Entry 240

Kent

The Old Kent Barn

At the end of a bumpy drive, a huge 200-year-old barn – a feast of beams from former ships. Be welcomed by Hilary and Roger into a gorgeous interior of flagstoned floors, muted colours and a minstrels' gallery with deep sofas and views. Bedrooms, three tucked between beams, have good beds, coordinated linen and fresh flowers. Wake to the smell of homemade bread, wander the large gardens, try your hand at tennis: come and go as you please. There's a small lake full of carp, a wooden gazebo, a dog called Kia and a cascading waterfall in the landscaped gardens. A short hop from Canterbury and Dover but in an AONB.

Price	£75-£95. Singles from £55.
Rooms	3: 2 doubles, 1 twin/double.
Meals	Pubs/restaurants within 10-minute drive.
Closed	Rarely.
Directions	M2/A2 London to Dover. A260 towards Folkestone. Left signed Swingfield St and Lydden. Left at x-roads; driveway to house 100 yds on right.

Hilary & Roger Simmons
The Old Kent Barn,
Smersole Farm, Swingfield,
Kent CT15 7HF
Tel   01303 844270
Mobile   07702 621191
Email   hilaryjanesimmons@zoom.co.uk
Web   www.theoldkentbarn.co.uk

Map 5   Entry 241

Kent

11a Admiralty Mews

No.11a, part of the grand 18th-century sweep of Deal's former Marine Barracks and music school, is crammed with fascinating fragile objects. Brian and Chan Loo have lived all over the world: he working for the British Council, she Chinese and from Malaysia (you'll be expected to wear slippers in the house). She is an accomplished cook and does the most exquisite embroidery. The guest bedroom has a pretty fireplace and a shower room across the landing. English breakfast is served on decorative china with pretty porcelain spoons and muesli in tiffin carriers – on the terrace on warm days.

Price	£50-£70.
Rooms	1 twin/double with separate shower.
Meals	Pubs/restaurants close by.
Closed	January & February.
Directions	A2 to A258 onto the Strand in Walmer. The Mews is behind wall on the left. Look out for clock tower; no 11a at rear.

Brian & Chan Loo Smith
11a Admiralty Mews,
The Strand,
Walmer,
Deal,
Kent CT14 7AZ
Tel   01304 389364
Email   chanloo.smith@btinternet.com

Map 5   Entry 242

Kent

Orchard Barn

Alison loves to spoil (big beds, fluffy towels, bread from the mill), David knows the wildlife. Now their twins have flown the nest, they are loving B&B. The big beautiful barn has been sympathetically restored and eclectically furnished, its middle section left open to create a stunning covered courtyard. You get two snug bedrooms up in the eaves – pale beams and pretty velux windows onto the garden, and a sweet bath (or shower) room. A delightful village here, the ancient port of Sandwich nearby and egrets, kingfishers, swallows and squirrels a walk away. *Children over seven welcome.*

Price	£65-£75. Singles from £40.
Rooms	2: 1 double, 1 twin/double.
Meals	Pubs/restaurants within 1.5 miles.
Closed	20 December-30 January.
Directions	A258 Sandwich to Deal. 1st right after Worth sign into Federland Lane; 0.5 miles concealed entrance on left, opp. black barn.

	David & Alison Ross
	Orchard Barn,
	Felderland Lane, Worth, Deal,
	Kent CT14 0BT
Tel	01304 615045
Mobile	07950 599304
Web	www.orchardbarn-worth.co.uk

Map 5   Entry 243

Kent

Park Gate

Who would not love it here? Peter and Mary make a delightful team and their conversation is informed and easy. Behind the wisteria-clad façade are two sitting rooms (one with chesterfield, one TV-free), ancient beams and polished wood. Bedrooms are freshly comfortable with views over the glorious garden to the fields beyond; bathrooms gleam, meals are delicious. More magic outside: croquet, tennis, foxgloves, wildlife and roses – and nine sheep to mow the paddock. Sir Anthony Eden lived here during WWII to be close to the Channel defences; now you have Channel Tunnel and ferry convenience.

Price	£65. Singles £35.
Rooms	3: 1 double, 1 twin; 1 single with separate shower.
Meals	Dinner £20. Pubs/restaurants 1 mile.
Closed	Christmas.
Directions	A2 Canterbury to Dover road; Barham exit. Through Barham to Elham. After Elham sign 1st right signed Park Gate 0.75 miles. Over brow of hill; house on left.

	Peter & Mary Morgan
	Park Gate,
	Elham,
	Canterbury,
	Kent CT4 6NE
Tel	01303 840304

Map 5   Entry 244

Kent

Woodmans

No traffic noise, just blissful peace – and you're no more than a short hop to Canterbury. Your cosy ground-floor bedroom has its own entrance via the glorious garden where there are plenty of places to sit when its sunny. Tuck into local bacon and eggs (from Sarah's own rescued hens) in the breakfast room with its old pine table, dresser and flowers – or decide to be lazy and let Sarah bring it to your room. You can eat delicious dinner here too, perhaps after some hearty walking on the Wye Downs with its magnificent Chalk Crown and far-reaching views to Dungeness and the coast.

Price	£65. Singles £35.
Rooms	1 double.
Meals	Dinner, 3 courses, £22.50. Packed lunch £6.50. Pub/restaurant 1 mile.
Closed	Rarely.
Directions	From A2, 2nd exit to Canterbury. Follow ring road & B2068 for Hythe. Over A2, through Lower Hardres, past Granville pub. Right to Waltham; 1.5 miles after Waltham, right into Hassell St; 4th on left.

Sarah Rainbird
Woodmans,
Hassell Street, Hastingleigh,
Ashford, Kent TN25 5JE
Tel   01233 750250
Mobile 07836 505575
Email   sarah.rainbird@googlemail.com

Map 5   Entry 245

Kent

Forstal House

Where to begin – the house or garden? Both are a rare delight. The house is beautiful, quietly traditional inside with muted colours, a riot of paintings and lots of interesting books. Cosy, welcoming bedrooms (it feels rather like staying with friends), one up, one down, look onto the gardens – graceful, formal, tantalising. Duncan, a painter, sculptor and printmaker, redesigned much of it after the 1987 hurricane. Fruit from the orchards goes into crumbles and pies and delicious breakfast jams. Your hosts enjoy their 17th- and 18th-century home and look after you well. *Children over seven welcome.*

Price	£70. Singles from £40.
Rooms	2: 1 twin/double, 1 double.
Meals	Dinner, 3 courses, £22.50. Pub/restaurant 2 miles.
Closed	Christmas.
Directions	From A257, Canterbury to Sandwich; left at Wingham, north towards Preston. In Preston, The Forstal is 2nd left; 500 yds to house.

Elizabeth Scott
Forstal House,
The Forstal,
Preston, Canterbury,
Kent CT3 1DT
Tel   01227 722282
Email   emscott@forstal.fsnet.co.uk

Map 5   Entry 246

Kent

Great Weddington

An enchanting home in a peaceful setting, and the garden a treat even in winter. The listed house of perfect proportions was built by a Sandwich brewer of ginger beer... the drawing room is gorgeous, bedrooms are desirable and cosy, bathrooms are small, snug and spotless, and Katie has decorated, sponged and stencilled to perfection. Much-loved antiques, shelves of books, fine watercolours, fresh flowers. Outside, stunning hedges and lawns and a terrace for tea and drinks in the summer. You are surrounded by farmland and the area hums with history. *Children over eight welcome.*

Price	£102–£106. Singles £68–£78.
Rooms	2 twins/doubles.
Meals	Dinner £30.
Closed	Christmas & New Year.
Directions	From Canterbury A257 for Sandwich. On approach to Ash, stay on A257 (do not enter village), then 3rd left at sign to Weddington. House 200 yds down on left.

Katie & Neil Gunn
Great Weddington,
Ash, Canterbury,
Kent CT3 2AR

Tel	01304 813407
Fax	01304 812531
Email	traveltale@aol.com
Web	www.greatweddington.co.uk

Map 5 Entry 247

Kent

Little Mystole

All is reassuringly traditional and peaceful in this corner of Kent. The small Georgian house and delightful garden is run with the lightest of touches by your well-travelled, charming hosts. Cosy, comfortable bedrooms have a touch of chintz, inviting beds and glorious views. Tuck into a delicious breakfast in the handsome dining room, relax in the beamed sitting room filled with antiques, plump sofas, gilt-framed portraits and pretty flower arrangements. Golf at Royal St George's can be arranged and there are walks through rolling downland, hop fields and orchards. *10 mins from Canterbury, 30 mins from ferry & tunnel.*

Price	£80. Singles £15–£46.
Rooms	2: 1 double with extra single bed, 1 twin.
Meals	Occasional dinner. Pubs/restaurants 1.5 miles.
Closed	Christmas & Easter.
Directions	A28 Canterbury-Ashford. Left to Shalmsford Street; right immed. after post office at Bobbin Lodge Hill. Road bends left, then right at T-junc.; 2nd drive on left at junc. with Pickelden Lane.

Hugh & Patricia Tennent
Little Mystole,
Mystole Park, Canterbury,
Kent CT4 7DB

Tel	01227 738210
Fax	01227 738210
Email	little_mystole@yahoo.co.uk
Web	www.littlemystole.co.uk

Map 5 Entry 248

Kent

7 Longport

A delightful, unexpected hideaway bang opposite the site of St Augustine's Abbey and a five-minute walk to the Cathedral. You pass through Ursula and Christopher's elegant Georgian house to emerge in a pretty courtyard, on the other side of which is the self-contained cottage. Downstairs is a cosy sitting room with pale walls, tiled floors and plenty of books, and a clever, compact wet room with mosaic tiles. Then up steep stairs to a swish bedroom with crisp cotton sheets on a handmade bed and views of magnolia and ancient wisteria. You breakfast in the main house or in the courtyard on sunny days. Perfect.

Price	£75. Singles £50.
Rooms	Cottage with 1 double & sitting room.
Meals	Restaurant 30 yds.
Closed	Rarely.
Directions	Follow ring road around Canterbury. Signs for Sandwich A257, at St George's r'bout turn for Dover. After 300 yds left for Sandwich. At mini r'bout, left; house on left just before corner.

Ursula & Christopher Wacher
7 Longport,
Canterbury,
Kent CT1 1PE
Tel   01227 455367
Email   ursula.wacher@btopenworld.com

Map 5   Entry 249

Kent

Frith Farm House

Eight beautifully tended acres of garden with pond, obelisk and orchards – yours to explore. Magnificent views, too – and a very pretty indoor pool that is heated all year round. The house is large, traditional, luxurious. Bold Traviata-type fabrics abound and walls are vividly coloured. Feel grand in the four-poster, enjoy Chinese carpets, oriental pictures, exotic antiques. There's a music room with an organ, too. Markham will play – but only if you will sing! He and Susan enjoy meeting new people over breakfast – local and delicious – and are lovely hosts. Canterbury and Leeds Castle are easily reached.

Price	£75. Singles £60.
Rooms	3: 1 double, 1 twin, 1 four-poster.
Meals	Pubs/restaurant nearby.
Closed	Christmas.
Directions	From A2 at Faversham, Brogdale road to Eastling. 1.5 miles past Carpenters Arms, right (by postbox). House 0.5 miles on right.

Susan & Markham Chesterfield
Frith Farm House,
Otterden, Faversham,
Kent ME13 0DD
Tel   01795 890701
Email   enquiries@frithfarmhouse.co.uk
Web   www.frithfarmhouse.co.uk

Map 5   Entry 250

Kent

Dadmans

Ease into a more gracious way of life at this listed Tudor dower house. Amanda is cheery company and enthuses about art history and her rare-breed hens – the breakfast eggs are ambrosial. There's good local food for dinner, too, served in the dining room on gleaming mahogany or in the Aga-warmed kitchen. Bedrooms have patterned fabrics, indulgent beds, fresh flowers and good bathrooms, one heavily beamed with a claw-foot bath. Ancient trees in the garden, orchards and fields all around, and Doddington Place with its gardens (and opera in summer) a five-minute drive. *Children over four welcome.*

Price	£80. Singles by arrangement.
Rooms	2: 1 twin;
	1 double with separate bath.
Meals	Dinner, 3 courses, £25. Supper from £12.50. Pubs/restaurants nearby.
Closed	Rarely.
Directions	M20 junc. 8, then east on A20; left in Lenham towards Doddington. At The Chequers in Doddington, left; house 1.7 miles on left before Lynsted.

Amanda Strevens
Dadmans,
Lynsted,
Sittingbourne,
Kent ME9 0JJ
Tel   01795 521293
Email   amanda.strevens@btopenworld.com
Web   www.dadmans.co.uk

Map 5   Entry 251

Kent

Little Dane

Acres of enchanting garden with pheasants and moorcocks roaming the lawn and a church next door… blissfully peaceful. It wasn't always so; built as a rectory in the 1830s, the house was taken over by the RAF in the war, turned into a market garden and finally run as a school. Now fresh flowers scent the air and light floods in through long windows revealing fine rugs, antique beds and comfy sofas. Bedrooms glow with bold colours and fabrics, bathrooms are full of goodies. The Ashdowns have achieved a gracious, traditional look with a crisp modern slant – and, quite often, Sonia's bread comes fresh from the Aga.

Price	£85-£110. Singles from £75.
Rooms	2 doubles.
Meals	Occasional supper. Pub 3-minute walk.
Closed	Rarely.
Directions	M20 exit 7 for Maidstone. At 2nd r'bout, follow signs for Bearsted. At shops, sharp left into Thurnham Lane. 1 mile up lane, after sign for church, house on left.

Sonia Ashdown
Little Dane,
Thurnham Lane, Thurnham,
Maidstone, Kent ME14 3LG
Tel   01622 730908
Mobile   07841 474595
Email   info@thurnhamoldrectory.co.uk
Web   www.thurnhamoldrectory.co.uk

Map 5   Entry 252

Kent

Pope's Hall

Wind through the charming village to this listed house that dates from 1212, with a madly sloping roof, uneven floors and a riot of beams and timber. Step down into the salmon-pink dining room for a breakfast of local produce served at a solid oak table; William and Veronica are cheerful and kind. Old-fashioned bedrooms are a good size and deeply comfortable; bathrooms are spanking clean and sport thick towels and lovely soaps. There are 3.5 acres of stunning gardens to explore with paddocks, orchard and ponds, so come to unwind – and it's only 40 minutes from the Channel tunnel.

Price	£55-£75.
Rooms	3: 1 twin;
	1 double, 1 twin sharing bath.
Meals	Pub 1.5 miles.
Closed	Rarely.
Directions	From M2, A249 towards Sittingbourne. 1st left at roundabout on A2; through Newington, 1st left to Hartlip.

William Wakeley
Pope's Hall,
The Street, Hartlip, Sittingbourne,
Kent ME9 7TL

Tel	01795 842315
Fax	01795 841746
Email	william.wakeley@btinternet.com
Web	www.popeshall-bedandbreakfast.co.uk

Map 5 Entry 253

Kent

Hartlip Place

The house resonates with a faded, funky grandeur. Family portraits and lovely pieces, a drawing room to die for, an antique table shimmering with potted hyacinths, sash windows with sweeping views and a garden intricate and special. After candlelit dinner, up the circular stair to your bedroom, delightful with big bed, garden views, decanter for sherry, proper old-fashioned bathroom and – huge treat – real winter fire. John is unflappable and a touch mischievous, Gillian cooks, daughter Sophie greets – you'll like the whole family. *Children over 12 welcome.*

Price	From £90. Singles £50.
Rooms	1 double.
Meals	Dinner £25.
Closed	Christmas & New Year.
Directions	From Dover, M2 to Medway Services. Into station, on past pumps. Ignore no exit signs. Left at T-junc., 1st left & on for 2 miles. Left at next T-junc. House 3rd on left.

**Gillian & John Yerburgh
& Sophie & Richard Ratcliffe**
Hartlip Place,
Place Lane,
Sittingbourne,
Kent ME9 7TR

Tel	01795 842323
Email	hartlipplace@btinternet.com

Map 5 Entry 254

Lancashire

Challan Hall

The wind in the trees, the boom of a bittern and birdsong. That's about as noisy as it gets. On the edge of the village, the Victorian former farmhouse overlooks fields, woods and Lake Haweswater. Deer, squirrels and Leighton Moss Nature Reserve are your neighbours. The Cassons are well-travelled and the house is filled with a colourful mish-mash of mementos. Comfortably traditional, there's a sofa-strewn sitting room, a smart red and polished-wood dining room and two cosily floral bedrooms. Morecambe Bay and the Lakes are on the doorstep – come back for peaceful views and stunning sunsets.

Price	£60-£70. Singles from £35.
Rooms	2: 1 twin/double; 1 twin with separate bath.
Meals	Packed lunch available. Pubs 2 miles.
Closed	Rarely.
Directions	M6 exit 35. Thro' Carnforth towards Warton. Past railway station, signed Silverdale. Over level crossing, right at T-junc, signs to Arnside. After 1 mile house on right.

Mrs Charlotte Casson
Challan Hall,
Silverdale,
Lancashire LA5 0UH
Tel   01524 701054
Fax   01524 701054
Email   cassons@btopenworld.com
Web   www.challanhall.co.uk

✕ ♀

Map 11   Entry 255

Lancashire

Northwood

The Victorian façade conceals a houseful of riches and light. Lofty rooms are a bold mix of traditional and modern – a red leather sofa, a polished stair, an original tiled floor. Your hosts happily find babysitters, advise on restaurants (then drive you there) and offer you maple syrup pancakes at breakfast, along with other treats; the whole place radiates humour and warmth. Bedrooms are generous: a palette of white, chocolate and grey, or a rich violet quilt and a view of the sea. Expect coir floors, baskets of blankets and towels, DVDs, tranquillity. Delightful St Annes lies outside the door.

Price	£80. Singles from £75.
Rooms	2: 1 double, 1 double/family room.
Meals	Restaurants 5-minute walk.
Closed	Christmas & New Year.
Directions	M6 exit 32 then M55 to Blackpool. Follow signs for Lytham St Annes then St Annes. Head for the promenade.

Shannon Kuspira
Northwood,
24 North Promenade,
St Annes on Sea,
Lancashire FY8 2NQ
Tel   01253 782356
Email   skuspira@hotmail.com
Web   www.24northwood.co.uk

🚶 🕊 ✕ � ♀ 🚲

Map 11   Entry 256

Lancashire

Peter Barn Country House

Wild deer roam – this is the Ribble Valley, an AONB that feels like a time-locked land. In this former 18th-century tithe barn, where old church rafters support the big yet cosy guest sitting room, you settle in among plump sofas, log fire and flat-screen TV. Bedrooms, too, are on the top floor – nicely private. The Smiths couldn't be more helpful and breakfast is a feast: jams and muesli are homemade, stewed fruits are from the gardens. Step outside: Jean has transformed a field into a riot of colour and scent, there are pretty corners, a meandering stream and water lilies bask in still pools. *Minimum stay two nights.*

Price	£60-£62. Singles £35.
Rooms	3: 1 double, 1 twin/double; 1 double with separate bath.
Meals	Restaurants 1.5 miles.
Closed	Christmas & New Year.
Directions	M6 junc. 31, A59 to Clitheroe. Through Clitheroe to Waddington. After village 0.5 miles, left on Cross Lane. 0.75 miles, past Colthurst Hall, house on left.

Jean & Gordon Smith
Peter Barn Country House,
Cross Lane/Rabbit Lane,
Waddington, Clitheroe,
Lancashire BB7 3JH
Tel   01200 428585
Mobile   07970 826370
Email   jean@peterbarn.co.uk

Map 12   Entry 257

Lancashire

Sagar Fold House

Helen transformed this 17th century dairy and created two perfect studio apartments, self contained, all mod cons, very here and now. Your own entrance leads to large, beamed spaces that bring together comfort, immaculate efficiency and unusual beauty. There are books, DVDs, and comfortable sofas to curl up on; continental breakfast is supplied, using homemade, organic or local produce whenever possible. Now gaze over the Italian knot garden, which ties in lines of a lovely landscape. Take wonderful walks in deeply peaceful countryside, and it's not far to top-notch places to eat.

Price	£70.
Rooms	Studio with 1 double & kitchenette.
Meals	Continental breakfast in fridge. Pubs/restaurants 1-2 miles.
Closed	Rarely.
Directions	A59 through centre of Whalley. At 2nd mini r'bout left to Mitton; 3 miles, Three Fishes pub on left. Right to Whitewell Chaigely; 1 mile, left to Whitewell Chaigely; 0.5 miles, 3rd drive left to house.

Helen & John Cook
Sagar Fold House,
Higher Hodder,
Clitheroe,
Lancashire BB7 3LW
Tel   01254 826844
Email   cookj@thomas-cook.co.uk

Map 12   Entry 258

Lancashire

Herris's Farm

A luxurious slice of peace and quiet in the Forest of Bowland – an Area of Outstanding Natural Beauty. Your hosts are full of friendly enthusiasm and their home glows with comfort and warmth. The private sitting room has three charming sofas, logs, books and art; the flagstoned shippon – the oldest part – guards a country table to which delectable breakfasts are brought. In summer, step onto the patio for eye-stretching views over the village and valley beyond. Up a stone stair past shelves full of maps and historic guides are cottagey bedspreads on luxurious beds. Brilliant value.

Price	£60. Singles £35.
Rooms	2: 1 double; 1 twin/double with separate bath/shower.
Meals	Pubs in nearby villages.
Closed	Christmas & New Year.
Directions	From A59 at Chatburn follow signs to Grindleton. In village, left at Duke of York pub. Follow Slaidburn road for 1.5 miles; pass Hayloft Country Kitchen; next right over cattle grid.

Vivien & Mark Leslie
Herris's Farm,
Smalden Lane,
Grindleton,
Lancashire BB7 4RX
Tel   01200 440725
Email info@herrisesfarm.co.uk
Web www.herrisesfarm.co.uk

Map 12   Entry 259

Leicestershire

The Grange

Behind the mellow brick exterior (Queen Anne in front, Georgian at the back) is a real family home. Log fires brighten chilly days and you are greeted with warmth and courtesy by Mary and Shaun, their two young children and a sweet dog called Marmite. Beautifully quiet bedrooms are hung with strikingly unusual wallpapers and furnished with excellent beds and pretty antiques, bathrooms are simple yet impeccable and there's a fireplace in the big, flagstoned hall decorated with sporting prints and deeds. The generous garden has shrubs, flowerbeds and a summer croquet lawn.

Price	£70. Singles £45.
Rooms	2: 1 twin, 1 double.
Meals	Pubs/restaurants 0.5-1.5 miles.
Closed	Christmas & New Year.
Directions	M1 exit 20; A4304 towards Market Harborough. First left after Walcote marked 'Gt Central Cycle Ride'; 2 miles, then right into Kimcote, pass church on left. On right after Poultney Lane.

Shaun & Mary Mackaness
The Grange,
Kimcote,
Leicestershire LE17 5RU
Tel   01455 203155
Fax   01455 203155
Email shaunandmarymac@hotmail.com
Web www.thegrangekimcote.co.uk

Map 8   Entry 260

Leicestershire

Curtain Cottage

A pretty village setting for this cottage on the main street, next door to Sarah's interior design shop. You have your own entrance by the side and through a large garden, which backs onto fields with horses and the National Forest beyond. A conservatory is your sitting room: wicker armchairs, wooden floors, a contemporary take on the country look. Bedrooms are light and fresh, linen from The White Company on sumptuous beds, a slate-tiled bathroom, stunning fabrics. Breakfast is anything, anytime, full English or fresh fruit and croissants from the local shop – all is delivered to you. Perfect privacy.

Price	£70. Singles £50.
Rooms	2: 1 double, 1 twin.
Meals	Pubs/restaurants 150 yds.
Closed	Rarely.
Directions	Gravel driveway to left of Barkers Interiors Design Showroom on Main Street. From car park, access to cottage via gate into garden at rear of showroom.

Sarah Barker
Curtain Cottage,92-94 Main Street,
Woodhouse Eaves,
Leicestershire LE12 8RZ
Tel   01509 891361
Fax   01509 890100
Email   barkerID@aol.com
Web   www.barkersinteriors.com

Map 8   Entry 261

Leicestershire

White House Fields Farm

A house with a very pretty front – Georgian with a leaded porch and sash windows – but you arrive at the back, past rather modern farm buildings. You have your own entrance from the courtyard garden into a light, beamed bedroom – painted a cheerful yellow, brightened with fresh flowers and soothing with linen and goose down. This is a comfortable, lived-in farm with no pretensions – but Charlotte gives you very special food indeed, either a smart affair in the dining room or a kitchen supper with her young family. Very convenient for Donington race track and East Midlands Airport, yet peaceful.

Price	£75-£85. Singles £50-£60.
Rooms	1 double.
Meals	Dinner, 3 courses with coffee & wine, £25. Pub/restaurant 0.5 miles.
Closed	Christmas & New Year.
Directions	M1 junc. 23a. Head towards East Midlands Airport, follow signs to Breedon on the Hill. Left signed Worthington. House 0.5 miles on right.

Mrs Charlotte Meynell
White House Fields Farm,
Worthington, Ashby de la Zouch,
Leicestershire LE65 1RA
Tel   01332 862312
Fax   01332 863827
Email   charlottemeynell@aol.com
Web   www.whitehousefieldsfarm.co.uk

Map 8   Entry 262

Leicestershire

The Gorse House

Passing cars are less frequent than passing horses – this is a peaceful spot in a pretty village. The lasting impression of this 17th-century cottage is of lightness, brightness and space. There's a fine collection of paintings and furniture, everything gleams and oak doors lead from dining room to guest sitting room. Bedrooms are restful and fresh, the largest with three views. The garden was designed by Bunny Guinness, the stables accommodate up to six horses and it's strolling distance to dinner at the village pub. The house is filled with laughter and the Cowdells are terrific hosts.

Price	From £55. Singles £30.
Rooms	3: 1 double, 1 family for 3. Stable: 1 triple & kitchenette.
Meals	Packed lunch £5. Pub 100 yds.
Closed	Rarely.
Directions	From A46 Newark-Leicester; B676 for Melton. At x-roads, straight for 1 mile; right to Grimston. There, up hill, past church. House on left, just after right-hand bend at top.

Mr & Mrs R L Cowdell
The Gorse House, 33 Main Street,
Grimston, Melton Mowbray,
Leicestershire LE14 3BZ

Tel	01664 813537
Mobile	07780 600792
Email	cowdell@gorsehouse.co.uk
Web	www.gorsehouse.co.uk

Map 9   Entry 263

Leicestershire

Littlefield Farm

A pond to picnic by, 850 acres to roam, a field for your horse, a games room for the children, an indoor pool, a newly laid tennis court – there's something to delight everyone at this 1860 traditional farmhouse. Luxurious bathrooms encourage hot soaks, big, comfortable bedrooms have sweeping views and the whole house is an Aladdin's cave of special things: oriental rugs, tapestry cushions, rich drapes, and paintings old and new. Nicky splits her time between Market Harborough and London, leaving her efficient housekeeper to look after you. *Children over 12 welcome.*

Price	£70-£80. Singles £45.
Rooms	3: 2 doubles; 1 twin with separate bath.
Meals	Pubs/restaurants nearby.
Closed	Rarely.
Directions	From A427 (Market Harborough to Corby) follow sign for East Carlton. House last on left in village.

Nicky Chaplin
Littlefield Farm,
East Carlton,
Market Harborough,
Leicestershire LE16 8YA

Tel	07860 201395
Fax	0207 7360456

Map 9   Entry 264

Lincolnshire

The Old Farm House

Hidden in the Lincolnshire Wolds, an 18th-century, ivy-covered house – and Nicola's father still farms the fields beyond the ha-ha. The stone-flagged, terracotta-washed hall gives a hint of warm colours to come; creamy walls show off tawny fabrics, prints and antiques; the beamed sitting/breakfast room has a big, rosy brick inglenook fireplace and tranquil views. Such a welcoming, tucked-away place, hopping with pheasant but just a 10-15-minute drive from shops, golf and racing in the nearby towns. Excellent value, and perfect if you fancy privacy and space. *Children over eight welcome.*

Price	£65. Singles £40.
Rooms	2: 1 double;
	1 triple with separate bath.
Meals	Pub 2 miles.
Closed	Christmas, New Year &
	occasionally.
Directions	M180 exit 5; A18 signed Louth.
	Past airport; 2.5 miles after
	junction of A46 take right signed
	Hatcliffe. House is third on right,
	before village.

Nicola Clarke
The Old Farm House,
Low Road,
Hatcliffe,
Lincolnshire DN37 0SH

Tel	01472 824455
Email	clarky.hatcliffe@btinternet.com
Web	www.oldfarmhousebandbgrimsby.co.uk

Map 13   Entry 265

Lincolnshire

Knaith Hall

This intriguing place, medieval church at its gate, dates from the 16th century. Lawns slope down to the river Trent, daffodils, lambs, a passing barge and waterfowl pattern the serenity. And the skyscapes are terrific! At night, a distant power station shines, actually enhancing that 'great rurality of taste' referred to in Pevsner. Indoors, diamond-paned windows, a domed dining room and fine furniture are softened by easy décor and a log fire. An appealing family house, with a relaxed atmosphere. Your own room is comfortable and restful with the very best of old-fashioned bedding.

Price	£70. Singles £40.
Rooms	2: 1 double with separate shower,
	1 twin with separate bath.
Meals	Dinner, 3 courses with wine, £20.
	Pub 4 miles.
Closed	Rarely.
Directions	Knaith 3 miles south of
	Gainsborough on
	A156 Lincoln-Gainsborough road.
	After Knaith signs, look for white
	gateposts on west side with sign
	for St Mary's Church.

John & Rosie Burke
Knaith Hall,
Knaith,
Gainsborough,
Lincolnshire DN21 5PE

Tel	01427 613005
Fax	01427 613005
Email	jandrburke@aol.com

Map 9   Entry 266

Lincolnshire

The Manor House

One guest's summing up reads: "Absolutely perfect – hostess, house, garden and marmalade." Ann loves having people to stay and makes you feel truly at home. You have the run of downstairs: neat, traditional, all family antiques, fresh flowers and space. Chintzy, carpeted bedrooms have dreamy views of the pretty gardens and duck-dabbled lake, and dinners are good value and delicious: game casserole, ginger meringue bombe... Perfect stillness at the base of the Wolds and a lovely one-mile walk along the route of the old railway that starts from the front door. Very special.

Price	From £58. Singles by arrangement.
Rooms	2: 1 double, 1 twin.
Meals	Dinner from £15. BYO. Pub/restaurant 2 miles.
Closed	Christmas.
Directions	From Wragby A157 for Louth. After approx. 2 miles, at triple road sign, right. Red postbox & bus shelter at drive entrance, before graveyard.

Ann Hobbins
The Manor House,
West Barkwith,
Lincolnshire LN8 5LF
Tel   01673 858253
Fax   01673 858253

Lincolnshire

The Grange

Wide open Lincolnshire farmland on the edge of the Wolds. This immaculately kept farm has been in the family for five generations; their award-winning farm trail helps you explore. Listen to birdsong, catch the sun setting by the trout lake, have supper before the fire in a dining room whose elegant Georgian windows are generously draped. Sarah is a young and energetic host and offers you delicious homemade cake on arrival. Comfortable bedrooms have spick and span bath or shower rooms and fabulous views that stretch to Lincoln Cathedral. A delightful couple running good farmhouse B&B.

Price	£60. Singles £40.
Rooms	2 doubles.
Meals	Supper from £13. Dinner, 3 courses, from £17. BYO. Packed lunch £6. (No meals at harvest time.) Pub/restaurant 1 mile.
Closed	Christmas & New Year.
Directions	Exit A157 in East Barkwith at War Memorial, into Torrington Lane. House 0.75 miles on right after sharp right-hand bend.

Sarah & Jonathan Stamp
The Grange,
Torrington Lane,
East Barkwith, Lincolnshire
LN8 5RY
Tel   01673 858670
Email   sarahstamp@farmersweekly.net
Web   www.thegrange-lincolnshire.co.uk

Lincolnshire

Baumber Park

Lincoln red cows and Longwool sheep ruminate in the fields around this rosy-brick farmhouse – once a stud that bred a Derby winner. The old watering pond is now a haven for frogs, newts and toads; birds sing lustily. Maran hens conjure delicious eggs and Clare, a botanist, is hugely knowledgeable about the area. Bedrooms are light and traditional, not swish, with mahogany furniture. There's a heart-stopping view through an arched window on the landing, a grass tennis court, a sitting room with a log fire, a dining room with local books. This is good walking, riding and cycling country, with quiet lanes.

Price	£58-£62. Singles from £35.
Rooms	3: 2 doubles; 1 twin with separate bath.
Meals	Pubs/restaurants 4 miles.
Closed	Christmas & New Year.
Directions	From A158 in Baumber take road towards Wispington & Bardney. House 300 yds down on right.

Mike and Clare Harrison
Baumber Park,
Baumber, Horncastle,
Lincolnshire LN9 5NE
Tel   01507 578235
Mobile   07977 722776
Email   baumberpark@amserve.com
Web   www.baumberpark.com

Map 9   Entry 269

Lincolnshire

Ryeland House

Farmer Mike and charming Caroline built this large red-brick and slate house on their own land and are much committed to the Countryside Stewardship programme; hang out of your bedroom window to watch waders, even deer, round the nearby pond. Inside is warm (thanks to underfloor heating) and spacious. Your bedroom has a boutique hotel feel in shades of cream and brown, while two beautifully lit sitting rooms are smoothly uncluttered and have comfortable armchairs. Pedal along those lovely flat lanes after breakfast, head to Lincoln and its cathedral or Horncastle for antiques. *Young people over 15 welcome.*

Price	From £65. Singles from £40.
Rooms	1 twin/double & sitting room.
Meals	Packed lunch from £2.50. Restaurant 0.5 miles.
Closed	Christmas, New Year & occasionally.
Directions	A15 Lincoln, Sleaford turn. Left at Mere onto B1178 for 3 miles; over staggered x-roads into Potterhanworth. At T-junc. right for 100 yds to War Memorial; left onto Barff Rd, 0.5 miles, driveway on left.

Michael & Caroline Norcross
Ryeland House,
Barff Road, Potterhanworth,
Lincoln, Lincolnshire LN4 2DU
Tel   01522 793563
Mobile   07977 590375
Email   norcross@ukfarming.co.uk
Web   www.ryelands-house.co.uk

Map 9   Entry 270

Lincolnshire

Churchfield House

The little house was built in the Sixties; inside glows with character and charm. Bridget is an interior decorator whose eye for detail and sense of fun inform the light-filled rooms. A small, snug bedroom sports fresh checks, warm colours, firm mattress, down pillows, interesting pictures, even a gilt-trimmed copy of a Louis XIV chair. The bathroom is spotless and inviting, and there's a conservatory mood to the brick-walled, stone-tiled dining room, where glass doors open to a large, lush garden in summer. You're close to good golf courses, Bridget cooks and chats with warmth and humour – this is a gem.

Price	£55. Singles £30.
Rooms	1 twin.
Meals	Dinner from £15. Pubs/restaurants 3 miles.
Closed	Christmas & New Year.
Directions	A607 Grantham to Lincoln road. On reaching Carlton Scroop 1st left for Hough Lane. Last house on left.

Mrs Bridget Hankinson
Churchfield House,
Carlton Scroop, Grantham,
Lincolnshire NG32 3BA

Tel   01400 250387
Fax   01400 250241
Email   info@churchfield-house.co.uk
Web   www.churchfield-house.co.uk

Map 9   Entry 271

Lincolnshire

Belvoir Vale Cottage

The Vale of Belvoir is gloriously quiet and you are just 200 yards from the Viking Way. Kindly Norman and Suzie have restored two old roadside cottages, charmingly; the emphasis is on warmth, lovely colours, beautifully arranged fresh flowers, good food and gorgeous views over the pretty garden to Belvoir Castle. Bedrooms and bathrooms are a good size and have thick carpets and new windows to keep out the blast; expect original brass beds, fluffy towels, crisp white linen. Start the day with a full English or undyed haddock with poached eggs; you'll be truly spoiled. *Children welcome if rooms let to one party.*

Price	£60-£85. Singles from £40.
Rooms	3: 1 double & sitting room; 1 double, 1 twin.
Meals	Dinner from £25. Packed lunch available. Pubs/restaurants 1.2 miles.
Closed	Rarely.
Directions	A52 Nottingham-Grantham. At Sedgebrook x-roads, turn for Stenwith & Woolsthorpe. After 1.5 miles cross double bridges - private car park 300 yds.

Suzie & Norman Davis
Belvoir Vale Cottage,
Stenwith, Woolsthorpe-by-Belvoir,
Grantham, Lincolnshire NG32 2HE

Tel   01949 842434
Mobile   07976 562845
Email   reservations@belvoirvale-cottage.co.uk
Web   www.belvoirvale-cottage.co.uk

Map 9   Entry 272

Lincolnshire

The White House

Right on the green in this fine conservation village is a tall, gravely beautiful Georgian house. It is even lovelier inside. Victoria and David, understandably passionate about the place, have filled the rooms with gorgeous things. Feel free to lounge on chaises longues in the library; admire the fine moulded fireplace and the etchings, the watercolours and the English and Chinese porcelain. The bedrooms, too, are striking, one with an antique four-poster canopied in green silk; bathrooms are fresh and appealing. Your charming hosts serve breakfast in the pretty little walled garden in summer.

Price	£70. Singles £45.
Rooms	2: 1 twin/double; 1 four-poster (with adjoining room if required) with separate bath.
Meals	Dinner, with wine, £25. Pub/restaurant round the corner.
Closed	Rarely.
Directions	A15 to Folkingham; on village green.

Victoria & David Strauss
The White House,
25 Market Place,
Folkingham, Sleaford, Lincolnshire
NG34 0SE

Tel	01529 497298
Email	victoria.strauss@btinternet.com
Web	www.bedandbreakfastfolkinghamlincolnshire.co.uk

Map 9   Entry 273

Lincolnshire

The Barn

Simon and Jane have farmed for 30 years and are the nicest people. Breakfasts are local and delicious, there are endless little extras and nothing is too much trouble. In this light-filled barn conversion old beams go well with new walls, floors, windows and the odd antique; a brick-flanked fireplace glows and heated flagged floors keep toes warm. Above the high-raftered main living/dining room is a comfy, good-sized double; in the adjoining stables, two further rooms, a crisp feel, sparkling showers, restful privacy. Views are to sheep-dotted fields and the Georgian village is a charmer.

Price	£70. Singles £40.
Rooms	3: 1 double, 1 twin/double; 1 single with separate bath/shower.
Meals	Supper, 2 courses, £15. Dinner, 3 courses, £20. BYO. Pub 2 miles.
Closed	Rarely.
Directions	Midway between Lincoln & Peterborough. From A15, in Folkingham, turn west into Spring Lane next to village hall; 200 yds on right.

Simon & Jane Wright
The Barn,
Spring Lane, Folkingham, Sleaford,
Lincolnshire NG34 0SJ

Tel	01529 497199
Mobile	07876 363292
Email	sjwright@farming.co.uk
Web	www.thebarnspringlane.co.uk

Map 9   Entry 274

Lincolnshire

Tanyard House

The old tanner's house (it dates from 1643) is listed and the Knights Templar convened in the cellar. Sloping ceilings, twisting stairs and tiny doors — a house of immense history which has been completely refurbished inside. Claire, full of enthusiasm for guests, gives you a long sunny living room overlooking a young garden, replete with dining table, generous sofas and deep sills. Upstairs are soft carpets, gentle hues, seductive linen, aromatic oils. One bedroom is in the old part (mullion windows, copse views), one (big and beautiful) in the new. Expect to be stylishly spoiled.

Price	£70. Singles £40.
Rooms	2 twins, each with separate bath/shower.
Meals	Occasional dinner with wine, £25. Pubs 0.75 miles.
Closed	Rarely.
Directions	North on A1, exit after Ram Jam Inn to S. Witham. Or: going south on A1, exit after Fox Inn to S. Witham; enter village, 1st right into Church Lane; 2nd drive on right.

Alex & Claire van Straubenzee
Tanyard House,
South Witham, Grantham,
Lincolnshire NG33 5PL

Tel	01572 767976
Mobile	07765 241354
Email	tanyardhouse@btinternet.com
Web	www.tanyardhouse.co.uk

Map 9   Entry 275

Lincolnshire

Cawthorpe Hall

Built in 1819, embellished later by Gardner of the RA, filled with original, unusual art, African carvings and swimming with light — a fascinating house, run by warm, relaxed owners. Gardner's remarkable studio has now been transformed into a vast sitting room, heated by a great wood-burning stove. Lots of fun here: chickens perching on the window sill, adorable pets, a long garden hedge fashioned into a train. The double rooms, a mix of traditional and floral with great bay windows and plenty of space, overlook fields of roses — and Ozric's genuine English rose water and confiture are for sale.

Price	£70–£80. Singles £35–£40.
Rooms	3: 2 doubles, 1 twin, each with separate bath/shower.
Meals	Pub/restaurant 1 mile.
Closed	Christmas & New Year.
Directions	From Bourne, A15 north for Sleaford, 1st hamlet on left signed to Cawthorpe. House last on right before road becomes track.

Ozric & Chantal Armstrong
Cawthorpe Hall,
Bourne,
Lincolnshire PE10 0AB

Tel	01778 423830
Fax	01778 426620
Email	chantal@cawthorpebandb.co.uk
Web	www.cawthorpebandb.co.uk

Map 9   Entry 276

Lincolnshire

Brook House

This two-storey stable conversion in warm stone is all yours, set in its own statue and bamboo-filled courtyard. Beyond is farmland as far as the eye can see. There's a fresh, stylish feel to the sitting room with Farrow & Ball 'matchstick' walls, a cream sofa, tumbled limestone floors with underfloor heating and your own fridge. Up thick biscuit carpets to a semi-galleried, spacious bedroom with white cane furniture, sloped ceiling, pretty fabrics and, from the bath, sunset views. Julian and Jenny have created a magical garden which is yours to explore – but stoke up with a hearty breakfast first. Wonderful.

Price	£86. Singles £60.
Rooms	Stables for 2: 1 double & sitting/dining room. Extra beds for children.
Meals	Pub 2 miles.
Closed	Christmas, Easter & New Year.
Directions	A1 north of Stamford; left just after South Witham exit, signed North Witham & Gunby. After Gunby village, house last after a sharp bend with walled garden visible from road.

Julian & Jenny McAlpine
Brook House,
Gunby,
Lincolnshire NG33 5LF

Tel	01476 860010
Fax	01476 860010
Email	julesmcalpine@aol.com
Web	www.honeyandmcalpine.co.uk

Map 9   Entry 277

London

29 Woodberry Crescent

London life, but not as we know it. A leafy suburb, an Edwardian house, a huge birdsung garden with a terrace and a thriving pond, delicious food grown on an allotment or bought from the farmers' market… you could be in the countryside but you can cycle to Hampstead Heath in 30 minutes. Inside is an eclectic mix of old and new, a comfortable sitting room with a wood-burner overlooking the garden and a bright bedroom upstairs with white walls and a modern metal bed. There are flowers from Edwina and Nigel's lovely garden, plenty of books, and on sunny days you can eat outside – a huge treat.

Price	£75. Singles £60-£65.
Rooms	1 double.
Meals	Dinner, 3 courses with wine, £25. Packed lunch £6-£7. Pubs/restaurants 200 yds.
Closed	Rarely.
Directions	Bus: 134 or 43. Tube: Highgate tube, exit Muswell Hill Rd. Owner will collect from tube station on request.

Edwina & Nigel Roberts
29 Woodberry Crescent,
Muswell Hill,
London N10 1PJ

Tel	020 8365 3639
Fax	020 8365 3639
Mobile	07957 680521
Email	edwinakellerman@btinternet.com

Map 4   Entry 278

London

30 King Henry's Road

Country-house luxury – great bed, lovely bathroom, digital TV, broadband connection in your bedroom – yet here you have the personal touch we so like. Breakfast on homemade bread and jams, bagels, croissants, yogurts and fruit salad in a large kitchen/dining room with real fire and garden views. Your room on the top floor has a brass bed, a sisal floor, good pictures, fine pieces of furniture and a wall of books. Shops, restaurants and sublime views of Primrose Hill are a five-minute stroll, and there's open-air theatre in Regent's Park in summer. Carole and Ted know London and will happily advise.

Price	£100. Singles £80.
Rooms	1 double.
Meals	Pubs/restaurants 2-minute walk.
Closed	Occasionally.
Directions	Tube: Chalk Farm 5-minute walk. Free parking weekends, ticket parking nearby.

	Carole Cox
	30 King Henry's Road,
	Primrose Hill,
	London NW3 3RP
Tel	020 7483 2871
Fax	020 7483 2871
Email	mail@carolecox.co.uk

Map 4 Entry 279

London

66 Camden Square

A modern, architect designed house made of African teak, brick and glass. Climb wooden stairs under a glazed pyramid to light-filled, Japanese-style bedrooms with low platform beds, modern chairs and adjacent sitting room/study. Sue and Rodger have travelled widely so there are pictures, photographs and ethnic pieces everywhere – and a parrot called Peckham. Share their lovely open-plan dining space at breakfast overlooking a bird-filled courtyard or eat outside on warmer days. Camden's bustling market and the zoo are near, and a huge choice of places to eat. *Children by arrangement.*

Price	£90-£100. Singles £50-£55.
Rooms	2: 1 double, 1 single sharing bath (2nd room let to same party only).
Meals	Pubs/restaurants nearby.
Closed	Occasionally.
Directions	Tube: Camden Town or Kentish Town. Parking free at weekends; meters during week.

	Sue & Rodger Davis
	66 Camden Square,
	Camden Town,
	London NW1 9XD
Tel	020 7485 4622
Fax	020 7267 1045
Email	rodgerdavis@btopenworld.com

Map 4 Entry 280

London

12A Evelyn Mansions

Your passport to Pimlico – one of the last 'villages' left in London with proper shops and a good choice of restaurants. Find comfort and elegance in this Edwardian mansion flat, its lovely drawing room sprinkled with interesting objects from Moranna's travels as the wife of a diplomat – she is a charming hostess. Your bedroom (double glazed) has a great view of the junction between Victoria Street and the station – a people-watcher's paradise – and is spoiling: goose down, easy chairs, good books, a shining white bathroom. It is the perfect city bolthole and good value too.

Price	£90. Singles £50.
Rooms	1 twin/double with separate bath.
Meals	After-theatre supper £15. Pubs/restaurants nearby.
Closed	Rarely.
Directions	3-minute walk to Victoria bus & tube; 5-minute walk to coach station. Carlisle Place is just off Victoria Street.

Moranna Colvin
12A Evelyn Mansions,
Carlisle Place,
London SW1P 1NH
Tel   020 7834 1889
Email   morannacolvin@yahoo.com

Map 4   Entry 281

London

4 First Street

This is a smart London home in one of London's most desirable quarters. You get the top floor to yourself, and some floor it is. You're nicely private, it's surprisingly quiet, there's masses of space and the luxuries are unremitting… trim carpets, comfy armchairs, traditonal pictures, stencilled borders, a bathroom of marble and mirrors – and a wall of glass opening to a tiny muralled balcony. Shirley is the kindest hostess. Breakfast in the basement by an open fire or catch the sun on the potted terrace. This is shop-till-you-drop land and you can't get posher. Charming.

Price	£110.
Rooms	1 double.
Meals	Continental breakfast. Pub/restaurant 2 mins.
Closed	Occasionally.
Directions	Tubes: Sloane Square; Knightsbridge; South Kensington. Nearest car park £25 for 24 hrs.

Shirley Eaton
4 First Street,
Chelsea,
London SW3 2LD
Tel   020 7581 8429
Mobile   07831 292888
Email   shirley@eaton3176.fsnet.co.uk

Map 4   Entry 282

London

20 Bywater Street

In a quiet, pretty cul-de-sac off the fashionable King's Road, a delightful pastel-coloured house and a welcoming B&B. Caroline and Richard give you a pretty, bright bedroom downstairs, with stripes and checks, a trim carpet and a wicker chair, fresh flowers, lots of magazines and a CD player. The private shower room is next door – fluffy towels, white tiles – while breakfast is taken across the hall in the kitchen/conservatory, a cheery room that swims in morning sun, whose doors open onto a smallish York-stone garden full of terracotta pots. The best of London laps at the door.

Price	From £95. Singles from £70.
Rooms	1 double with separate shower.
Meals	Continental breakfast. Pubs & restaurants nearby.
Closed	Occasionally.
Directions	Tube: Sloane Square 5-minute walk (down King's Road, 6th street on right). Parking available locally.

Caroline & Richard Heaton–Watson
20 Bywater Street,
Chelsea, London SW3 4XD
Tel   020 7581 2222
Fax   020 7581 2222
Email caheatonw@aol.com
Web   www.20bywaterstreet.com

� ✗ ⚲

Map 4   Entry 283

London

90 Old Church Street

In a quiet street facing the Chelsea Arts Club, an enticing, contemporary haven. Softly spoken Nina is passionate about the arts, knows Chelsea inside out and takes real pleasure in looking after her guests. Antique shop spoils stand alongside more modern delights, the attention to detail is amazing and there are plentiful bunches of flowers. A lush carpet takes you up to the second floor and your super-private, surprisingly peaceful and deliciously designed bedroom. Breakfast – an array of fresh fruit, yogurts and croissants – is shared with Nina in the kitchen. We love this place.

Price	From £110. Singles from £95.
Rooms	1 double.
Meals	Continental breakfast. Restaurants nearby.
Closed	Occasionally.
Directions	Tube: South Kensington 10-minute walk.

Nina Holland
90 Old Church Street,
Chelsea,
London SW3 6EP
Tel   020 7352 4758
Mobile 07831 689167
Email ninastcharles@btinternet.com

✗ ⚲

Map 4   Entry 284

London

37 Trevor Square

A fabulous find, luxury in the middle of Knightsbridge. The square is impossibly pretty, unexpectedly peaceful and a three-minute walk from Hyde Park or Harrods. Margaret runs an interior design company – rather successfully, by the look of things. You breakfast in the dining room (smoked salmon with scrambled eggs, if you wish) elegant with toile de Jouy walls, stone busts, warm rugs and fire in winter. Upstairs: electric blankets, duvets, a maple table, a gorgeous marbled bathroom, a minibar, DVDs and CDs. There's a snug conservatory/sitting room you're welcome to use, too.

Price	£140. Singles £100.
Rooms	2: 1 double, 1 twin sharing bath & shower (2nd room let to same party only).
Meals	Restaurants 200 yds.
Closed	Occasionally.
Directions	Tube: Knightsbridge. Nearest car park £25 for 24 hrs (closed overnight).

Margaret & Holly Palmer
37 Trevor Square,
Knightsbridge, London SW7 1DY
Tel 020 7823 8186
Fax 020 7823 9801
Email margaret@37trevorsquare.co.uk
Web www.37trevorsquare.co.uk

Map 4 Entry 285

London

Hyde Park Gate

Virginia Woolf was born in the sitting room (there's a library of her books here) which entitles this smart London house to a blue plaque – in fact it has three! Jasmyne is well-travelled, cultured, and gives you a full English breakfast (smoked salmon on Sundays) in a deep green and blue dining room. Your bedroom sits quietly at the back, sweetly decorated in corals and with fresh flowers, fruit, chocolates and a tea tray with proper china; the compact shower room sparkles. You are a step away from the Albert Hall, Kensington Gardens, Hyde Park and Knightsbridge – an excellent choice of restaurants too.

Price	From £75. Singles from £55.
Rooms	1 double.
Meals	Pubs/restaurants nearby.
Closed	Occasionally.
Directions	Tube: Gloucester Road; Kensington High Street. Bus: 9, 10, 52, 452, 70. Car park £25 per 24 hrs.

Jasmyne King-Leeder
Hyde Park Gate,
Flat 3, Kensington,
London SW7 5DH
Tel 020 7584 9404
Email jkingleeder@yahoo.co.uk
Web www.22hydeparkgate.com

Map 4 Entry 286

London

6 Oakfield Street

Margaret and Simon take it in turns to cook breakfast at the weekends so they can each be sure of a lie-in! This district dates from the mid-1660s and Simon, who knows his Chelsea onions, has maps to prove it. Enter their 1860s house and you glimpse a collection of Egyptian prints — they once lived in Cairo. There's an open-plan feel to the kitchen and a roof terrace where you can sit in summer under a smart green umbrella. Bedrooms are at the top of the house. The twin is tiny but, being at the back, is silent at night; the double has a big wooden bed and an antique armoire.

London

50a Penywern Road

In a grand central London street, a luxurious slice of peace. Past potted pansies and down limestone steps to warm, smiling, Irish Breege, who leads you into a light lower ground-floor space zinging with art and good taste. Off the kitchen is the guest bedroom. Find a huge bed, chrome chairs, subtle lights, white walls splashed with art and through to your own magnificent shower that designer Breege drove with Jack all the way to Paris to claim. More steps up to a lovely garden where statues peep out of bushes and seats beckon. Easy, fun and *so* spoiling — readers are full of praise. *Minimum stay two nights.*

Price	£80. Singles £60.
Rooms	2: 1 double, 1 twin.
Meals	Restaurants nearby.
Closed	Occasionally.
Directions	Tube: Earl's Court 15-minute walk. Nearest car park £25 for 24 hrs. South Kensington 20-minute walk.

Price	£85. Singles £60.
Rooms	1 double.
Meals	Continental breakfast.
Closed	Christmas & New Year.
Directions	Tube: Earl's Court 2-minute walk. Pay and display parking 8.30-6.30 Mon-Sat. Free at all other times in P&D bays and on yellow lines.

	Margaret & Simon de Maré
	6 Oakfield Street,
	Little Chelsea, London SW10 9JB
Tel	020 7352 2970
Mobile	07990 844008
Email	demare@easynet.co.uk
Web	www.athomeinnchelsea.com

	Breege Collins
	50a Penywern Road,
	Earl's Court, London SW5 9SX
Tel	020 7610 4532 (day)
	020 7244 7178 (night)
Fax	020 8568 1273
Email	info@breegecollins.com

Map 4   Entry 287

Map 4   Entry 288

London

26 Hillgate Place

You are in luxurious, bohemian Notting Hill: a movie at the Coronet, a pint at the Windsor Castle, the best Thai at the Churchill and the chic-est shops. Whatever you do, roll back to Hilary's easy-going home for a bit of eastern spice; Indian textiles, old teak dressers, the odd wooden elephant, wildly colourful art (Hilary paints). The bigger double has a Caribbean influence and shares a bathroom up a flight of stairs; the small one is smarter – immaculate, actually – with a sofa and a claw-foot bath. Both rooms come with bathrobes and small fridge, and there are two gardens to look out on, one on a roof.

Price	£70-£95. Singles £60-£75.
Rooms	2: 1 double; 1 double/twin sharing family bath.
Meals	Pubs/restaurants nearby.
Closed	Occasionally.
Directions	Tube: Notting Hill Gate 5-minute walk.

Hilary Dunne
26 Hillgate Place,
Notting Hill Gate,
London W8 7ST
Tel   020 7727 7717
Email   hilary.dunne@virgin.net
Web   www.26hillgateplace.co.uk

Map 4   Entry 289

London

101 Abbotsbury Road

The area is one of London's most desirable and Sunny's family home is opposite the borough's loveliest park, with open-air opera in summer. The whole top floor is generally given over to visitors. Cosy, spotless bedrooms are in gentle yellows and greens, with pale carpets, white duvets, pelmeted windows and a dressing table in the double. The bathroom, marble-tiled and sky-lit, shines. You are well placed for Kensington High Street, Olympia, Notting Hill, Portobello Market, Kensington Gardens, the Albert Hall, Knightsbridge and Piccadilly. Feel free to come and go. *Children over ten welcome.*

Price	£100. Singles from £50.
Rooms	2: 1 double, 1 single, sharing bath.
Meals	Continental breakfast. Pubs/restaurants 5-minute walk.
Closed	Occasionally.
Directions	Tube: Holland Park 7-minute walk. Off-street parking sometimes available.

Sunny Murray
101 Abbotsbury Road,
Holland Park,
London W14 8EP
Tel   020 7602 0179
Mobile   07768 362562
Email   sunny.murray@googlemail.com

Map 4   Entry 290

London

Sterndale Road

This is a mildly eccentric, very welcoming home-from-home for people travelling alone in the capital, and Maggie, who likes fast cars and drives an MG, pretty much gives you the run of the place. Have a sundowner in the garden, bring food home and cook a light meal at night – the cupboards are all labelled so you can find what you want. Spotless bedrooms are super value: nothing too fancy, just fresh flowers, padded headboards, floral curtains, painted wardrobes and trim carpets. There's a sitting room packed with books and TV, or a drawing room upstairs if you want peace and quiet.

Price	£65–£75. Singles £40–£45.
Rooms	5: 1 double, 4 singles, sharing 3 baths. Separate bathrooms by arrangement.
Meals	Continental breakfast. Pubs/restaurants nearby.
Closed	Occasionally.
Directions	Tubes: Hammersmith; Shepherd's Bush.

	Maggie Clarke-Campbell Sterndale Road, Brook Green, London W14 0HX
Tel	020 7602 9768
Fax	020 7603 4751
Email	maggie.cc@virgin.net

Map 4   Entry 291

London

31 Rowan Road

Terrific value for money in Brook Green, and perfect privacy. Vicky's top-floor pied-à-terre is big and airy and delightfully decorated in white, pink and lime-green. Under the eaves are a sofa, a window seat spilling cushions, a big comfy bed and a bathroom with a deep cast-iron bath from which you can gaze out at the birds. A continental breakfast is popped into the fridge the night before. The larger, lower-ground-floor studio, furnished in contemporary style, is equally inviting and has its own wisteria-strewn entrance. There's a garden full of blossom and super restaurants close by.

Price	£60–£85. Extra person £10.
Rooms	2 studios for 2-3: with twin or twin/double & kitchen or kitchenette.
Meals	Continental breakfast. Pubs/restaurants 2 mins.
Closed	Occasionally.
Directions	Tube: Hammersmith. Off-street parking £10 a day.

	Vicky & Edmund Sixsmith 31 Rowan Road, Brook Green, London W6 7DT
Tel	020 8748 0930
Mobile	07966 829359
Email	vickysixsmith@btconnect.com
Web	www.abetterwaytostay.co.uk

Map 4   Entry 292

London

21 Barclay Road

The grand piano is a magnet for conductors and music professors from around the world. Charlotte, who does something unspeakably high-powered by day, happily advises on the best of London. You pretty much get the run of the house: a large sitting room with open fire, two compact but well laid-out bedrooms (quiet for London), waffle bathrobes, a book-filled guest bathroom, a decanter of sherry. Breakfast on homemade muffins, French toast, fresh fruit, even apple fritters, and good coffee – eat on the tree-top terrace in summer. Delightful people, a great city find. *Use of grand piano by arrangement.*

London

8 Parthenia Road

Caroline, an interior designer, mixes the sophistication of the city with the feel of the countryside and her handsome big kitchen is clearly the engine-room of the house. It leads through to a light breakfast room with doors onto a pretty brick garden with chairs and table – hope for fine days. The house is long and thin, Fulham style, and reaches up to a large, sloping-ceilinged bedroom in the eaves that is sunny and bright. A surprisingly quiet place to stay in an accessible part of town, near the King's Road with its antique and designer shops and Chelsea Football ground. *Broadband connection.*

Price	£85. Singles £65.
Rooms	2 doubles sharing bathroom.
Meals	Food & music evenings Thursdays. Restaurants 2-minute walk.
Closed	Occasionally.
Directions	Tube: Fulham Broadway 2-minute walk. Parking free 8pm-9am & all Sunday. 9am-8pm pay & display.

Price	£80-£100. Singles from £75.
Rooms	1 twin/double.
Meals	Continental breakfast. Restaurants nearby.
Closed	Rarely.
Directions	Tube: Parsons Green 4-minute walk. Parking £12.80 per day in street. Bus: no. 22, 2-minute walk.

Charlotte Dexter
21 Barclay Road,
Fulham, London SW6 1EJ
Tel   020 7384 3390
Mobile   07767 420943
Email   info@barclayhouselondon.com
Web   www.barclayhouselondon.com

Caroline & George Docker
8 Parthenia Road,
Fulham,
London SW6 4BD
Tel   020 7384 1165
Fax   020 7371 8819
Email   carolined@angelwings.co.uk

Map 4   Entry 293

Map 4   Entry 294

London

22 Marville Road

Smart railings help a pink rose climb, orange lilies add a touch of colour and breakfast is in the back garden in good weather, with lavender, rose and clematis for company. Tess – the spaniel – and Christine – music lover, traveller, rower – make you feel at home. A generous single on the first floor shares the main bathroom (claw-foot bath, huge shower). The big en suite room in elegant French grey comes with a chaise longue; it was tested and vacated with regret. Treasures from Chrisine's travels, crisp linen, good mattresses... and the famous White Horse at Parson's Green only a five-minute stroll.

Price	£80–£90. Singles from £40.
Rooms	2: 1 twin/double; 1 single with shared bath/shower. Extra single bed.
Meals	Occasional dinner. Pubs nearby.
Closed	Rarely.
Directions	At Fulham Rd junc. with Parson's Green Lane, turn down Kelvedon Rd. Cross Bishop Rd into Homestead Rd; 1st left into Marville Rd.

Christine Drake
22 Marville Road,
Fulham, London SW6 7BD
Tel   020 7381 3205
Mobile   07973 113757
Email   christine.drake@btinternet.com
Web   www.londonguestsathome.com

🕮 ♟ 🐾 🚲

Map 4   Entry 295

London

15 Delaford Street

A pretty Victorian terraced home, unassuming from the front but with space and charm inside. In a tiny, sun-trapping courtyard you can have continental breakfast in good weather – tropical fruits are a favourite; a second miniature garden bursts with life at the back. The bedroom, up a spiral staircase, looks down on it all. Expect perfectly ironed sheets, a quilted throw, books in the alcove, a sunny bathroom and fluffy white towels. The tennis at Queen's is in June and on your doorstep. Tim and Margot – she's from Melbourne – are fun, helpful and happy to pick you up from the nearest tube.

Price	£80. Singles £55.
Rooms	1 double.
Meals	Restaurants nearby.
Closed	Occasionally.
Directions	Tube: West Brompton. Parking free eves/weekends; otherwise pay & display. 74 bus to West End nearby.

Margot & Tim Woods
15 Delaford Street,
Fulham,
London SW6 7LT
Tel   020 7385 9671
Fax   020 7385 9671
Email   woodsmargot@hotmail.co.uk

🕮

Map 4   Entry 296

London

49 Quarrenden Street

A satisfyingly quiet, tree-lined street of late Victorian houses, just a few minutes walk from good shops and restaurants, and a lovely park. Gudrun looks after you well but you can come and go as you please and use the kitchen for tea and coffee when you like. You breakfast (fresh fruit salad, full English) in the dining room overlooking the pretty garden, or outside in good weather. Your large and light bedroom is on the first floor; find creamy yellow walls, good thick curtains, plenty of hanging space and a modern, gleaming bathroom with walk-in shower. Comfortable, good value and close to the tube.

Price	£75.
Rooms	1 double/twin.
Meals	Restaurants/pubs within walking distance.
Closed	Occasionally.

Stop Press
No longer doing B&B

🐦 ✕ 🐈

Map 4   Entry 297

London

33 Barmouth Road

Good value, family-friendly B&B in a smart 1880s terraced house of which only the exterior walls survive. Everything else is new, from the four flights of stairs to the Farrow & Ball paints. Expect neutral colours, a refined elegance, old pine dressers and a bit of helping yourself to things like breakfast. Uncluttered bedrooms at the top have good linen and all mod cons, the kitchen's floors are warm underfoot, there's a pretty Arts and Crafts feel and curtains made by Nessie. She, a fashion designer, and Duncan, a sports editor on a national paper, are most welcoming and full of enthusiasm for their B&B.

Price	From £50. Singles from £35.
Rooms	2: 1 twin/double, 1 double.
Meals	Continental breakfast. Pubs/restaurants nearby.
Closed	Occasionally.
Directions	From A217 at Wandsworth r'bout into Trinity Rd; under bypass & right at lights into Windmill Rd; right at lights into Heathfield Rd; 1st left into Westover Rd; Barmouth Rd 3rd right. Wandsworth station 10-min walk.

	Nessie & Duncan Maclay
	33 Barmouth Road,
	Wandsworth Common,
	London SW18 2DT
Tel	020 8877 0331
Mobile	07885 379136
Email	beds@maclayworld.com
Web	www.maclayworld.com

🐦 ✕ 🚃 🍷 🚲

Map 4   Entry 298

London

The Coach House

A rare privacy: you have your own coach house, separated from the Notts' home by a stylish terracotta-potted courtyard with Indian sandstone paving and various fruit trees (peach, pear, nectarine). Breakfast in your own sunny kitchen, or let Meena treat you to an all-organic full English in hers (she makes fine porridge, too). The big main attic bedroom has toile de Jouy bedcovers, cream curtains, rugs on dark polished floors; the brick-walled ground-floor twin is pleasant, light and airy, and both look over the peaceful garden. *Minimum stay three nights; two nights in Jan/Feb.*

Price	£75–£165.
Rooms	Coach House for 2–5 (1 family room; 1 twin with separate shower). Same-party bookings only.
Meals	Pub/restaurant 200 yds.
Closed	Occasionally.
Directions	From r'bout on south side of Wandsworth Bridge, south down Trinity Rd on A214. At 3rd set of lights, 1.7 miles on, left into Upper Tooting Park. 4th left into Marius Rd, then 3rd left.

Meena & Harley Nott
The Coach House,
2 Tunley Road, Balham,
London SW17 7QJ

Tel	020 8772 1939
Fax	08701 334957
Email	coachhouse@chslondon.com
Web	www.coachhouse.chslondon.com

Map 4   Entry 299

London

108 Streathbourne Road

It's a handsome house in a conservation area that manages to be both elegant and cosy. The cream-coloured double bedroom has an armchair, a writing desk, pretty curtains and a big, comfy walnut bed; the twin is light and airy. The dining room overlooks a secluded terrace and garden and there are newspapers at breakfast. Dine in – David, who works in the wine trade, always puts a bottle on the table – or eat out at one of the trendy new restaurants in Balham. A friendly city base on a quiet, tree-lined street – maximum comfort and good value for London. Delightful. *Minimum stay two nights.*

Price	£80–£90. Singles £65–£75.
Rooms	2: 1 double with separate bath; 1 twin sharing bath (let to same party only).
Meals	Dinner £27.50. Restaurants 5-minute walk.
Closed	Occasionally.
Directions	Tube: Tooting Bec 7-minute walk. Free parking weekends, otherwise meters or £6 daily.

Mary & David Hodges
108 Streathbourne Road,
Balham,
London SW17 8QY

Tel	020 8767 6931
Fax	020 8672 8839
Email	mary.hodges@virgin.net
Web	www.streathbourneroad.com

Map 4   Entry 300

London

20 St Philip Street

Come for peace and undemanding luxury: the 1890 Victorian cottage with delightful courtyard garden protects you from the frenzy of city life. You breakfast in the dining room on freshly squeezed juice, homemade bread and jams, organic full English; across the hall is the sitting room, with gilt-framed mirrors, wooden blinds, plump-cushioned sofas and a piano you are welcome to play. Upstairs is a bright and restful bedroom with pretty linen and a cloud of goose down to snuggle into. Your bathroom next door is fabulous with its porthole windows and huge mirror. Nothing has been overlooked.

Price	£95. Singles £65.
Rooms	1 double with separate bath & shower.
Meals	Restaurants 200 yds.
Closed	Occasionally.
Directions	Nearby r'way stations (6-min ride Waterloo, 3-min ride Victoria). Or 137 & 452 bus (Sloane Sq) & 156 (Vauxhall) tubes 10 mins. Parking limited to 4 hrs (£1.80 per hr) or £10 day ticket, 9.30-5.30 Mon-Fri. Otherwise free.

Barbara Graham
20 St Philip Street,
Battersea,
London SW8 3SL
Tel   020 7498 9967
Email   stay@bed-breakfast-battersea.co.uk
Web   www.bed-breakfast-battersea.co.uk

Map 4   Entry 301

London

39 Telford Avenue

A very pretty Edwardian home, a family enclave, with logs piled high at the front door and a fire in the hall on cold afternoons. Warm interiors come with stripped floors, bright colours, fresh flowers and a piano in the dining room. There's a sofa in the homely double bedroom, a wall of good books and an electric pink bathroom two paces across the landing. Breakfast is a treat: homemade bread and yogurt, the full cooked works, a good selection of teas. Richard, an architect, loves his cricket; prints of Lords hang on the walls. You can be in Victoria in 15 minutes, and there's off-street parking, too.

Price	£60. Singles £30.
Rooms	2: 1 twin/double, 1 single each with separate bath.
Meals	Restaurants 2-minute walk.
Closed	Occasionally.
Directions	Train: Streatham Hill (to Victoria) 5-minute walk. Or ring on arrival at Clapham South tube (Northern line) & you will be collected.

Katharine & Richard
Wolstenholme
39 Telford Avenue,
Streatham Hill,
London SW2 4XL
Tel   020 8674 4343
Email   rwolstenholme@aol.com

Map 4   Entry 302

London

Bowling Hall

Once an Irish drinking den, now a wonderland of cool lines and soothing colours. The mix of old and new is delicious: rugs on limestone tiles, a satinwood chest, old prints – Peter has renovated with style. Stand at the front door and look through the house: 160-feet deep, the view floats seamlessly through each room. On the walls, dazzling art, much of it Katherine's. You stay in a lovely self-contained apartment at the front of the house – maple floors, linen curtains, light colours – opening onto an Indian courtyard garden stuffed with lavender and bamboo, and you are walking distance to both Tates!

Price	£90. Singles £50.
Rooms	Apartment with 1 double, 1 single, sitting room & kitchenette.
Meals	Continental breakfast. Pubs/restaurants 5-minute walk.
Closed	Occasionally.
Directions	Details on booking. Near underground & bus routes.

Peter Camp & Katherine Virgils
Bowling Hall,
346 Kennington Road,
London SE11 4LD

Tel	020 7840 0454
Fax	020 7840 0454
Email	bowlinghall@freenet.co.uk

Map 4   Entry 303

London

24 Fox Hill

This part of London is full of sky, trees and wildlife; Pissarro captured on canvas the view up the hill in 1870 (the painting is in the National Gallery). There's good stuff everywhere – things hang off walls and peep over the tops of dressers; bedrooms are stunning, with antiques, textiles, paintings and big, firm beds. Sue, a graduate from Chelsea Art College, employs humour and intelligence to put guests at ease and has created a special garden, too. Tim often helps with breakfasts. Frogs sing at night, woodpeckers wake you in the morning, in this lofty, peaceful retreat. *Victoria is 20 minutes by train.*

Price	£85. Singles £50.
Rooms	3: 1 twin/double; 1 double, 1 twin sharing shower.
Meals	Dinner £30-£35. Pubs/restaurants 5-minute walk.
Closed	Rarely.
Directions	Train: Crystal Palace (7-min. walk). Collection possible. Good buses to West End & Westminster.

Sue & Tim Haigh
24 Fox Hill,
Crystal Palace,
London SE19 2XE

Tel	020 8768 0059
Email	suehaigh@hotmail.co.uk
Web	www.foxhill-bandb.co.uk

Map 4   Entry 304

London

113 Pepys Road

Anne and Tim, full of life, well-travelled, live on the side of a hill above a carpet of London lights. Hats on the hat stand, batiks on the walls, orchids... the place sparkles. The downstairs room has plush carpets, a huge bed, bamboo blinds; pad into your gorgeous marble bathroom kimono-clad. Upstairs, two more lovely rooms, one in country-house style, the other in elegant yellow. Anne also cooks brilliantly and will do you a steaming hot oriental cooked breakfast or the 'full English'. The garden has two splendid magnolias and it's a short walk downhill to buses, tubes and trains. Special.

Price	£90-£100. Singles from £60.
Rooms	3: 1 double, 1 twin/double; 1 twin with separate bath.
Meals	Dinner £30. BYO. Restaurant 0.5 miles.
Closed	Rarely.
Directions	Directions on booking.

Anne & Tim Marten
113 Pepys Road,
New Cross,
London SE14 5SE

Tel	020 7639 1060
Fax	020 7639 8780
Email	annemarten@pepysroad.com
Web	www.pepysroad.com

Map 4   Entry 305

London

16 St Alfege Passage

The approach is along the passage between the Hawksmoor church and its graveyard, away from the village's hubbub. At the end of the lane is a 'cottage' set about with greenery, lamp posts and benches. Inside, a cup of tea and flapjack await you in the eccentrically furnished (stuffed cat on dentist chair, huge parasol) sitting room. Bedrooms are cosy and colourful, with double beds (not huge) that positively encourage intimacy. Breakfast is in the basement, another engagingly furnished room awash with character. Robert, an actor, is easy, funny, chatty – and has created an unusual and attractive place.

Price	From £75. Singles from £50.
Rooms	3: 1 four-poster, 1 double, 1 single.
Meals	Pubs/restaurants 2-minute walk.
Closed	Rarely.
Directions	3-minute walk from Greenwich train & Docklands Light Railway station or Cutty Sark DLR station. Parking free from 5pm (6pm Sundays) to 9am.

Nicholas Mesure & Robert Gray
16 St Alfege Passage,
Greenwich,
London SE10 9JS

Tel	020 8853 4337
Email	info@st-alfeges.co.uk
Web	www.st-alfeges.co.uk

Map 4   Entry 306

London

No 74

Hop on board for an experience not to be missed – but hey, if you do, there'll probably be two more not far behind. Enter a long sitting room where two rows of sofas dressed in velveteen tartan await – their backs artily daubed with marker pen. Climb the precipitous staircase to the top floor and prepare to be amazed: wraparound windows have views straight onto a hedge and dead branches. You may be seated next to fellow guests but try not to start up a convo: it's generally regarded as suspicious. Food is not on offer although the odd apple core may occasionally roll past. Pay up front. This is B&B without the B or the B.

Price	No notes, change not given.
Rooms	2: sleeps 108 with some standing room.
Meals	Second-hand chewing gum on seat in front.
Closed	Limited Sunday service.
Directions	On request.

Buster Knightsbridge
No 74,
The Depot, Upper Tooting,
London HP0 0NN

Tel	000 007 400
Email	hopon@topdeck.bus
Web	www.convo-buster-.tk.et

Map 10   Entry 307

Norfolk

Bagthorpe Hall

Among the wholesomeness of Norfolk – all birdwatching, boats, salt marshes and crab nets – beats the heart of this dynamic household. Tid is a pioneer of organic farming and good things from his 700 acres wing their way monthly to the farmers' market. Gina's passions are music, dance and gardens and she organises open days and concerts for charity. Theirs is a large, elegant house with a mural in the hall chronicling their family life. It's fascinating, and beautiful. Wonderful colours, good beds, generous curtains and excellent food – maybe fresh raspberries for breakfast.

Price	£65-£75. Singles £40.
Rooms	3: 1 double; 1 double with separate shower, 1 twin with separate bath.
Meals	Dinner £20-£25; in winter only. Pubs/restaurants 2 miles.
Closed	Rarely.
Directions	From King's Lynn for A148 to Fakenham. Left at East Rudham by Cat & Fiddle pub. 3.5 miles to Bagthorpe. Past farm on left, wood on right, white gates set back from trees. At top of drive.

Gina Morton
Bagthorpe Hall,
Bagthorpe, King's Lynn,
Norfolk PE31 6QY

Tel	01485 578528
Fax	01485 578151
Email	dgmorton@hotmail.com
Web	www.bagthorpehall.co.uk

Map 10   Entry 308

Norfolk

Glebe Farmhouse

After a wild walk on Holkham Beach, return to a house filled with warmth and colour. Life revolves around the big, square farmhouse kitchen: a painted dresser brimming with bright china, well-cushioned sofas, books, paintings, gentle fabrics, wooden floors and French windows to the garden. Mary, a painter, designer and thoughtful host, gives you a delicious breakfast here, or on the terrace in summer. Bedrooms are peaceful and cosy, with views to garden or fields and woodland. Mary and Jeremy have been doing B&B since renovating their traditional Norfolk farmhouse back in 1991.

Price	£65. Singles £40.
Rooms	2: 1 double, 1 twin/double. Extra fold-up bed for child.
Meals	Pub 5-minute walk.
Closed	Rarely.
Directions	A148 King's Lynn to Cromer, north onto B1355 just west of Fakenham. 6.5 miles to North Creake. Right after red phone box, then 300 yds. On right.

Mary & Jeremy Brettingham Smith
Glebe Farmhouse,
Wells Road, North Creake,
Fakenham, Norfolk NR21 9LG
Tel 01328 730133
Mobile 07818 041555
Email enquiries@glebe-farmhouse.co.uk
Web www.glebe-farmhouse.co.uk

Map 10 Entry 309

Norfolk

Fern Cottage

An elegant Georgian house a short walk from the bustling harbour and shops. Linda and Richard have thought of everything to make you happy. Peaceful bedrooms look onto the courtyard and have large beds, dear little fireplaces, good linen and modern art; bathrooms are light and fresh. A traditional English breakfast sets you up for walks, fishing, golfing and cycling (there's bike storage), a steam train to Walsingham or a day on the beach in your very own candy-striped hut. Birdwatchers will love it here, especially in autumn when the pink-footed geese arrive. *Min. stay two nights. Beach hut £15.*

Price	£70. Singles £55.
Rooms	2: 1 double; 1 double with separate bath.
Meals	Pubs/restaurants 2-5 minute walk.
Closed	Rarely.
Directions	B1105 (Fakenham); right into Polka Rd; over Station Rd to top of Standard Rd. Just after Cobblers Guest House, small alleyway. Gate on right leads to blue front door. Off street parking at rear.

Linda & Richard Pearce
Fern Cottage, Standard Road,
Wells next the Sea,
Norfolk NR23 1JU
Tel 01328 710306
Fax 01328 710874
Email enquiries@ferncottage.co.uk
Web www.ferncottage.co.uk

Map 10 Entry 310

Norfolk

The Old Vicarage

Norfolk at its best in this fine Georgian vicarage....huge skies, views that stretch forever, absolute peace. A curved staircase springs from the flagstoned inner hall lit by a cupola high above. Two traditional bedrooms (one with a view to Walsingham) have good beds and fine furniture, pretty china, fresh flowers. Enjoy hearty, home-produced breakfast in the sunlit dining room; wander through French windows to the garden. Sandy beaches, marsh walks and the seal colony are near; on your return a log fire and the lure of Rosie's scrumptious candlelit dinner will tempt you to stay put. *French spoken.*

Norfolk

Holly Lodge

The mock-medieval house and B&B gleams – from the tooled leather dining chairs to the pewter collection to the suit of armour, 'Dudley', at the foot of the stair. The three snug guest cottages flourish smart iron bedsteads and rugs on stone tiles, neat little shower rooms and tapestry-seat chairs, books, music, TV. Make the most of the Mediterranean garden with pond and decking in summer, the handsome conservatory and the utter peace. Your hosts are delightful – Jeremy who cooks three-course meals enthusiastically, ethically and with panache, and Canadian-raised Gill.

Price	From £55. Ask for singles' rates.
Rooms	2: 1 twin/double; 1 double with separate bath.
Meals	Dinner, 2-3 courses, £18-£22. BYO. Pub 2 miles.
Closed	Christmas & New Year.
Directions	A148 Fakenham to Cromer for 6 miles. Left at Crawfish Inn into Hindringham, down hill & left before church, into Blacksmith's Lane. Follow lane, bear right, house on left at top of hill; flint-wall entrances.

	Rosie & Robin Waters
	The Old Vicarage,
	Blacksmith's Lane,
	Hindringham,
	Norfolk NR21 0QA
Tel	01328 878223
Fax	01328 878223
Email	watersrobin@hotmail.com

Map 10   Entry 311

Price	£80-£120. Singles from £60-£100.
Rooms	3 cottages for 2.
Meals	Dinner, 3 courses with wine, £17.50. Pubs/restaurants 1 mile.
Closed	January.
Directions	From Fakenham A148, Fakenham-Cromer road; 6 miles; left at Crawfish pub. Signs to Thursford Collection, past village green; 2nd drive on left.

	Jeremy Bolam
	Holly Lodge,
	Thursford Green,
	Norfolk NR21 0AS
Tel	01328 878465
Fax	01328 878465
Email	info@hollylodgeguesthouse.co.uk
Web	www.hollylodgeguesthouse.co.uk

Map 10   Entry 312

Norfolk

Burgh Parva Hall

Sunlight bathes the Norfolk longhouse on summer afternoons; the welcome from the Heals is as warm. The listed house is all that remains of the old village of Burgh Parva, deserted after the Great Plague. It's a handsome house and warmly inviting... old furniture, rugs, books, pictures and Magnet the terrier-daschund. Large guest bedrooms face the sunsets and the garden annexe makes a sweet hideaway. Breakfast eggs are from the garden hens, vegetables are home-grown, fish comes fresh from Holt and the game may have been shot by William. Settle down by the fire and tuck in.

Price	£55-£75. Singles from £35.
Rooms	3: 1 double, 1 twin; 1 twin with separate bath.
Meals	Dinner £22. Pub/restaurant 4 miles.
Closed	Rarely.
Directions	Fakenham A148 for Cromer. At Thursford B1354 for Aylsham. Just before Melton, speed bumps, left immed. before bus shelter; 1st house on right after farmyard.

Judy & William Heal
Burgh Parva Hall,
Melton Constable,
Norfolk NR24 2PU
Tel   01263 862569
Email   judyheal@dsl.pipex.com

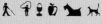

Map 10   Entry 313

Norfolk

Incleborough House

A listed, mellow-bricked 17th-century house which faces a pretty, bird-filled, walled garden. Nick and Barbara have done a terrific restoration job and give you sumptuous bedrooms with huge beds, beautiful linen, super views, shining contemporary bathrooms, chocolates and wine. There's an elegant sitting room for tea and cakes, with an open fire and books to read. Breakfast at white linen-topped tables in the conservatory is a treat – try slow baked marmalade ham with poached eggs. You are only 300 yards from the sea and the local walks are fabulous. *Min. two nights at weekends; check for late availability.*

Price	£140-£150. Singles £105-£112.50.
Rooms	3: 2 doubles, 1 twin/double.
Meals	Occasional dinner, with wine, £22.50. Restaurant 150 yds.
Closed	Never.
Directions	From Sheringham head for Cromer. In East Runton, 1st right into Felbrigg Road. House 200 yds on left behind oak trees.

Nick & Barbara Davies
Incleborough House,
Lower Common, East Runton,
Cromer, Norfolk NR27 9PG
Tel   01263 515939
Mobile 07738 241672
Email   enquiries@incleboroughhouse.co.uk
Web   www.incleboroughhouse.co.uk

Map 10   Entry 314

Norfolk

Stable Cottage

In a privately owned village stands one of Norfolk's finest Elizabethan houses, Heydon Hall. In the Dutch-gabled stable block, fronted by Cromwell's Oak (a frequent visitor, he once scaled it while escaping a bull!), is this cottage – fresh, sunny and enchanting. Each room is touched by Sarah's warm personality and love of country things; seagrass floors and crisp linen, toile de Jouy walls and pretty china. Bedrooms are cottagey and immaculate, there are fresh fabrics, baskets of toiletries in the bathrooms, delicious food on your plate. All this in a serene parkland setting: a rare treat.

Price	£80. Singles £45.
Rooms	2 twins/doubles.
Meals	Dinner, 3 courses, from £18. BYO. Pub 1 mile.
Closed	Christmas.
Directions	From Norwich, B1149 for 10 miles. 2nd left after bridge, for Heydon. 1.5 miles, right into village, over cattle grid, into park. Pass Hall on left, cottage in front of you; left over cattle grid and into stable yard.

Sarah Bulwer-Long
Stable Cottage,
Heydon Hall,
Heydon,
Norfolk NR11 6RE

Tel	01263 587343
Mobile	07780 998742

Map 10   Entry 315

Norfolk

Highfield Farm

Elizabeth is capable and funny – a winning combination. She got the local church bells ringing again after years of silence: tractor grease did the trick. Reached by a long lane and blissfully quiet, this is a working family farm and the house is elegant inside – antiques, silver, porcelain and paintings. After a candlelit dinner, retire to floral sofas, games and good books – there are many. Bedrooms are a generous size, with tall sash windows, huge bath towels, views. Breakfasts are worth getting up for – eggs from organic hens, home fruits in season – and there may be Elizabeth's lemon cake for tea. Wonderful.

Price	£60-£70. Singles in high season, £40.
Rooms	2: 1 twin; 1 double with separate bath.
Meals	Dinner, 3 courses, £20 (winter only). Pub 2.5 miles.
Closed	Christmas & New Year.
Directions	From Fakenham B1146 for East Dereham. After 2 miles, left to Gt. Ryburgh. In village, 2nd left up Highfield Lane opp. pink cottage & on for 0.5 miles; house on right.

Elizabeth Savory
Highfield Farm,
Great Ryburgh, Fakenham,
Norfolk NR21 7AL

Tel	01328 829249
Fax	01328 829422
Web	www.broadland.com/highfield.html

Map 10   Entry 316

Norfolk

Lower Farm

This house reflects its farming owners – natural, laid-back, delightful. Enter a flagstoned hall with wooden settle, rosewood tallboy and pine doors stripped down by Amanda. The drawing room is shared but there are sofas in the bedrooms if you prefer privacy. These are more homely than lavish: two vast and high-ceilinged with good views from long windows, and the twin at the end of a long corridor. The garden is lovely and there are dogs and horses galore (stabling available); the walls bear the proof of success at point-to-points and shows. Breakfasts are ample.

Price	£60. Singles £35.
Rooms	3: 2 doubles; 1 twin with separate bath/shower.
Meals	Pub/restaurant 800 yds.
Closed	Rarely.
Directions	From King's Lynn, A148 for Cromer. 3 miles after Hillington, 2nd of 2 turnings right to Harpley (no signpost) opp. Houghton Hall sign. 200 yds on; over x-roads, house 400 yds on left.

Amanda Case
Lower Farm,
Harpley,
King's Lynn,
Norfolk PE31 6TU
Tel 01485 520240
Fax 01485 520240

Map 10 Entry 317

Norfolk

Manor House Farm

In the stable wing of this traditional Norfolk farmhouse, surrounded by four acres of lovingly tended gardens, are two beautiful fresh rooms with wildly comfortable beds and their own sitting room; antiques, colourful rugs and fresh flowers. Breakfast, served in the elegant dining room of the main house, is home grown and delicious: fruit, eggs from the Welsummer hens, bacon and sausages from their own happy pigs. Libby and Robin have won conservation awards for the farm – and the North Norfolk coast is 20 minutes away. *Gardens open for NGS. Children over ten welcome.*

Price	£75–£80. Singles £40–£50.
Rooms	2: 1 double, 1 twin/double.
Meals	Pub 1.5 miles.
Closed	Rarely.
Directions	A1065 Swaffham-Fakenham road. 6 miles on, through Weasenham. After 1 mile, right for Wellingham. House on left, next to church.

Elisabeth Ellis
Manor House Farm,
Wellingham, Fakenham,
King's Lynn, Norfolk PE32 2TH
Tel 01328 838227
Fax 01328 838348
Web www.manor-house-farm.co.uk

Map 10 Entry 318

Norfolk

Litcham Hall

For the whole of the 19th century this was Litcham's doctor's house; the red-brick Hall is still at the centre of the community. The big-windowed guest bedrooms look onto the stunning gardens with yew hedges, a lily pond and herbaceous borders. This is a thoroughly English home with elegant proportions – the hall, drawing room and dining room are gracious and beautifully furnished. The hens lay the breakfast eggs, the garden fills the table with soft fruit in season and John and Hermione are friendly and most helpful. There's a sitting room for guests. *Children & dogs by arrangement.*

Price	£60-£80. Singles by arrangement.
Rooms	3: 1 double, 1 twin; 1 twin with separate bath.
Meals	Occasional dinner, £25. Pub/restaurant 3 miles.
Closed	Christmas.
Directions	From Swaffham, A1065 north for 5 miles, then right to Litcham on B1145. House on left on entering village. Georgian red-brick with stone balls on gatepost.

John & Hermione Birkbeck
Litcham Hall,
Litcham,
King's Lynn,
Norfolk PE32 2QQ
Tel   01328 701389
Fax   01328 701164

Map 10   Entry 319

Norfolk

Kesmark House

Sheena and James continue to conserve their beautiful Georgian village house and garden. In the French bedroom – chintz, old armoire, carved bed – you lie in stylish comfort; the twin room is beamed, freshly decorated and very private. Delicious breakfast is served in the dining room, striking with old pamment floor and wood-burner; linger in comfort over the papers. The atmosphere is informal, your hosts relaxed. The listed house sits in two acres and you may picnic in the secluded top garden. Two traditional pubs in the village and the wonderful Norfolk coast an easy drive. *Stable Cottage used for overflow guests.*

Price	From £60. Singles £35.
Rooms	2: 1 double; 1 twin with separate bath.
Meals	Pub 5 minute-walk.
Closed	Christmas.
Directions	B1147 north of Dereham to Swanton Morley. There, 500 yds after Angel Pub, house on right with white railings.

Sheena & James Willis
Kesmark House,
Swanton Morley,
Dereham, Norfolk NR20 4PP
Tel   01362 637663
Email   stay@kesmarkhouse.co.uk
Web   www.kesmarkhouse.co.uk

Map 10   Entry 320

Norfolk

College Farm

Lavender has done B&B for years and looks after her stupendous listed house single-handedly. Over afternoon tea, she tells colourful stories of the house and her family's local history: from 1349 until the Dissolution of the Monasteries the house was a college of priests and there's stunning Jacobean panelling in the dining room. Bedrooms are big and lived-in, two of the bathrooms are tiny, all have lovely views over the garden with its pingos (ice age ponds). Come for history and architecture and friendly Lavender, and breakfast from the farm shop down the road. *Children over seven welcome.*

Price	From £60. Singles £30.
Rooms	3: 1 twin, 1 twin/double; 1 double with separate bath. Extra shower available.
Meals	Afternoon tea included. Pub 1 mile.
Closed	Rarely.
Directions	From Thetford, A1075 north for Watton. After 9 miles, left to Thompson at 'Light Vehicles Only' sign. After 0.5 miles, 2nd left at red postbox on corner. Left again, house at end.

Lavender Garnier
College Farm,
Thompson, Thetford,
Norfolk IP24 1QG

Tel	01953 483318
Fax	01953 483318
Email	collegefarm83@amserve.net

Map 10 Entry 321

Norfolk

The Buttery

At the end of a farm track, a little treasure: a thatch-and-flint octagonal dairy house just for you. Built on the Georgian and listed Berry Hall Estate, it has been perfectly restored by the best local craftsmen and is as neat as a new pin. You get a little kitchen and a fridge that Deborah stocks with delicious things for a full breakfast, a terracotta-tiled sitting room and a luxurious sofabed, a romantic mezzanine bedroom reached by a steep wooden stair, a jacuzzi bath and a sun terrace. Surrounded by birds, deer, sheep and peace, you may walk from the door into parkland and woods.

Price	£75-£90.
Rooms	Cottage with 1 double, sitting room & kitchenette.
Meals	Pub 10-minute walk.
Closed	Rarely.
Directions	From A47 Barnham Broom/Weston Longville x-roads, south towards Barnham Broom. After 150 yds, 1st farm track on right. Left at T-junc., left again, house on left.

Deborah Meynell
The Buttery,
Berry Hall, Honingham, Norwich,
Norfolk NR9 5AX

Tel	01603 880541
Fax	01603 880887
Email	thebuttery@paston.co.uk

Map 10 Entry 322

Norfolk

Sallowfield Cottage

In the drawing room, gorgeous prints and paintings, unusual furniture and decorative lamps: Caroline's cottage is so crammed with family treasures it takes time to absorb the splendour. One bedroom, not huge but handsome, has a Regency-style canopied bed and decoration to suit the house (1850); the attic room is large and lovely but there are steep stairs. Drift into the fascinating garden to find hedged rooms and a jungly pond that slinks between the trees. Caroline – and pets – loves having guests and if you have friends living locally she can do lunch or dinner for up to ten. *Children over nine welcome.*

Price	From £55. Singles £35.
Rooms	3: 1 double; 1 double with separate bath, 1 single with separate shower.
Meals	Lunch £10. Dinner from £20. Pub 2 miles.
Closed	Christmas & New Year.
Directions	A11 Attleborough-Wymondham. Take Spooner Row sign. Over x-roads beside Three Boars pub. 1 mile; left at T-junc. to Wymondham for 1 mile. Look for rusty barrel on left, turn into farm track.

	Caroline Musker Sallowfield Cottage, Wattlefield, Wymondham, Norfolk NR18 9PA
Tel	01953 605086
Mobile	07778 316616
Email	caroline.musker@tesco.net
Web	www.sallowfieldcottage.co.uk

Map 10   Entry 323

Norfolk

Washingford House

Tall octagonal chimney stacks and a Georgian façade give the house a stately air. In fact, it's the friendliest of places to stay: Paris and Nigel love entertaining and give you a delicious breakfast. The house, originally Tudor, is a delightful mix of old and new. Large light-filled bedrooms have loads of good books and views over the four-acre garden, a favourite haunt for local birds. Beyond, sheep graze equably on acres of green. Bergh Apton is a conservation village seven miles from Norwich and you are in the heart of it. *Children over 12 welcome.*

Price	£70. Singles £40.
Rooms	2: 1 twin; 1 single with separate bath.
Meals	Occasional dinner with wine, £15-£25. Packed lunch £4.50. Pubs/restaurants 4-6 miles.
Closed	Rarely.
Directions	A146 from Norwich to Lowestoft for 4 miles. Right after Gull Pub, signed Slade Lane. First left, then left at T-junc for 1 mile. Straight over x-roads; house on left past post office.

	Paris & Nigel Back Washingford House, Cookes Road, Bergh Apton, Norwich, Norfolk NR15 1AA
Tel	01508 550924
Mobile	07900 683617
Email	parisb@waitrose.com

Map 10   Entry 324

Norfolk

Sloley Hall

A grand and gracious yellow-brick Georgian house with formal gardens and tree-studded parkland – only the swishing-tailed horses are missing. Of course there are flagstoned floors, Persian rugs, gleaming circular tables with vases of garden-grown flowers but your hosts aren't snooty – Barbara was married here and is charmingly easy-going and helpful. A huge light-flooded dining room is perfect for breakfast; the drawing room is comfy but uncluttered in pinks, with a marble fireplace and long views. Bedrooms are large and elegant with room for seats, and bathrooms warm and generous.

Price	£60–£80. Singles from £40.
Rooms	3: 1 double; 1 double with separate bath; 1 twin with separate shower. Extra child bed available.
Meals	Pub/restaurant 2-4 miles.
Closed	Rarely.
Directions	From Norwich ring road, B1150 through Coltishall/Scottow. Right after Three Horseshoes pub (byway to Upper St); across staggered junc., 1st drive on right.

Mrs Barbara Gorton
Sloley Hall,
Norwich,
Norfolk NR12 8HA
Tel   01692 538582
Mobile   07748 152079
Email   babsgorton@hotmail.com
Web   www.sloleyhall.com

Map 10   Entry 325

Norfolk

The Old Rectory

Conservation farmland all around; acres of wild heathland busy with woodpeckers and owls; the coast two miles away. Life in the handsome 17th-century rectory revolves around the great kitchen and the draw of the Aga is irresistible on bread-baking days: Fiona loves to cook and food is seasonal and good. Comfortable bedrooms have *objets* from diplomatic postings, and the larger double has armchairs so you can settle in with a good book. Super views, three friendly dogs, a drawing room to share, masses of space and a family buzz when the teenagers come home.

Price	From £50. Singles £35.
Rooms	2: 1 twin/double; 1 double sharing bath & shower.
Meals	Dinner from £15. Pubs 2 miles.
Closed	Rarely.
Directions	From Norwich A1151 for Stalham. Just before Stalham, left to Happisburgh. Left at T-junc; 3 miles; 2nd left after E. Ruston church, signed by-way to Foxhill. Right at x-roads; 1 mile on right.

Peter & Fiona Black
The Old Rectory,
Ridlington,
Norfolk NR28 9NZ
Tel   01692 650247
Email   blacks7@email.com
Web   www.oldrectory.northnorfolk.co.uk

Map 10   Entry 326

Norfolk

Manor Farmhouse

A family buzz and candlelight in the farmhouse where you eat, peace in the 17th-century barn where you stay. All rooms lead off its charming, stylish, vaulted sitting room with cosy winter fire. You have a chunky four-poster and a tiny en suite shower on the ground floor, then two narrow stairs to two bedrooms upstairs – small, quirky, fun, with a tucked-up-in-the-roof feel. Come for a sunny courtyard garden, billiards in the stable, fresh flowers, lovely hosts, gorgeous food – and you may come and go as you please. Great value, a perfect rural retreat. *Children over seven welcome.*

Price	From £50. Singles by arrangement.
Rooms	3: 1 double, 1 twin/double, 1 four-poster.
Meals	Dinner, 3 courses, £16. BYO. Pubs 1 mile.
Closed	Christmas & New Year.
Directions	From Norwich, A1151/A149 almost to Stalham. Left for Walcott. At T-junc. left again. 1 mile on, right for H'burgh. Next T-junc., right. Next T-junc., left. Road bends right, look for house sign by fence.

	David & Rosie Eldridge
	Manor Farmhouse,
	Happisburgh,
	Norfolk NR12 0SA
Tel	01692 651262
Fax	01692 650220
Email	manorathappisburgh@hotmail.com
Web	www.northnorfolk.co.uk/manorbarn

Map 10   Entry 327

Norfolk

Manor House

Sally looks after you beautifully in this elegant house on the edge of Halvergate marshes. Excellent walking – the Weavers Way runs past the farmhouse door – and there is good birdwatching; spot pink-footed geese in winter. Your sitting room is an open landing outside the bedroom with comfortable chairs, TV, books, guides and fresh flowers. Bedrooms are traditional and spotless with soft colours, splashes of colour from cushions and curtains and touches of luxury; mattresses are firm, bathrooms sparkle. Breakfast bacon and sausages are from the farm shop – wonderful – and jams and marmalades are homemade.

Price	£70–£80. Singles £40.
Rooms	2: 1 double with separate bath; 1 twin sharing bath (let to same party only).
Meals	Packed lunch £6.50. Pub 3 miles.
Closed	Christmas & New Year.
Directions	A47 towards Great Yarmouth. After Acle, right signed Halvergate. Into village, past Red Lion pub on right, take 3rd right signed Tunstall only. After 0.5 miles, farmhouse on left before the ruined church.

	Sally More
	Manor House,
	Tunstall, Halvergate, Norwich,
	Norfolk NR13 3PS
Tel	01493 700279
Fax	01493 700279
Email	smore@fsmail.net
Web	www.manorhousenorfolk.co.uk

Map 10   Entry 328

Norfolk

The Old Rectory

Soft pale brick, striking ogee arched windows, curtains of wisteria and acres of garden. This Victorian rectory is as handsome out as in. High-ceilinged rooms are flooded with light, furnished with a comfy contemporary and traditional mix and Lucy's paintings. Large bedrooms have pale colours and Portuguese embroidered bedspreads. Pick your spot in the garden, perhaps the bench by the pond or the vine-covered pergola, as John and Lucy prepare dinner. Fruit and vegetables from the garden, beef from their own herd, homemade bread: great food in a rural oasis.

Price	From £75. Singles £50.
Rooms	3: 1 double, 1 twin/double, 1 twin.
Meals	Dinner, 3 courses, from £25. Pub 2.5 miles.
Closed	Rarely.
Directions	A143 Harleston bypass to Beccles/Yarmouth; 3rd left after 2nd r'bout; up Station Rd; right at T-junc; right at x-roads opp. pillar box up School Rd. Left up driveway just before T-junc.

Lucy & John Hildreth
The Old Rectory,
Alburgh, Harleston,
Norfolk IP20 0BW

Tel   01986 788408
Fax   01986 788192
Email   lucy@alburgholdrectory.com
Web   www.alburgholdrectory.com

Map 10   Entry 329

Norfolk

Rushall House

Blue-shelled eggs for breakfast, homemade cake for tea. Plenty to delight eyes and tummy at this comfortable Victorian rectory. High rooms are classically decorated with a contemporary touch, airy bedrooms have pale walls, rich fabrics, crisp bed linen and simple but choice furniture; radios and books are pleasing touches. Sink into the sitting room's sofa in front of a crackling fire. Walk off breakfast – a feast of local produce – around the garden, or cycle, antiques browse, birdwatch... children will love collecting eggs from the hens. Jane and Martin are relaxed but efficient hosts.

Price	From £65. Singles £40.
Rooms	3: 1 double; 1 double, 1 twin, sharing bath/shower.
Meals	Dinner £20. BYO. Pubs/restaurants 0.5-3 miles.
Closed	Rarely.
Directions	Turn off A140 at r'bout to Dickleburgh; right at village store. After two miles pass Lakes Rd & Vaunces Lane, on right. Shortly after z-bend sign, house on right.

Martin Hubner & Jane Gardiner
Rushall House,
Dickleburgh Road, Rushall, Diss,
Norfolk IP21 4RX

Tel   01379 741557
Fax   01379 740148
Email   janegardineruk@aol.com
Web   www.rushallhouse.co.uk

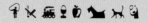

Map 10   Entry 330

Norfolk

Le Grys Barn

Light pours into this 17th-century threshing barn – a jewel of a conversion in peaceful Norfolk. Julie lived in Hong Kong and her house glows with warmth, colour and oriental touches. Glass-topped tables increase the sense of space, Persian carpets beautify beech floors, golden buddhas rest in quiet corners. Across a courtyard, two very private, beamed and raftered bedrooms are stunningly equipped: guidebooks and glossies, easy chairs and Thai silk, music, flowers and mini fridge. Bathrooms have Italian tiles and breakfast, served on a Chinese altar table, is as delicious as all the rest.

Price	£65-£70. Singles from £45.
Rooms	2: 1 double, 1 twin/double.
Meals	Packed lunch available. Pub 5-minute drive.
Closed	Christmas & New Year.
Directions	From A140 at Long Stratton, take Flowerpot Lane (opp. Shell garage) to Wacton; at x-roads left by phone box, past swings; 500 yds to telegraph pole with sign: left turn up 'Private Rd', over cattle grid to end of lane.

Mrs Julie Franklin
Le Grys Barn,
Wacton Common, Long Stratton,
Norfolk NR15 2UR

Tel	01508 531576
Fax	01508 532124
Email	jm.franklin@virgin.net
Web	www.legrys-barn.co.uk

Map 10   Entry 331

Northamptonshire

Coton Lodge

Hidden at the end of a mile-long drive, a handsome, wisteria-clad farmhouse surrounded by enchanting gardens, ancient sycamores, horse chestnuts and limes. This is Joanne's childhood home to which she has returned with Peter – to run the farm and carry on the gardens her mother started 30 years ago. The elegant, early 19th-century rooms are filled with light and look out across the beautiful valley beyond. Bedrooms are softly decorated, utterly comfortable and spotless. Wake to birdsong and a delicious breakfast of waffles, fresh eggs from the farm and homemade jams. *Children over 12 welcome.*

Price	From £90. Singles from £70.
Rooms	3: 2 doubles, 1 twin.
Meals	Packed lunch £5. Pub 3 miles.
Closed	January.
Directions	From M1 junc. 18 follow signs for Crick & W. Haddon. Bypass W. Haddon following signs to Guilsborough. After 0.5 miles fork right to Guilsborough, Coton Lodge 0.75 miles on right.

Joanne de Nobriga
Coton Lodge,
West Haddon Road, Guilsborough,
Northamptonshire NN6 8QE

Tel	01604 740215
Fax	01604 743515
Email	jo@cotonlodge.co.uk
Web	www.cotonlodge.co.uk

Map 8   Entry 332

Northamptonshire

Colledges House

Huge attention to comfort here, and a house full of laughter. Liz clearly derives pleasure from sharing her 300-year-old stone thatched cottage, immaculate garden, pretty conservatory and converted barn with guests. Bedrooms and bathrooms are luxurious and there is something special wherever you turn: a Jacobean trunk, a Bechstein piano, a beautiful bureau in the bathroom. Cordon Bleu dinners are elegant affairs – and great fun. Guests have said that staying here is "like staying with a good friend". Stroll around the conservation village of Staverton – delightful. *Children over eight & babes in arms welcome.*

Price	£98–£102. Singles £62.50–£65.
Rooms	4: 1 double, 1 single.
	Cottage: 1 double, 1 twin.
Meals	Dinner, 3 courses, £29.50–£31.
	Pub 4-minute walk.
Closed	Rarely.
Directions	From Daventry, A425 to Leamington Spa. 100 yds past Staverton Park Conference Centre, right into village, then 1st right. Keep left, & at 'Give Way' sign, sharp left. House immed. on right.

	Liz Jarrett
	Colledges House,
	Oakham Lane, Staverton, Daventry,
	Northamptonshire NN11 6JQ
Tel	01327 702737
Mobile	07710 794112
Email	liz@colledgeshouse.co.uk
Web	www.colledgeshouse.co.uk

Map 8   Entry 333

Northamptonshire

The Vyne

Weighed down by wisteria, this 16th-century cottage rests in a honey-hued conservation village. There's not a straight line in the cosy oak-beamed cottage, its rooms filled with good antiques and eclectic art. The twin is enchanting, tucked under the rafters, its beds decorated in willow-pattern chintz, its walls glinting with gilded frames; the double has a Georgian four-poster and a sampler-decorated bathroom that's a quick flit next door. Warm and charming, Imogen not only works in publishing but is a dedicated gardener and Cordon Bleu cook – enjoy supper in her sunny secluded garden. *Babies welcome.*

Price	£72. Singles from £45.
Rooms	2: 1 twin;
	1 four-poster with separate bath.
Meals	Supper £18. Dinner £28. BYO.
	Pub 2-minute walk.
Closed	Christmas & New Year.
Directions	M40 exit 11. A422 to Northampton, left onto B4525. 2 miles, left to Thorpe Mandeville. 3 miles, left to Culworth. After Culworth, right to Eydon.

	Imogen Butler
	The Vyne,
	High Street,
	Eydon, Daventry,
	Northamptonshire NN11 3PP
Tel	01327 264886
Fax	01327 260735
Email	imogen@ibutler2.wanadoo.co.uk

Map 8   Entry 334

Northamptonshire

The Coach House

Sunlight and flower-scent fill this sprawling, rosy-brick home. Originally a coach house and stabling, it's now a series of elegant, light-filled ground-floor rooms around a central courtyard. Sarah's eye for colour and design shows in the clever mix of modern and traditional, gingham curtains, pretty fabrics and striking lampshades. Bedrooms ooze country-house luxury with antique lace pillowcases, thick towels, glossy magazines and doors to garden or courtyard. Relax here – or on the tennis court – after a day at Silverstone or Towcester races. And there's homemade bread for breakfast!

Price	£90. Singles from £45.
Rooms	2: 1 double, 1 twin.
Meals	Packed lunch on request. Pub/restaurant within 5 miles.
Closed	Rarely.
Directions	From A43 dual carriageway, A5 North for Hinckley. After 1.1 miles sharp left to Duncote. First house on left, 300 yds, 2nd gate.

Sarah Baker Baker
The Coach House,
Duncote,
Towcester,
Northamptonshire NN12 8AQ

Tel	01327 352855
Mobile	07875 215705
Email	sarah@duncote.plus.com

Map 8   Entry 335

Northumberland

Chain Bridge House

The kitchen is the hub of Livvy's home, and the house, mid-19th century, is the last in England; the historic Union Chain Bridge crosses an idyllic stretch of the Tweed just across the road. Anglers fish for salmon and the walks are wonderful: look out for otters and the occasional seal. Expect books and log fires in the sitting room, a revolving summer house in the garden with views, white towels on heated rails, goose down duvets in lovely bedrooms… bliss. Breakfasts and dinners are as seasonal and organic as can be, Livvy is a fantastic cook and babies and children get as big a welcome as anyone.

Price	£70-£75. Singles £40-£45.
Rooms	2: 1 double, 1 twin.
Meals	Dinner £25. Supper £15. Packed lunch from £5. Pubs/restaurants 5-7 miles.
Closed	Rarely.
Directions	A698; exit from A1 at East Ord, west of Berwick. After 1 mile, right for Horncliffe; follow signs for Honey Farm; past farm 200 yds; house on right.

Livvy Cawthorn
Chain Bridge House,
Horncliffe, Berwick-upon-Tweed,
Northumberland TD15 2XT

Tel	01289 386259
Fax	01289 386259
Email	info@chainbridgehouse.co.uk
Web	www.chainbridgehouse.co.uk

Map 16   Entry 336

Northumberland

West Coates

Slip through the gates of this Georgian townhouse and you're in the country. Two acres of leafy gardens, with shady or sunny spots to relax, belie the closeness of Berwick's centre. As surprising are the indoor pool and hot tub tucked in the corner. From the lofty ceilings and sash windows to the soft colours, gleaming furniture and handsome sporting prints, the house has a calm, ordered elegance. Bedrooms have antiques and garden views; two have roll top baths; fruit, homemade cakes, flowers welcome you. Warm, friendly Karen is a stunning cook, inventively using local produce and spoiling you.

Price	£90-£100. Singles from £50.
Rooms	3: 1 double, 1 twin/double; 1 twin/double with separate bath/shower.
Meals	Dinner £30. Pub/restaurant 15-minute walk.
Closed	Christmas & New Year.
Directions	From A1 take A6105 into Berwick. House 300 yds on left. Stone pillars at end of drive.

Karen Brown
West Coates, 30 Castle Terrace,
Berwick-upon-Tweed,
Northumberland TD15 1NZ

Tel	01289 309666
Mobile	07814 281973
Email	karenbrownwestcoates@yahoo.com
Web	www.westcoates.co.uk

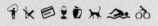

Map 16   Entry 337

Northumberland

Hethpool

Spot wild goats on the hills of this valley, whose private roads are virtually car-free (vehicles are restricted). It's remote, rugged and breathtakingly beautiful. Inside, old family pieces, honeysuckle chintz, hunting gear, milling dogs – and Martin and Eildon who have lived here for years and look after you with ease. Bedrooms, neat and tidy, comfy and clean, share a sitting room; after one of Eildon's fine dinners, settle in in front of the fire. There's a 16th-century peel tower in the garden and the National Park beyond. Bring your horse and let your hosts be your guide!

Price	From £60.
Rooms	2: 1 twin; 1 double with separate bath.
Meals	Dinner, 2-3 courses, £15-£20. Pub 8 miles.
Closed	Rarely.
Directions	From Wooler A697 towards Coldstream; 2 miles left onto B6351. After 4 miles left to Hethpool; 1.5 miles, left at 'Private Drive' sign; 3rd on right.

Eildon & Martin Letts
Hethpool,
Wooler,
Northumberland NE71 6TW

Tel	01668 216232
Email	eildon@hethpoolhouse.co.uk
Web	www.hethpoolhouse.co.uk

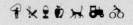

Map 16   Entry 338

Northumberland

Broome

A totally surprising one-storey house, full of beautiful things. It is an Aladdin's cave and sits in the middle of a coastal village with access to miles of sandy beaches. The garden/breakfast room is its hub and has a country cottage feel; enjoy locally smoked kippers here, award-winning 'Bamburgh Bangers' and home-cured bacon from the village butcher. There's also a sun-trapping courtyard full of colourful pots for breakfasts in the sun. Guests have a cheerful sitting/dining room and bedrooms with fresh flowers and good books. Mary is welcoming and amusing and has stacks of local knowledge.

Price	£70–£90. Singles £50–£60.
Rooms	2: 1 double, 1 twin, sharing separate bath/shower (2nd room let to same party only).
Meals	Pubs/restaurants 2-minute walk.
Closed	Christmas & New Year.
Directions	From Newcastle north on A1; right for Bamburgh on B1341. To village, pass 30mph sign & hotel; 1st right at Victoria Hotel. House 400 yds on right.

Mary Dixon
Broome,
22 Ingram Road,
Bamburgh, Northumberland
NE69 7BT
Tel   01668 214287
Mobile   07956 013409
Email   mdixon4394@aol.com

Map 16   Entry 339

Northumberland

Bilton Barns

A solidly good farmhouse B&B whose lifeblood is still farming. The Jacksons know every inch of the countryside and coast that surrounds their 1715 home; it's a pretty spot. They farm 400 acres of mixed arable land that sweeps down to the coast yet always have time for guests. Dorothy takes pride in creating an easy and sociable atmosphere – three couples who were introduced to each other one weekend returned for a reunion! Bedrooms are big, carpeted, fresh and comfortable, a conservatory leads onto the garden and there's an airy guests' sitting room with an open fire and views to the sea.

Price	£60–£70. Singles £30–£40.
Rooms	3: 1 double, 1 twin, 1 four-poster.
Meals	Packed lunch from £4. Pub/restaurant 1.5 miles.
Closed	Christmas & New Year.
Directions	From Alnwick, A1068 to Alnmouth. At Hipsburn r'bout follow signs to station & cross bridge. 1st lane to left, 0.3 miles down drive.

Brian & Dorothy Jackson
Bilton Barns,
Alnmouth, Alnwick,
Northumberland NE66 2TB
Tel   01665 830427
Mobile   07939 262028
Email   dorothy@biltonbarns.com
Web   www.biltonbarns.com

Map 16   Entry 340

Northumberland

Thistleyhaugh

Enid thrives on hard work and humour, her passions are pictures, cooking and people and if she's not the perfect B&B hostess, she's a close contender. Certainly you eat well – local farm eggs at breakfast and their own beef at dinner. Choose any of the five large, lovely bedrooms and stay the week; they are awash with old paintings, silk fabrics and crisp white linen. But if you do stray downstairs, past the log fire and the groaning table, there are 720 acres of organic farmland to discover and a few million more of the Cheviots beyond that. Wonderful hosts, house and region.

Price	£75. Singles £50-£75.
Rooms	5: 4 doubles, 1 twin.
Meals	Dinner, 3 courses, £20. Pub/restaurant 2 miles.
Closed	Christmas & New Year.
Directions	Leave A1 for A697 for Coldstream & Longhorsley; 2 miles past Longhorsley, left at Todburn sign; 1 mile to x-roads, then right; on 1 mile over white bridge; 1st right, right again, over cattle grid.

	Henry & Enid Nelless
	Thistleyhaugh,
	Longhorsley, Morpeth,
	Northumberland NE65 8RG
Tel	01665 570629
Fax	01665 570629
Email	thistleyhaugh@hotmail.com
Web	www.thistleyhaugh.co.uk

Map 16   Entry 341

Northumberland

East Hepple Farmhouse

In the farmhouse sitting room, a huge cast-iron range blazes away in winter and the shelves are groaning with books – bibliophile heaven. And the suite has its own sitting room – with more books, and a wood-burner. The peace is so deep in the Coquet valley that you may sleep until the whiff of sizzling local bacon hits your nostrils. Beds are firm, old pine pieces pretty, pillows feathery soft and views over the river to the Simonside hills abundant. Joan and Brian are expert at looking after you, will drive you to dinner and guide you the next day to the beaches, Cragside, Alnwick Castle and fabulous walking.

Price	£55-£60. Singles £40.
Rooms	2: 1 suite; 1 twin (let to same party only).
Meals	Packed lunch £3-£4. Pubs/restaurants 2.5 miles.
Closed	End of October to end of March.
Directions	West from Rothbury on B6341. In Hepple, pass church on left; next right, then immediate hard right into driveway.

	Joan & Brian Storey
	East Hepple Farmhouse,
	Hepple,
	Morpeth,
	Northumberland NE65 7LH
Tel	01669 640221
Email	joanstorey@coquetdale.net
Web	www.easthepplefarmhouse.co.uk

Map 16   Entry 342

Northumberland

Shieldhall

You stay in recently converted 18th-century farm buildings, each with an entrance into a central courtyard. Stephen and his sons make and restore antique furniture and there are examples of their artistry throughout. Bedrooms are compact and named after the wood used within, bathrooms are spacious and there's a sitting room/library that's shared. Meals are taken in the beamed dining room of the main house – once home to the family of Capability Brown. Celia is friendly and attentive and loves cooking – and most ingredients are locally sourced. There's also a secret bar and a small but varied wine list.

Price	£76. Singles £50.
Rooms	3: 1 double, 1 twin, 1 four-poster.
Meals	Dinner, 4 courses, £25. Pub 7 miles.
Closed	Rarely.
Directions	From Newcastle A696 for Jedburgh. 5 miles north of Belsay, right onto B6342. On left after 500 yds (turn into front courtyard).

Celia & Stephen Robinson-Gay
Shieldhall,
Wallington, Morpeth,
Northumberland NE61 4AQ

Tel 01830 540387
Fax 01830 540490
Email robinson.gay@btconnect.com
Web www.shieldhallguesthouse.co.uk

Map 16   Entry 343

Northumberland

Lansdown House

The arched coach house doors to this 1600s house are still right on the pavement on the busy market town street. But nip down a side corridor and you could be in deep countryside; a delightfully long town garden and your own entrance give you independence and bubbly Lesley is on hand to make sure you have all you need. Fab breakfasts (in bed if you want) set you up for miles of sandy beaches, cycling, shooting, fly fishing, Alnwick Castle and horse riding. Lazy lumps can just loll in a sumptuous bed admiring the Designers Guild wallpaper, the TV (flat-screen, naturally) and the fine pieces of furniture.

Price	£70-£80. Singles from £48.
Rooms	2: 1 double, 1 twin.
Meals	Dinner, 3 courses, £22.50. Packed lunch £5. Pubs/restaurants walking distance.
Closed	Rarely.
Directions	The house is on the main thoroughfare through Morpeth, on right heading north, next to Sour Grapes wine bar. Easy free parking.

Lesley Mantel
Lansdown House,
90 Newgate Street,
Morpeth, Northumberland
NE61 1BU

Tel 01670 511129
Email kitchendiva@gmail.com
Web www.lansdownhouse.co.uk

Map 16   Entry 344

Northumberland

The Hermitage

A magical setting, only three miles from Hadrian's wall. Through ancient woodland, up the long drive and over the burn to this beautiful Georgian house. Inside is supremely comfortable and elegant but still homely. Large, carpeted and delightful bedrooms are furnished with antiques, prints and superb beds; bathrooms have large roll top baths. There's a walled garden, and breakfasts (delicious) can be served on the terrace. Katie grew up in this lovely house, looks after you brilliantly and knows all there is to know about the area. *Guests back please by 11pm. Children over seven & babes in arms welcome.*

Northumberland

Bog House

It's too quiet for some townies – and thank goodness! If you've had it with bustle, bury yourself in the depths of Northumberland, two miles from Hadrian's Wall. Here is an immaculate barn conversion that's mercifully free from the usual modern furniture; what you have is a contemporary, airy feel and an open-raftered space stuffed with antiques. Rosemary has created a stunning place. Breakfast sausages are local (organic where possible), the peace total and the welcome disarming; you have your own entrance and may come and go as you please. An indulgent, wonderful retreat.

Price	From £75. Singles from £45.
Rooms	3: 1 double, 1 twin; 1 twin with separate bath.
Meals	Pub 2 miles.
Closed	October-February.
Directions	7 miles north of Corbridge on A68. Left on A6079 for 1 mile, then right through lodge gates with arch. House 0.5 miles down drive.

Price	£80-£90. Singles £45-£50.
Rooms	2: 1 twin, 1 double.
Meals	Dinner, 2 courses, £15-£18. Pubs/restaurants 15-minute drive.
Closed	Rarely.
Directions	A68; 5 miles north of Corbridge, right onto B6318. After 3.5 miles, left signed Moorhouse. On for 1 mile, right; left to Bog House after 1 mile. Last farm on left.

Simon & Katie Stewart
The Hermitage,
Swinburne,
Hexham, Northumberland
NE48 4DG
Tel   01434 681248
Fax   01434 681110
Email   katie.stewart@themeet.co.uk

Rosemary Stobart
Bog House,
Matfen,
Northumberland NE20 0RF
Tel   01661 886776
Mobile   07850 375535
Email   rosemary.stobart@btinternet.com
Web   www.boghouse-matfen.co.uk

Map 16   Entry 345

Map 16   Entry 346

Northumberland

Matfen High House

Bring the wellies! You are 25 miles from the border and the walking is a joy. Struan and Jenny are amusing company, love country pursuits and will drive you to Matfen Hall for dinner. Expect tasselled lampshades and festoon blinds in comfortable bedrooms, coloured towels in bright bathrooms, pictures, books and choice pieces in the drawing room; the sturdy stone house of 1735 is a pleasant, pretty place to stay. You are served delicious breakfast at a mahogany table and may try out French and Spanish on your fluent hostess. The Roman Wall and the great castles of Alnwick and Bamburgh beckon.

Price	£60–£70. Singles £30–£35.
Rooms	4: 1 double, 1 twin; 1 double, 1 twin sharing bath.
Meals	Packed lunch £3.50. Restaurant 2 miles.
Closed	Rarely.
Directions	A69 at Heddon on the Wall, onto B6318 past Robin Hood Inn; 500 yds, right to Moorhouse; right at next junction signed High House Brewery; past Hadrian Pet Hotel; 300 yds, right, opp. cottages.

Struan & Jenny Wilson
Matfen High House,
Matfen,
Corbridge,
Northumberland NE20 0RG

Tel	01661 886592
Fax	01661 886847
Email	struan@struan.enterprise-plc.com

Map 12   Entry 347

Nottinghamshire

The Old Vicarage

Jillie's grandmother studied at the Slade and her paintings line the walls; glass and china adorn every surface. This wisteria-clad Victorian vicarage next to the 12th-century church was falling down when the Steeles bought it; now it's an elegant, traditional country home. Long windows are generously draped, two of the bedrooms are spacious, baths have claw feet and a number of friendly cats and dogs wait to welcome you. Jerry bakes the bread and all the vegetables come from the garden, where you may play tennis or croquet. Mary Queen of Scots is reputed to have stayed at Langford as guest of the Earl of Shrewsbury.

Price	£70–£80. Singles £45–£50.
Rooms	3: 1 double, 1 small double, 1 twin.
Meals	Dinner (min. 4). £22.50. Pub/restaurant 1.5 miles.
Closed	Rarely.
Directions	From A1, A46 to Lincoln & left onto A1133 for Gainsborough. Through Langford, 0.5 miles on, then left for Holme. House 100 yds on, on right, by church.

Jerry & Jillie Steele
The Old Vicarage,
Langford,
Newark,
Nottinghamshire NG23 7RT

Tel	01636 705031
Email	jillie.steele@virgin.net
Web	www.langfordoldvicarage.co.uk

Map 9   Entry 348

Nottinghamshire

The Yellow House

A butter-yellow 30s semi in a quiet, tree-lined street. Suzanne, a well-travelled ex-model, and Misza her lovely dog, welcome you in. Colour schemes are cool, peaceful, with the occasional oriental touch. Your bedroom in the eaves – a charming, cossetting, cottagey hideaway with a good big bed – is crisply decorated in bold cream-and-olive florals, and has a good shower. Suzanne offers breakfast on the terrace in fine weather and has loads of info on walks. Nottingham's attractions are three miles away, the great oaks of Sherwood Forest are 12 miles north.

Price	£55. Singles £35.
Rooms	1 double.
Meals	Pubs/restaurants 1 mile.
Closed	Rarely.
Directions	From A60 main Mansfield road going north, at junc. with Vale Pub right onto Thackerey's Lane; at r'bout straight on; after 100 yds right into Whernside Rd. Left at x-roads into Littlegreen Rd; house on left.

Suzanne Prew-Smith
The Yellow House,
7 Littlegreen Road, Woodthorpe,
Nottingham,
Nottinghamshire NG5 4LE
Tel   01159 262280
Email   suzanne.prewsmith1@btinternet.com
Web   www.theyellowhousenottingham.co.uk

Map 8   Entry 349

Oxfordshire

Home Farmhouse

The house is charming, with low, wobbly ceilings, exposed beams, stone fireplaces and winding stairs; the bedrooms, perched above their own staircases like crows' nests, are decorated with extravagant swathes of rich floral chintz. All rooms are unusual, old and full of character, but luxurious; lavish curtains embellish one bath. The family's history and travels are evident all over, the barn room has its own entrance and the Grove-Whites – who are super – run their B&B as a team. Two delightful dogs, too – Ulysses and Goliath. It's all so laid-back you'll find it hard to leave.

Price	£78. Singles £50.
Rooms	3: 2 twins/doubles; 1 twin/double with separate bath.
Meals	Dinner £26. Supper £18. Pub 100 yds.
Closed	Christmas.
Directions	M40 junc. 10, A43 for Northampton. After 5 miles, left to Charlton. There, left & house on left, 100 yds past Rose & Crown.

Rosemary & Nigel Grove-White
Home Farmhouse,
Charlton, Banbury,
Oxfordshire OX17 3DR
Tel   01295 811683
Fax   01295 811683
Email   grovewhite@lineone.net
Web   www.homefarmhouse.co.uk

Map 8   Entry 350

Oxfordshire

The Old Post House

Great natural charm in the 17th-century Old Post House: shiny flagstones, rich dark wood and mullion windows combine with luxurious fabrics, papers, colours and fine furniture. Bedrooms are big, with antique wardrobes, oak headboards and an old-fashioned feel. The walled gardens are lovely – rich with espaliered fruit trees and there's a pool for sunny evenings. Christine, a well-travelled ex-pat, has an innate sense of hospitality – as do her two Springer spaniels – and breakfasts are delicious. There's village traffic but your sleep should be sound, and Deddington is delightful. *Children over 12 welcome.*

Price	£75. Singles £50.
Rooms	3: 1 double, 1 twin/double, 1 four-poster.
Meals	Occasional dinner. Pubs/restaurants in village.
Closed	Rarely.
Directions	A4260 Oxford-Banbury. In Deddington, on right next to cream Georgian house. Park opposite.

Christine Blenntoft
The Old Post House,
New Street, Deddington,
Oxfordshire OX15 0SP

Tel	01869 338978
Fax	01869 338978
Email	kblenntoft@aol.com

Map 8   Entry 351

Oxfordshire

Buttermilk Stud

At the top of an avenue of limes, enveloped by 70 beautiful acres, is this rambling farmstead with orchards and vegetable gardens, wildlife, roses and foxgloves. George is a painter and the house is filled with vibrant art; Victoria looks after the three children and the small farm. Inside is a happy assemblage of family furniture, flowers from the garden, children, dogs and harmonious colours. Your bedroom is old-fashioned and comfortable, with beautiful views over rolling pasture. Outside are geese, horses, cows... and chickens. The marvellous Falkland Arms at Great Tew is an hour's stride across fields.

Price	From £80. Singles £50.
Rooms	1 double/twin.
Meals	Packed lunch £10. Supper, 2 courses, £25. Dinner, 3 courses, £30. Pub 1 mile.
Closed	Rarely.
Directions	From A361 Banbury/Chipping Norton road, take turn to 'The Barfords' at South Newington; on for 1 mile; house on right up avenue of limes.

Victoria Irvine
Buttermilk Stud,
Barford St Michael, Banbury,
Oxfordshire OX15 0PL

Tel	01295 722929
Mobile	0780 3907238
Email	buttermilk@btconnect.com

Map 8   Entry 352

Oxfordshire

Buttslade House

A gorgeous ground-floor retreat for couples who need to catch up with each other. You get a smart, private bedroom across the courtyard from the 17th-century farmhouse with its barns and stables. A clever melody of ancient and contemporary style romps through your summer sitting room with ancestral portraits and modern Spanish art, antique sofas, fluorescent cushions and a comfortable wooden bed with a Rajasthan cover and feather pillows. Diana is fun and will pamper you or leave you, there's a blissful garden to stroll through, food is fresh and local and it's a hop to the village pub.

Price	£70. Singles £45.
Rooms	1 double & sitting room.
Meals	Dinner, 3 courses, £25. Lunch £7. Pub 200 yds.
Closed	Rarely.
Directions	From B4035 look for signs to Wykham Arms. Buttslade is 2nd house beyond pub, going down hill.

Diana Thompson
Buttslade House,
Temple Mill Road, Sibford Gower,
Banbury, Oxfordshire OX15 5RX
Tel   01295 788818
Email   janthompson50@hotmail.com
Web   www.buttsladehouse.co.uk

Map 8   Entry 353

Oxfordshire

Minehill House

Bump your way up the track (mind the car!) to the top of a wild and windswept hill and a gorgeous family farmhouse with views for miles and young, energetic Hester to care for you. Little people will adore the ping-pong table and the trampoline; their parents will enjoy the well-polished flags, colourful oil paintings, wood-burning stove and seriously sophisticated food. Rest well in the big double room with Sanderson oak-leaved paper and stunning views, and a cubby-hole door through to extra twin beds; bathrooms are sparklingly clean and spacious. Bracing walks straight from the door.

Price	£50–£80. Singles from £45.
Rooms	1 double/family.
Meals	Dinner, 3 courses, from £25. Supper £15. Packed lunch available. Pubs 1-5 miles.
Closed	Christmas & New Year.
Directions	From Banbury B4035 to Brailes; after 10 miles take road signed Hook Norton; 0.5 miles, right onto unmarked uphill farm track to house.

Hester & Ed Sale
Minehill House,
Lower Brailes, Banbury,
Oxfordshire OX15 5BJ
Tel   01608 685594
Mobile   07890 266441
Email   ed_and_hester@lineone.net

Map 8   Entry 354

Oxfordshire

The Glebe House

This is a truly relaxing place. Beyond the idyllic garden and the honey-stone walls are charmingly renovated rooms, the friendliest people and all the character and elegance you'd expect from a couple with art and architecture running through their veins. A comfy light-filled sitting room, sweet fresh bedrooms, flowers from Clare's lovely garden, organic meals in a colourful dining room, glorious views and a gem of a village. There are wonderful walks, a children's tree "fort" to discover, ponies and bikes to ride and masses for all ages to do. Readers love this place. *Self-catering cottage attached.*

Price	£60–£85. Singles £45–£60.
Rooms	4: 2 doubles, each with separate bath; 2 singles sharing bath.
Meals	Dinner, with wine, £20–£25. Pubs/restaurants 2 miles.
Closed	Rarely.
Directions	From Burford, A40 for Cheltenham. 1st left, for Westwell. 2 miles to T-junc., then right, through village. Right to Aldsworth; 1st right onto concrete drive. On to gateway at end of drive.

Clare & Robin Dunipace
The Glebe House,
Westwell, Burford,
Oxfordshire OX18 4JT

Tel	01993 822171
Fax	01993 824125
Email	clare.dunipace@amserve.net
Web	www.oxford-cotswold-holidays.com

Map 8   Entry 355

Oxfordshire

Caswell House

A handsome 15th-century manor house with an ancient orchard, walled gardens, smooth lawns and a moat brimming with trout. Guest wing quarters are spacious, beamed and comfortable, with a log fire and views over the garden from leaded windows. Bedrooms are spoiling and large with the best linen, thick towels and warm bathrooms. Amanda and Richard are generous and easy-going – a game of snooker is a must! – and seasonal produce is sourced from the farm shop and cooked on the Aga. A great place to relax; for heartier souls there are 450 acres of rolling farmland.

Price	£75. Singles £55.
Rooms	3: 2 doubles, 1 twin.
Meals	Pubs/restaurants nearby.
Closed	Rarely.
Directions	A40 Burford to Oxford. Right after 1.8 miles to Brize Norton, left at staggered x-roads. Right at r'bout, left at mini-r'bout for Curbridge; on for 1.2 miles, house on right.

Mrs Amanda Matthews
Caswell House,
Caswell Lane, Brize Norton,
Oxfordshire OX18 3NJ

Tel	01993 701064
Fax	01993 774901
Email	stay@caswell-house.co.uk
Web	www.caswell-house.co.uk

Map 8   Entry 356

Oxfordshire

The Craven

Roses and clematis cover this pretty 16th-century thatched cottage where breakfast in the farmhouse kitchen is served at a long pine table by a dresser laden with china. Cosy beamed bedrooms have embroidered sheets and country views; the room on the ground floor with antique four-poster is charming, the room in the stable block has a Victorian half-tester and bathrooms promise gold taps and fluffy towels. More beams and pretty chintz sofas in the sitting room, where you sip tea or wine around a huge log fire. Carol's daughter Katie creates prize-winning dinners – and there are walks from the door.

Price	£75-£95.
Rooms	3: 2 doubles, 1 four-poster.
Meals	Dinner, 3 courses, from £24.50.
Closed	Rarely.
Directions	M4 junc. 14 to A338, then B4001. Thro' Lambourn, 1 mile north of village, fork left; 3 miles to Kingston Lisle, left to Uffington. Thro' village, right after church. House 0.3 miles out, on left.

Carol Wadsworth
The Craven,
Fernham Road, Uffington,
Oxfordshire SN7 7RD

Tel	01367 820449
Fax	01367 820351
Email	carol@thecraven.co.uk
Web	www.thecraven.co.uk

Map 3 Entry 357

Oxfordshire

Rectory Farm

Come for the happy buzz of family life. It's relaxed and informal and you are welcomed with tea and homemade shortbread by Mary Anne. The date above the entrance stone reads 1629 and bedrooms, light and spotless, have beautiful stone-arched and mullioned windows. The huge twin has ornate plasterwork and views over the garden and church; the double is cosier with a carved pine headboard; both have good showers and large fluffy towels. The pedigree North Devon cattle are Robert's pride and joy and his family has farmed here for three generations. It's a treat to stay.
Minimum stay two nights at weekends.

Price	£65-£70. Singles £48-£50.
Rooms	2: 1 double, 1 twin.
Meals	Pub 2-minute walk.
Closed	Mid-December-mid-January.
Directions	From Oxford, A420 for Swindon for 8 miles & right at r'bout, for Witney (A415). Over 2 bridges, immed. right by pub car park. Right at T-junc.; drive on right, past church.

Mary Anne Florey
Rectory Farm,
Northmoor, Witney,
Oxfordshire OX29 5SX

Tel	01865 300207
Mobile	07974 102198
Email	pj.florey@farmline.com
Web	www.oxtowns.co.uk/rectoryfarm

Map 8 Entry 358

Oxfordshire

Manor Farmhouse

Helen and John radiate pleasure and good humour. Blenheim Park is a short walk down the lane and this soft old stone house is perfect for any delusions of grandeur: good prints and paintings, venerable furniture, gentle fabrics, nothing cluttered or overdone. Shallow, curvy, 18th-century stairs lead past grandfather's bronze bust to the splendid double; the other small bedroom has its own challenging spiral stair to a cobbled courtyard. Breakfast is by the rough-hewn fireplace and the ancient dresser. Wander through the lovely garden in spring and summer; the village is palpably quiet.

Price	£66–£75. Singles from £50.
Rooms	2 doubles, sharing shower room.
Meals	Pub within walking distance.
Closed	Christmas.
Directions	A44 north from Oxford's ring road. At r'bout, 1 mile before Woodstock, left onto A4095 into Bladon. Last left in village; house on 2nd bend in road, with iron railings.

Helen Stevenson
Manor Farmhouse,
Manor Road, Bladon, Woodstock,
Oxfordshire OX20 1RU

Tel	01993 812168
Fax	01993 812168
Email	helstevenson@hotmail.com
Web	www.oxlink.co.uk/woodstock/manor-farmhouse/

Map 8   Entry 359

Oxfordshire

Langsmeade House

Marianne has applied talent and her Dutch background to make her 1920s house irresistibly comfortable and perfect for house parties. There are two sitting rooms, velvet and tapestry sofas, wooden floors, panelling, excellent beds, some lovely Dutch furniture and lawns to loll on in the summer. Big-hearted Marianne imposes few rules, prepares terrific breakfasts and gives lifts in her London cab to Oxford's Park & Ride, the Ridgeway *and* to restaurants; she will collect you up until 1am! Traffic noise from the nearby M40 is constant – loud outside, audible inside – but we defy you not to be charmed.

Price	£80. Singles £45.
Rooms	3: 1 double; 2 doubles sharing bath/shower (let to same party only).
Meals	Lunch £5. Dinner £17.50. Packed lunch £3.50. Pub 2 miles.
Closed	Rarely.
Directions	M40 from London, junc. 7 for Thame, right then left for Milton Common. Pass Belfry Hotel on right. House on left down 'No Through Road'.

Mrs M Aben
Langsmeade House,
Milton Common, Thame,
Oxfordshire OX9 2JY

Tel	01844 278727
Fax	01844 279256
Email	enquiries@langsmeadehouse.co.uk
Web	www.langsmeadehouse.co.uk

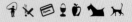

Map 8   Entry 360

Oxfordshire

Cowdrays

Birdsong and sunlight find their way into every room and Margaret, genuinely welcoming, bends to the needs of all guests; the downstairs room, complete with piano, is perfect for wheelchair-users. There are chickens, geese, dogs and, in the lovely garden – a corner of which is Gertrude Jekyll-inspired – a tennis court and pool. This is a homely, endearingly timeworn sort of place, neither smart nor stylish, but with good furniture, masses of books, clean bathrooms, a little sitting room... even a kitchen area in which to prepare a snack if you prefer not to walk to the historic village's pubs.

Price	From £70. Singles £35.
Rooms	5: 2 doubles;
	1 twin with separate shower;
	1 twin, 1 single sharing bath/shower.
Meals	Packed lunch £5.
	Pubs 7-minute walk.
Closed	Rarely.
Directions	Off A417, 3 miles from Wantage going east. Right into East Hendred; 3rd right into Orchard Lane; past pub; at x-roads, left into Cat St; house behind wall/gates.

Margaret Bateman
Cowdrays,
Cat Street, East Hendred, Wantage,
Oxford, Oxfordshire OX12 8JT

Tel	01235 833313
Mobile	07799 622003
Email	cowdrays@virgin.net
Web	www.cowdrays.co.uk

Map 4 Entry 361

Oxfordshire

Hernes

The lovely rambling farmhouse has been in the family for over a century and has a warmly individual flavour. Pre-Raphaelite Aunt Connie looks down on you in the dimly-lit hall, the billiard room, with log-burning stove and comfortable chairs, is vast, and more ancestors keep an eye on you at breakfast. High-ceilinged bedrooms come without the usual arctic chill and have long views and country-house charm. The garden is wonderful, the surroundings peacefully rural and there's home-produced honey and marmalade for breakfast. Perfect for exploring Henley and some gorgeous *Vicar of Dibley* countryside.

Price	£95-£97.50. Singles from £65.
	Single-night bank holiday surcharge.
Rooms	3: 1 twin/double, 1 four-poster;
	1 double with separate bath.
Meals	Pub & restaurants 1 mile.
Closed	December-mid-January & occasionally.
Directions	Over lights in centre of Henley as far as Town Hall. Left through carpark; right onto Greys Rd for 2 miles; 300 yds after 30mph zone, 2nd drive on right; signed drive to main house.

Richard & Gillian Ovey
Hernes,
Henley-on-Thames,
Oxfordshire RG9 4NT

Tel	01491 573245
Fax	01491 574646
Email	governor@herneshenley.com
Web	www.herneshenley.com

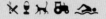

Map 4 Entry 362

Oxfordshire

Uplands House

Come to be spoiled at this 'farmhouse' built in 1875 for the Earl of Jersey's son and completely renovated by this talented couple. It's elegant and sumptuously furnished with large, light bedrooms, crisp linen, thick towels, spoiling bathrooms and long bucolic views from the Orangery where you have tea and cake. Relax here with a book as the sounds and smells of the garden waft by, or chat to charming Poppy while she creates a delicious dinner. Breakfast is Graham's domain – try smoked salmon with scrambled eggs and red caviar. You're well placed for exploring but you may find it hard to leave.

Price	£90–£150. Singles £55–£90.
Rooms	3: 1 double, 1 twin/double, 1 four-poster.
Meals	Dinner, 2-4 courses, £20–£30. Pub 1.25 miles.
Closed	Rarely.
Directions	M40 junc.11; thro' Banbury, A422 thro' Wroxton, pass 'Warwickshire' & 'Upton House 200 yds' signs. Turn right after 10 yds down drive signed Uplands Farm; 1st entrance on right.

Poppy Cooksey & Graham Paul
Uplands House,
Upton,
Banbury,
Oxfordshire OX15 6HJ
Tel   01295 678663
Email   poppy@cotswolds-uplands.co.uk
Web   www.cotswolds-uplands.co.uk

Map 4   Entry 363

Oxfordshire

Fyfield Manor

One of the most fabulous houses in Oxfordshire (once owned by Simon de Montfort) with vast water gardens created by the Browns. Through the grand wood-panelled hall enter a beamed dining room with high-backed chairs and brass rubbings; you breakfast (local, free-range, organic) through the 12th-century arch… or al fresco. Bedrooms are large, warm and light with snowy bed covers and views. Oxford Park & Ride is nearby, there's walking from the door and delightful Christine has wangled you a free glass of wine in the local pub if you walk or cycle. *Min. stay two nights at weekends. Children over ten welcome.*

Price	£65–£70. Singles £45–£55.
Rooms	3: 1 twin/double; 1 double with separate bath. Cloisters: 1 double.
Meals	Pubs within 1 mile.
Closed	Rarely.
Directions	M4 junc. 8/9; A4130 thro' Henley to Wallingford. Turn off for Benson; cont. thro' village 1 mile. Last house on right, behind 6 foot-high brick wall.

Christine Brown
Fyfield Manor,
Benson, Wallingford,
Oxfordshire OX10 6HA
Tel   01491 835184
Fax   01491 825635
Email   chris_fyfield@hotmail.co.uk
Web   www.fyfieldmanor.co.uk

Map 4   Entry 364

Rutland

Old Hall Coach House

A rare and special setting on the edge of Rutland Water, with far-reaching lake and church views. Inside: high ceilings, stone archways, fine antiques and a conservatory overlooking a lovely garden and croquet lawn. Bedrooms are traditional with modern touches and very comfortable; the double and single have super new bathrooms. Rutland is a mini-Cotswolds of stone villages and gentle hills, the lake encourages you to sail, fish, walk or ride, and Georgian Stamford, Burghley House and Belvoir Castle are nearby. Hard to imagine anyone who would not love it here: Cecilie is charming and a terrific cook.

Price	From £80. Singles £40.
Rooms	3: 1 double; 1 twin, 1 single, each with separate bath.
Meals	Dinner £25. Pub/restaurant 5-minute walk.
Closed	Occasionally.
Directions	From A1 Stamford bypass A606 for Oakham for 3 miles. Fork left for Edith Weston; past village sign; 1st right, Church Lane; past church, right down hill; on right on left bend.

Cecilie Ingoldby
Old Hall Coach House,
Edith Weston, Oakham,
Rutland LE15 8HQ
Tel   01780 721504
Email   cecilieingoldby@aol.com,
           cecilieingoldby@yahoo.co.uk
Web   www.oldhallcoachhouse.co.uk

Map 9   Entry 365

Shropshire

Cleeton Court

A tiny lane leads to Cleeton Court, charming Ros and homemade cake. With views over meadows and heathland, the part 14th-century farmhouse feels immersed in countryside – rare peace. You have a private entrance to your rooms, and the use of the drawing room, prettily striped in yellow and cream, elegantly comfortable with sofas and log fire. Beamed bedrooms are delightfully furnished, one with a magnificent, chintzy four-poster and a vast bathroom; recline in the cast-iron bath, gaze on views from the window as you soak. Bring your boots: the walking is superb. *Children over five welcome.*

Price	From £70. Singles £45.
Rooms	2: 1 twin/double, 1 four-poster.
Meals	Pubs/restaurants 4 miles.
Closed	Christmas & New Year.
Directions	From Ludlow, A4117 for Kidderminster for 1 mile; left on B4364 for Cleobury North; on for 5 miles. In Wheathill, right for Cleeton St Mary; on for 1.5 miles; house on left.

Rosamond Woodward
Cleeton Court,
Cleeton St Mary, Ludlow,
Shropshire DY14 0QZ
Tel   01584 823379
Fax   01584 823379
Email   roswoodward@talktalk.net
Web   www.cleetoncourt.co.uk

Map 7   Entry 366

Shropshire

Timberstone Bed & Breakfast

The house is young, engaging and fun – as are Tracey and Alex. She, once in catering, is a reflexologist and new generation B&Ber. Come for logs in winter, charming bedrooms under the eaves, a double ended or claw-foot bath, chunky beams with a modern feel, pale colours, white cotton… and the Bowen Technique (massage) in the garden studio or the relaxing sauna. In the warm guest sitting room – brimming with art – are books, kilims on aged oak boards, a wood-burner. Eggs come from their hens, breakfasts are special; have an excellent home-cooked supper or head for Ludlow and its clutch of Michelin stars.

Shropshire

Shortgrove

A unique, late 15th-century listed house on a gated common away from all roads. It's gloriously homely inside with buckled beams (some padded!) and creaky, carpeted floors; the two sitting rooms, one in the old cider mill end, have plump chairs and an inglenook fire for chilly nights. Bedrooms, cottagey not grand, sit cosily and comfortably under the eaves, their lovely leaded windows overlooking the two-acre garden and much of Shropshire beyond. All this, a super dog and kind, generous Beryl producing fine breakfasts – and marmalade – from her Aga, make this a very comforting place to stay.

Price	£60-£80. Singles £30-£40.
Rooms	3: 1 double; 1 twin, 1 family, both with separate bathroom.
Meals	Dinner, 3-4 courses, £21-£25. Supper £15. Pubs/restaurants 5 miles.
Closed	Rarely.
Directions	B4364 Ludlow-Bridgnorth. After 3 miles, right to Clee Stanton; on for 1.5 miles; left at signopst to Clee Stanton; 1st house on left.

Price	From £75. Singles £46.
Rooms	2: 1 twin; 1 double with separate bath.
Meals	Pub 1 mile.
Closed	November-Easter.
Directions	Off A49, 1 mile south of Woofferton into School Lane. Immed. left at 2nd School Lane sign. Through gate onto common. Fork left where track divides and cont. to end of track.

	Tracey Baylis Timberstone Bed & Breakfast, Clee Stanton, Ludlow, Shropshire SY8 3EL
Tel	01584 823519
Mobile	07905 967263
Email	enquiry@timberstoneludlow.co.uk
Web	www.timberstoneludlow.co.uk

	Beryl Maxwell Shortgrove, Brimfield Common, Ludlow, Shropshire SY8 4NZ
Tel	01584 711418
Web	www.shortgrove-ludlow-bb.co.uk

Map 7 Entry 367

Map 7 Entry 368

Shropshire

Rosecroft

A pretty, quiet, traditional house with charming owners, well-proportioned rooms and an elegant sitting room. But there's not a trace of pomposity and breakfasts are huge enough to set you up for the day: Pimhill organic muesli, smoked or unsmoked local bacon, black pudding, delicious jams. The garden is a delight to stroll through – in summer you can picnic here – and serious walkers are close to the Welsh borders. Bedrooms and bathrooms are polished to perfection, you have fresh flowers, homebaked cakes and biscuits when you arrive, and medieval Ludlow is five miles away. *Children over 12 welcome.*

Price	£65–£70. Singles £40–£42.
Rooms	2: 1 double; 1 double with separate bath.
Meals	Packed lunch £5. Pub 200 yds.
Closed	Rarely.
Directions	Between Ludlow & Leominster on A49, turn onto B4362 at Woofferton. After 1.5 miles, left into Orleton. Past school & small green, house on right, opp. vicarage.

Mrs Gail Benson
Rosecroft,
Orleton, Ludlow,
Shropshire SY8 4HN
Tel   01568 780565
Fax   01568 780565
Email   gailanddavid@rosecroftorleton.freeserve.co.uk
Web   www.stmem.com/rosecroft

Map 7   Entry 369

Shropshire

Upper Buckton

Hayden and Yvonne have lived on this working farm for 40 years, and make your stay special. Bedrooms are large with huge beds made to perfection with lovely linen and proper blankets; bathrooms sport robes and treats. Standing in lush gardens that slope peacefully down to a millstream, meadows and river, the house has a motte and bailey castle site, a heronry, a point-to-point course and a ha-ha. Yvonne's cooking using local produce is upmarket and creative, Hayden's wine list is a treat – marvellous for walkers returning from a day in the glorious Welsh Borders. *Children by arrangement.*

Price	£76–£90. Singles £48–£55.
Rooms	3: 1 double; 2 twins/doubles, each with separate bath.
Meals	Dinner, 4 courses, £25. Pub/restaurant 5 miles.
Closed	Rarely.
Directions	From Ludlow, A49 to Shrewsbury. At Bromfield, A4113. Right in Walford for Buckton, on to 2nd farm on left. Large sign on building.

Hayden & Yvonne Lloyd
Upper Buckton,
Leintwardine,
Craven Arms, Ludlow,
Shropshire SY7 0JU
Tel   01547 540634
Fax   01547 540634
Email   ghlloydco@btconnect.com

Map 7   Entry 370

Shropshire

Hopton House

You won't be surprised to know that Karen runs courses on how to do B&B; she looks after her guests with such competence and care. The attractive house has been converted from a granary and its mix of old beams, high ceilings and twinkling fire creates a fresh, uplifting feel. Bedrooms are warm and charming, each with a decanter of sherry, flat-screen TV, digital radio and good lighting; bathrooms are spoiling, one with a double-ended bath and walk-in shower. Breakfast is a treat with Ludlow sausage, home-laid eggs and homemade jams, dinner is local and home-grown and Karen is happy to collect you from the station.

Price	£70–£95. Singles from £50.
Rooms	2 doubles.
Meals	Light supper £12.50. Restaurant 3 miles.
Closed	23 December–2 January & occasionally.
Directions	A49 Craven Arms exit, B4368 west. After 1 mile, left signed Hopton Heath. At Hopton Heath x-roads, right over bridge, follow road right. House 2nd on left.

Karen Thorne
Hopton House,
Hopton Heath,
Craven Arms,
Shropshire SY7 0QD
Tel   01547 530885
Email   info@shropshirebreakfast.co.uk
Web   www.shropshirebreakfast.co.uk

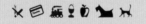

Map 7   Entry 371

Shropshire

Clun Farm House

These young owners make a good team: Susan the cook (award-winning marmalade at breakfast, seasonal produce at dinner), Anthony the guide, happy to show you the historic village and the heavenly hills beyond. Both are enthusiastic collectors of country artefacts and have filled their listed, late 15th-century farmhouse with eye-catching things – not every kitchen range has a cowboy's saddle above it and this one echoes Susan's roots. Old polished oak contrasts beautifully with chic florals and bold walls. Walk the Shropshire Way; return to a cosy woodburner, a warm smile and a delicious dinner.

Price	From £65. Singles by arrangement.
Rooms	2: 1 double (with extra bunk-bed room); 1 twin/double with separate shower.
Meals	Dinner from £25. Packed lunch £3.50. Pubs/restaurants nearby.
Closed	Occasionally.
Directions	A49 from Ludlow & onto B4368 at Craven Arms, for Clun. In High St on left 0.5 miles from Clun sign.

Anthony & Susan Whitfield
Clun Farm House,
High Street, Clun,
Shropshire SY7 8JB
Tel   01588 640432
Fax   01588 640432
Mobile   07885 261391
Web   www.clunfarmhouse.co.uk

Map 7   Entry 372

Shropshire

The Birches Mill

Just as a mill should be, tucked in the nook of a postcard valley. It ended Gill and Andrew's search for a refuge from the city; it is a treat to share its seclusion and natural beauty where the only sounds are watery ones from the river. The fresh, breezy rooms in the 17th-century part have elegant brass beds, goose down duvets, fine linen and one has an original, very long, roll top bath; the new stone and oak extension blends beautifully and has become a large, attractive twin. Gill and Andrew are affable hosts, and have brought artistic flair to this stunning valley of meadowland and woods. *Children over 12 welcome.*

Price	£76–£84. Singles by arrangement.
Rooms	3: 1 double, 1 twin; 1 double with separate bath.
Meals	Packed lunch £6. Pub 3 miles.
Closed	November–March.
Directions	From Clun A488 for Bishops Castle. 1st left, for Bicton. 2nd left for Mainstone, then narrow winding lane for 1.5 miles. Up bank to farm, then 1st right for Burlow. House at bottom of hill on left by river.

Gill Della Casa & Andrew Farmer
The Birches Mill,
Clun, Craven Arms,
Shropshire SY7 8NL

Tel	01588 640409
Fax	01588 640409
Email	gill@birchesmill.fsnet.co.uk
Web	www.birchesmill.co.uk

Map 7 Entry 373

Shropshire

Jinlye

Wuthering Heights in glorious Shropshire — and every room with a view. There's comfort too, in the raftered lounge with its huge open fire, the swish dining room for fun breakfasts, the conservatory scented in summer — and the spacious bedrooms with their deep-pile carpets, new mattresses and sumptuous touches... expect faux-marble reliefs, floral sinks, boudoir chairs and spotless *objets*. Sheltered Jinlye sits in lush landscaped gardens surrounded by hills, rare birds, wild ponies and windswept ridges. Kate, Jan and their little papillon dogs look after you well.

Price	£64–£84. Singles £54–£62.
Rooms	6: 3 doubles, 2 twins/doubles, 1 twin.
Meals	Packed lunch on request. Pubs 1 mile.
Closed	Christmas Day.
Directions	From Shrewsbury A49 to Church Stretton past Little Chef & right towards All Stretton. Right, immed. past phone box, up a winding road, up the hill to Jinlye.

Jan & Kate Tory
Jinlye, Castle Hill,
All Stretton, Church Stretton,
Shropshire SY6 6JP

Tel	01694 723243
Fax	01694 723243
Email	info@jinlye.co.uk
Web	www.jinlye.co.uk

Map 7 Entry 374

Shropshire

Hannigans Farm

High on the hillside, a mile up the drive, the views roll out before you – stunning. Privacy and peace are yours in the converted dairy and barn across the flower-filled yard. Big, carpeted, ground-floor rooms have comfy beds and new sofas; one has views that roll towards the setting sun. In the morning Fiona and Alistair, delightful, easy-going and fun, serve you home eggs, fruit, honey and jam in the book-lined dining room of their farmhouse. Feel free to take tea in the garden with its little hedges and manicured lawns, feel restored in this quiet Shropshire corner.

Price	£60. Singles by arrangement.
Rooms	2 twins.
Meals	Pub 1.25 miles.
Closed	Rarely.
Directions	From Bridgnorth, A458 to Shrewsbury. 0.5 miles after Morville, right onto stone road & follow signs for 1 mile, to farm.

Mrs Fiona Thompson
Hannigans Farm,
Morville, Bridgnorth,
Shropshire WV16 4RN
Tel   01746 714332
Fax   01746 714332
Email   hannigansfarm@btinternet.com
Web   www.hannigans-farm.co.uk

Map 7   Entry 375

Shropshire

Acton Pigot

Elegance abounds and yet there's a family farmhouse feel. The fine old house sits well on its ancient piece of ground, its sash windows looking across to the site of England's first parliament. The delightful Owens spoil you with afternoon tea before a log fire in the sitting room (and in the lovely garden in summer). Come for deep beds, soft lights, fine linen, hand-printed wallpaper and English oak in stair, beam and floor. Bedrooms are inviting and cosy. The two-acre garden hugs the house – a treat with rare plants, croquet lawn, shady spots and pool for summer. A restorative place run by special people.

Price	From £70. Singles £45.
Rooms	3: 1 double, 1 twin/double, 1 family room.
Meals	Dinner from £15. Pub 2 miles.
Closed	Christmas.
Directions	From A5 & Shrewsbury, onto A458 for Bridgnorth; 200 yds on, right to Acton Burnell. Entering Acton Burnell, left to Kenley; 0.5 miles, left to Acton Pigot; house 1st on left.

John & Hildegard Owen
Acton Pigot,
Acton Burnell, Shrewsbury,
Shropshire SY5 7PH
Tel   01694 731209
Mobile 07850 124000
Email   acton@farmline.com
Web   www.actonpigot.co.uk

Map 7   Entry 376

Shropshire

Meole Brace Hall

The Hathaways take B&B to a new state of excellence and love having guests in their heavenly house: Georgian and listed, with manicured gardens. It is the quintessence of English period elegance. Joan is a terrific cook who radiates courtesy and charm; Charles cheerfully assumes the role of 'mine host'. Their sumptuous home is rich with antiques, polished mahogany and eye-catching wallpapers and fabrics, and the Blue Room has an elegant half-tester bed. Summer breakfasts are taken in the conservatory, as is afternoon tea. A 20-minute stroll from Abbey and town, but it feels a million miles away.

Price	From £75. Singles from £59.
Rooms	3: 2 doubles, 1 twin.
Meals	Restaurants 1 mile.
Closed	Rarely.
Directions	A5/A49 junc. (south of bypass), follow signs to centre. Over 1st mini r'bout, 2nd exit at next; 2nd left into Upper Rd; 150 yds on at bend, left & immed. right into Church Lane. Drive at bottom on left.

Joan Hathaway
Meole Brace Hall,
Shrewsbury,
Shropshire SY3 9HF

Tel	01743 235566
Fax	01743 236886
Email	hathaway@meolebracehall.co.uk
Web	www.meolebracehall.co.uk

Map 7   Entry 377

Shropshire

Mulberry Lodge

In the middle of its own rambling, informal garden this was once the gardener's cottage to Hawkstone – a Catholic retreat. Nearly a mile from any road, the silence is extraordinary – but this is smarter than country style. Stunning modern oil paintings, huge vases of fresh flowers, good antiques, thick carpets and a cosseting bedroom with enormous walk-in shower and deep deep bath – all in great order and designed to spoil. Sue and Simon are young, charming and unpretentious; food is homemade and often home-grown. Tons to do, from walking in the private park to exploring Shrewsbury.

Price	£70. Singles from £50.
Rooms	2 doubles.
Meals	Pubs/restaurants 10-20 min. drive.
Closed	Rarely.
Directions	Take A442 into Marchamley, on bend turn for 'Hawkstone Hall Centre'. House is 1st on left after 0.75 miles.

Sue Marsh
Mulberry Lodge,
Hawkstone Park, Marchamley,
Shrewsbury, Shropshire SY4 5LF

Tel	01630 685481
Mobile	07870 375235
Email	sue@mulberrylodge.co.uk
Web	www.mulberrylodge.co.uk

Map 7   Entry 378

Shropshire

Brimford House

Tucked under the Breidden Hills, farm and Georgian farmhouse have been in David's family for four generations. Views stretch all the way to the Severn; the simple garden does not try to compete. Bedrooms are spotless and fresh: a half-tester with rope-twist columns and Sanderson fabrics, a twin with Victorian wrought-iron bedsteads, a double with a brass bed and huge bathroom with roll top bath. Liz, friendly and helpful, serves you breakfast round the tulip-legged table: tuck into fresh farm eggs and homemade preserves. Farmhouse comfort, great value and walks from the door.

Price	£55-£65. Singles £40-£60.
Rooms	3: 2 doubles, 1 twin.
Meals	Packed lunch £4.50. Pub 3-minute walk.
Closed	Rarely.
Directions	From Shrewsbury A458 Welshpool road. After Ford, right onto B4393. Just after Crew Green, left for Criggion. House 1st on left after Admiral Rodney pub.

Liz & David Dawson
Brimford House,
Criggion, Shrewsbury,
Shropshire SY5 9AU
Tel   01938 570235
Mobile 07801 100848
Email   info@brimford.co.uk
Web   www.brimford.co.uk

Map 7   Entry 379

Shropshire

Top Farmhouse

A house with a huge heart, to which the loyal return. The house is ancient, magpie-gabled and rambling, the church and pound are 800 years old and Pam is theatrical, gregarious and fun. Downstairs is attractive, warm and cosy, a lattice of beams dividing the dining room from the drawing room where wine and conversation flow. Upstairs, floors rise, fall and creak, beds are brass or varnished pine, trays are filled with treats and windows are double-glazed. Pam's breakfasts are as generous as her spirit. Chirk and Powys castles are close by. *Children over 11 welcome.*

Price	£60-£70. Singles from £35.
Rooms	3: 1 double, 1 twin, 1 double/family room.
Meals	Packed lunch available. Pub 2.5 miles.
Closed	Rarely.
Directions	From Shrewsbury, A5 north. Through Nesscliffe & after 2 miles, left to Knockin. Through Knockin, past Bradford Arms. House 150 yds on left.

Pam Morrissey
Top Farmhouse,
Knockin,
Oswestry,
Shropshire SY10 8HN
Tel   01691 682582
Email   p.a.m@knockin.freeserve.co.uk
Web   www.topfarmknockin.co.uk

Map 7   Entry 380

Shropshire

Pinfold Cottage

Heart-warming B&B. Vintage toys and games add to the merry clutter, illustrations from children's books cover the walls, bedrooms are charming, simple and homely. But the biggest treat is Sue. Generous with her time, spirit and home cooking, she quickly engages you in lively conversation, her laughter echoed by Polly the parrot. Other natural sounds are provided by the well-fed birdlife and the trickle of the stream that meanders through the enchanting garden. Take a glass of wine to the grassy bank and revel in the peace. Breakfasts are healthy and delicious, the value is superb.

Price	£50. Singles £30.
Rooms	2: 1 double, 1 single, each with separate shower. Extra bath available.
Meals	Dinner, 3 courses, from £15. Packed lunch £7. Restaurant 0.5 miles.
Closed	Rarely.
Directions	From Oswestry, A483 from A5 for Welshpool. 1st left to Maesbury; 3rd right at x-roads with school on corner; 1st house on right.

Mrs Sue Barr
Pinfold Cottage,
Newbridge,
Maesbury,
Oswestry,
Shropshire SY10 8AY
Tel 01691 661192
Email suebarr100@hotmail.com

Map 7 Entry 381

Somerset

North Wheddon Farm

Pootle through the vibrant green patchwork of Exmoor National Park and bowl down a pitted track to land in Blyton-esque bliss – a classic Somerset farmyard, crackling with geese and hens, round which is the gentleman farmer's house. Bedrooms are airy and calming with grand views, books, fresh flowers and small, but neat-as-a-pin bathrooms. Bring children and they will be in heaven, with eggs to collect and pigs to pat, or come just for yourself and a bit of indulgence. Food is 'River Cottage' style and much is home reared, the walking is fabulous for miles and kind Rachael sends you off with a thermos of tea.

Price	£55-£60. Singles £27.50-£30.
Rooms	3: 1 double, 1 twin/double; 1 single with separate bath.
Meals	Dinner, 3 courses, £18.50. Cold/hot packed lunch £6.75-£9.75.
Closed	Rarely.
Directions	From Minehead A396 to Wheddon Cross. Pass pub on right & Moorland Hall on left. North Wheddon is next driveway on right.

Rachael Abraham
North Wheddon Farm,
Wheddon Cross,
Somerset TA24 7EX
Tel 01643 841791
Email northwheddonfarm@aol.com
Web www.go-exmoor.co.uk

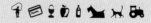

Map 2 Entry 382

Somerset

Emmetts Grange

A superb landscape — the rugged real deal. And if you love huntin', shootin' and fishin' this is your place, high on the moor. At the end of a long drive, a listed country house; be greeted by a peacock (stuffed!) in the hall and a portrait of an ancestor in wig and ermine. Tom and Lucy have boys, dogs, ponies, hens, and raise Red Devon cattle; the Grange is their sideline. Bedrooms and bathrooms are large and comfortable with an old-fashioned feel but you are here for the outdoors: 900 acres of moorland asking to be discovered. Tom is the cook and, not surprisingly, is pretty keen on the local beef.

Price	£70–£94. Singles from £40.
Rooms	3: 1 twin/double, 1 twin, 1 four-poster.
Meals	Dinner, 3 courses, £25. Pub 2 miles.
Closed	Christmas, New Year & occasionally.
Directions	M5 exit 27. A361 towards South Molton. 25 miles then right to A399 Ilfracombe. 1 mile, right towards Simonsbath. 6 miles, entrance to Grange on right.

Tom & Lucy Barlow
Emmetts Grange,
Simonsbath, Minehead,
Somerset TA24 7LD
Tel 01643 831138
Fax 01643 831093
Email causewaybb@aol.com
Web www.emmettsgrange.co.uk

Map 2   Entry 383

Somerset

Higher Orchard

A little lane tumbles down to the centre of lovely old Dunster (the village is a two minute-walk) yet here you have open views of fields, sheep and sea. Exmoor footpaths start behind the house and Janet encourages explorers, by bike or on foot; ever helpful and kind, she is a local who knows the patch well. The 1860s house keeps its Victorian features, bedrooms are quiet and simple and the double has a view to Blue Anchor Bay and Dunster castle and church. All is homely, with stripped pine, cream curtains, fresh flowers, garden fruit and home-laid eggs for breakfast. *Children & pets by arrangement.*

Price	£55. Singles from £30.
Rooms	3: 1 double, 2 twins/doubles.
Meals	Packed lunch from £3.50. Restaurants 2-minute walk.
Closed	Christmas.
Directions	From Williton, A39 for Minehead for 8 miles. Left to Dunster. There, right fork into 'The Ball'. At T-junc. at end of road, right. House 75 yds on right.

Mrs Janet Lamacraft
Higher Orchard,
30 St George's Street,
Dunster,
Somerset TA24 6RS
Tel 01643 821915
Email lamacraft@higherorchard.fsnet.co.uk
Web www.higherorchard.fsnet.co.uk

Map 2   Entry 384

Somerset

The Old Priory

The 12th-century priory leans against its church, has a rustic gate, a walled garden, a tumble of flowers. Both house and hostess are dignified, unpretentious and friendly. Here are old oak tables, flagstones, panelled doors, higgledy-piggledy corridors and large bedrooms in the softest colours. But a perfect English house in a sweet Somerset village needs a touch of pepper and relaxed, cosmopolitan Jane adds her own special flair with artistic touches here and there, and books and dogs for company. Dunster Castle towers above on the hill, walks start from the door.

Somerset

No.7

Feast on homemade biscuits, croissants and local whortleberry jam. Feast, too, on the views of the wooded valley. Then drink in the calm – TV-free! – of Lucy and Jean-Christophe's young, cosy, uncluttered 'cottage hotel': a peace punctuated only by the chimes of the ancient church. Bedrooms are light, not large, and airy, with goosefeather pillows, patchwork quilts and pretty iron beds – but mind your head on the beams. Bathrooms are immaculately white. Down the 17th-century spiralling wooden staircase to sofa and wood-burner below – or for a seat at a crisply white table for Jean-Christophe's delicious dinner.

Price	£75-£80. Singles by arrangement.
Rooms	3: 1 twin, 1 four-poster; 1 double with separate shower.
Meals	Restaurants/pubs 5-minute walk.
Closed	Christmas.
Directions	From A39 into Dunster, right at blue sign 'Unsuitable for Goods Vehicles'. Follow until church; house adjoined.

Price	£60-£75. Singles from £45.
Rooms	3: 2 doubles; 1 double with separate shower.
Meals	Dinner, 3 courses, £21. Afternoon tea from £5. Packed lunch from £5.50.
Closed	Christmas.
Directions	M5 exit 25. A358 towards Minehead, then A39 to Dunster. Thro' village past church, 200 yds; house on left.

Jane Forshaw
The Old Priory,
Dunster,
Somerset TA24 6RY
Tel 01643 821540
Web www.theoldpriory-dunster.co.uk

Lucy Paget-Tomlinson
No.7,
7 West Street, Dunster,
Somerset TA24 6SN
Tel 01643 821064
Mobile 07736 375232
Email info@no7weststreet.co.uk
Web www.no7weststreet.co.uk

Map 2   Entry 385

Map 2   Entry 386

Parsonage Farm

Breakfast beside the open fire is a feast: homemade bread and jam, eggs from the hens, juices from the orchard, pancakes and porridge from the Aga. This is an organic smallholding and your enthusiastic hosts have added an easy comfort to their 17th-century rectory farmhouse – quarry floors, log fires, books, maps and piano in the cosy sitting room. Suki, from Vermont, has turned a stable into a studio, and her pots and paintings add charm to the décor. Big bedrooms have fresh flowers and tranquil views. Wonderful walking and cycling in the Quantock Hills, and the new Coleridge Way starts down the lane.

There's a large organic walled vegetable and soft fruit garden and an apple orchard with many old and rare varieties. Meals are made with the freshest of produce from the garden and apples are pressed into juice in the barn. In the bathrooms are organic cotton towels, and locally-made soaps. Recycling is emphasised, low energy bulbs used and a wood burning central heating boiler is being installed through a renewable energy grant from Eco-Exmoor. Those who arrive without a car can expect a 5% discount.

Price	£55-£65. Singles £35-£50.
Rooms	3: 1 double (extra sofabed), 1 twin/double (extra pull-out bed); 1 double sharing bath.
Meals	Supper £10. Dinner, 2-3 courses, £20-£25.
Closed	Christmas Day.
Directions	A39 Bridgwater-Minehead. 7 miles on, left at Cottage Inn for Over Stowey; 1.8 miles; house on right after church.

SPECIAL
GREEN ENTRY
see page 17

	Susan Lilienthal Parsonage Farm, Over Stowey, Bridgwater, Somerset TA5 1HA
Tel	01278 733237
Fax	01278 733511
Email	suki@parsonfarm.co.uk
Web	www.parsonfarm.co.uk

Map 2 Entry 387

Somerset

Wyndham House

The Vincents have made the house 'smile' again; charming and Georgian, it overlooks the marina within sight and sound of the sea. Bedrooms are pleasantly traditional, the blue double looking onto a pretty courtyard, the twin, with chintz valances and curtains, looking out to Bristol Channel. Breakfasts at the gleaming dining table are generous – Susan loves to cook. The garden has palm trees, ponds, burgeoning borders and a revolving summer house; the steam railway at the bottom runs through the Quantock Hills. Watchet and its marina are being gently revived. *Children by arrangement.*

Somerset

Blackmore Farm

Come for atmosphere and architecture: the Grade I-listed manor-farmhouse is remarkable. Medieval stone walls, a ceiling open to a beamed roof, ecclesiastical windows, a fire blazing in the Great Hall. Ann and Ian look after guests and farm (900 acres plus dairy) with equal enthusiasm. Furnishings are comfortable not lavish, bedrooms are cavernous and the oak-panelled suite (with secret stairway intact) takes up an entire floor. Breakfast at a 20-foot polished table in the carpeted but baronial Great Hall, store your bikes in the chapel, book in for a wedding. A rare place.

Price	From £65. Singles from £35.	Price	£70-£85. Singles £45-£55.
Rooms	2: 1 twin; 1 double with separate bath.	Rooms	4: 1 double, 1 twin, 1 four-poster, 1 suite.
Meals	Pub/restaurants a short walk.	Meals	Pubs/restaurants 5-minute walk.
Closed	Christmas.	Closed	Rarely.
Directions	From railway station & footbridge in Watchet, up South Rd (for Doniford). After 50 yds, left into Beverly Drive. House 50 yds on left with gravel parking area.	Directions	From Bridgwater, A39 west around Cannington. After 2nd r'bout, follow signs to Minehead; 1st left after Yeo Valley creamery; 1st house on right.

Susan & Roger Vincent
Wyndham House,
4 Sea View Terrace,
Watchet,
Somerset TA23 0DF

Tel   01984 631881
Fax   01984 631881
Email rhv@dialstart.net

Ann Dyer
Blackmore Farm,
Cannington, Bridgwater,
Somerset TA5 2NE

Tel   01278 653442
Fax   01278 653427
Email dyerfarm@aol.com
Web   www.dyerfarm.co.uk

Map 2   Entry 388

Map 2   Entry 389

Somerset

Tilbury Farm

The highest B&B in Somerset – up with the buzzards and the wind. Renovation is the Smiths' business and their conversion is exemplary. Reclaimed flags and seasoned oak enhance the natural beauty of the old farmhouse and barns; Pamela is a perfectionist, full of life and plans. Antiques on seagrass floors, dusky pink walls and crisp linen, a sitting room cosy with log fires in winter, a wonderfully monastic dining room for delicious breakfasts. And the setting is spectacular: 20 acres of fields and woodland, wildlife lake and spring. On a clear day can you see for 30 miles. *Children over seven welcome.*

Price	£55–£60. Singles £35–£40.
Rooms	3: 2 doubles, 1 twin.
Meals	Pubs 0.5 miles.
Closed	Rarely.
Directions	From Taunton, A358 north for Williton. Approx. 7 miles on, right for West Bagborough. Through village, up hill for 0.5 miles. Farm on left.

Mrs Pamela Smith
Tilbury Farm,
West Bagborough,
Taunton,
Somerset TA4 3DY
Tel   01823 432391

Map 2   Entry 390

Somerset

Bashfords Farmhouse

A feeling of warmth and happiness pervades the exquisite 17th-century farmhouse in the Quantock hills. The Ritchies love doing B&B even after 14 years, and there's a homely feel with splashes of style – well-framed prints, good fabrics, comfortable sofas. Rooms are pretty, fresh and large and look over the cobbled courtyard or open fields; the sitting room has an inglenook, sofas and books. Charles and Jane couldn't be nicer, know about local walks (the McMillan Way runs past the door) and love to cook: local meat and game, tarte tatin, homemade bread and jams. A delightful garden rambles up the hill.

Price	£60–£65. Singles £35–£37.50.
Rooms	3: 1 double; 1 double with separate shower; 1 twin with separate bath.
Meals	Dinner £25. Supper £20.
Closed	Rarely.
Directions	M5 junc. 25. A358 for Minehead. Leave A358 at West Bagborough turning. Through village for 1.5 miles. Farmhouse 3rd on left past pub.

Charles & Jane Ritchie
Bashfords Farmhouse,
West Bagborough,
Taunton,
Somerset TA4 3EF
Tel   01823 432015
Email   info@bashfordsfarmhouse.co.uk
Web   www.bashfordsfarmhouse.co.uk

Map 2   Entry 391

Somerset

Causeway Cottage

Robert and Lesley are ex-restaurateurs, so guests heap praise on their food, most of which is sourced from a local butcher and fishmonger; charming Lesley also runs cookery courses. This is the perfect Somerset cottage, with an apple orchard outside and views to a lofty church across a cottage garden and a field. The bedrooms are light, restful and have a country-style simplicity with their green check bedspreads, white walls and antique pine furniture. A great hideaway for food-lovers with easy access to the M5 and a quiet, rural feel. Very special. *Children over ten welcome.*

Price	From £66. Singles by arrangement.
Rooms	3: 1 double, 2 twins.
Meals	Supper from £20. Pub/restaurant 0.75 miles.
Closed	Christmas.
Directions	From M5 junc. 26, West Buckland road for 0.75 miles. 1st left just before stone building. Bear right; 3rd house at end of lane, below church.

Lesley & Robert Orr
Causeway Cottage,
West Buckland, Wellington,
Somerset TA21 9JZ
Tel   01823 663458
Fax   01823 663458
Email   causewaybb@aol.com
Web   www.causewaycottage.co.uk

Map 2   Entry 392

Somerset

Saltmoor House

An abundance of Georgian elegance and comfort: fresh flowers, beautiful pictures and Italianate murals, an 18th-century French mirror and Empire chairs, checks, stripes and toile de Jouy… all exist in perfect harmony. Gorgeous, light bedrooms have thick bathrobes and fat pillows; bathrooms thrill with roll top baths, soaps and scents. Elizabeth's cooking is sublime and imaginative and she uses plenty of home-grown produce. You are in the heart of the Somerset Moors and Levels, surrounded by mystical views and countryside of huge environmental significance: wonderful.

Price	From £100. Singles £50.
Rooms	3: 1 twin; 2 doubles, each with separate bath.
Meals	Dinner, 3-4 courses, £25-£30. BYO. Pub 5 miles.
Closed	Rarely.
Directions	M5, junc. 24; 5 miles via Huntworth to Moorland; 2 miles after Moorland, house on right after sharp right-hand bend.

Crispin & Elizabeth Deacon
Saltmoor House,
Saltmoor,
Burrowbridge, Bridgwater,
Somerset TA7 0RL
Tel   01823 698092
Email   saltmoorhouse@aol.com
Web   www.saltmoorhouse.co.uk

Map 2   Entry 393

Somerset

Church Cottage

Partly clothed in English garden and with views to the church, this 400-year-old cottage has wooden beams, low ceilings and wonky walls. Ignore the modern house on the other side of the road and restore your senses with blue lias flagstones, neutral colours, soft cushions, a flash of Thompson gazelle skin, the whiff of woodsmoke and floppy roses on a scrubbed table. Caroline is artistic and rustles up a fine breakfast in her calm kitchen. Bedrooms are small and simple – pine furniture, cool colours; the Potting Shed is a private, generous nest for two. Miles of walking straight from the door.

Price	£60-£85. Singles £50-£75.
Rooms	3: 2 doubles; 1 double with separate bath/shower.
Meals	Packed lunch available. Pubs 1 mile.
Closed	Rarely.
Directions	M5 exit 23 to A39. 7 miles; left to Shapwick. Cottage on left next to church.

Caroline Hanbury-Bateman
Church Cottage,
Station Road,
Shapwick,
Bridgwater,
Somerset TA7 9NH
Tel   01458 210904
Email   caroline@shapwick.fsnet.co.uk

Map 3   Entry 394

Somerset

Church House

Eggs from the hens, organic sausages, homemade preserves served at a long table on Villeroy & Boch china – great attention to detail at this Georgian rectory. All is pristine, sparkling, light and fresh; walls are cream, goose down duvets as soft as a cloud, bathrooms stylish and sumptuous and each bedroom has a harmonious blend of new furniture – rattan, Provençal or classic. There is the odd caravan visible but this is a world away from Weston, with sweeping views across Bristol Channel. Close to airport and roads, the perfect gathering point for friends – warm, inviting, professional B&B.

Price	From £75. Singles from £55.
Rooms	5: 4 doubles, 1 twin.
Meals	Pubs 400 yds.
Closed	Rarely.
Directions	M5 junc. 21, follow signs for Kewstoke. After Old Manor Inn on right, left up Anson Rd. At T-junc. right into Kewstoke Rd. Follow road for 1 mile; church on right; drive between church & church hall.

Jane & Tony Chapman
Church House, 27 Kewstoke Road,
Kewstoke, Weston-super-Mare,
Somerset BS22 9YD
Tel   01934 633185
Fax   01934 633185
Email   churchhouse@kewstoke.net
Web   www.churchhousekewstoke.co.uk

Map 2   Entry 395

Somerset

Rolstone Court Barn

A converted Victorian grainstore, full of light, good family furniture, portraits and interesting finds. It's down a narrow lane on the Somerset Levels — fabulous walking country — and has a big, Mendip-view garden. Two prettily decorated bedrooms are under the eaves, the other on the first floor, there's a lovely sitting room with open fire and a smart dining room for delicious breakfasts of organic bacon and sausages. Kathlyn, who extends her welcome to children and dogs, will collect from or deliver to Bristol airport, thus saving you airport parking. An attractive stopover for the Cornwall route.

Somerset

Barton Drove Cottage

Come for the setting and the views — on a clear day you can see all the way to the Black Mountains. The pretty cottage extension is tucked into the hill so the first-floor drawing room opens directly to the terrace. All is polished and spotless inside and the guest bedroom traditional: patterned rugs on soft carpet, a crisp white bed, two gorgeous views. The bathroom has a corner bath (and a loo with more view!). Charming Sarah enjoys her guests and her garden and grows flowers for the house. Roe deer in the field, primroses in the woods, wonderful walking on Wavering Down.

Price	£70. Singles £45.
Rooms	3: 1 double; 1 double, 1 family room sharing bath/shower.
Meals	Pubs/restaurants 4 miles.
Closed	Rarely.
Directions	M5 junc. 21; north onto A370 towards Bristol. Take 2nd right to Rolstone, then 1st left into Balls Barn Lane. House 3rd & last.

Price	£60. Singles £30.
Rooms	1 double.
Meals	Supper £15. Packed lunch £5. Pubs within 3 miles.
Closed	Rarely.
Directions	From A38 0.5 miles up Winscombe Hill. When road begins to descend, left between houses onto unmade track. Cottage 100 yds on the left.

Kathlyn Read
Rolstone Court Barn,
Rolstone, Hewish,
Weston-super-Mare,
Somerset BS24 6UP

Tel   01934 820129
Email   read@rolstone-court.co.uk
Web   www.rolstone-court.co.uk

Sarah Gunn
Barton Drove Cottage,
Winscombe Hill, Winscombe,
Somerset BS25 1DJ

Tel   01934 842373
Mobile   07736 417363
Email   sarahgunn2000@hotmail.com
Web   www.bartondrovecottage.info

Map 3   Entry 396

Map 3   Entry 397

Somerset

Harptree Court

One condition of Linda's moving to her husband's family home was that she should be warm! She is, and you will be, too. Linda has softened the 1790 house and imbued the rambling rooms with an upbeat elegance — they're sunny and sparkling with beds and windows dressed in delicate fabrics in perfect contrast to solid antique pieces. On one side of the soaring Georgian windows, 17 acres of parkland with ponds, an ancient bridge and carpets of spring flowers; on the other, the log-fired guest sitting room and extravagant bedrooms. An excellent breakfast sets you up to walk the grounds. Relaxing and easy.

Price	£90–£100. Singles from £70.
Rooms	3: 2 doubles; 1 twin/double with separate shower.
Meals	Dinner, 2-3 courses, £17.50–£25. Pub 400 yds.
Closed	Rarely.
Directions	Turn off A368 onto B3114 towards Chewton Mendip. After approx. 0.5 miles, right into drive entrance, straight after 1st x-roads. Left at top of drive.

	Linda Hill
	Harptree Court,
	East Harptree, Bristol,
	Somerset BS40 6AA
Tel	01761 221729
Mobile	07970 165576
Email	location.harptree@tiscali.co.uk
Web	www.harptreecourt.co.uk

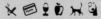

Map 3   Entry 398

Somerset

Manor Farm

Rosalind loves bringing people together and, as a geologist and walking enthusiast, can shed new light on the area. The place is stuffed with books and maps... pet sheep, chickens, ducks and friendly cats. The garden suite, adapted for wheelchair users, is accessible from its pretty and secluded walled garden and has an inglenook fireplace in its private sitting room and 17th century charm. The others are homely and old-fashioned — not swish — with a mix of new pine and white units. Breakfast on duck eggs and admire the views of Wells — why not walk to Evensong?

Price	£65–£90. Singles from £40.
Rooms	4: 2 doubles, 1 suite; 1 twin/double with separate bath & shower.
Meals	Packed lunch & light snacks. Pub 1 mile.
Closed	November–February.
Directions	From Wells, A371 for Shepton Mallet for 1 mile; left onto B3139. In Dulcote, left at fountain. House 4th on right after Manor Barn.

	Rosalind Bufton
	Manor Farm,
	Dulcote, Wells,
	Somerset BA5 3PZ
Tel	01749 672125
Fax	01749 672125
Email	manorfarm@wells-accommodation.co.uk
Web	www.wells-accommodation.co.uk

Map 3   Entry 399

Somerset

Hillview Cottage

Don't tell too many of your friends about this place. It's an unpretentious ex-quarryman's cottage presided over by Catherine – a warm-spirited and cultured host who'll make fresh coffee, chat about the area, even show you around Wells Cathedral (she's an official guide). This is a comfy, tea-and-cakes family home with rugs on wooden floors, antique patchwork quilts, an old Welsh dresser in the kitchen and elevated views. The bedrooms have a French feel, and there's a sitting room with books and magazines. Walk from the door, or play tennis (on grass!) or croquet. Wonderful, modest and excellent value.

Price	£70. Singles £35.
Rooms	2: 1 twin/double, 1 twin sharing bath (2nd room let to same party only).
Meals	Pubs 0.25 miles.
Closed	Rarely.
Directions	From Wells A371 to middle of Croscombe. Right at red phone box & then immed. right into lane. House up on left after 0.25 miles. Straight ahead into signed drive.

Michael & Catherine Hay
Hillview Cottage,
Paradise Lane,
Croscombe,
Wells,
Somerset BA5 3RN
Tel   01749 343526
Email   cathyhay@yahoo.co.uk

Map 3   Entry 400

Somerset

The Manor House

Tucked into a hamlet, the house oozes tranquillity. Late medieval, owned by Glastonbury monks, an architectural flourish at every turn: plasterwork ceiling, Jacobean staircase, Tudor fireplace. English country-house furnishings are gorgeously mixed with Indian textiles and antiques. Three bedrooms in a private wing share a boldly stylish bathroom and are prettily feminine with hand-crafted bedheads, antiques and rich fabrics. The garden delights with rose pergola, knot garden and fish pond. Local bread and organic meats for breakfast, and Harriet and Bryan cultured and engaging.

Price	£80. Singles £40.
Rooms	3: 2 doubles, 1 single all sharing bath (let to same party only).
Meals	Pub 2 miles.
Closed	15 December-15 January.
Directions	A361 Shepton Mallet-Glastonbury. At Pilton, turn between village stores and Crown Inn onto Totterdown Lane; 1 mile; right at T-junc. in W. Compton; next right 100 yds onto lane. On left.

Harriet Ray
The Manor House,
West Compton,
Shepton Mallet,
Somerset BA4 4PB
Tel   01749 890582
Fax   01749 890582
Email   jbr-halr.westcompton@virgin.net

Map 3   Entry 401

Somerset

Pennard House

Pennard has been in Susie's family since the 17th century – the cellars date from then and the superstructure is stately, lofty and Georgian. Multi-lingual Martin runs an antiques business from here and he and Susie obviously enjoy having guests in their home. You have the run of the library, drawing room, magnificent billiard room, 60-acre orchard, meadows, woods, grass tennis court and six acres of garden with a spring-fed pool (swim with the newts). Bedrooms are large and have good views; one is oval with a corner bath in the room. Although this is a big house it still feels warm and comfortably lived in.

Price	From £90. Singles from £45.
Rooms	3: 1 double, 1 twin; 1 twin/double with separate bath/shower.
Meals	Pub 2 miles.
Closed	Rarely.
Directions	From Shepton Mallet south on A37, through Pylle, over hill & next right to East Pennard. After 500 yds, right & follow lane past church to T-junc. at very top. House on left.

Martin & Susie Dearden
Pennard House,
East Pennard, Shepton Mallet,
Somerset BA4 6TP

Tel   01749 860266
Fax   01749 860700
Email   susie.d@ukonline.co.uk

Map 3   Entry 402

Somerset

Broadgrove House

In lushest Somerset, at the end of a long lane, tranquillity: a 17th-century stone house, a walled cottage garden, fruit trees and horses. Inside is just as special. Beams, flagstones and inglenook fireplaces have been sensitively restored; rugs, pictures, comfy sofas and polished antiques add warmth and serenity. The twin, at the end of the house, has its own front door. Breakfast on homemade and farmers' market produce before exploring Longleat, Stourhead, Wells. Sarah, engaging, well-travelled and a great cook, looks after guests and horses with equal enthusiasm. *Shooting available. Children by arrangement.*

Price	From £80. Singles £50.
Rooms	2: 1 twin & sitting room; 1 double with separate bath.
Meals	Dinner, 3 courses, from £25. Pub/restaurant 1 mile.
Closed	Christmas & New Year.
Directions	Directions on booking.

Sarah Voller
Broadgrove House,
Leighton, Frome,
Somerset BA11 4PP

Tel   01373 836296
Mobile   07775 918388
Email   broadgrove836@tiscali.co.uk

Map 3   Entry 403

Claveys Farm

For the artistic seeker of inspiration and the adventurous, not those who thrill to standardised luxury. Fleur is a talented artist, Francis works for English Heritage, both have a passion for art, real food and lively conversation. Rugs are time-worn, panelling and walls are distempered with natural pigment, bedrooms are better than simple, beds have white linen. From the warm kitchen of this 18th-century house come delicious home-grown meals, breakfast eggs from the hens and oak-smoked bacon from Fleur's rare-breed pigs. Acres of fields, footpaths and woodland await for long walks and Mells is a dream.

The Kellys use only local and organic food stuffs, producing their own hams, oak-smoked bacon, sausages, pork, lamb, vegetables, fruit (for delicious compotes and jams) and nuts. They recycle with real enthusiasm, the chickens and the compost heap playing their part. No artificial fertilisers are used and only animal manure goes on the garden. Organic flour for your freshly baked bread at breakfast is left to prove overnight in the Aga, and only environmentally friendly cleaning products are used.

Price	£65. Singles £32.50.
Rooms	2: 1 double/family, 1 twin sharing separate bathroom.
Meals	Dinner, 3 courses, £15. BYO. Occasional lunch. Packed lunch £5. Pub/restaurant 0.5 miles.
Closed	Rarely.
Directions	At Mells Green on Leigh-on-Mendip road SW from Mells (NGR ST718452). Past red phone box; house last on right before speed de-restriction signs. If lost, Mells PO, by the village pond, has map outside.

Fleur & Francis Kelly
Claveys Farm, Mells,
Frome, Somerset BA11 3QP

Tel	01373 814651
Mobile	07968 055398
Email	bandb@fleurkelly.com
Web	www.fleurkelly.com/bandb

SPECIAL
GREEN ENTRY
see page 17

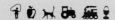

Map 3 Entry 404

Somerset

Chalice Hill House

You can see St John's spire poking out over the treetops: vibrant Glastonbury buzzes just below. Fay's contemporary artistic flair mingles naturally with the classical frame of this Georgian house; grand mirrors, wooden floors, gentle colours and loads of books create an interesting feel. The bedrooms are enchanting, not at all understated; carved oak Slavic sleigh beds, embroidered Indian cotton bedspreads and views of the dovecote, wedding cake tree and Chalice Hill beyond. Weekend breakfasts are leisurely, served with panache (and optional chilli sauce!). Exotic, comfortable elegance – and a lovely hostess.

Price	£90. Singles £75.
Rooms	2: 1 double, 1 twin.
Meals	Occasional dinner. Pubs/restaurants 5-minute walk.
Closed	Rarely.
Directions	From top of Glastonbury High Street, right; 2nd left into Dod Lane. Past Chalice Hill Close; right into driveway.

Fay Hutchcroft
Chalice Hill House,
Dod Lane, Glastonbury,
Somerset BA6 8BZ
Tel   01458 830828
Mobile   07976 959409
Email   mail@fayhutchcroft.co.uk
Web   www.chalicehill.co.uk

Map 3   Entry 405

Somerset

Estate Farmhouse

A warm, interesting, artistic house with owners to match. The Burnhams, one of whom worked in fashion, have an eye for colour, material and form; coir matting sits stylishly with well-loved antiques and bedrooms feel fresh and new. Floorboards bend and creak, ceilings dip and wave, there are plump white duvets, pictures, prints and lots of well-thumbed books. The twin is the bigger, its bathroom comfortable and close. Breakfasts (some produce from their daughter's organic deli) are served at a long table in a charming dining room, overseen by ancestors. *Children by arrangement.*

Price	£70. Singles £55.
Rooms	2: 1 double; 1 twin with separate bath.
Meals	Pub 300 yds.
Closed	Christmas.
Directions	From Somerton Lake B3153 for Langport. Right after 2 miles for Pitney, just before Halfway Inn. Down to bottom of road; house last but one on right, with dark green railings.

Peter & Jane Burnham
Estate Farmhouse,
Pitney,
Langport,
Somerset TA10 9AL
Tel   01458 250210

Map 3   Entry 406

Somerset

The Lynch Country House

Peace, seclusion and privacy at this immaculate Regency house in lush Somerset. First-floor bedrooms are traditionally grand, second-floor rooms snug but as smart; those in the coach house have a more modern feel. Deep warm colours prevail, fabrics are flowery and carpets soft green. You'll feel as warm as toast and beautifully looked after. A stone stair goes right to the top where the observatory lets in a cascading light; the flagged hall, high ceilings, long windows and private tables at breakfast create a country-house hotel feel. The vast, lovely grounds are rich in trees and wildlife.

Price	£70–£100. Singles £60–£70.
Rooms	9: 1 double, 1 twin, 2 four-posters; 1 double (extra single bed) with separate bath. Coach house: 3 doubles, 1 twin.
Meals	Restaurants 5-minute walk.
Closed	Never.
Directions	From London, M3 junc. 8, A303. At Podimore r'bout A372 to Somerton. At junc. of North St & Behind Berry.

Mr Roy Copeland
The Lynch Country House,
4 Behind Berry, Somerton,
Somerset TA11 7PD
Tel   01458 272316
Fax   01458 272590
Email   the_lynch@talk21.com
Web   www.thelynchcountryhouse.co.uk

Map 3   Entry 407

Somerset

Mill House

Two and a half hours from London, peace and serenity on the Somerset Levels. A stream flows under one end of the listed building into the Brue and you can fish without leaving the grounds. Rita and Michael took on the handsome mill house five years ago and gave it antique elegance and period colours. Bedrooms are carpeted and comfortable, mattresses new; views sail over the mill stream to fields. Aga-fresh breakfasts are brought to a smart dining table, the marmalades are Rita's and the attention to detail is wonderful. *Children over ten welcome.*

Price	£60–£88. Singles from £34.
Rooms	3: 1 twin/double, 1 double, 1 single.
Meals	Pub 1 mile.
Closed	January.
Directions	A303; A37 towards Bristol; onto B3153 at Lydford. Right at Keinton Mandeville, down Coombe Hill; right at T-junc, bottom of hill. House 1st on right.

Michael & Rita Knight
Mill House,
Mill Road,
Barton St David,
Somerset TA11 6DF
Tel   01458 851215
Email   b&b@millhousebarton.co.uk
Web   www.millhousebarton.co.uk

Map 3   Entry 408

Somerset

Bratton Farmhouse

A place full of delicious paradoxes – a gorgeous old (1600) house which is at the same time calm and full of life: cosy and fresh, ancient yet modern. Quietly amusing Australian host Suellen has created an airy, vital effect throughout and the bedrooms are a joy. One, in the main house, has oak-panelled walls and a vast bed with old French embroidered linen. Another, in a newly converted studio across the courtyard, has its own living room with wood-burner. There's stabling for your horse and the pretty garden spills over into open countryside, promising walks and rides galore.

Price	From £80. Singles from £50.
Rooms	3: 1 double/twin & sitting room; 2 doubles, each with separate bath/shower.
Meals	Lunch £10. Dinner, 3 courses, £25. Packed lunch £5. Pub 2 miles.
Closed	Rarely.
Directions	A303 then A371 signed Wincanton & Castle Cary. Follow signs to Castle Cary. After approx. 2.5 miles, right to Bratton Seymour. House 0.4 miles on right.

	Suellen Dainty
	Bratton Farmhouse,
	Bratton Seymour, Wincanton,
	Somerset BA9 8BY
Tel	01963 32458
Mobile	07780 848567
Email	sdainty52@googlemail.com
Web	www.brattonfarmhouse.co.uk

Map 3   Entry 409

Somerset

Lower Farm

The Good Life in the depths of Somerset, and a delightful family. The Dowdings have converted an old stone barn into a self-contained apartment with lime-washed walls and lovely bedrooms with views across the garden to fields. Perfect for a larger party – the cosy oak-floored sitting room comes with a woodburner and extra beds. The whole place has a charmingly French feel – hens strut around the orchard, Charles grinds their own wheat for daily bread-making, kind Susie can bring you a delicious, organic breakfast: homemade apple juice and yogurt, local bacon, their own eggs. A place to do your own thing.

Price	From £75.
Rooms	2: 1 double, 1 twin. Extra beds in shared sitting room; extra shower.
Meals	Pub 0.5 miles.
Closed	Rarely.
Directions	From junction of A371 and A359 for Bruton. Right to Shepton Montague. At x-roads by pub follow sign to church and village hall. Sharp bend at church, house 100 yds on right. Park in yard behind house.

	Charles & Susie Dowding
	Lower Farm,
	Shepton Montague,
	Wincanton,
	Somerset BA9 8JG
Tel	01749 812253
Email	enquiries@lowerfarm.org.uk
Web	www.lowerfarm.org.uk

Map 3   Entry 410

Somerset

Rectory Farm House

A mile off a fairly main road but as peaceful as can be. Lavinia has showered love and attention on her early Georgian house and garden in a landscape that has changed little since the 18th century. Beams, sash windows, wood fires and high ceilings are the backdrop for gleaming family furniture, paintings and delightfully arranged flowers. Good-sized bedrooms in restful colours have starched linen, fluffy bathrobes and binoculars for watching wildlife; spot deer, badgers, foxes, hares, buzzards. Breakfast is so local it could walk to the table – and includes homemade marmalade and jams.

Price	£84. Singles £52.
Rooms	3: 1 double; 1 twin/double, 1 double sharing bath (let to same party only).
Meals	Dinner £25. Pub 0.5 miles.
Closed	Rarely.
Directions	From the east, exit A303 on to B3081 for Bruton. After 1 mile, left into Rectory Lane. House 0.25 miles on right.

Michael & Lavinia Dewar
Rectory Farm House,
Charlton Musgrove, Wincanton,
Somerset BA9 8ET

Tel	01963 34599
Mobile	07775 651868
Email	mike@oneismore.com
Web	www.rectoryfarmhouse.com

Map 3 Entry 411

Somerset

Yarlington House

A mellow Georgian manor surrounded by impressive parkland, formal gardens, rose garden, apple tree pergola and laburnum walk. Your hosts are friendly and flexible, artists with an eye for detail; her embroideries are everywhere. Something to astound at every turn: fine copies of 18th-century wallpapers, 18th-century fabric around the canopied bed and a bedroom whose Regency striped wallpaper extends across the entire ceiling creating the effect of a Napoleonic tent. There are elegant antiques, proper 50s bathrooms, log fires, a heated pool (summer only). Surprising, unique. *Children by arrangement.*

Price	£100. Singles £50.
Rooms	2: 1 double, 1 twin.
Meals	Pubs/restaurants nearby.
Closed	August.
Directions	From Wincanton, 2nd left on A371, after Holbrook r'bout. Then 3rd right; 1st gateposts on left.

Countess Charles de Salis
Yarlington House,
Wincanton,
Somerset BA9 8DY

Tel	01963 440344
Fax	01963 440335
Email	carolyn.desalis@yarlingtonhouse.com
Web	www.yarlingtonhouse.com

Map 3 Entry 412

Somerset

The Dairy House

A captivating place, tucked under Cadbury Hill. What were once 17th-century stables have been transformed by perfectionist Emma. Step through a smoky-blue stable door into a little cottage – all yours. The sitting room has a grey slate floor, pale walls, interesting art and smart seagrass-covered stairs winding up to an airy, sloping-ceilinged bedroom. It is subtle, understated and beautifully restful. The cottage stands in its own pretty orchard but you're also welcome to explore Emma's gorgeous walled garden. Breakfast is served in the Dairy House. *Children over ten welcome.*

Price	£80. Singles £50.
Rooms	Cottage with 1 twin/double; sofabed; extra shower.
Meals	Pub/restaurant 1.5 miles.
Closed	Occasionally.
Directions	From Wincanton A303 west, exit Chapel Cross for Sparkford. Right for Sparkford, left for Little Weston. House 0.25 miles on left, sign on wooden gate.

Emma & Graham Barnett
The Dairy House,
Little Weston,
Sparkford,
Somerset BA22 7HP
Tel   01963 440987
Fax   01963 441200
Email   grahambarnett@lineone.net

Map 3   Entry 413

Somerset

Barwick Farm House

A proper old-fashioned smallholding with Dorset sheep, hens, horses and all the attendant wildlife. Angela and Robin (charming, and passionate about the soil) have saved ancient elm floorboards, exposed the sandstone linterns of the original fireplaces, stuck to traditional materials, then limewashed the walls in vibrant colours. Roomy bedrooms have ironed cotton sheets and a comforting mishmash of styles; one bathroom is painted bubble-gum pink and has a free-standing bath with views over fields. Wake to birdsong and the sizzle of bacon; good walking and cycling start from the door.

Price	£60-£75. Singles from £35.
Rooms	2: 1 double, 1 family room.
Meals	'Early Bird' packed breakfasts also available. Restaurant 100 yds.
Closed	Rarely.
Directions	A37 to Dorchester; 0.25 miles outside Yeovil, 1st exit off r'bout (opp. Red House pub) following signs to Little Barwick House restaurant. Farmhouse in the fork of the road.

Angela Nicoll
Barwick Farm House,
Barwick, Yeovil,
Somerset BA22 9TD
Tel   01935 410779
Mobile   07967 385307
Email   info@barwickfarmhouse.co.uk
Web   www.barwickfarmhouse.co.uk

Map 3   Entry 414

Somerset

Chinnock House

Fiona's flair has revived the grand little flax merchant's house – Regency, listed and buried down a tangle of lanes. She is charming and it's a delightful set-up. In the house, two big light bedrooms with high beds, thick eiderdowns and fine print wallpapers. In the coach house, two equally delightful sun-filled bedrooms and a super sitting room under the eaves with deep comfy sofas and chairs. Breakfast is at your hosts' gleaming dining table. You are surrounded by a glorious garden – French formality meets English profusion – in a hamlet that could be in France. *Children over eight welcome.*

Price	£70–£120. Singles from £42.
Rooms	4: 1 double;
	1 twin with separate bath.
	Coach house: 2 twins, sharing bath.
Meals	Pubs/restaurants 1 mile.
Closed	Christmas & New Year's Eve.
Directions	Take either of two lanes off A30. Follow sign for West Chinnock but ignore left turn to West Chinnock itself. House on right about 100m after Middle Chinnock church on left.

Fiona Wynn-Williams
Chinnock House,
Middle Chinnock,
Crewkerne,
Somerset TA18 7PN
Tel   01935 881229
Fax   01935 881066
Email fionaww@btinternet.com

Map 3   Entry 415

Staffordshire

Manor House

A rambling, Jacobean, time-capsule farm house with mullioned windows, aged oak and the most sloping floors. The dim interior is crammed with curios, pewter, pictures and settles, gorgeously glowing in the light from winter's roaring fire. There's a bird-filled garden with sculptures, tennis and croquet and a summer house that sports a turret from Sheffield Infirmary. Rooms with views have four-posters; bathrooms flaunt lace, drapes and tassels. Chris and Margaret are easy-going hosts but cook the best breakfasts. If you can leave the table unassisted you are welcome to make yourselves very much at home.

Price	£52–£58. Singles from £32.
Rooms	4: 3 four-posters, 1 double.
Meals	Pubs/restaurants within 4 miles.
Closed	Christmas.
Directions	From Uttoxeter, B5030 for Rocester. Beyond JCB factory, left onto B5031. At T-junc. after church, right onto B5032. 1st left for Prestwood. Farm 0.75 miles on right over crest of hill, through arch.

Chris & Margaret Ball
Manor House,
Prestwood, Denstone, Uttoxeter,
Staffordshire ST14 5DD
Tel   01889 590415
Fax   01335 342198
Email cm_ball@yahoo.co.uk
Web   www.4posteraccom.com

Map 8   Entry 416

Staffordshire

Chartley Manor

The rare Tudor manor has beams, warm colours, fun touches and fresh flowers. Jeremy was born here and deals in antiques (the rooms are filled with polished oak and pewter), Sarah is great at breakfasts; both are generous and enthusiastic hosts. In the Sudbury Yellow drawing room are family portraits and delicious sofas, while bedrooms are cosily carpeted and heavily beamed. One has oak panelling, buttery damask hangings and a secret door to the shower. There's a nature trail in the woodland and masses of history: Mary Queen of Scots was incarcerated in the castle opposite.

Price	£60-£80. Singles £40.
Rooms	2 doubles, each with separate bath/shower.
Meals	Pubs/restaurants 1 mile.
Closed	Christmas & New Year.
Directions	Halfway between Stafford & Uttoxeter on A518, just past Chartley Castle ruin on left & at top of hill, on right.

Jeremy & Sarah Allen
Chartley Manor,
Chartley, Stafford,
Staffordshire ST18 0LN
Tel   01889 270891
Mobile   07958 304836
Email   jeremy.allen4@btopenworld.com
Web   www.chartleymanor.co.uk

Map 8   Entry 417

Staffordshire

Slab Bridge Cottage

A 19th-century cottage in a quiet setting beside the Shropshire Union Canal – one of England's prettiest waterways. Bedrooms have floral curtains and all is spotless and homely, with open fires, polished copper and brass, old oak furniture, pretty bathrooms, fresh flowers. Eat outside on the terrace overlooking the canal, or on the narrowboat on an evening cruise – but do book! Diana makes her own bread, biscuits, cakes and jams and has five llamas, including a baby called Scrumpy; David cuts fresh vegetables and salads from the garden. On a good day for the hens there are home-laid eggs, too.

Price	£65. Singles £45.
Rooms	2: 1 double with separate bath; 1 double with separate shower.
Meals	Dinner £17.50. Packed lunch £5. Pub 2 miles.
Closed	Christmas & New Year.
Directions	M6 junc. 12; A5 west to r'bout; straight on. 1 mile to Stretton x-roads, right then 1st left (Lapley Lane); 3 miles to small x-roads at white house; left. Cottage 0.5 miles, on right.

Diana Walkerdine
Slab Bridge Cottage,
Little Onn,
Church Eaton, Staffordshire
ST20 0AU
Tel   01785 840220
Fax   01785 840220
Email   ddwalkerdine@btinternet.com

Map 8   Entry 418

Suffolk

Haughley House

A timber-framed, medieval manor in three acres of garden overlooking 30 acres of farmland. The attractive village is in a conservation area; your hosts: the Lord of the Manor and his wife. They also happen to be accomplished cooks and use the finest ingredients – their own beef, game and eggs, and vegetables and soft fruits from the kitchen garden. You'll find genuine country-house style here, tea and homemade cake on arrival, flowery wallpapers, much charm and sparkling shower rooms – there's even a stairlift. Ask Jeffrey to show you the manorial records and the priest hole. Aga-cooked breakfasts are a feast.

Price	From £80. Singles from £60.
Rooms	3: 2 doubles, 1 twin.
Meals	Dinner, 4 courses, £25.
Closed	Rarely.
Directions	From A14 exit 48, after 0.5 miles take right hand fork; house 100 yds on right.

Jeffrey & Caroline Bowden
Haughley House,
Haughley,
Suffolk IP14 3NS
Tel   01449 673398
Fax   01449 673170
Email   bowden@keme.co.uk
Web   www.haughleyhouse.co.uk

Map 10   Entry 419

Suffolk

The Old Vicarage

Up the avenue of fine old horse chestnut trees to find just what you'd expect from an old vicarage: a Pembroke table in the flagstoned hall, a log fire which warms the sitting room for tea and homemade cake, a refectory table sporting copies of *The Field*... an inviting sofa, a piano, hunting scenes and silver pheasants. Bedrooms are large, chintzy and handsomely furnished, and the double has hill views. Weave your way through the branches of the huge copper beech to the garden that Jane loves. She grows her own vegetables, and keeps hens and house with equal talent. *Children over seven welcome.*

Price	From £70. Singles £40.
Rooms	2: 1 double; 1 twin, each with separate bath. Extra single room off twin.
Meals	Dinner £20. BYO. Packed lunch £6. Pub/restaurant 2 miles.
Closed	Christmas Day.
Directions	From Cambridge, A1307 for Haverhill. Left to Withersfield. At T-junc., left. Almost 3 miles on, high yew hedge; at 'Concealed Entrance' sign on left, sharp turn into drive.

Jane Sheppard
The Old Vicarage,
Great Thurlow,
Newmarket,
Suffolk CB9 7LE
Tel   01440 783209
Fax   01638 667270
Email   s.j.sheppard@hotmail.co.uk

Map 9   Entry 420

Suffolk

The Manse

Unmissable in its coat of rich red paint, the beamed, 16th-century Manse overlooks a historic village green. The owners will ply you with fresh fruit, muesli, bread and marmalade – home-grown and homemade – and provide a different posy of garden flowers each day. Robin, ex diplomatic service, has a passion for opera; Bridget organises the church choir. The guest quarters are completely private and deliciously cosy; there are polished antiques, fine porcelain, a rose-tumbled garden for breakfast on fine days, and a chivalrous black labrador called Tristan, always happy to take guests for a walk.

Price	£65–£70. Singles from £40.
Rooms	1 twin/double & sitting room.
Meals	Pub/restaurant in village.
Closed	Rarely.
Directions	From Bury St. Edmunds, A413 to Haverhill; left on to B1066 for Glemsford. 6 miles to Hartest; house on far side of green, opp. red telephone box.

Bridget & Robin Oaten
The Manse,
The Green,
Hartest,
Suffolk IP29 4DH
Tel   01284 830226
Mobile   07910 857446
Email   theoatens@tiscali.co.uk

ᠲ ⚓ ⚑ ⚲ ๘

Map 10   Entry 421

Suffolk

The Old Manse Barn

A loft-style apartment in sleepy Suffolk; this living/eating/sleeping space of blond wood, white walls and big windows has an urban feel yet overlooks countryside. Secluded from the main house, in a timber-clad barn, the style is thrillingly modern: leather sofas, glass dining table, stainless steel kitchenette. Floor lights dance off the walls while CD surround-sound creates mood. The fridge is well-stocked – homemade granola, local bread and ham – so breakfast when you want. There's peace for romance, solitude for work, a garden to sit in and friendly Sue to suggest the best pubs.

Price	£70.
Rooms	Studio with 1 double & kitchenette.
Meals	Pubs/restaurants within walking distance.
Closed	Rarely.
Directions	A134 towards Bury St Edmunds & Sudbury; A1141 Lavenham, left after 1.4 miles towards Cockfield & Stowmarket; 1.2 miles on right.

Sue Jones
The Old Manse Barn,
Chapel Road, Cockfield,
Bury St Edmunds, Suffolk IP30 0HE
Tel   01284 828120
Mobile   07931 753996
Email   bookings@theoldmansebarn.co.uk
Web   www.theoldmansebarn.co.uk

⚓ ⚑ ⚲

Map 10   Entry 422

Suffolk

The Red House

An exceptional town and you are in the heart of it. The Victorian house tumbles with books, photos, plants and flowers; Diana was once a stage manager so there's a stylish feel. The sitting room is terracotta and cosy, bedrooms are simple and comfortable, with pale walls, pine furniture and pretty bedcovers. The garden is bursting with roses – enjoy a sunny breakfast, a glass of wine or a pot of tea outside while the cats bask in the sun. Outside the door: a historic church, splendid Guildhall and pretty houses and shops await your discovery. *Minimum stay two nights at weekends.*

Price	£75.
	Singles from £50 (Mon-Thur only).
Rooms	3: 2 doubles, 1 twin.
Meals	Pubs/restaurants a short walk.
Closed	Christmas.
Directions	From Sudbury, B1115 to Lavenham. Pass Swan Hotel on right, next right into Market Lane, cross Market Place, right, then left. House on right next to school. Off-street parking.

Diana Schofield
The Red House,
29 Bolton Street,
Lavenham,
Suffolk CO10 9RG

Tel	01787 248074
Email	redhouse-lavenham@amserve.com
Web	www.lavenham.co.uk/redhouse

Map 10   Entry 423

Suffolk

16 Bolton Street

Gillian and Bill have moved round the corner to Bolton Street and the welcome is as warm as ever. The house is 15th century, the mood is relaxed, and Lavenham, part medieval, part Tudor, has been voted the fifth finest man-made wonder in England. Low-ceilinged rooms ooze books, pictures and Gillian's fine stitchwork; oak stairs lead to traditional bedrooms nicely beamed, lush fabrics and plump pillows. Gillian likes nothing better than to spoil her guests with Suffolk breakfasts of local sausages and bacon, potato cakes, tasty mushrooms and fresh fruit. Wholly delightful.

Price	£80-£85.
Rooms	2: 1 twin/double, 1 double.
Meals	Packed lunch £6.
	Pubs/restaurants close by.
Closed	Rarely.
Directions	From the market square in Lavenham, pass The Great House Restaurant, then left into Bolton Street. Long pink house at bottom on right.

Bill & Gillian de Lucy
16 Bolton Street,
Lavenham,
Suffolk CO10 9RG

Tel	01787 249046
Email	gdelucy@aol.com
Web	www.guineahouse.co.uk

Map 10   Entry 424

Suffolk

Milden Hall

Over five generations of Hawkins have lived in this seemingly grand 16th-century hall farmhouse with its smooth wooden floors, enormous windows and vast fireplaces. Bedrooms range from big to huge, are elegantly old-fashioned and filled with interesting tapestries, wall hangings and lovely furniture; it's a bit of a trek to the loo from the family room so you need to be nimble. Juliet is a passionate conservationist, full of ideas for making the most of the surrounding countryside, on foot or by bicycle. Expect delicious home-grown bacon, sausages, bantam eggs and fruit compotes for breakfast.

Price	£60–£80. Singles from £40.
Rooms	3: 2 twins, 1 family room, all sharing bathroom.
Meals	Supper £15. Dinner, 2 courses, £20. BYO. Pubs/restaurants 2-3 miles.
Closed	Rarely.
Directions	From Lavenham, A1141 for Monks Eleigh. After 2 miles, right to Milden. At x-roads, right to Sudbury on B1115. Hall's long drive 0.25 miles on left.

Juliet & Christopher Hawkins
Milden Hall,
Milden,
Lavenham,
Suffolk CO10 9NY
Tel   01787 247235
Email   hawkins@thehall-milden.co.uk
Web   www.thehall-milden.co.uk

Map 10   Entry 425

Suffolk

Wood Hall

Susan greets you with the warmest of welcomes. Janus-like, her house looks both ways, Georgian to the front, and beamed Tudor behind. Breakfast on summer mornings on the terrace in the walled garden on homemade marmalade, jams and fruit compotes; in winter, settle beside the fire with a cup of tea. The bedrooms, one delicately floral, the other with cream walls, are elegant with padded headboards, thick curtains, armchairs, writing desks, candles, standard lamps, books and an ample tea tray. Wander through the garden to find a Victorian greenhouse with two types of vine. *Bridge classes offered to groups of four.*

Price	From £80. Singles £45 (Sun-Thurs only).
Rooms	2: 1 double, 1 twin/double.
Meals	Dinner £20 (not Sat). BYO. Pub 150 yds.
Closed	Christmas/New Year.
Directions	B1115 for Lavenham from Sudbury 3.5 miles; right to Little Waldingfield; house on left, 200 yds beyond The Swan. Parking at rear of house.

Mrs Susan Nisbett
Wood Hall,
Little Waldingfield, Lavenham,
Suffolk CO10 0SY
Tel   01787 247362
Fax   01787 248326
Email   susan@woodhallbnb.fsnet.co.uk
Web   www.thewoodhall.com

Map 10   Entry 426

Suffolk

Nether Hall

The garden cascades with old English roses in summer. This is a charming 16th-century home in a valley made famous by John Constable; make the most of this delightful area. The River Box borders the garden, the house, barn and stables are old, the tennis court newer and inside is warmly enticing. Find elegance and period charm in uneven floors and ancient doors, little windows and wonky beams, woodsmoke from the inglenook, chintz and checks on the chairs. And there's a downstairs bedroom with its own entrance. Jennie immediately puts you at ease and is renowned for her breakfasts.

Price	£80–£85. Singles £60.
Rooms	3: 1 double, 1 twin/double; 1 single with separate bath.
Meals	Pubs 1 mile.
Closed	Rarely.
Directions	3 miles from A12, on B1068 between Higham & Stoke-by-Nayland. On south side of road, 300 yds east of Thorington Street.

Patrick & Jennie Jackson
Nether Hall,
Thorington Street,
Stoke-by-Nayland,
Suffolk CO6 4ST
Tel 01206 337373
Fax 01206 337496
Email patrick.jackson7@btopenworld.com

Map 10 Entry 427

Suffolk

Mulberry Hall

Delight in the characterful architecture and uneven tread of this handsome hall house of 1523; it was owned by Cardinal Wolsey and has Henry VIII's coat of arms above the fire. It rambles round corners, is rich in beams and beloved family pieces, and has two winding stairs. Penny, gentle and well-travelled, gives you tea and cakes in the drawing room and lights a log fire on chillier days. In the garden: old roses, pear pergola and mulberry tree; in the bedrooms: leaded windows, beamed walls, good beds. Homemade jam on home-baked bread when you wake, soft robes for the bath before bed.

Price	From £60. Singles from £35.
Rooms	2: 1 twin; 1 double with separate shower.
Meals	Supper £8–£12. Pubs/restaurants 5–8 miles.
Closed	Rarely.
Directions	5 miles west of Ipswich (off A1071). 200 yds after village Post Office Stores, left; next to farmyard.

Penny Debenham
Mulberry Hall,
Burstall,
Ipswich,
Suffolk IP8 3DP
Tel 01473 652348
Fax 01473 652110
Email pennydebenham@hotmail.com

Map 10 Entry 428

Suffolk

The Old Granary Cottage

A watery idyll of bobbing boats, weatherboarded buildings and the whole of lovely Woodbridge to explore. The cottage was once part of a grain store, and you enter through a narrow hallway and up the stairs to a sun-filled sitting/dining room with limewashed cladding, interesting books and paintings and stunning views of river and mill pond. Your bedroom is up another flight of stairs — white walls, French furniture, a grand bed with crisp linen, soft red toile de Jouy, long views. Bryony lays on traditional English as well as jugged kippers, eggs florentine and homemade muesli. *Min. stay two nights at weekends.*

Price	£85. Singles from £55.
Rooms	1 double with separate bath.
Meals	Restaurants & pubs 400 yds.
Closed	Rarely.
Directions	A12 for Woodbridge; signs for Tide Mill. Turn into Tide Mill Way, signed 'Dead End'. Carry on to Tide Mill. Cottage on left, before marina.

Bryony Hebson
The Old Granary Cottage,
Tide Mill Way,
Woodbridge,
Suffolk IP12 1BY
Tel   01394 383793
Email   bryony.hebson@virgin.net
Web   www.theoldgranarycottage.co.uk

Map 10   Entry 429

Suffolk

Melton Hall

There's more than a touch of theatre to this beautiful listed house. The dining room is opulent red; the drawing room, with its delicately carved mantelpiece and comfortable George Smith sofas, has French windows to the terrace. There's a four-poster in one bedroom, an antique French bed in another and masses of fresh flowers and books. The seven acres of garden include an orchid and wildflower meadow designated a County Wildlife Site. River walks, the coast and Sutton Hoo — the Saxon burial site — are close by. Cindy, her delightful children and their little dog, Snowball, give a great welcome.

Price	£95–£110. Singles from £40.
Rooms	3: 1 double; 1 double, 1 single, sharing bath.
Meals	Dinner, 1-3 courses, £16–£34. BYO. Pubs/restaurants nearby.
Closed	Rarely.
Directions	From A12 Woodbridge bypass, exit at r'bout for Melton. Follow for 1 mile to lights; there, right. Immediately on right.

Mrs Lucinda de la Rue
Melton Hall,
Woodbridge,
Suffolk IP12 1PF
Tel   01394 388138
Mobile   07775 797075
Email   cindy@meltonhall.co.uk
Web   www.meltonhall.co.uk

Map 10   Entry 430

Suffolk

The Hayloft

Romantics, walkers, birdwatchers and those who need to get away from it all will be in heaven. In the old hayloft is a self-contained and stunningly stylish apartment: a raftered sitting room with a sweeping oak floor, cream sofas and a window to trumpet the view. The bedroom is uncluttered and cosy with a big leather bed, gorgeous linen and feathered bedside lights. Continental breakfast is in the fridge (homemade jams, local honey, their own fruits in summer, home-baked rolls), there are ten idyllic acres of gardens, meadows and wildlife, and bikes to borrow. Farmers' markets and festivals abound.

Price	£120. Singles £80.
Rooms	Studio with 1 double & sitting room.
Meals	Restaurants 4 miles.
Closed	Christmas.
Directions	North of Woodbridge on A12, take road signed Bredfield. At T-junc with B1078 (3 miles), left, then 1st right into Martins Lane. Farm House on right, gravel parking on left.

Adrian & Jane Stevensen
The Hayloft,
Valley Farm House, Clopton,
Woodbridge, Suffolk IP13 6QX

Tel	01473 737872
Fax	01473 737880
Email	info@thehayloftsuffolk.co.uk
Web	www.thehayloftsuffolk.co.uk

Map 10   Entry 431

Suffolk

The Old Butchers Shop

Artist Sarah has cleverly converted this old butcher's shop: you're right on the main street of an undisturbed brick and timber estuary village, a hop from the sea for birdwatching or walks, and Snape for music lovers. Bedrooms, not huge, are pretty and light with proper linen on supremely comfortable beds and views over the maturing garden or the street and fine Norman church. Two happy cats lie comatose in the drawing room with its gay kilims and bright checks, books jostle for space with pictures. Sarah is laid-back and fun and cooks a mean breakfast: homemade yogurt and stewed fruits, local kippers.

Price	£60-£70. Singles from £40.
Rooms	3: 1 twin/double, 1 double; 1 twin/double with separate bath/shower.
Meals	Pubs/restaurants 5-minute walk.
Closed	Rarely.
Directions	From A12, signs to Orford. Left-hand bend after King's Head pub towards quay. House on opposite side of road with green door. Park in Market Sq.

Mrs Sarah Holland
The Old Butchers Shop,
111 Church Street, Orford,
Woodbridge, Suffolk IP12 2LL

Tel	01394 450517
Fax	01394 459436
Email	sarah@oldbutchers-orford.co.uk
Web	www.oldbutchers-orford.co.uk

Map 10   Entry 432

Suffolk

Priory House

A soft, 16th-century Suffolk combination of bricks and beams; drink in the peace of house and garden all day if you wish. The house is friendly and informal, with antique furniture, gleaming brass and William Morris-style floral sofas and chairs; the fascinating, heavily timbered dining room was once a cheese room where 'Suffolk Bang' was made. Expect white walls in the bedrooms and a wood-burning stove in the guest sitting room, along with books and comfy chairs. Plan your days with friendly Rosemary – the Southwold coast is half an hour away. *Children over ten welcome. Minimum stay two nights July-October.*

Price	From £60. Singles £35.
Rooms	3: 1 double; 1 double, 1 twin, each with separate bath.
Meals	Pubs/restaurants 8-minute walk.
Closed	Christmas week.
Directions	From Scole, A140, right onto A143 for Gt Yarmouth. After 7 miles, right at Harleston. B1116 to Fressingfield. Pass church & Fox & Goose on left. At top of hill, right, then left into Priory Rd.

	Stephen & Rosemary Willis
	Priory House,
	Priory Road,
	Fressingfield,
	Eye,
	Suffolk IP21 5PH
Tel	01379 586254
Fax	01379 586254

Map 10   Entry 433

Suffolk

Valley Farm Vineyards

Start the day with a Wissett Sparkler: bubbly from the vineyard that yields a startling variety of wines, all produced by sustainable viticultural methods. The Crafts organise wine tours and give you great home cooking, big beds, good cotton sheets and excellent bathrooms – one with a roll top bath. The Tudor bedroom, pretty in pink, has five leaded windows and exposed beams. In the Victorian extension there are two lofty bedrooms and a sumptuous drawing room. Aga-cooked fresh breakfasts include a choice of spoiling pancakes and you dine overlooking the pretty garden. *Minimum stay two nights.*

Price	£70-£80. Singles from £50.
Rooms	3: 2 doubles; 1 double/twin with separate bath/shower.
Meals	Dinner, 3 courses with wine, £25. Pub/restaurant 1 mile.
Closed	Christmas & New Year.
Directions	From Halesworth, Wissett road. Through Wissett, towards Rumburgh. Pass church on left & after 0.5, miles turn for Valley Farm on left.

	Janet Craft
	Valley Farm Vineyards,
	Wissett, Halesworth,
	Suffolk IP19 0JJ
Tel	01986 785535
Fax	01986 785281
Email	valleyfarmvineyards@tiscali.co.uk
Web	www.valleyfarmvineyards.com

Map 10   Entry 434

Suffolk

Church Farmhouse

Come for the good Suffolk light, peaceful views, lots of books and a relaxed atmosphere. The listed Elizabethan farmhouse sits in a quiet hamlet opposite a thatched church with Southwold and the coast nearby. Restful, uncluttered bedrooms have fresh flowers and laundered linen; bathrooms are modern, well-lit and warm. No sitting room, but a delightful beamed dining room with a generous square table at which you may linger, or have tea in the pretty garden in summer. Sarah, well-travelled and entertaining, is a terrific cook. *Children over 12 welcome. Min. stay two nights at weekends in summer.*

Price	From £70. Singles from £45.
Rooms	3: 1 double, 1 twin; 1 single (double bed) with separate bath.
Meals	Dinner £25-£28. Pub/restaurants within 4 miles.
Closed	Christmas.
Directions	A12 for Wangford; left signed Uggeshall; house 1 mile on left before church.

Sarah Jupp
Church Farmhouse,
Uggeshall,
Southwold,
Suffolk NR34 8BD

Tel	01502 578532
Email	sarah-jupp@lineone.net
Web	www.uggeshall.fsnet.co.uk

Map 10   Entry 435

Suffolk

Grange Farm

The tennis court and garden are surrounded by a 12th-century listed moat – this is a glorious old place. Ancient stairs rise and fall all over the 13th-century house, there are sloping floors and honey-coloured beams and a lovely dining room that was once the dairy. Bedrooms are large, comfortable and traditional; the sitting room is cosy with baby grand, log fire, fresh flowers, books, puzzles and games, and the views are to a garden full of birds. Delightful Elizabeth spoils you with homemade cake, local honey, own bread and homemade marmalade for breakfast. Good value, great fun.

Price	£50. Singles £25.
Rooms	2: 1 twin/double, 1 twin, sharing bath.
Meals	Pub 2-mile walk.
Closed	December-February.
Directions	A1120 (Yoxford to Stowmarket) to Dennington. B1116 north for approx. 3 miles. Farm on right 0.9 miles north of Owl's Green & red phone box.

Elizabeth Hickson
Grange Farm,
Dennington,
Woodbridge,
Suffolk IP13 8BT

Tel	01986 798388
Mobile	07774 182835
Web	www.grangefarm.biz

Map 10   Entry 436

Suffolk

Sandpit Farm

Idyllic views of the wide Alde valley from this deeply comfortable, listed farmhouse. The river borders their 20 acres of beautiful meadows, orchard, gardens, tennis court, ponds and remains of brick-lined moat. Be charmed by family antiques and portraits, easy colour schemes, some beams and open fires, and every cossetting thing in the pretty bedrooms, one with its own sitting room. Susie and her Aga will cook a scrumptious breakfast of homemade and local produce. Near the coast, Snape for concerts, great birdwatching, walks and cycling. Peaceful and so relaxing. *Painting classes possible.*

Price	£65-£80. Singles from £45.
Rooms	2: 1 double, 1 twin.
Meals	Pub/restaurant 1.5 miles.
Closed	Rarely.
Directions	From A1120, Yoxford to Stowmarket, east to Dennington; take B1120, Framlingham. First left; house 1.5 miles on left.

Mark & Susie Marshall
Sandpit Farm,
Bruisyard,
Saxmundham,
Suffolk IP17 2EB
Tel   01728 663445
Email   smarshall@aldevalleybreaks.co.uk
Web   www.aldevalleybreaks.co.uk

Map 10   Entry 437

Suffolk

The Old Methodist Chapel

Atmosphere and architecture – easy to see what seduced Jackum and David into converting this listed Victorian chapel into a home. Bedrooms have their own entrance and are charming – one, with access to conservatory and courtyard garden, has pale walls, oak floors and beams; the flag-floored Retreat Room sports bright rugs and bedcovers from far-flung places. The chapel is comfortably, cosily cluttered and the Browns are easy-going. Potions and lotions by your bath, videos, DVDs and music in your room, books and flowers in every corner, and famous bacon from Peasenhall. *Minimum stay two nights at weekends.*

Price	£75-£90. Singles £50-£65.
Rooms	2: 1 twin; 1 double with separate bath.
Meals	Pubs/restaurants within walking distance.
Closed	Rarely.
Directions	From A12 in Yoxford, A1120 signed Peasenhall & Stowmarket. Chapel 200 yds on right.

Jackum & David Brown
The Old Methodist Chapel,
High Street, Yoxford,
Suffolk IP17 3EU
Tel   01728 668333
Mobile   07887 580139
Email   browns@chapelsuffolk.co.uk
Web   www.chapelsuffolk.co.uk

Map 10   Entry 438

Suffolk

Arch House

Arch House stands in three acres of garden, meadow and woodland by the river Hundred, home to the delightful and fun-loving Araminta and Hugh. He, a keen member of the Soil Association, shoots, fishes and grows his own veg; she is involved in the Healing Hands projects; both are great cooks. They are also complementary therapists, so book a treatment in advance! The décor is traditional, the bedrooms are colourful, and the casually elegant drawing/dining room has a boudoir grand piano you're very welcome to play. Trout, salmon or game for dinner; at breakfast, eggs from the hens. Great value.

Price	£55-£65. Singles £30.
Rooms	2: 1 double with separate bath; 1 double (same party only).
Meals	Dinner from £15. BYO. Pub 200 yds.
Closed	Rarely.
Directions	From A12, A1094 into Aldeburgh. Left at r'bout onto B1122 to Leiston. On left, 0.5 miles after Aldringham sign.

Araminta Stewart & Hugh Peacock
Arch House,
Aldeburgh Road,
Aldringham,
Suffolk IP16 4QF
Tel   01728 832615
Email amintys@aol.com

✗ ♀ 🐾

Map 10   Entry 439

Suffolk

Dunan House

You may get wild mushrooms for breakfast and new-laid eggs from the chickens. This is an unusual, invigorating place to stay, with a joyful décor. Ann is a potter and her artistry is apparent everywhere: even the hens live in hand-painted houses. Bedrooms are upbeat and attractive, with woven rugs, crisp linen and imaginative, decorative touches, and the double at the top is a wonderful eyrie, with its own little sitting room and long views. Ann and Simon, an illustrator, are entertaining company. It is excellent value and wonderfully close to town and sea. *Minimum stay two nights at weekends.*

Price	From £80. Singles from £50.
Rooms	2: 1 twin/double; 1 double & sitting room with single sofabed.
Meals	Pubs & restaurants 6-minute walk.
Closed	Christmas & New Year.
Directions	From A1094 drive towards town from r'bout. First right towards hospital, through 'Private Road' gate. House 100 yds on left, opp. tennis courts.

Mr Simon Farr & Ms Ann Lee
Dunan House,
41 Park Rd, Aldeburgh,
Suffolk IP15 5EN
Tel   01728 452486
Fax   01728 452486
Email dunanhouse@btinternet.com
Web   www.dunanhouse.co.uk

🐔 ✗ ♀ 🐈

Map 10   Entry 440

Suffolk

Ocean House

Wraparound sea views – you are almost on the beach. Phil, from Zimbabwe, and Juliet are easy-going hosts. The furniture is Victorian, some mahogany, some walnut; no sitting room, but a dining room that is cosily lit by paraffin lamps at dinner. Upstairs, white cotton crocheted bedspreads come from the market at Victoria Falls; here are old things, good taste, books and magazines galore, rugs on wooden floors, biscuits on the bedside coffee/tea tray, a rattan chair or a window seat from which to watch TV or admire the view. You can borrow bikes, play table tennis in the cellar, and sail.

Price	£70-£80. Singles £60-£70.
Rooms	2: 1 double, 1 twin.
Meals	Dinner £12.50-£15. Restaurant 20 yds.
Closed	Rarely.
Directions	From Ipswich A12 north. Right onto A1094 after 20 miles. House in centre of Aldeburgh seafront, between two lookout towers, with parking outside.

Juliet & Phil Brereton
Ocean House,
25 Crag Path,
Aldeburgh,
Suffolk IP15 5BS
Tel   01728 452094
Email   jbreroh@aol.com
Web   www.oceanhousealdeburgh.co.uk

Map 10   Entry 441

Surrey

Swallow Barn

A squash court and stables, once belonging to the next-door manor, have become a happy, homely house. Full of family memories and run by interesting and helpful people, it has a mature charm – and lovely trees in the garden, a paddock and a summer pool. Given the hushed tranquillity you are surprisingly close to the airports and the M25. The bedrooms are small but one has its own entrance, another the use of a sunny sitting room, the third a balcony; beds are firm and have super duvets, garden views are pretty and breakfasts are both generous and scrumptious. *Children over eight welcome.*

Price	£85. Singles £55.
Rooms	3: 1 double & sitting room, 1 twin; 1 twin with separate shower.
Meals	Pub/restaurant 0.75 miles.
Closed	Rarely.
Directions	From M25, exit 11, A319 into Chobham. Left at T-junc.; left at mini-r'about onto A3046. After 0.7 miles, right between street light & postbox. House 2nd on left.

Joan & David Carey
Swallow Barn,
Milford Green, Chobham, Woking,
Surrey GU24 8AU
Tel   01276 856030
Fax   01276 856030
Email   swallowbarn@web-hq.com
Web   www.swallow-barn.co.uk

Map 4   Entry 442

Surrey

Old Great Halfpenny

It feels as rural as Devon, yet you are perfectly placed for airports and easy access to London. The 16th-century listed farmhouse sits on a country lane beneath the Pilgrim's Way. Beyond the pretty garden – Michael's passion – roll the North Downs and wooded hills with hardly a house in sight; there are fabulous walks right from the door. You have your own entrance with fairly steep steps to beautifully furnished bedrooms (Alison is an interior designer) with lovely fabrics and French antique beds. You will be treated to breakfast on the terrace in the summer and large log fires in winter. Special.

Price	£75-£85. Singles £65.
Rooms	2 doubles, each with separate bath.
Meals	Pub 0.5 miles.
Closed	Rarely.
Directions	From London, exit A3 before Guildford, signed Burpham. Ring for detailed directions - 2 miles.

Michael & Alison Bennett
Old Great Halfpenny,
Halfpenny Lane, St Martha,
Guildford, Surrey GU4 8PY

Tel	01483 567835
Fax	01483 303037
Mobile	07768 745765
Email	bennettbird@gmail.com

Map 4   Entry 443

Surrey

The Old Bothy

A fine house in a foliage-rich garden with a glorious view. Willo is Canadian and a potter, Tom an old car enthusiast and keen plantsman; interesting, much travelled people. Breakfast (superb) is taken in the first-floor, barrel-vaulted living room surrounded by paintings and sculpture collected worldwide. One bedroom is downstairs: pale blue walls, good lighting, an Art Deco headboard painted with moon and stars, curtains of maroon silk and a small but perfect bathroom with aquamarine tiles. An intriguing mix of old and new, remarkably peaceful and Gatwick an eight-minute drive. *Packed breakfast for early departures.*

Price	From £70. Singles from £50.
Rooms	2: 1 double; 1 single sharing bath (let to same party only).
Meals	Packed lunch £5. Pub 400 yds.
Closed	Occasionally.
Directions	M23 onto A23. At Longbridge r'bout, A217 towards Reigate, left for Norwood Hill. 1 mile, left into Collendean Lane; house on right after 0.75 miles.

Willo & Tom Heesom
The Old Bothy,
Collendean Lane, Norwood Hill,
Horley, Surrey RH6 0HP

Tel	01293 862622
Fax	01293 863185
Email	willo@heesom.fsnet.co.uk
Web	www.theoldbothy.co.uk

Map 4   Entry 444

Surrey

Lower Eashing Farmhouse

A homely place with a lovely walled garden and super hosts; Gillian, who speaks French, German and Spanish, enjoys welcoming people from all over the world. The house, 16th to 19th century, has exposed timbers, books and bold colours. The dining room is red; the guest sitting room – with open fire and decorated with fascinating artefacts from around the world – is big enough for a small company meeting, or a wedding group. Your hosts, who are great fun, run an efficient and caring ship. In the walled garden, sipping tea, the distant rumble of the A3 reminds you how well placed you are for Gatwick and Heathrow.

Price	From £70. Singles from £45.
Rooms	4: 1 twin/double; 1 twin/double with separate bath/shower; 2 singles sharing shower.
Meals	Pub 300 yds.
Closed	Occasionally.
Directions	A3 south. 5 miles after Guildford, Eashing signed left at service station. House 150 yds on left behind white fence.

David & Gillian Swinburn
Lower Eashing Farmhouse,
Lower Eashing,
Godalming,
Surrey GU7 2QF
Tel   01483 421436
Fax   01483 421436
Email   davidswinburn@hotmail.com

Map 4   Entry 445

Surrey

High Edser

Ancient wattle and daub, aged timbers and bags of character – it really does ramble. Built in 1532, High Edser sits in 2.5 acres of smooth lawns beyond which lie the village and the Surrey hills. But, unlike many houses of a certain age, this one is light and inviting and has the sort of family clutter that makes you feel at home. Bedrooms are full of character; kind Patrick and Carol leave you plenty of space to gently unfurl. The carved wooden fireplace in the stone-flagged dining room is spectacular, and there's a snug study just for guests. Very peaceful in an AONB, yet close to both airports.

Price	£60-£65. Singles £25-£35.
Rooms	3: 2 doubles, 1 twin, all sharing bath.
Meals	Pub/restaurant 300 yds.
Closed	Christmas.
Directions	From A3, 1st exit after M25, for Ripley. Through Ripley & West Clandon, over dual c'way (A246) onto A25. 3rd right to Shere. There, right to Cranleigh. House 5 miles on left, 1 mile past The Windmill.

Patrick & Carol Franklin Adams
High Edser,
Shere Road, Ewhurst, Cranleigh,
Surrey GU6 7PQ
Tel   01483 278214
Fax   01483 278200
Email   carol@highedser.co.uk
Web   www.highedser.co.uk

Map 4   Entry 446

Surrey

Greenaway

An enchanting cottage. People return time and again – for the house, the dovecote, the garden, the countryside, and Sheila and John. The sitting room is vast with restful rich colours and textures. A sturdy, turning oak staircase leads to the sweet bedrooms – and newly decorated bathrooms with roll tops; a peek at them all will only confuse you: each one is gorgeous. There's an ornate bedstead in the Chinese room and, in another, an oak bedstead and beams. An exceptional place and a delightful village with glorious walks on the Greensand Way, yet so close to London and the airports.

Price	£75-£90. Singles from £55.
Rooms	3: 1 double; 1 double, 1 twin, sharing bath.
Meals	Hotel restaurant 0.25 miles.
Closed	Rarely.
Directions	A3 to Milford, then A283 for Petworth. At Chiddingfold, Pickhurst Road off green. House 3rd on left, with large black dovecote.

Sheila & John Marsh
Greenaway,
Pickhurst Road,
Chiddingfold,
Surrey GU8 4TS
Tel 01428 682920
Fax 01428 685078
Email jfmarsh@gotadsl.co.uk

Map 4   Entry 447

Surrey

Hunters

Impossible to believe London is 45 minutes away. Surrounded by lawns, woodland and a palm-dotted terrace, the house feels buried deep in sunny countryside. Large and relaxed, it makes the most of the natural light: rugs on polished wood, flagstones, creamy colours, elegant furniture. Bedrooms (one with balcony) have a smooth, luscious, contemporary feel with bold shots of colour, Ros's vibrant paintings, perhaps an ethnic touch or a modern sculpture. Bathrooms are chic spaces of stone and natural wood. Take walks, play golf, relax over those woodland views, return to a delicious dinner.

Price	From £80. Singles from £65.
Rooms	3: 2 doubles sharing shower; 1 double with separate bath.
Meals	Dinner £20. Pub 4 miles.
Closed	Christmas.
Directions	From A3 onto B3002 towards Bordon; 1 mile; through Grayshott; church on right, drive on left.

Mrs Ros Richards
Hunters,
Grayshott,
Surrey GU26 6DL
Tel 01428 606623
Mobile 07788 420439
Email rosrichards@hotmail.com

Map 4   Entry 448

Sussex

Boonshill Farm

A glorious farmhouse down a cinder track with a duck pond, brick and weatherboard outbuildings, flouncing flower beds and charming Lisette, a garden designer from London who has achieved something different. Large bedrooms have original wide wood flooring, old garden gates for headboards, reclaimed windows as beautiful mirrors, comfortable chairs, pale colours and views across green fields. Outside are acres of lawns, a wildflower garden, chickens and handsome Berkshire pigs; breakfast here is special. You're ten minutes from the cobbled streets of Rye with its smart shops, and the walking's great, too.

Price	£80. Singles £50. Child £10.
Rooms	2: 1 double, 1 twin. Extra child bed.
Meals	Pub 1 mile.
Closed	Rarely.
Directions	Grove Lane opposite The Bell in Iden. Down lane for 1 mile, then left immediately before oast house, down track. Boonshill is at end of track, on left, white gate.

Lisette Pleasance
Boonshill Farm,
Grove Lane,
Iden, Rye,
Sussex TN31 7QA
Tel   01797 280533
Mobile   07706 054787
Email   boonshillfarm@yahoo.co.uk

Map 5   Entry 449

Sussex

Wellington House

The house is a warm marriage of Victorian red-brick front and 16th-century coach house rear. Inside, the friendly Brogdens have worked an informal magic, and comfort rules, from the cosy guests' sitting room to the big peaceful bedrooms above. These are creamy-walled and carpeted, with new mattresses, antique bed linen, pristine shower rooms and good toiletries. Lovely breakfasts – homemade yogurts and fresh fruits as well as full English – and afternoon tea and cakes in the garden. You can visit Bodiam by river boat, comb Camber Sands – or walk to Christopher Lloyd's gardens at Great Dixter up the road.

Price	£70. Singles £50.
Rooms	2 doubles.
Meals	Supper, 3 courses, from £18 (min. 4). Pubs within 2 miles.
Closed	Christmas & New Year.
Directions	Follow brown tourist signs in Northiam village for Great Dixter House & Gardens to Dixter Rd. At main road end, next to opticians.

Fanny & Vivian Brogden
Wellington House,
Dixter Road,
Northiam, Rye,
Sussex TN31 6LB
Tel   01797 253449
Mobile   07989 928236
Email   fanny@frances14.freeserve.co.uk

Map 5   Entry 450

Sussex

Farthings Farm

Perfectly ordinary-looking Edwardian farmhouses tend not to thrill and certainly not in tranquil Sussex. But John and Penny have created something different, light and contemporary; it will appeal to all but hard-nosed traditionalists. Stunning furniture made by John, beautiful smooth wooden floors laid by John, pictures painted by Penny. This talented pair will also offer you privacy in your green or blue bedroom – think minimalist – and a banquet of a breakfast. French windows lead to a fecund abundance in the garden, equally well designed, and Battle is a 20-minute walk on the 1066 footpath.

Price	£70.
Rooms	2 twins/doubles.
Meals	Pub/restaurant 1 mile.
Closed	Rarely.
Directions	A271 from Battle, left onto B2204 for 1 mile. Left after nursery; 0.5 miles down farm track, left at sign for Farthings. Past farm building to house.

Penny & John Rodgers
Farthings Farm,
Catsfield,
Battle,
Sussex TN33 9BA
Tel   01424 773107
Email   penny.rodgers@btinternet.com
Web   www.farthingsfarm.co.uk

Map 5   Entry 451

Sussex

Fox Hole Farm

Whitewashed, carpeted and beamed, a wood-burner twinkling in its inglenook, the pretty tile-hung farmhouse is as cosy as can be. Come for stacks of woody character, a rolling hillside real farm setting and lovely hosts whose kindness goes beyond the call of duty. There are woodpeckers outside the window, nightingales in the wood and low-beamed bedrooms with latch cupboards, mellow boards and latticed windows that reveal sheep and hill views. A really lovely breakfast (eggs straight from the hens) will set you up for a two-mile woodland walk to the small historic town of Battle.

Price	£63. Singles £40.
Rooms	3: 2 doubles, 1 triple.
Meals	Restaurant 1.5 miles.
Closed	24 December-1 February.
Directions	From Battle on A271, 1st right to Heathfield. After 0.75 miles, right into drive.

Paul & Pauline Collins
Fox Hole Farm,
Kane Hythe Road,
Battle,
Sussex TN33 9QU
Tel   01424 772053
Fax   01424 772053
Email   foxholefarm@kanehythe.orangehome.co.uk

Map 5   Entry 452

Sussex

Globe Place

A listed 17th-century house beside the church in a tiny village, ten minutes from Glyndebourne. Alison — a former chef to the Beatles — is a great cook and can provide you with a delicious and generous hamper, and tables and chairs too. Willie is a former rackets champion who gives tennis coaching; there's a court in the large, pretty garden, and a pool. Relax by the inglenook fire in the drawing room after a walk on the Cuckoo Trail or the South Downs, then settle down to a great supper — local fish, maybe, with home-grown vegetables. An easy-going, fun and informal household. *Children over 12 welcome.*

Price	£80. Singles £40–£45.
Rooms	4: 1 double, 1 single sharing bath (single for same party); 1 double, 1 single sharing bath (single for same party).
Meals	Dinner £25. BYO. Hamper £30–£32.50. Pub 10-minute drive.
Closed	Christmas.
Directions	From Boship r'bout on A22, A267. 1st right to Horsebridge & immed. left to Hellingly. Past the church, left into Mill Lane. Next to church. Parking at top of drive.

	Alison & Willie Boone
	Globe Place,
	Hellingly,
	Sussex BN27 4EY
Tel	01323 844276
Mobile	07870 957608
Email	aliboone@globeplace.plus.com

Map 5   Entry 453

Sussex

Ocklynge Manor

On the top of a hill overlooking Eastbourne, a charming 18th-century house. Once a commandery for the Knights of St John of Jerusalem, it was later home of children's illustrator Mabel Lucie Attwell. Now it is the home of Wendy, talented maker of breads, cakes and jams, immaculate seamstress and delightful hostess. Creamy carpeted bedrooms create a mood of relaxed indulgence and are full of thoughtful touches: dressing gowns, DVDs, your own fridge. The day starts with a superb breakfast overlooking the lovely walled garden, and ends in a pretty chintz sitting room just for guests.

Price	£70–£80. Singles from £45.
Rooms	3: 1 twin, 1 family suite for 3; 1 double with separate shower.
Meals	Pub 5-minute walk.
Closed	Rarely.
Directions	From Eastbourne General Hospital, over r'bout on A2021. 1st right to Kings Ave; house at top.

	Wendy Dugdill
	Ocklynge Manor,
	Mill Road, Eastbourne,
	Sussex BN21 2PG
Tel	01323 734121
Mobile	07979 627172
Email	ocklyngemanor@hotmail.com
Web	www.ocklyngemanor.co.uk

Map 5   Entry 454

Sussex

Hailsham Grange

Come for elegance and ease. Noel welcomes you into his lovely Queen 'Mary Anne' home (1701-1705) – set back from the road in a town where they still hold two cattle markets a week. No standing on ceremony here, despite the décor: classic English touched with chinoiserie in perfect keeping with the house. Busts on pillars, swathes of delicious chintz, books galore and bedrooms a treat: a sunny double and a romantic four-poster. Summery breakfasts are served on the flagged terrace, marmalades and jams on a silver salver. The town garden, with its box parterre and bank of cherry trees, is an equal joy.

Price	£75-£110. Singles from £60.
Rooms	4: 1 double, 1 four-poster. Coach house: 1 double, 1 twin/double.
Meals	Pub/restaurants 300 yds.
Closed	Rarely.
Directions	From Hailsham High St, left into Vicarage Rd. House 200 yds on left. Park in coach yard.

Mr Noel Thompson
Hailsham Grange,
Hailsham,
Sussex BN27 1DL
Tel   01323 844248
Email   noel-hgrange@amserve.com
Web   www.hailshamgrange.co.uk

Map 5   Entry 455

Sussex

Old Whyly

Rich colours, lush fabrics, deep sofas, fine oils – there's an effortless elegance to this manor house, once home to one of King Charles's Cavaliers. Bedrooms are atmospheric, one in French style, and the treats continue outside to a beautiful flower garden annually replenished with 5,000 tulips, a lake and orchard, a stunning swimming pool and new tennis court – fabulous. Dine under the pergola in summer; food is a passion and Sarah's menus are adventurous with a modern slant. Glyndebourne is close so make a party of it and take a divine 'pink' hamper with blankets or a table and chairs included.

Price	£90-£130. Singles by arrangement.
Rooms	3: 2 twins/doubles; 1 twin/double with separate bath.
Meals	Dinner, 3 courses, £30. Hampers £35. Pub/restaurant 7 miles.
Closed	Rarely.
Directions	0.5 miles past Halland on A22, south from Uckfield; 1st left off Shaw r'bout towards E. Hoathly; on for 0.5 miles. Drive on left with postbox; central gravel drive.

Sarah Burgoyne
Old Whyly,
East Hoathly,
Sussex BN8 6EL
Tel   01825 840216
Fax   01825 840738
Email   stay@oldwhyly.co.uk
Web   www.oldwhyly.co.uk

Map 5   Entry 456

Sussex

The Grange

There's a time-worn feel to this dreamy home. Books are stuffed into shelves, walls are decorated with years of paintings and wooden African hippos guard the stairs. A mainly Queen Anne rectory in a secluded spot beside the church, the house is beautifully old-fashioned with oak stairs, antique swords, an ancient tapestry and your own comfortable sitting room. The bedroom is light and traditional with an iron bedstead and lovely views over the paddock; a single room is next door. Bunny will look after you perfectly and there's wonderful walking in Pooh Bear country.

Price	From £65. Singles £38.
Rooms	1 double & sitting room.
Meals	Pubs 200 yds.
Closed	Occasionally.
Directions	In the centre of Hartfield, take road (Church Street) between The Haywagon & The Anchor pubs. Pass church on left; house is beyond church, on left.

Bunny & James Murray Willis
The Grange,
Hartfield,
Sussex TN7 4AG
Tel 01892 770259
Email bunnymw@hotmail.co.uk

Map 5   Entry 457

Sussex

Park Cottage

A thoroughly charming, small country house, with a courtyard at the front and a quiet, walled garden at the back, each a riot of colour in spring and summer. When you arrive you are offered tea and homemade cake – a lovely start. Bedrooms are bright and fresh, with sumptuous linen on big beds, good furniture and homemade biscuits on the tea tray. Lucy fills the house with flowers – you'll feel beautifully looked after. Wander from the garden to parkland behind; only birdsong disturbs the peace. Handy for opera lovers, with Glyndebourne so close. *Minimum stay two nights during Glyndebourne.*

Price	£90. Singles from £80.
Rooms	2: 1 double, 1 twin/double.
Meals	Packed lunch £10. Pub 1 mile.
Closed	Christmas & New Year.
Directions	A26 for Uckfield; straight at Little Horsted r'bout for Ridgewood. 1st right down New Road; at phone box right down concealed drive. House 2nd on left.

Mrs Lucy Ann
Park Cottage,
Ridgewood, Uckfield,
Sussex TN22 5TG
Tel 01825 767104
Email l.ann@btinternet.com
Web www.bedandbreakfastslewes.co.uk

Map 4   Entry 458

Sussex

South Paddock

A real one off, with hosts who cater to your every whim. Jennifer enjoys helping you plan your day and books tables at the village pub; Graham makes his own jams and marmalades and, ex-Army, has created a regimental 'museum' in the downstairs loo. Visitors from 59 nations have enjoyed the comforts of this unspoilt, wisteria-clad 1930s bastion of old-Englishness. Bedrooms are Seventies' comfy with good beds, log fires crackle in winter and the garden is a treat, its fruit and veg plot big enough to feed an army. Borrow boots and visit 'Pooh' bridge for a game of sticks. *Children over ten welcome.*

Price	From £78. Singles from £47.
Rooms	3: 1 double, 1 twin, each with separate bath; 2nd twin available.
Meals	Pub in village.
Closed	Rarely.
Directions	From M25, A22 to Maresfield. At mini-r'bout in centre of village, under stone arch opp. church & pub, & over 5 speed bumps. House 1st on left.

Graham & Jennifer Allt
South Paddock,
Maresfield Park,
Uckfield,
Sussex TN22 2HA
Tel   01825 762335

Map 4   Entry 459

Sussex

The Cider House

A stand-alone converted apple store on two levels, promising peace and blissful privacy. Expect books, fridge, sofabed, country views (deer pad down to the pretty garden) and a beautifully uncluttered space. The bedroom upstairs is softly cream with a vaulted ceiling, good furniture and own basin and wc; the sitting room and limestone-tiled bathroom are downstairs. Breakfast is local and brought to you so you have the best of both worlds – Christina and Lawrence leave you to your own devices but are on hand if you need them. It's so quiet you can hear owls at night, yet you're only ten miles from Gatwick.

Price	£110–£120. Singles £80–£90.
Rooms	Cottage for 2–4: 1 double & sofabed in sitting room.
Meals	Supper £20. Packed lunch £15. Pubs/restaurants 2.5 miles.
Closed	Mondays & occasionally.
Directions	B2028; 1st left after Ardingly signed Highbrook, Horsted Keynes & West Hoathly; continue 0.5 miles. Low hedge, gate, post & rail fence and white weather boarded house on right. Right into driveway, house straight ahead.

Christina & Lawrence Flowers
The Cider House, North Cottage,
Upper Sheriff Farmhouse,
Hammingden Lane,
Ardingly, Sussex RH17 6SR
Tel   01444 891340
Mobile   07836 322227
Email   reservations@ciderhousesussex.com
Web   www.ciderhousesussex.com

Map 4   Entry 460

Sussex

Little Lywood

On the ground floor you feel nicely private; the bathroom is a couple of steps from your door. The softly-lit, unfussy room, which overlooks the drive and then the road, has a pine dressing table, rattan chairs, matching curtains and duvet covers, and fresh flowers. No guest sitting room but you breakfast in the old part of this Elizabethan forester's cottage with its small mullioned windows and ancient timbers – Jeannie and Nick will leave you to come and go as you please. Within easy reach of the Ashdown forest and Sussex's great gardens; the one here is lovely, too. *Minimum stay two nights at weekends in summer.*

Price	£65. Singles £45.
Rooms	1 double with separate bath.
Meals	Pubs 2.5 miles.
Closed	Rarely.
Directions	From Haywards Heath, B2028 to Lindfield. House on left, 1.5 miles after passing church at north end of Lindfield.

Jeannie & Nick Leadsom
Little Lywood,
Ardingly Road,
Lindfield,
Sussex RH16 2QX
Tel   01444 892571
Email   nick@nleadsom.plus.com

Map 4   Entry 461

Sussex

Highbridge Mill

Many humorous touches here – a 'No Diving' mat by the bath, a life-size family of pigs by the door – courtesy of Sue and Joffy, your mildly eccentric, extremely charming hosts. The old part of the house – attractive from the rear – was a flour mill (1810-1930) and there's a rusted wheel to prove it; the interiors are joyfully new. A red-Aga kitchen with wrought-iron chandelier, a ruby sitting room with an open fire, bedrooms with quilts and happy colours. Sue has cooked at various posh places and spoils you rotten; breakfast honey comes from the village via their own woodland bees. Huge fun.

Price	£70. Singles £45.
Rooms	2: 1 twin/double; 1 double with separate bath/shower.
Meals	Dinner, 3 courses, £30. Pubs within 10 min. drive.
Closed	15 December-15 January.
Directions	A23, then A272 for Haywards Heath. Pass Ansty Cross pub, downhill towards Cuckfield Rd. Drive to house on right opposite the r'bout sign.

Sue Clarke
Highbridge Mill,
Cuckfield Road, Ansty,
Sussex RH17 5AE
Tel   01444 450881
Mobile 07850 271606
Web   www.highbridgemill.com

Map 4   Entry 462

Sussex

Blakehurst Farm

Immerse yourself in the warmth of family and farming life. Alex and Claire, a hardworking and friendly couple with young children, are the third generation of Locks to farm here and have created a delightful place to stay. Inside the late 18th-century house all is natural and unpretentious. Fine wildlife photographs decorate the guest sitting room, while bedrooms are immaculate and restful, with crisp white linen and views over farmland or across the fields to Arundel Castle. Your breakfast egg comes from the back garden, you can walk or cycle straight onto the South Downs, and the sea is five miles away.

Price	£70. Singles from £35.
Rooms	2: 1 double, 1 twin/double, sharing bath.
Meals	Pubs/restaurants 2-3 miles.
Closed	December-March.
Directions	From Arundel east; first left-hand turning off dual carriageway A27, signed Blakehurst. Farm 0.5 miles on left.

Claire and Alex Lock
Blakehurst Farm,
Arundel,
Sussex BN18 9QG
Tel   01903 889562
Mobile   07786 160307
Web   www.blakehurstfarm.co.uk

Map 4   Entry 463

Sussex

The Well House

A delightful hideaway – your Normandy-styled annexe to a listed Georgian house leads into its own large walled garden and has a private entrance. In the 17th century it was a humble shelter but the thatch and beams are immaculate now. Marilyn's style reflects her warm personality – you have white bedding on a big brass bed, a rich rug on dark boards, small armchairs and an open stove, a hat stand for clothes and a fine chest of drawers. It's luxurious but cosy, with a shower room to match; even your own small dining room. An unspoilt beach, with dunes, is a seven-minute walk. Perfect. *Minimum stay two nights.*

Price	From £85.
Rooms	1 double.
Meals	Pub/restaurants 2-10-minute walk.
Closed	Rarely.
Directions	A259 Littlehampton/Bognor. Left towards sea signed Climping Street & Beach. House 4th on right with private lay-by opposite.

Marilyn Craine
The Well House,
Climping Street, Climping,
Littlehampton, Sussex BN17 5RQ
Tel   01903 713314
Email   info@baronshall.co.uk
Web   www.baronshall.co.uk

Map 4   Entry 464

Sussex

The Flint House

Calm, kind Vivien feeds the birds from the stable door, then turns breakfasts (from the organic farm shop) into an early-morning house party – later there are delicious cakes for tea. The garden has a tennis court and lovely views; the house, built by Napoleonic prisoners of war, was once part of the Goodwood estate. Two sunny, ground-floor bedrooms in the converted cattle byre (with a reading room and pool table) have white bedspreads and chintz curtains; bathrooms have huge hot towel rails and spoiling treats. You are close to Goodwood, and husband Tim manages a thoroughbred stud. *Children over 12 welcome.*

Price	£80–£100. Singles £50.
Rooms	2: 1 double, 1 twin.
Meals	Pubs in village, 1 mile.
Closed	Christmas & New Year.
Directions	A272 to Midhurst, A286 to Singleton. Left for Goodwood; over downs, past racecourse, next right for Lavant; 0.5 miles, house 1st on right.

Tim & Vivien Read
The Flint House,
Pook Lane, East Lavant, Chichester,
Sussex PO18 0AS

Tel	01243 773482
Mobile	07860 244396
Email	theflinthouse@ukonline.co.uk

Map 4   Entry 465

Sussex

Lordington House

On a sunny slope of the Ems valley, life ticks by peacefully as it has always done… apart from a touch of turbulence in the 16th century. The house is vast and impressive, with majestic views past clipped yew, box, pillared gates and walled garden to the AONB beyond. Inside is engagingly old-fashioned: Edwardian beds with firm mattresses and floral bedspreads, carpeted Sixties-style bathrooms, shepherdess wallpapers up and over wardrobe doors. Tea cosies and homemade marmalade at breakfast, big log fires and a panelled drawing room. *Children over five welcome. Dogs by arrangement.*

Price	From £75. Singles from £40.
Rooms	4: 1 double; 1 twin/double with separate bath/shower; 1 double, 1 single sharing bath/shower.
Meals	Dinner £20. Packed lunch from £5. Pub 1 mile.
Closed	Rarely.
Directions	Lordington (marked on some road maps) west side of B2146, 6 miles south of South Harting, 0.5 miles south of Walderton. Enter thro' white railings by letterbox; fork right after bridge.

Mr & Mrs John Hamilton
Lordington House,
Lordington, Chichester,
Sussex PO18 9DX

Tel	01243 375862
Fax	01243 375862
Email	audreyhamilton@onetel.com

Map 4   Entry 466

Sussex

Church Gate

Janie has added a conservatory and sunny, friendly 'live-in' kitchen to her 1930s house. Smiling and bubbly, she rustles up eggs from her black hens at breakfast, and may even treat guests to home-baked bread or croissants, served on the terrace in summer. The house is adorned with Nigerian musical instruments and Janie's photographs from ex-pat days; the sun-streamed, practically furnished bedrooms are brightened with garden flowers. Polish your serve on the tennis court (bring the raquets), or set off for Chichester with its theatre and shops. Or pretty Itchenor, a mecca for sailors.

Sussex

Itchenor Park House

The Duke of Richmond reportedly built Itchenor Park for his French mistress in 1783. If he was hoping to hide her away, he succeeded – the listed Georgian house sits in beautiful formal gardens on a vast 700-acre farmed estate. It is remote, wonderfully tranquil, and a field path brings you to Chichester harbour for boat trips and sailing bustle. More walks to the beach and around the village. You stay in a graceful self-contained apartment in the cricket pavilion wing with private sitting room and use of the walled garden (breakfast is in the fridge). Your hosts are gracious and energetic people.

Price	From £70. Singles from £40.
Rooms	4: 1 double; 1 twin with separate bathroom. Cottage: 1 double, 1 twin & sitting room.
Meals	Pub 0.5 miles.
Closed	Christmas & occasionally.
Directions	From A27 at Chichester take A286 Witterings; 5 miles; at r'bout bear right onto B2179. 0.5 miles turn right to Itchenor. 1 mile, house opp. church.

Price	£80. Singles from £40.
Rooms	1 twin/double & sitting room with sofabed & kitchenette.
Meals	Continental breakfast. Pub 5-minute walk.
Closed	Rarely.
Directions	A27 at Chichester onto A286 towards the Witterings. At Birdham, right at garage onto B2179; 500 yds, right to Itchenor. Driveway on left past church, signed.

	Mrs Janie Impey
	Church Gate,
	Itchenor, Chichester,
	Sussex PO20 7DL
Tel	01243 514700
Email	janie.allen@btinternet.com
Web	www.chichesterbandb.co.uk

	Susie Green
	Itchenor Park House,
	Itchenor, Chichester,
	Sussex PO20 7DN
Tel	01243 512221
Mobile	07718 902768
Email	susie.green@lineone.net

Map 4   Entry 467

Map 4   Entry 468

Sussex

Crede Farmhouse

Lesley, once a dancer, is vivacious and kind; Peter helps cook delicious Aga breakfasts. This fine flint house (1810) is a cottagey haven inside: all is fresh, peaceful and beautifully maintained. One bedroom is primrose and white with green views, the sweet smaller double has a wrought-iron bed and overlooks a barn. Crackling fires, ticking clocks and breakfast overlooking the terrace in winter; a pool and garden in summer. Your hosts' easy generosity and delectable Bosham (history, harbour, sailing boats) make this special. Chichester Theatre is up the road; Portsmouth ferry port 30 minutes away.

Price	£70–£90. Singles £55–£60.
Rooms	2: 1 double; 1 small double with separate bath.
Meals	Pubs/restaurants 5-minute walk.
Closed	Christmas.
Directions	From Chichester, A259 west for Bosham; through Fishbourne, past garden centre, left into Walton Lane. After sharp bend, right into Crede Lane; 200 yds to end of lane. On left, with white garage.

Mrs Lesley Hankey
Crede Farmhouse,
Crede Lane,
Bosham,
Sussex PO18 8NX
Tel 01243 574929
Email lesley@credefarmhouse.fsnet.co.uk

Map 4   Entry 469

Sussex

Castle Cottage

However beautiful the countryside and the walks, you will be most enchanted by what your hosts have achieved. In birdsung woodland is a small house with a separate weather-boarded family barn and a cobbled conservatory. The barn's A-frame roof draws in the light and the front views, and there are perfect decorative touches: Persian carpets, dashing blue paints, a wrought-iron staircase, sculptures, handmade paper, superb lighting. The double in the house has the same magic. But the treehouse upstages all, high in a giant chestnut, with vast bed, veranda, sauna and shower room. Beautifully built… ineffable.

Price	£90–£125.
Rooms	3: 1 double with separate bath/shower. Barn: 1 family suite. Treehouse: 1 double.
Meals	Pubs/restaurants 1.5 miles.
Closed	Rarely.
Directions	From Fittleworth, south on B2138. Right onto Coates Lane; 1 mile, then right onto 'private drive'. Right at castle, right again & immed. left.

Alison Wyatt
Castle Cottage,
Coates Castle, Fittleworth,
Sussex RH20 1EU
Tel 01798 865001
Fax 01798 865032
Email alison@castlecottage.info
Web www.castlecottage.info

Map 4   Entry 470

Sussex

Fitzlea Farmhouse

A wooded track leads to the beautiful, mellow, 17th-century farmhouse with tall chimneys and a cluster of overgrown outbuildings. Wood-panelled walls and ancient oak beams, a vast open fireplace, mullioned windows and deep sofas create an atmosphere of relaxed country-house charm. Maggie welcomes you to a delicious breakfast in her Aga-warm farmhouse kitchen; in spring, the scent of bluebells wafts through open doors. A winding staircase leads to comfortable timbered bedrooms which overlook fields, rolling lawns and woodland where you can stroll in peace. Heavenly. *Children by arrangement.*

Price	£50-£80. Singles by arrangement.
Rooms	3: 1 family room; 1 double, 1 twin, sharing bath.
Meals	Packed lunch available. Pubs/restaurants 2 miles.
Closed	Christmas.
Directions	Directions on booking.

Maggie Paterson
Fitzlea Farmhouse,
Selham,
Petworth,
Sussex GU28 0PS
Tel   01798 861429

Map 4   Entry 471

Sussex

Beauchamp Cottage

In the market town of Petworth, with a tucked-away feel, a cosy retreat for two. The owners, who live nearby, have sensitively restored the little two-storey cottage with its brewery connections. Up the pine stair, under open rafters, is a light and airy sitting room with wooden floors and sofabed; downstairs, carved antique beds and fine linen, a super shower room and sweet garden views. Breakfast waits for you in the little kitchen with microwave and fridge. Petworth House, with paintings, history and summer concerts in the park, is a treat. *Off-street parking. Two nights minimum stay preferred.*

Price	From £85.
Rooms	Cottage with 1 twin/double, sitting room & kitchen area.
Meals	Pubs/restaurants 1.25 miles.
Closed	Never.
Directions	In Petworth, follow one-way system to end of East St. Straight ahead onto Middle St; at T-junc. with High St, driveway opposite, thro' arch.

Dr David Parsons
Beauchamp Cottage,
c/o Fairfield House,
High Street, Petworth,
Sussex GU28 0AU
Tel   01798 345110
Fax   01798 345110
Email beauchampcottage@btinternet.com

Map 4   Entry 472

Sussex

Amberfold

Down the secluded, wooded lane and through a stone archway to find a glorious terraced garden and a listed 17th-century house; the perfect hideaway. Bedrooms are in individual annexes so you can come and go as you please. Step in to vibrant colours, large beds, interesting art, a refreshing lack of clutter and space for comfy armchairs; showers only do full pelt and towels are plentiful. Erling (who adores music and, clearly, gardening) is dedicated to your happiness, making this the perfect place to recharge the batteries in peace and quiet; breakfast on the terrace in summer.

Price	£65-£95. Singles £55-£75.
Rooms	2 doubles.
Meals	Pubs 1-4 miles.
Closed	Rarely.
Directions	From Midhurst, A286 for Chichester. After Royal Oak pub on left, Greyhound on right, on for 0.5 miles, left to Heyshott. On for 2 miles, do not turn off, look for white posts & house sign on left.

Erling Sorensen
Amberfold,
Heyshott, Midhurst,
Sussex GU29 0DA

Tel	01730 812385
Mobile	07802 415639
Email	erlingamberfold@aol.com
Web	www.amberfold.co.uk

Map 4   Entry 473

Sussex

The Quag

Buried in a birchwood, The Quag feels remote, yet Midhurst – "the second most attractive town in England" – is only two miles away. Feel private in your own space with bedroom, striking bathroom with chequerboard floor, pine-floored sitting room with futon, useful fridge and separate stairs to garden and pool. You breakfast in the main house at a long wooden table with antique wheatsheaf-back chairs. Views are to the lawns that run romantically down to the stream, then across to the South Downs. Mark works for Christie's and Loveday looks after you. A happy, relaxed atmosphere.

Price	From £70. Singles £50.
Rooms	1 twin & sitting room.
Meals	Pubs/restaurants nearby.
Closed	Occasionally.
Directions	A272 Midhurst-Petersfield; 2 miles from Midhurst, left signed Minsted. Count 7 telegraph poles, then 1st left. White house 1st on right.

Loveday & Mark Wrey
The Quag,
Minsted,
Midhurst,
Sussex GU29 0JH

Tel	01730 813623
Fax	01730 817844
Email	beds@wrey.co.uk

Map 4   Entry 474

Sussex

Severals House

In a sunny clearing deep in the woods stands a mellow house in a garden filled with lavender. The Fairlies happened upon it years ago and fell in love with it. Originally two woodcutters' cottages – an old brick path still leads to the well – it was built in the year of Trafalgar. Jock is a rug weaver and a writer so there's a fine collection of books, and he and Serena are the loveliest hosts. The fresh-feeling, green and white bedroom is large, comfy and totally peaceful; breakfast includes Midhurst Royal sausages and homemade marmalade. Walk through a little garden gate into bird-filled woods.

Price	£70-£80. Singles from £45.
Rooms	1 double.
Meals	Pubs/restaurants 1-2 miles.
Closed	Rarely.
Directions	From centre of Midhurst, A272 to Petersfield. 1 mile on, see Woolbeding on right; go past. Carry on A272; 300 yds on, left into wood. Blue 'Single Track Road' sign. House 300 yds on right.

Serena & Jock Fairlie
Severals House,
Severals Wood,
Midhurst,
Sussex GU29 0LX
Tel   01730 812771

Map 4   Entry 475

Sussex

Redford Cottage

In a tiny village, an enchanting house – home to much-loved books and very kind hosts. The immense inglenook dates back to 1510 and the guest rooms are exceptionally private. The room in the main house, cosy, old-worldly and floral, has a private sitting room with a woodburner and access to undulating lawns; the barn has the woody spaciousness of a ski chalet and is perfect for friends… old rugs, new pine, games, views and (up open stairs) beds tucked under a sloped ceiling. The silence is filled with birdsong and you are surrounded by wildlife and the rolling South Downs. Breakfasts are a treat.

Price	From £85. Singles from £55.
Rooms	3: 1 double & sitting room. Barn: 2 twins/doubles & sitting room.
Meals	Pubs/restaurants 2.5-4 miles.
Closed	Christmas.
Directions	On old A3, north from Petersfield, at Hill Brow right for Rogate, left after 300 yds to Milland. Follow lane through woods for 6 miles; right for Midhurst & Redford. On right, 150 yds beyond Redford sign.

Caroline & David Angela
Redford Cottage,
Redford,
Midhurst,
Sussex GU29 0QF
Tel   01428 741242
Fax   01428 741242

Map 4   Entry 476

Sussex

Park Farm

Through a farm gate to a gravelled forecourt and a super home: Nigel and Cathy's 18th-century dairy farmhouse and your annexe. Bedrooms, let to one party only, are pale and pretty, deeply comfortable and huge: one with elegant family pieces, both with field views. There are soft carpets, fat duvets and – luxury – your own sitting/dining room (breakfast here on eggs from Cathy's hens). French windows lead to a patio, then the garden with wild areas and paddocks. Your friendly and humorous hosts know all about walking (borrow Potter the chocolate lab) and run a wine business from here. *Children over eight welcome.*

Price	From £80. Singles from £40.
Rooms	2 twins sharing bath & sitting room (same party only).
Meals	Pub within walking distance.
Closed	Christmas–mid-January.
Directions	From x-roads in centre of Milland by the Rising Sun pub, take Petersfield road; Park Farm 0.25 miles on right on leaving village.

Nigel & Cathy Johnson-Hill
Park Farm,
Milland,
Liphook,
Sussex GU30 7JT
Tel   01428 741389
Fax   01428 741368
Email   cathy@vintry.co.uk

Map 4   Entry 477

Warwickshire

Mows Hill Farm

From the flagstoned kitchen, peep through the stable door at the cattle munching in their stalls – perfect for nature lovers! The place has been in the family for generations and the late-Victorian farmhouse has a warm, uplifting feel. Lynda and Edward have completely redecorated: the sitting and dining rooms are elegant and comfortable, the family room (with shower) is a symphony of lavender and white, the double room dramatic cream and navy. You get a proper farmhouse breakfast in the new, warm conservatory – homemade bread and jams, home-reared bacon, just-laid eggs – and field views reach out from every window.

Price	£75. Singles from £45.
Rooms	2: 1 family room; 1 double with separate bath.
Meals	Pub/restaurant 3 miles.
Closed	Rarely.
Directions	A3400 Hockley Heath; B4101 (Spring Lane); left into Umberslade Rd. At 2nd triangle, keep right & onto Mows Hill Rd; 0.25 miles on right.

Mrs Lynda Muntz
Mows Hill Farm, Mows Hill Road,
Kemps Green, Tanworth in Arden,
Warwickshire B94 5PP
Tel   01564 784312
Fax   01564 783378
Email   mowshill@farmline.com
Web   www.b-and-bmowshill.co.uk

Map 8   Entry 478

Warwickshire

Salford Farm House

Beautiful within, handsome without. Thanks to subtle colours, oak beams and lovely old pieces, Jane has achieved a seductive combination of comfort and style. A flagstoned hallway and an old rocking horse, ticking clocks, beeswax, fresh flowers: this house is well-loved. Jane was a ballet dancer, Richard has green fingers and runs a fruit farm nearby – you may expect meat and game from the Ragley Estate and delicious fruits in season. Bedrooms have a soft, warm elegance and flat-screen TVs, bathrooms are spotless and welcoming, views are to garden or fields. Wholly delightful.

Price	£85. Singles £52.50.
Rooms	2 twins/doubles.
Meals	Dinner £25.
Closed	Rarely.
Directions	A46 from Evesham or Stratford; exit for Salford Priors. On entering village, right opp. church, for Dunnington. House on right, approx. 1 mile on, after 2nd sign on right for Dunnington.

Jane & Richard Beach
Salford Farm House,
Salford Priors,
Evesham,
Warwickshire WR11 8XN
Tel   01386 870000
Email   salfordfarmhouse@aol.com
Web   www.salfordfarmhouse.co.uk

Map 8   Entry 479

Warwickshire

Cross o' th' Hill Farm

From the veranda you can see the church where Shakespeare is buried. (A footpath across the fields gets you there – and Stratford – in 12 minutes.) There's been a farm on this rural spot since before Shakespeare's time but part of the house is Victorian. Built around 1860, it's full of light, with wall-to-ceiling sash windows, glass panelling in the roof, large uncluttered bedrooms and smart, newly decorated bathrooms. The garden, full of trees and birds, dates from the same period – there's even a sunken croquet lawn. Decima grew up here; she and David are gentle hosts, and passionate about art and architecture.

Price	£76-£80. Singles £57-£60.
Rooms	3: 2 doubles; 1 double with separate bath.
Meals	Pubs/restaurants 20-minute walk.
Closed	20 December-February.
Directions	From Stratford south on A3400 for 0.5 miles, 2nd right on B4632 for Broadway Rd for 500 yds. 2nd drive on right for farm.

Decima Noble
Cross o' th' Hill Farm, Broadway Rd,
Stratford upon Avon,
Warwickshire CV37 8HP
Tel   01789 204738
Mobile   07973 971067
Email   decimanoble@hotmail.com
Web   www.crossothhillfarm.com

Map 8   Entry 480

Warwickshire

Blackwell Grange

Sheep-dotted views entice you from mullioned windows, Wyandotte bantams strut the summer lawns, and the peace is profound. The mellow stone farmhouse surrounded by fields is a homely and unstuffy place to stay; there are flagstones, beams and floorboards that creak, and a guest sitting room that invites you with books, magazines, comfy sofas and open fire. Generous-sized bedrooms have well-loved furniture and touches of chintz, bathrooms are well-equipped and the room on the ground floor is perfect for wheelchairs. Footpaths, bridleways and lanes radiate from the door.

Price	From £75-£80. Singles from £35.
Rooms	3: 2 twins/doubles, 1 single.
Meals	Pubs 1-1.5 miles.
Closed	Rarely.
Directions	From Stratford upon Avon, A3400 for Oxford. After 5 miles, right by church in Newbold on Stour & follow signs to Blackwell. Fork right on entering Blackwell. Entrance beyond thatched barn.

Liz Vernon Miller
Blackwell Grange,
Blackwell, Shipston-on-Stour,
Warwickshire CV36 4PF

Tel	01608 682357
Fax	01608 682856
Email	sawdays@blackwellgrange.co.uk
Web	www.blackwellgrange.co.uk

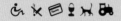

Map 8   Entry 481

Warwickshire

Loxley Farm

The gentle kind Hortons love their home – a thatched cruck house from 1501 – and their guests; they will even drive you to the theatre. The main house is all you'd hope for in Shakespeare country, the woodland garden is a treat, and the bedrooms, in a listed 17th-century barn, are peaceful, private and charming. The Garden Suite has its own sun-streamed conservatory – ideal for watching the birds – while the beamy Hayloft has a little sitting room and a kitchenette. Generous breakfasts are served in the main house by Anne, at a beautiful antique table. It is a delight to stay here.

Price	£75. Singles £50.
Rooms	2: 1 suite with sitting room & kitchenette; 1 suite.
Meals	Pub 3-minute walk.
Closed	1 December-7 January.
Directions	From Stratford, A422 Banbury road for 4 miles; turn for Loxley; through village, left at bottom of hill; 3rd house on right.

Mrs Anne Horton
Loxley Farm,
Loxley, Warwick,
Warwickshire CV35 9JN

Tel	01789 840265
Fax	01789 840645
Email	loxleyfarm@hotmail.com
Web	www.loxleyfarm.co.uk

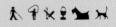

Map 8   Entry 482

Warwickshire

Drybank Farm

Behind the high, worn, red-brick facia of the farmhouse lies a cool, impressive hall, where Angela – beautifully organised and helpful – welcomes you. Honey coloured beams, lush fabrics and jugs of fresh flowers make for a perfectly serene feel, and the countrified bedrooms and bathrooms are superb. If it's action you're after, your host will flawlessly arrange shooting, quad biking, horse riding – whatever you wish. Family horses Roger and Jack will be waiting for you at the end of the day, as will a deep bath, French soaps, fluffy dressing gowns ('his' and 'hers') and a feather duvet. Wonderful!

Price	From £76. Singles £55.
Rooms	3: 1 double, 1 twin/double, 1 suite.
Meals	Packed lunch from £9. Pub 0.5 miles.
Closed	Christmas.
Directions	A422 from Stratford to Ettington; thro' village, past Chequers pub on left. Right at x-roads; house on left over brow of hill.

Angela Winter
Drybank Farm, Fosseway,
Ettington, Stratford upon Avon,
Warwickshire CV37 7PD
Tel   01789 740476
Mobile   07966 332299
Email   drybank@btinternet.com
Web   www.drybank.co.uk

Map 8   Entry 483

Warwickshire

Oxbourne House

Hard to believe the house is new, with its beamed ceilings, fireplaces and antiques. Bedrooms are fresh, crisp, cosy and cared for, the family room with an 'up in the attic' feel; lighting is soft, beds excellent, bath and shower rooms top of the range and views far-reaching. In the garden are tennis, sculpture and Graeme's beautiful handmade pergola. Wake to birdsong and fresh eggs from village ducks and hens; on peaceful summer nights, watch the dipping sun. Posy and Graeme are hugely likeable and welcoming: a most comforting place to stay. *Dogs by arrangement.*

Price	£65-£75. Singles from £45.
Rooms	3: 1 double, 1 family room for 3; 1 twin/double with separate bath.
Meals	Dinner from £20. Pub 2-minute walk.
Closed	Rarely.
Directions	A422 from Stratford-on-Avon for Banbury. After 8 miles, right to Oxhill. Last house on right on Whatcote Road.

Graeme & Posy McDonald
Oxbourne House,
Oxhill, Warwick,
Warwickshire CV35 0RA
Tel   01295 688202
Mobile   07753 661353
Email   graememcdonald@msn.com
Web   www.oxbournehouse.co.uk

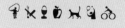

Map 8   Entry 484

Warwickshire

The Old Manor House

Jane, a Cordon Bleu cook, runs her 16th- and 17th-century house with huge energy and efficiency. The A-shaped double in the main part of the house has ancient beams, oak furniture and a lovely bathroom; a newly decorated twin and a single in the other wing are private and self-contained with a large and elegant drawing and dining room for all visitors to share. Breakfasts are carefully prepared here and the river Stour flows through the beautiful landscaped garden. In warm weather enjoy a drink on the terrace surrounded by old, scented roses; dinner will be excellent and locally sourced. *Children over seven welcome.*

Price	From £80. Singles from £45.
Rooms	3: 1 double with separate bath; 1 twin, 1 single sharing bath (2nd room let to same party only).
Meals	Dinner from £25. Restaurants nearby.
Closed	Rarely.
Directions	From Stratford, A422 for 4 miles for Banbury. After 4 miles, right at r'bout onto A429 for Halford. There, 1st right. House with black & white timbers straight ahead.

Jane Pusey
The Old Manor House,
Halford, Shipston-on-Stour,
Warwickshire CV36 5BT

Tel	01789 740264
Fax	01789 740609
Email	info@oldmanor-halford.fsnet.co.uk
Web	www.oldmanor-halford.co.uk

Map 8   Entry 485

Warwickshire

Abbey Farm

Views sweep lakewards and upwards to Merevale Hall… there are abbey ruins in the back garden. Tim, Ali and family arrived five years ago, drawn to this ethereal place and its many acres. Hospitable and generous, they whip up great meals and Aga-cooked breakfasts: Old Spot bacon, black pudding, vine tomatoes, home eggs. Everywhere is charmingly uncluttered with plain Georgian mantles, mullioned and arched windows, fat sofas, scrubbed pine tables; bedrooms are simple country style and a good size. This is family-friendly B&B: cots if you need them, coots on the lake, happy hosts and acres of space.

Price	£59–£79. Singles from £45.
Rooms	3: 2 doubles; 1 double with separate bath/shower.
Meals	Dinner, 3 courses, from £18. Pubs/restaurants 2 miles.
Closed	Rarely.
Directions	M42 exit J10. Head east on A5 towards Atherstone Nuneaton Hinckley. At 3rd r'bout, right into Merevale Lane (B4116). House 1st on left about 0.3 miles, just after 50mph signs.

Tim & Alison Jones
Abbey Farm,
Merevale Lane,
Atherstone,
Warwickshire CV9 2LA

Tel	01827 715091
Email	tim@abbeyfarmbandb.co.uk
Web	www.abbeyfarmbandb.co.uk

Map 8   Entry 486

Warwickshire

Hardingwood House

Close to Stratford and with a theatrical, Tudor feel. Denise, warm and delightful, spoils guests with big bedrooms, dressing rooms, good linen and deep gold-tapped baths. There are books, flowers, antique clocks and plush sofas; tapestry and velvet curtains frame leaded windows; dark timbers and reds and pinks abound. The 1737 barn is immaculate inside and out: the kitchen gives onto a stunning patio, while bedrooms have views to garden or fields. Much rural charm, yet close to Birmingham – and there's a self-catering cottage for two if you like your independence. *Advance booking essential.*

Price	£75. Singles £50.
Rooms	3: 1 double, 2 twins.
Meals	Pub 1 mile.
Closed	Rarely.
Directions	M6 junc. 4; A446 for Lichfield. Into right lane & 1st exit towards Coleshill. From High St, turn into Maxstoke Lane. After 4 miles, right. 1st drive on left.

Mrs Denise Owen
Hardingwood House,
Hardingwood Lane,
Fillongley, Coventry,
Warwickshire CV7 8EL
Tel 01676 542579
Fax 01676 541336
Email denise@hardingwoodhouse.fsnet.co.uk

✗ ᐁ

Map 8   Entry 487

Warwickshire

Park Farm House

Fronted by a circular drive, the warm red-brick farmhouse is listed and old – it dates from 1655. Linda is friendly and welcoming, a genuine B&B pro. There's a stylish, spotless guest sitting room with oriental touches and three bedrooms in apple pie order: new mattresses on mahogany and brass beds, fine fabrics, duvets or blankets on request, heaps of towels. No decorative excesses, just a smart country feel, and breakfasts and dinners that spoil you with the best local produce. A haven of rest from the motorway (morning hum only), and convenient for Birmingham, Warwick and Stratford.

Price	£70-£72. Singles from £42.
Rooms	3: 2 doubles, 1 twin.
Meals	Dinner, 3 courses, from £22. Supper £18. Pub/restaurant 1.5 miles.
Closed	Rarely.
Directions	M6/M69 exit 2; B4065 through Ansty to Shilton; left at lights then next left. Over m'way; after telephone box, right to Barnacle; through village, left into Spring Road, house at end.

Linda Grindal
Park Farm House,
Barnacle, Shilton, Coventry,
Warwickshire CV7 9LG
Tel 0247 6612628
Fax 0247 6616010
Mobile 07786 667900
Web www.parkfarmguesthouse.co.uk

✗ ♀ ᐁ 🚜

Map 8   Entry 488

Warwickshire

Shrewley Pools Farm

A charming, eccentric home and fabulous for families, with space to play and animals to see: sheep, turkeys, geese, Saddleback pigs. A fragrant, romantic garden, too, and a fascinating house (1640), all low ceilings, aged floors and steep stairs. Timbered passages lead to large, pretty, sunny bedrooms (all with electric blankets) with leaded windows and polished wooden floors and a family room with everything needed for a baby. In a farmhouse dining room Cathy serves sausages, bacon, pork, game and lamb from the farm, and is happy to do teas for children. Buy a day ticket and fish in the lake.

Price	From £55. Singles from £40.
Rooms	3: 1 family room (& cot); 1 twin with separate bath, 1 single sharing bath (let to same party only).
Meals	Packed lunch £4. Child's high tea £4. Pub/restaurant 1.5 miles.
Closed	Christmas & New Year.
Directions	From M40 junc. 15, A46 for Coventry. Left onto A4177. 4.5 miles to Five Ways r'bout. 1st left, on for 0.75 miles; signed, opp. Farm Gate Poultry: track on left.

Cathy Dodd
Shrewley Pools Farm,
Five Ways Road, Haseley, Warwick,
Warwickshire CV35 7HB

Tel	01926 484315
Mobile	07818 280681
Email	cathydodd@btinternet.com
Web	www.shrewleypoolsfarm.co.uk

Map 8   Entry 489

Warwickshire

Wethele Manor Farm

Swish and comfortable. And that's the owner, Simon. His clever mum has overseen the dramatic conversion of this once dilapidated house with Georgian façade and older behind into a seriously smart place to stay. Leave your car here and helicopter to Silverstone, or take in a point-to-point. Bedrooms are warm, large and kitted out with good furniture, the best beds, heavy spreads and swish bathrooms — perfect for weddings or house parties. The sitting room is uncluttered and flawless, the food is decently homemade. Bring your children, horses or dogs – all will be beautifully looked after.

Price	£70-£125. Singles from £55.
Rooms	9: 3 doubles, 2 twins, 2 four-posters, 2 family rooms.
Meals	Dinner, 3 courses, £25. Pubs/restaurants under 1 mile.
Closed	Rarely.
Directions	From B4455 go to Hunningham. Left at T-junc. with B4453 thro' Weston-under-Wetherley. House on right on road to Cubbington.

Simon Moreton
Wethele Manor Farm,
Weston-Under-Wetherley,
Leamington, Warwickshire CV33 9BZ

Tel	01926 831772
Mobile	07932 156806
Email	simonmoreton@wethelemanor.com
Web	www.wethelemanor.com

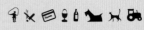

Map 8   Entry 490

Warwickshire

Marston House

A generous feel pervades this lovely family home; Kim's big friendly kitchen is the hub of the house. She and John are easy-going and kind and there's no standing on ceremony. Feel welcomed with tea on arrival, delicious homemade breakfasts, oodles of interesting facts about what to do in the area. The house is big and sunny; old rugs cover parquet floors, soft sofas tumble with cushions and sash windows look onto the smart garden packed with interesting plants and birds. Bedrooms are roomy, traditional and supremely comfortable. A special place with a big heart and great walks straight from the house.

Price	From £80. Singles from £50.
Rooms	3: 1 double, 1 twin/double, each with separate bath; 1 twin/double with separate shower.
Meals	Kitchen supper £22. Dinner £30 (min. 4). Pub 5-minute walk.
Closed	Rarely.
Directions	M40 exit 11. From Banbury, A361 north for 7 miles; at Byfield village sign, left into Twistle Lane; on to Priors Marston; 5th on left with cattle grid, after S-bend (3 miles from A361).

Kim & John Mahon
Marston House,
Priors Marston, Southam,
Warwickshire CV47 7RP

Tel	01327 260297
Fax	08703 835445
Email	kim@mahonand.co.uk
Web	www.ivabestbandb.co.uk

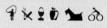

Map 8   Entry 491

Wiltshire

Manor Farm

Farmyard heaven in the Cotswolds. A 17th-century manor farmhouse in 550 arable acres; horses in the paddock, dozing dogs in the yard, tumbling blooms outside the door and a perfectly tended village, with duck pond, a short walk. Beautiful bedrooms are softly lit, with muted colours, plump goose down pillows and the crispest linen. Breakfast in front of the fire is a banquet of delights, tea among the roses is a treat, thanks to charming, welcoming Victoria. This is the postcard England of dreams, with Castle Combe, Lacock, grand walking and gardens to visit. *Children over 12 welcome.*

Price	From £70. Singles from £38.
Rooms	3: 2 doubles; 1 twin with separate bath.
Meals	Pub 1 mile. Wild venison suppers by special arrangement.
Closed	Christmas.
Directions	From M4 A429 to Cirencester (junc. 17). After 200 yds, 1st left for Grittleton; there, follow signs to Alderton. Farmhouse near church.

Victoria Lippiatt-Onslow
Manor Farm,
Alderton, Chippenham,
Wiltshire SN14 6NL

Tel	01666 840271
Mobile	07721 415824
Email	victoria.lippiatt@btinternet.com
Web	www.themanorfarm.co.uk

Map 3   Entry 492

Wiltshire

The Coach House

In an ancient hamlet a few miles north of Bath, an impeccable conversion of an early 19th-century barn. Bedrooms are fresh and cosy with sloping ceilings; the drawing room is elegant with porcelain and chintz, its pale walls the ideal background for striking displays of fresh flowers. Sliding glass doors lead to a south-facing patio... then to a well-groomed croquet lawn bordered by flowers, with vegetable garden, tennis court, woodland and paddock beyond. Helga and David are delightful and there's lots to do from here; the splendours of Bath, Castle Combe and plenty of good golf courses are all near.

Price	£60-£70. Singles from £35.
Rooms	2: 1 double with separate bath/shower; 1 twin/double let to same party only.
Meals	Dinner, 3 courses, £20. Pubs/restaurants 1 mile.
Closed	Rarely.
Directions	From M4 junc. 17, A350 for Chippenham. A420 to Bristol (East) & Castle Combe. After 6.3 miles, right into Upper Wraxall. Sharp left opp. village green; at end of drive.

Helga & David Venables
The Coach House,
Upper Wraxall,
Chippenham,
Wiltshire SN14 7AG

Tel	01225 891026
Email	david@dvenables.co.uk
Web	www.upperwraxallcoachhouse.co.uk

Map 3   Entry 493

Wiltshire

Alcombe Manor

Down a maze of magical lanes discover this hamlet and its 17th-century manor house: a deeply romantic hideaway with panelling, wooden floors, a couple of medieval windows, deep sofas, log fires, a galleried hall, shelves of books and plenty of places to sit. A fine oak staircase leads to large, light bedrooms, reassuringly old-fashioned; carpeted floors creak companionably and every ancient leaded window has a dreamy garden view... five acres of English perfection, no less, with topiary and a stream dashing through. Your hosts are kind, the peace is palpable, and you are just five miles from Bath.

Price	From £75. Singles £45.
Rooms	3: 2 twins, each with separate bath/shower; 1 single sharing bath.
Meals	Occasional dinner. Pubs nearby.
Closed	Rarely.
Directions	M4 junc. 17; A4 to Bath through Box; right for Middle Hill & Ditteridge; 200 yds, left signed Alcombe. Up hill for 0.5 miles, fork right; 200 yds on left.

Simon & Victoria Morley
Alcombe Manor,
Box,
Corsham,
Wiltshire SN13 8QQ

Tel	01225 743850
Mobile	07887 855634
Email	morley@alcombebox.fsnet.co.uk

Map 3   Entry 494

Wiltshire

Bullocks Horn Cottage

Up a country lane to this hidden-away house which the Legges have turned into a haven of peace and seclusion. Liz loves fabrics and mixes them with flair, Colin has painted a colourful mural – complete with macaws – in the conservatory. Bedrooms are quiet with lovely views, the sitting room with log fire has large comfy sofas, and the garden, which has been featured in various magazines, is exceptional. Home veg and herbs and local seasonal food are used at dinner which, in summer, you can eat in the cool shade of the arbour, covered in climbing roses and jasmine. *Minimum stay two nights July/August.*

Wiltshire

Glebe House

An attractive restoration of a 19th-century cottage, with landscaped garden and very English views to Spye Park; you are in a quiet hamlet near Avebury, Bath and Lacock. Bill and Ginny will serve you dinner while their ancestors watch over; retire to the delightful drawing room with log fires, coral sofas with fine needlepoint cushions and a lifetime's collection of pieces. Bedrooms are small but prettily dressed; linen is perfectly pressed. Breakfast marmalade and bread are homemade, hundreds of birds sing in the garden, and parrot Biggles chats by the Aga.

Price	From £75. Singles from £35.
Rooms	2: 1 twin;
	1 twin with separate bath.
Meals	Dinner £20-£25. BYO. Pub 1.5 miles.
Closed	Christmas & Easter.
Directions	From A429, B4040 through Charlton, past Horse & Groom. 0.5 miles, left signed 'Bullocks Horn No Through Road'. On to end of lane. Right; 1st on left.

Price	From £65. Singles from £35.
Rooms	2: 1 double, 1 twin.
Meals	Dinner, 3 courses, from £20.
Closed	Christmas & New Year.
Directions	From Devizes-Chippenham A342. Follow Chittoe & Spye Park. On over crossroads onto narrow lane. House 2nd on left.

Colin & Liz Legge
Bullocks Horn Cottage,
Charlton,
Malmesbury,
Wiltshire SN16 9DZ

Tel	01666 577600
Email	legge@bullockshorn.clara.co.uk
Web	www.bullockshorn.co.uk

Bill & Ginny Scrope
Glebe House,
Chittoe, Chippenham,
Wiltshire SN15 2EL

Tel	01380 850864
Mobile	07767 608841
Email	gscrope@aol.com
Web	www.glebehouse-chittoe.co.uk

Map 3   Entry 495

Map 3   Entry 496

Wiltshire

Oaklands

It was the first house in Warminster to have a bathroom. The bathrooms have multiplied since and the interiors have had a recent (delightful) makeover; easy to see why this lovely spacious 1880s house has been in the family forever. Andrew, retired headmaster, and Carolyn, quietly charming, are used to catering for large numbers and serve delicious breakfasts in an elegant room. Bedrooms, most comforting and welcoming, overlook churchyard and trees; fresh fabrics, soft colours, cosy bathroom, family antiques. Deep comfort, lovely people, a big garden for summer and Bath not too far away.

Price	£65-£85. Singles from £55.
Rooms	2: 1 double, 1 twin/double (rooms can interconnect).
Meals	Occasional dinner (min. 4). Pub/restaurant 3 miles.
Closed	Christmas & rarely.
Directions	From Warminster centre direction Salisbury. On right, opp. end of St John's churchyard.

Carolyn & Andrew Lewis
Oaklands,
88 Boreham Road,
Warminster,
Wiltshire BA12 9JW
Tel   01985 215532
Mobile   07850 158302
Email   apl1944@yahoo.co.uk

Map 3   Entry 497

Wiltshire

Woodside Cottage

Not your average B&B. Barbette is an artist, house restorer and chef and there's a quirkiness to the house (and your arrangements in it) that reflects her character – she's quite happy to stay and look after you or leave you alone! This Edwardian cottage has been restored beautifully and simply, from the old brick paving in the courtyard to the beams and the limed doors. Bedrooms have wooden floors, dusky walls, French bed linen and, in one, a lunette painting of the Medici palace on the headboard. The food is truly sublime: osso bucco, risotto, fish from the market, veg from the garden. A treat.

Price	£65-£80. Singles £35.
Rooms	4: 2 doubles; 1 twin with shared shower. Annexe: 1 family suite.
Meals	Dinner, 3 courses, £25. Packed lunch £10. Pub 1 mile.
Closed	Rarely.
Directions	A36 Bath-Warminster. At Standerwick, left to Rudge & Brokers Wood. In Rudge, right at Full Moon pub. House 1 mile on right, just before green tin church.

Barbette Saunders
Woodside Cottage,
Brokers Wood, Westbury,
Wiltshire BA13 4EG
Tel   01373 827082
Mobile   07796 687806
Email   barbettesaunders@onetel.com
Web   www.cottagenet.co.uk/woodside.htm

Map 3   Entry 498

Wiltshire

Crockerton House

A 1669 listed house, once part of the Longleat estate. White walls soak up light, rugs cover stripped floors, a fire burns in the sitting room. Airy bedrooms are delightful, two are huge, all come in Farrow & Ball hues with bowls of fruit, quilted covers, crisp white linen and bathrobes. Best of all is the garden with its large vegetable patch that Enid tends with undying enthusiasm. Its healthy yield provides much for the table, so dinner here is a treat. Breakfast is served communally overlooking the front lawn. Stonehenge is close as are the gardens at Stourhead.
Minimum two nights most weekends.

Price	£85–£129.
Rooms	3: 2 twins/doubles; 1 double with separate bath.
Meals	Dinner, 3 courses, £28. Not Sundays.
Closed	Christmas.
Directions	South from Warminster on A350. Left after half a mile at tiny green. On left.

Christopher & Enid Richmond
Crockerton House,
Crockerton Green,
Warminster,
Wiltshire BA12 8AY

Tel	01985 216631
Email	stay@crockertonhouse.co.uk
Web	www.crockertonhouse.co.uk

Map 3   Entry 499

Wiltshire

The Limes

Through the electric gates, past the gravelled car park and the pretty, box-edged front garden and you arrive at the middle part of a 1620 house divided into three. The beams, stone mullions and leaded windows are charming, and softly spoken Ellodie is an exceptional hostess. Light bedrooms have pretty curtains and fresh flowers, tiled bathrooms have good soaps and thick towels, logs glow in the grate, and breakfasts promise delicious Wiltshire bacon, prunes soaked in orange juice and organic bread. You are on the busy main road leading out of Melksham – catch the bus to Bath from right outside the door.

Price	£50–£70. Singles £30–£35.
Rooms	3: 2 doubles, 1 twin/double.
Meals	Dinner £15–£20. Packed lunch £3–£5.
Closed	Rarely.
Directions	Leave Melksham on A365 to Bath. After Victoria Motors, sharp left at school sign, brown gates will open slowly. Park on left, follow path to house.

Ellodie van der Wulp
The Limes,
Shurnhold House,
Shurnhold,
Melksham,
Wiltshire SN12 8DG

Tel	01225 790627
Mobile	07974 366892

Map 3   Entry 500

Wiltshire

Merlin House

Whether named after a mystery bird or King Arthur's legendary wizard, this elegant 1760 Georgian town house is stylish, warm and comfortable. Exquisitely decorated throughout, the rich fabrics complement fine antiques and original features are lovingly restored. The garden, designed and created by Penny, an artist, is a revelation, and amiable Richard is the perfect host with good local knowledge. Bedrooms are deeply peaceful; a soak in the huge Victorian bath, with original fittings, is a memorable experience. Delve into delicious breakfasts served in the conservatory, or under the old apple tree in summer.

Price	£80. Singles £45.
Rooms	2 doubles sharing bath (let to same party only).
Meals	Pubs/restaurants in village.
Closed	Christmas and occasionally.

Stop Press
No longer doing B&B

Map 3   Entry 501

Wiltshire

Perrior House

This listed, one-time butcher's shop has been in Darea's family for years. Charmingly cluttered, sparkingly clean, there are beautiful objects and lovely pieces at every turn. Darea's enthusiasm for books and travel is undimmed: she can identify every rich and rare specimen in her garden, keeps detailed diaries and albums of her travels and has thrown nothing away. Your chintzy bedrooms are seductively cosy; one looks over the delightful cottage garden. The village has an excellent pub and lies in a fascinating corner of England – Stonehenge, Longleat, Stourhead and Salisbury are nearby. *Pets by arrangement.*

Price	£70-£75. Singles £40-£45.
Rooms	2: 1 twin; 1 twin/double with separate bath.
Meals	Pub 50 yds.
Closed	Rarely.
Directions	Exit A303 at junc. with A36 for Wylye. In village, cross river & round sharp left-hand bend. House 25 yds on right.

	Mrs Darea Browne
	Perrior House,
	Wylye,
	Warminster,
	Wiltshire BA12 0QU
Tel	01985 248228
Email	dareabrowne@aol.com

Map 3   Entry 502

Wiltshire

The Duck Yard

Your own terrace, your own entrance, your own sitting room, your own wing – a treat. A beautiful conversion and everything as fresh as a daisy. Peaceful too, at the end of the lane, with a colourful cottage garden, a summerhouse and roaming bantams. Unflappable Harriet makes wedding cakes, looks after guests and cheerfully rustles up fine meals at short notice; breakfasts, too, are delicious, with eggs from happy hens. Your carpeted bedroom and pristine bathroom are under the eaves, the sitting room is bright and cheerful. Warm, generous, good value B&B.

Wiltshire

Baverstock Manor

Instantly gracious – the 15th-century honey stone that lights up in sunlight, the Jacobean 'extension', the wisteria, the solidity… Inside it is creaky, friendly, engagingly chaotic, full of well-worn antiques and lovely faded rugs. If you're travelling with family, choose the roomy twin that connects with the little single, its small, florally-dressed windows overlooking gardens and pheasants. The twin/double has a pretty bed and an ancient stone fireplace. Come for history not luxury, oodles of character and a pool and a tennis court nearby. *Children over eight welcome.*

Price	£65. Singles £45.
Rooms	1 twin/double & sitting room.
Meals	Dinner, 3 courses, £20. Packed lunch £7. Pub 2 miles.
Closed	Christmas & New Year.
Directions	A303 to Wylye, then for Dinton. After 4 miles left at x-roads, for Wilton & Salisbury. On for 1 mile, down hill, round sharp right bend, signed Sandhills Rd. 1st low red brick building on left. Park in space on left.

Harriet & Peter Combes
The Duck Yard,
Sandhills Road, Dinton,
Salisbury, Wiltshire SP3 5ER

Tel	01722 716495
Fax	01722 716163
Mobile	07729 777436
Email	harriet.combes@googlemail.com

Map 3   Entry 503

Price	£80. Singles £40.
Rooms	3: 1 twin/double with separate bath; 1 twin/double, 1 single sharing bath.
Meals	Packed lunch £6. Pubs within 4 miles.
Closed	December–January.
Directions	From Salisbury, A36 to Wilton, then A30 (to Shaftesbury). After 3 miles, in Barford St Martin, right onto B3089; after 2 miles, right to Baverstock; after 0.75 miles stone gateway on right, on S-bend.

Tim & Belinda Hextall
Baverstock Manor,
Dinton,
Salisbury,
Wiltshire SP3 5EN

Tel	01722 716206
Fax	01722 716510
Email	hextallbavers@hotmail.com

Map 3   Entry 504

Wiltshire

Little Langford Farmhouse

A rare treat to have your milk fresh from the cow – the Helyers have pedigree cattle. The bedrooms of this rather grand Victorian-gothic farmhouse are large and pretty with period furniture and crisp linen; there are impressive countryside views, a baby grand and a billiard room. Everything is elegant and polished yet cosy, and terrace doors are thrown open for delicious al fresco breakfasts in summer. The farm, part of which is an SSSI, is treasured for its glorious walks, wild flowers and butterflies, and the Helyers are immensely welcoming. *Minimum stay two nights at weekends. Children by arrangement.*

Price	£68-£75. Singles £50-£60.
Rooms	3: 1 double, 1 twin/double; 1 twin with separate shower.
Meals	Pub/restaurant 1.75 miles.
Closed	Christmas & New Year.
Directions	Exit A303 at A36 junc; follow signs for Salisbury. 2 miles; right for The Langfords. In Steeple L, right for Hanging L. At T-junc. opp. village hall, left for Little Langford. House 0.75 miles on left.

	Patricia Helyer
	Little Langford Farmhouse,
	Little Langford, Salisbury,
	Wiltshire SP3 4NP
Tel	01722 790205
Fax	01722 790086
Email	bandb@littlelangford.co.uk
Web	www.littlelangford.co.uk

Map 3   Entry 505

Wiltshire

Dowtys

A stunning setting and a newly converted farmhouse up a long drive, with fabulous views south over the Nadder valley. Bedrooms are all large and very private – one has its own sun room and terrace – with Vi-spring mattresses, rafters and beams, antiques and smart bathrooms. The sitting room has a contemporary feel with frameless windows, modern open fireplace, sliding oak patio windows and underfloor heating. Relax on the terrace, stroll through the espaliered limes in the smart garden, or dip into the National Trust woods behind the house. Footpaths start from the door and the wildlife is abundant.

Price	£65-£75. From £45.
Rooms	3: 1 double; 1 double, 1 twin both with separate bath/shower.
Meals	Packed lunch on request. Pub 0.25 miles.
Closed	Christmas & New Year.
Directions	B3089 approaching Dinton from east (Barford St Martin). Take 1st turn right after village sign & 30 mph, signed Wylye. 100 yds; 1st right up Dowtys Lane to house.

	Mrs Di Verdon-Smith
	Dowtys,
	Dowtys Lane,
	Dinton,
	Salisbury,
	Wiltshire SP3 5ES
Tel	01722 716886
Email	dowtys.bb@gmail.com

Map 3   Entry 506

Wiltshire

The Mill House

In a tranquil village next to the river is a house surrounded by water meadows and wilderness garden. Roses ramble, marsh orchids bloom and butterflies shimmer. This 12-acre labour of love is the creation of Diana, now in her 80s, and her son Michael. Their home, the time-worn 18th-century miller's house, is packed with country clutter – porcelain, teddy bears, ancestral photographs above the fire – while bedrooms are quaint, old-fashioned and flowery, with firm, comfy beds. The family has lived here over 46 years and have been doing B&B for 26 of them. *Children over five welcome.*

Price	From £75. Singles from £40.
Rooms	5: 3 doubles, 1 family room; 1 twin with separate bath.
Meals	Pub 5-minute walk.
Closed	Never.
Directions	From A303 take B3083 at Winterbourne Stoke to Berwick St James. Go through the village, past the Boot Inn and the church. Turn into yard just before the sharp left bend. Coming from A36 (B3083), house is first on right.

**Diana Gifford Mead &
Michael Mertens**
The Mill House,
Berwick St James, Salisbury,
Wiltshire SP3 4TS
Tel   01722 790331
Fax   01722 790753
Web   www.millhouse.org.uk

Map 3   Entry 507

Wiltshire

Bolhays

Fresh flowers and the smell of irresistible freshly baked bread fill the rooms of this smartly cosy Victorian villa. Sisters Bar and Sue have kept period details – pine doors, marble fireplaces – but updated the look with Farrow & Ball paints and oatmeal carpets. Bedrooms are light and restful with white and brass bedsteads, bed linen is impeccable and bathrooms sparkle. The breakfast room overlooks the pretty, pocket-handkerchief garden and there's a very comfy front parlour to come back to. A treat to be in the centre of Salisbury, staying with such lovely, easy-going people. *Children over 12 welcome.*

Price	£62. Singles £42.
Rooms	2: 1 double; 1 double with separate bathroom.
Meals	Pubs/restaurants 5-minute walk.
Closed	Rarely.
Directions	From r'bout where A345 meets A36 on the N. side of Salisbury, take City Centre exit. Wyndham Rd 2nd left.

Bar Barbour & Sue Lemin
Bolhays,
48 Wyndham Road,
Salisbury,
Wiltshire SP1 3AB
Tel   01722 320603
Email   info@bolhays.com
Web   www.bolhays.com

Map 3   Entry 508

Wiltshire

The Priory

There's enough in Salisbury to keep you busy for a week and you can do it all on foot. Michael and Sarah are intuitive and will give you space; you have your own door from the ground-floor bedroom with its floral drapes and large sofa into the bird-filled garden (breakfast here on sunny days) and then a lane to the Cathedral. It would be a pity though to miss out on their dazzling company – among other things they ran a coffee farm in Jamaica. Partly Jacobean, the house is stunning with a 25ft-wide carved fireplace in the sitting-room, white marble statues and glorious furniture. *Minimum stay two nights.*

Price	From £75-£80. Singles from £60.
Rooms	1 twin.
Meals	Pub/restaurant 100 yds.
Closed	Rarely.
Directions	Enter town's one-way system. From north side of Market Sq, right into Brown St. Through 2 sets of lights; house on left, set back from road.

Michael & Sarah Credland
The Priory,
95 Brown Street,
Salisbury,
Wiltshire SP1 2BA
Tel   01722 502337
Email   credland@btopenworld.com
Web   www.lcv.ne.jp/~credland/index.htm

Map 3   Entry 509

Wiltshire

85 Exeter Street

The dreaming spire of the cathedral is a two-minute walk away but, tantalisingly, the bedrooms look over a quiet tiny courtyard. You are so central here that you can wander on foot (having parked by the house or walked from the station). Susan is refreshingly enthusiastic about her new 'career' and determined to keep any weary professionalism at bay. Bedrooms are simple, traditional and attractive: William Morris curtains, a five-foot bed and a shower cabinet in one; a single bed with spare roll-out bed in the other. The breakfast room has one big table plus sofas, and encourages conviviality.

Price	From £75. Singles from £50.
Rooms	2: 1 double; 1 single/twin with separate bath/shower.
Meals	Pubs & restaurants nearby.
Closed	Rarely.
Directions	Ring road round Salisbury to south of city; past r'bout to Southampton; at next r'bout (Exeter St Roundabout), 3rd exit on to Exeter St (signed Old George Mall). No 85 near city centre. Park opp. house; ask for permit on arrival.

Susan Orr-Ewing
85 Exeter Street,
Salisbury,
Wiltshire SP1 2SE
Tel   01722 417944
Mobile   07904 814408
Email   susan.orr-ewing@virgin.net
Web   www.85exeterstreet.co.uk

Map 3   Entry 510

Wiltshire

Fisherman's House

Watch ducks shoot the rapids of the Kennet River as it swooshes past the lawns of this exquisitely decorated home. It looks every inch a doll's house, but Jeremy and Heather add a deft human touch. The elegance of excellent breakfasts taken in the conservatory is balanced by the comforting hubbub emanating from the family kitchen. There's a guests' sitting room with an open fire and, upstairs, ornately and generously decorated bedrooms. Time slips by effortlessly here, many people come to visit the crop and stone circles and Marlborough is a hop away.

Price	£80. Singles £40.
Rooms	4: 2 doubles sharing bath (2nd room let to same party only); 1 twin, 1 single sharing bath.
Meals	Lunch/packed lunch from £3. Pub 500 yds.
Closed	Christmas.
Directions	From Hungerford, A4 for Marlborough. After 7 miles, right for Stitchcombe, down hill (bear left at barn) & left at T-junc. On entering village, house 2nd on left.

Jeremy & Heather Coulter
Fisherman's House,
Mildenhall, Marlborough,
Wiltshire SN8 2LZ

Tel	01672 515390
Fax	01672 519009
Email	heathercoulter610@btinternet.com
Web	www.fishermanshouse.co.uk

Map 3   Entry 511

Wiltshire

Westcourt Farm

Rozzie and Jonny left London to restore a medieval, Grade II* cruck truss hall house (beautifully) and wildflower meadows, hedgerows and ponds. They are delightful people, and eager to welcome you. Rooms are freshly decorated, crisp yet traditional; the country furniture is charming, the crucks and trusses a carpenter's delight. Bedrooms have comfortable beds and fine linen, bathrooms are spot-on, there's a lovely dining room and a barn for corporate meetings. Encircled by footpaths and fields, Westcourt is the oldest house in a perfect village, two minutes from an excellent pub.

Price	£80. Singles £40.
Rooms	2: 1 twin with separate bath; 1 double with separate shower.
Meals	Pub/restaurant in village.
Closed	Christmas & New Year.
Directions	A338 Hungerford-Salisbury; after 4 miles signed Shalbourne; through village & fork left at pub; 150 yds, 2nd drive on right.

Jonny & Rozzie Buxton
Westcourt Farm,
Shalbourne,
Marlborough,
Wiltshire SN8 3QE

Tel	01672 871399
Email	info@westcourtfarm.com
Web	www.westcourtfarm.com

Map 3   Entry 512

Wiltshire

Puckshipton House

An intriguing name, Puckshipton: it means Goblin's Barn. The house is deep in the lush countryside of the Vale of Pewsey, reached by a long tree-lined drive. You stay in the Georgian end, with a private entrance that leads to a Regency-blue hall. Rooms are stylish and uncluttered, an attractive mix of old and new with good beds, crisp linen and bathrooms that are cossetting, one with a roll top bath. The dining and sitting rooms have wood-burners both. James, a forester, and Juliette have young children, a walled garden and a thatched hen house from which to fetch your breakfast egg.

Price	£75. Singles £50.
Rooms	2: 1 four-poster; 1 twin/double with separate bath/shower.
Meals	Pubs & restaurant 5-minute drive.
Closed	Christmas.
Directions	Devizes A342 towards Rushall; left to Chirton, right to Marden & through village. On for 0.25 miles; right into private drive.

Juliette & James Noble
Puckshipton House,
Beechingstoke,
Pewsey,
Wiltshire SN9 6HG
Tel 01672 851336
Email noble.jj@gmail.com
Web www.puckshipton.co.uk

Map 3   Entry 513

Wiltshire

The Manor

Isabel is a delight and a great cook (she used to run a chalet in the Swiss Alps), happy to chat by the Aga as she rustles up huge breakfasts. She has decorated her beautifully converted home in style: the drawing room is elegant, with a cosy fire and a touch of the orient, bedrooms are prettily papered in pale pink and blue, mattresses are of the finest quality. Breakfast is eaten at a polished oak table, glazed doors thrown open to the garden in summer. This is a treat of a 17th-century brick-and-flint manor in a beguiling spot by the river Avon; good walking and plenty of wildlife.

Price	£80. Singles from £40.
Rooms	2 twins/doubles.
Meals	Pub/restaurant 2-minute walk.
Closed	Rarely.
Directions	From Upavon towards Andover on A342. Manor 3rd house on right & last before bridge.

Isabel Green
The Manor,
Upavon, Pewsey,
Wiltshire SN9 6EB
Tel 01980 635115
Mobile 07919 278334
Email isabelgreen@hotmail.com
Web www.themanorupavon.co.uk

Map 3   Entry 514

Worcestershire

Home Farm

A half-moated house in a magical spot: the timbered part — 14th-century and listed — peeps through the trees as you approach. Gorgeous in summer (terrace, gardens, ducks), relaxing all year round: a special B&B. Antiques, soft colours and an open fire in the guest sitting room, fresh fabrics and uncluttered comfort in the bedrooms and peaceful views to the Abberley Hills and beyond. Roger and Anne are generous hosts and give you local bacon at breakfast, stewed fruits and jam from their plums. Make time for Great Witley, the finest baroque church in England. *Children over ten welcome.*

Price	£70–£80. Singles £40–£45.
Rooms	3: 1 twin; 1 single, 1 twin each with separate bath/shower.
Meals	Pubs within 5 miles.
Closed	Christmas & New Year.
Directions	On entering Great Witley from Worcester on A443, left onto B4197 to Martley; after 0.25 miles 1st right on sharp left-hand bend by grass triangle/chevrons; up hill 1st house on right.

Roger & Anne Kendrick
Home Farm,
Great Witley, Worcester,
Worcestershire WR6 6JJ
Tel   01299 896825
Fax   01299 896176
Email anniekendrick@hotmail.com
Web   www.homefarmbandb.com

Map 8   Entry 515

Worcestershire

Harrowfields

Tucked just off the high street this compact cottage is surprisingly stylish with contemporary colours and old beams, great books and a cosy feel. Bedrooms large enough to lounge in are delightful (one even has a wood-burner) with crisp, jump-on-me beds, sound systems, super bathrooms, pump-action lotions, antique pine furniture and garden views. Susie and Adam (who cooks) are natural and charming, hens cluck in the garden, breakfast is local and seasonal, you can walk for miles or just to the pub. Young, romantic couples will be in heaven here; uncork the wine, light the fire, turn up the music.

Price	£60–£65. Singles from £40.
Rooms	2: 1 double; 1 double with separate shared bath.
Meals	Packed lunch from £5. Pubs in village.
Closed	Rarely.
Directions	Enter Eckington from Bredon (M5 junc. 9). Turn 1st right by village shop. House on left before Anchor pub.

Susie Alington & Adam Stanford
Harrowfields,
Cotheridge Lane,
Eckington, Worcestershire
WR10 3BA
Tel   01386 751053
Email susie@harrowfields.co.uk
Web   www.harrowfields.co.uk

Map 8   Entry 516

Old Country Farm

Ella's passion for this remote, tranquil place – and the environment in general – is infectious. She believes the house was once home to a Saxon chief. Certainly, it has beams dating from 1400; now it's a rambling mix of russet stone and colour-washed brick, with a warm and delightfully cluttered kitchen, wooden floors, lovely rugs. Friendly, low-ceilinged bedrooms are simple and rustic. Ella's parents collected rare plants and the garden is full of hellebores and snowdrops; roe deer and barn owls flit about in the surrounding woods. A wonderful retreat for nature lovers, birdwatchers and walkers.

No wonder Ella has a Green Business Award and a Gold Wildlife Award from Herefordshire Nature Trust; the whole farm is managed for the benefit of the landscape and its wildlife. Here you are encouraged to understand better our relationship – physical, spiritual and creative – with the natural world. At least 80% of the food is organic – the farm is run through several environmental schemes – and a WET sewage system provides the perfect pool for ducks and moorhens, with hovering dragonflies and swaying grasses.

Price	£60–£90. Singles £35–£55.
Rooms	3: 1 double; 1 double with separate bath; 1 double with separate shower.
Meals	Pubs/restaurants 3 miles.
Closed	Rarely.
Directions	From Worcester A4103 for 11 miles; B4220 for Ledbury. After leaving Cradley, left at top of hill for Mathon, right for Coddington; house 0.25 miles on right.

SPECIAL
GREEN ENTRY
see page 17

Ella Quincy
Old Country Farm,
Mathon, Malvern,
Worcestershire WR13 5PS

Tel	01886 880867
Email	ella@oldcountryhouse.co.uk
Web	www.oldcountryhouse.co.uk

Map 8 Entry 517

Worcestershire

Bidders Croft

Completely rebuilt in 1995 from 200-year-old bricks, this solid house has a hand-carved mahogany hall pillar, oak-framed loggias and an enormous conservatory where you eat overlooking the garden, an orchard and the Malvern hills. Traditional bedrooms with padded headboards and skirted dressing tables are warm and comfortable; bathrooms are spick and span. Bill and Charlotte give you a log fire, books and magazines in the sitting room and an Aga-cooked breakfast or candlelit dinner with home-grown vegetables and fruit. The hills beckon walkers, the views soar and you're near the Malvern theatres.

Yorkshire

Village Farm

Tucked behind the houses and shops, this was once the village farm with land stretching to the coast; the one-storey buildings overlooking a courtyard are now large immaculate bedrooms in gorgeous colours with luxurious touches. Baths are deep, beds crisply comfortable, heating is underfoot. Delicious breakfasts are served at wooden tables in a light room with a contemporary feel; wicker sofa and chairs, terracotta floors, white walls. Justin and Alison are friendly and helpful but give you complete privacy; stride the cliffs, watch birds at Flamborough Head or make for Spurn Point – remote and lovely.

Price	£75. Singles £45.
Rooms	2: 1 twin with separate bath, 1 double with separate shower.
Meals	Dinner, 4 courses, £27.50 (for min. 4). Pub/restaurant 250 yds.
Closed	Christmas, New Year & Easter.
Directions	From Upton-upon-Severn, A4104 dir. Little Malvern & Ledbury. After 3 miles, pass Anchor Inn on right; drive is 250 yds on left, house signed.

Price	£70. Singles from £39.95.
Rooms	3: 2 doubles, 1 twin.
Meals	Pubs/restaurants within 2 miles.
Closed	Rarely.
Directions	A165 Beverley to Bridlington. At Beeford x'roads, right onto B1249 to Skipsea. There, pass church on left, at x'roads, straight across to Back Street. On right, opp. pub.

Bill & Charlotte Carver
Bidders Croft,
Welland, Malvern,
Worcestershire WR13 6LN

Tel	01684 592179
Fax	01684 594866
Email	carvers@bidderscroft.com
Web	www.bidderscroft.com

Justin & Alison Thorn
Village Farm,
Skipsea,
Yorkshire YO25 8SW

Tel	01262 468479
Mobile	07813 612803
Email	info@villagefarmskipsea.co.uk
Web	www.villagefarmskipsea.co.uk

Map 9   Entry 518

Map 13   Entry 519

Yorkshire

Crown House

Scarborough... bracing walks, salty air, fresh fish and buckets and spades. But this is no typical guest house – the Firths have one of those charming listed houses in respectable South Cliff, moments from the Esplanade. Inside, good proportions, light rooms, polished banisters and contemporary furniture. Barbara, thoughtful and fun, serves the very best breakfasts (and juices just-squeezed) at a good square table that seats eight. Bedrooms are cream, stylish and restful. Coastline and castles by day, home baking on your return. Books and CDs to borrow, cats to admire, and a theatre just down the road.

Price	From £80.
Rooms	3 doubles.
Meals	Supper £15. Dinner £25. Packed lunch available. Restaurants 10-minute walk.
Closed	Rarely.
Directions	From station, A165 signed Filey. Right over Valley Bridge, left at end; immed. right on Belmont Road. At green, right again; left into Crown Terrace.

Barbara Firth
Crown House,
6 Crown Terrace, Scarborough,
Yorkshire YO11 2BL
Tel   01723 375401
Mobile   07736 626289
Email   barbara@crownhousescarborough.co.uk
Web   www.crownhousescarborough.co.uk

Map 13   Entry 520

Yorkshire

Foulsyke Farmhouse

The pretty village of Scalby is on the edge of the North Yorkshire Moors, close to Scarborough with its sweeping bays and Whitby – a great little town to explore. Jayne and John do perfect B&B, give you afternoon tea, a heart-warming breakfast with eggs from the hens and sausages from the butcher, and charming cosy bedrooms with a country-cottage feel. Your sitting room is packed with magazines, books and maps; plan your walking or cycling routes here and Jayne will sort out the bikes. Leave the car and take the bus to Scarborough – John will happily collect – or you can get the bus by the duck pond!

Price	£56. Singles £33.
Rooms	3: 1 twin/double, 1 double; 1 double with separate shower.
Meals	Light supper £6. Packed lunch £5. Tea room open weekends & bank holidays. Pubs 0.5 miles.
Closed	Never.
Directions	A171 Scarborough-Whitby. 0.5 miles past entrance to Scalby, left onto Barmoor Lane (signed Suffield/Harwood Dale). House 1st right after pond.

Jayne Pickup
Foulsyke Farmhouse,
Barmoor Lane,
Scalby, Scarborough,
Yorkshire YO13 0PG
Tel   01723 507423
Email   info@foulsykefarmhouse.co.uk
Web   www.foulsykefarmhouse.co.uk

Map 13   Entry 521

Yorkshire

Holly Croft

Huge kindness and thoughtful touches (hot water bottles, lifts to the pub, cake and tea on arrival) make this home special. The décor is Edwardian plush – wallpapers striped and floral, curtains lavish – the comfort indisputable. The double has an elaborate floral-and-rose headboard with matching drapes, there are bathrobes in fitted wardrobes, big showers and generous breakfasts – own jams, Yorkshire teas, kippers if you choose – are served round the polished mahogany table. After a bracing clifftop walk return to a homely sitting room overlooking the garden. Whitby is 20 minutes away.

Price	From £65. Singles from £40.
Rooms	2: 1 twin;
	1 double with separate bath.
Meals	Pub 600 yds.
Closed	Rarely.
Directions	A171 from Scarborough to Whitby; at Scalby x-roads, by tennis courts, take road on right. Signed 500 yds on right.

John & Christine Goodall
Holly Croft,
28 Station Road, Scalby,
Scarborough, Yorkshire YO13 0QA
Tel 01723 375376
Mobile 07759 429706
Email christine.goodall@tesco.net
Web www.holly-croft.co.uk

Map 13 Entry 522

Yorkshire

Portobello Farm

Among a flurry of geese and hens discover this old farmhouse with pretty sash windows, varied floor levels and huge kitchen hung with dried flowers, pots, platters and paintings. All has a warm, bohemian feel with floor stencils, oak furniture, books, vibrant art and a log-burning stove in the sitting room. Bedrooms have traditional iron beds, patchwork quilts, painted floors, small shower rooms (and a quirky bathroom with stone walls). The garden slips away to fields where sheep slowly munch; Lynne gives you the heartiest of breakfasts at a round table in the hallway and you're 20 minutes from York.

Price	£55. Singles £33.
Rooms	3: 2 doubles;
	1 twin with separate bath.
Meals	Pubs 3-6 miles.
Closed	Christmas & New Year.
Directions	Take unclassified road from Norton to Stamford Bridge & Pocklington. 1st turn right after 30 mph sign, lane signed Menethorpe; 1 mile along farm drive, signed.

Lynne Cole
Portobello Farm,
Welham, Norton,
Malton,
Yorkshire YO17 9QY
Tel 01653 658518
Email portobello.farm@tiscali.co.uk
Web www.portobellofarm.co.uk

Map 13 Entry 523

Yorkshire

Low Penhowe

With the Turners at the helm, you are on a safe ship. They see to everything so perfectly – the crispness of the breakfast bacon, the freshness of the eggs from their hens, the homemade bread, the bowls of flowers, the fire in the guest drawing room. Traditional, comfortable bedrooms face south and overlook the garden – lap up the views in summer while birds soar and twitter, Christopher's Highland cattle peer over the fence and the chickens strut and scratch. Castle Howard and the North Yorks Moors are in front of you and all around are abbeys, castles, rivers, ruins and woods. *Children over ten welcome.*

Price	£70-£80. Singles £50.
Rooms	2: 1 double; 1 twin/double with separate bath.
Meals	Packed lunch £6. Pubs 1.5 miles.
Closed	Christmas.
Directions	A64 at Whitwell on the Hill, right for Kirkham. Over crossing & Derwent, pass Kirkham Priory & Stone Trough Inn. Right at T-junc, left for Burythorpe, over x-roads, 700 yds; right up drive.

	Christopher & Philippa Turner
	Low Penhowe,
	Burythorpe, Malton,
	Yorkshire YO17 9LU
Tel	01653 658336
Mobile	07900 227000
Email	LowPenhowe@btinternet.com
Web	www.bedandbreakfastyorkshire.co.uk

Map 13   Entry 524

Yorkshire

Manor Farm

Pass the stables into the scullery and the sweet smell of saddles and tack; enter a warm kitchen where muslin-wrapped hams hang to dry. This is special: a thriving and immaculate working farm with a relaxed, artistic owner. Low-ceilinged bedrooms are stuffed with colour, old armchairs and thick rugs, books and rose china. There's a garden room for summer breakfasts – home-baked bread and muesli from the Side Oven Bakery, hen and duck from the farm – and a charming garden tucked deep in the wedge of Thixendale. Wonderful for those seeking a remote escape. *Please book by phone.*

Price	From £70. Singles £35.
Rooms	2: 1 twin & sitting room; 1 double sharing bath (let to same party).
Meals	Packed lunch £7.50. Pub in village.
Closed	Rarely.
Directions	Left at top of Garrowby Hill A166; 4 miles to Thixendale. Thro' village, farm on left. 10 miles from Malton, through Birdsall on unclassified roads.

	Gilda & Charles Brader
	Manor Farm,
	Thixendale, Malton,
	Yorkshire YO17 9TG
Tel	01377 288315
Fax	01377 288315
Email	info@manorfarmthixendale.co.uk
Web	www.manorfarmthixendale.co.uk

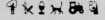

Map 13   Entry 525

Yorkshire

Barugh House

In a friendly village, a listed Georgian house that is a joy for sybarites. The well-travelled Woods look after you immaculately – hot cinnamon toast and tea by the fire, plump pillows and towelling robes, fresh flowers and magazines, treats for your dog and superb breakfasts for you. Bedrooms are strikingly elegant, views sweep over the garden to the moors and the sitting room has an open fire. Colourful lupins stand proud in the garden that is Janie's delight; massed roses and dreamy sunsets vie for your attention. In summer sit under the old apple tree with a glass of homemade lemonade. Special.

Price	£80. Singles £40.
Rooms	2: 1 twin/double, 1 double sharing bath (2nd room let to same party only).
Meals	Packed lunch £6. Pub 50 yds.
Closed	Rarely.
Directions	From Malton, B1257 for Helmsley. Through Amotherby then right to Kirkbymoorside. On for 3.25 miles. At Great Barugh, left at T-junc. House on right, 50 yds past pub.

Janie Wood
Barugh House,
Great Barugh,
Malton,
Yorkshire YO17 6UZ
Tel   01653 668615
Email   barughhouse@aol.com

Map 13   Entry 526

Yorkshire

Hunters Hill

The moors lie behind this solid, stone farmhouse, five yards from the National Park, in farmland and woodland with fine views... marvellous walking country. The house is full of light and flowers; bedrooms are pretty but not overly grand. The attractive sitting room has deeply comfortable old sofas, armchairs and fine furniture, while rich colours, hunting prints and candles at dinner give a warm and cosy feel. The Orr family has poured a good deal of affection into this tranquil house and the result is a home that's happy, charming and remarkably easy to relax in... Wonderful.

Price	£80. Singles from £45.
Rooms	2: 1 twin/double; 1 twin/double with separate bath.
Meals	Dinner, 3 courses, £30. Pub/restaurant 500 yds.
Closed	Rarely.
Directions	From A170 to Sinnington. On village green, keep river on left, fork right between cottages, sign to church. Up lane, bearing right up hill. House past church beyond farm buildings.

The Orr Family
Hunters Hill,
Sinnington,
York,
Yorkshire YO62 6SF
Tel   01751 431196
Email   ejorr@tiscali.co.uk

Map 13   Entry 527

Yorkshire

Sproxton Hall

Drive through a stone archway into an old courtyard: the 17th-century beamed farmhouse, once attached to Rievaulx Abbey, is still part of a working farm – complete with rare-breed Belted Galloways. Inside, a handsome grandfather clock and a genuine welcome from Margaret and Andrew. The guests' sitting and dining rooms have 18th-century country antiques and the bedrooms are traditional and comfortable, with lovely views; the double has a half-tester with floral canopy. Sensible, hearty breakfasts prepare you for a day on the peaceful North Yorkshire Moors. *Children over ten welcome.*

Price	£66–£76. Singles £46.
Rooms	3: 1 twin, 1 double; 1 twin with separate bath & shower.
Meals	Pubs/restaurants 1-3 miles.
Closed	Christmas & New Year.
Directions	From Thirsk A170 for 12 miles. Right onto B1257 (1 mile before Helmsley); 50 yds on, left by church. House at end of 'No Through Road'.

Margaret & Andrew Wainwright
Sproxton Hall,
Sproxton, Helmsley,
Yorkshire YO62 5EQ
Tel 01439 770225
Fax 01439 771373
Email sproxtonhall@btinternet.com
Web www.sproxtonhall.co.uk

Map 13   Entry 528

Yorkshire

No 54

The welcome tea and homemade cakes sets the tone for your stay; this is a happy place. No. 54 was once two cottages on the Duncombe estate; now it's a single house and Lizzie has made the most of the space. Buttermilk walls, be-rugged flagged floors, country furniture, open fires and a stylish lack of clutter. A single-storey extension has been fashioned into three extra bedrooms around a secluded courtyard. Thoughtful extras – magazines, cafetiere, an umbrella – make you feel cherished, and the breakfasts will fuel the most serious of walks. Make a house party and bring your friends!

Price	£80. Singles from £35.
Rooms	4: 2 doubles, 1 twin; 1 single with separate shower.
Meals	Dinner, 2-3 courses, £28-£35. Restaurants 10-minute walk.
Closed	Christmas & New Year.
Directions	A170 to Helmsley; right at mini r'bout in centre, facing The Crown; house 500 yds along A170, on right.

Lizzie Would
No 54,
Bondgate, Helmsley,
Yorkshire YO62 5EZ
Tel 01439 771533
Fax 01439 771533
Email lizzie@no54.co.uk
Web www.no54.co.uk

Map 13   Entry 529

Yorkshire

Shallowdale House

Phillip and Anton have a true affection for their guests so you will be treated like angels. Sumptuous bedrooms dazzle in yellows, blues and limes, acres of curtains frame wide views over the Howardian Hills, bathrooms are gleaming and immaculate. Breakfast on the absolute best; fresh fruit compote, dry-cured bacon, homemade rolls – and walk it off in any direction straight from the house. Return to an elegant drawing room, with a fire in winter, and an enticing library. Dinner is out of this world and coffee and chocolates are all you need before you crawl up to bed. Bliss. *Children over 12 welcome.*

Price	£87.50-£107.50. Singles £70-£80.
Rooms	3: 2 twins/doubles; 1 double with separate bath/shower.
Meals	Dinner, 4 courses, £32.50.
Closed	Christmas & New Year.
Directions	From Thirsk, A19 south, then 'caravan route' via Coxwold & Byland Abbey. 1st house on left, just before Ampleforth.

Anton van der Horst & Phillip Gill
Shallowdale House,
West End, Ampleforth,
Yorkshire YO62 4DY

Tel	01439 788325
Fax	01439 788885
Email	stay@shallowdalehouse.co.uk
Web	www.shallowdalehouse.co.uk

Map 12   Entry 530

Yorkshire

Braythorne Barn

Absolute independence here with your own entrance; inside are paintings, fine furniture, colourful fabrics and rugs. Beams and floors are light oak, windows and doors hand-crafted and sunlight dances around the rooms. Trina has given the bedroom a Scandinavian stripes-and-gingham feel. The bathroom is spotless, the sitting room – all yours – generously furnished. Walk the Priests Way, from Bolton Abbey to Knaresborough. Buttercup the donkey, chickens and great breakfasts – perhaps brandy-soaked fruit compote... a rural idyll with a contemporary twist. *Children over 12 welcome. Minimum stay two nights.*

Price	£80. Singles from £50.
Rooms	1 twin & sitting room.
Meals	Packed lunch £6. Pubs/restaurants 2-4 miles.
Closed	Rarely.
Directions	From Pool-in-Wharfedale, A658 over bridge towards Harrogate. 1st left to Leathley; right opp. church to Stainburn (1.5 miles). Bear left at fork; house next on left.

Petrina Knockton
Braythorne Barn,
Stainburn, Otley,
Yorkshire LS21 2LW

Tel	0113 284 3160
Fax	0113 284 2297
Email	homerelocation@aol.com
Web	www.braythornebarn.co.uk

Map 12   Entry 531

Yorkshire

Sunnybank

A Victorian gentleman's residence just a short walk up the hill from the centre of bustling *Last of the Summer Wine* Holmfirth, still with its working picturedrome (touring bands too), and arts and folk festivals, restaurants and shops. Peter and Anne look after you beautifully. Big peaceful bedrooms are a fresh mix of contemporary, Art Nouveau and Art Deco pieces, caramel cream velvets and silks, spoiling bathrooms and lovely views. A huge Yorkshire breakfast will set you up for a lazy stroll round the charming gardens, or a brisk yomp through rural bliss. *Min. stay two nights at weekends.*

Price	£65–£85. Singles from £50.
Rooms	3: 2 doubles, 1 twin/double (with extra single bed).
Meals	Supper snacks £7. Packed lunch £7. Pubs/restaurants 500 yds.
Closed	New Year & occasionally.
Directions	A6024 signed Glossop out of Holmfirth centre. Take right in between Ashley Jackson Studio & Worthingtons into Upperthong Lane. House on drive on right just past church.

Peter & Anne White
Sunnybank,
78 Upperthong Lane,
Holmfirth,
Yorkshire HD9 3BQ

Tel	01484 684857
Email	info@sunnybankguesthouse.co.uk
Web	www.sunnybankguesthouse.co.uk

Map 12   Entry 532

Yorkshire

Field House

You drive over bridge and beck to this listed, 1713 farmhouse – expect comfort, homeliness and open fires. Pat and Geoff love showing guests their hens, horses, goats and lambs, and will tell you about the 14 circular walks or lend you a torch so you can find the pub across the fields! Ramblers will be in heaven – step out of the front door, past the lovely walled garden and you're in rolling, Bronte countryside. Good big bedrooms are in farmhouse style, one bathroom has a roll top bath, another a 70s blue suite, and Geoff's breakfasts are generous in the finest Yorkshire manner.

Price	£56–£64. Singles £32–£40.
Rooms	3: 1 double, 1 twin; 1 twin with separate bath/shower.
Meals	Dinner from £10. Packed lunch available. Pub/restaurant 200 yds.
Closed	Rarely.
Directions	1 mile from Halifax on A58 Leeds road. Turn between Stump Cross Inn car park & Clarence Smith's carpet shop. 100 yds to gates.

Pat & Geoff Horrocks-Taylor
Field House,
Staups Lane,
Stump Cross, Halifax,
Yorkshire HX3 6XW

Tel	01422 355457
Email	stayatfieldhouse@yahoo.co.uk
Web	www.fieldhouse-bb.co.uk

Map 12   Entry 533

Yorkshire

Thurst House Farm

This solid Pennine farmhouse, its stone mullion windows denoting 17th-century origins, is English to the core. Your warm, gracious hosts give guests a cosy and carpeted sitting room with an open fire in winter; bedrooms are equally generous, with inviting brass beds, antique linen and fresh flowers. Outside: clucking hens, two friendly sheep and a hammock in a garden with beautiful views. Tuck into homemade bread, marmalade and jams at breakfast, and good traditional English dinners, too – just the thing for walkers who've trekked the Calderdale or the Pennine Way. *Children over eight welcome.*

Price	£70. Singles by arrangement.
Rooms	2: 1 double, 1 family room.
Meals	Dinner, 4 courses, £25. Packed lunch £5. Restaurants within 0.5 miles.
Closed	Christmas & New Year.
Directions	Ripponden on A58. Look for brown Beehive sign and then right up Royd Lane 100 yds before lights; right at T-junc. opp. Beehive Inn; on for 1 mile. House on right, gateway on blind bend, reverse in.

David & Judith Marriott
Thurst House Farm,
Soyland, Rippond
en, Sowerby Bridge, Yorkshire
HX6 4NN

Tel   01422 822820
Mobile   07759 619043
Email   thursthousefarm@bushinternet.com

Map 12   Entry 534

Yorkshire

Holme House

A delightful Georgian house in bustling Hebden Bridge: with its artists, musicians, book shops, real ale pubs and commitment to Fair Trade, it's the Totnes of the Pennines. Perfect if you enjoy the outdoor life – walks along the Calder Valley start from the door – but prefer to be based in town. Inside, you will be spoiled with classic proportions, a light-filled hallway, sometimes local art and a comfortable sitting room with leather sofas. Fresh flowers, chocolates, great beds and cool, creamy colours encourage you to linger in bed, but Sarah's locally sourced breakfasts will set you up for anything.

Price	£70-£85. Singles £55.
Rooms	3: 2 doubles, 1 twin.
Meals	Packed lunch from £7.50. Pubs/restaurants 100 yds.
Closed	Christmas Day & Boxing Day.
Directions	On corner of New Road (main road thro' town) & Holme Street. Car park on left as you turn into Holme Street, thro' black railings.

Sarah & Charles Eggleston
Holme House,
New Road, Hebden Bridge,
Yorkshire HX7 8AD

Tel   01422 847588
Fax   01422 847354
Email   mail@holmehousehebdenbridge.co.uk
Web   www.holmehousehebdenbridge.co.uk

Map 12   Entry 535

Yorkshire

Ponden House

Brenda's sturdy new house of reclaimed stone sits high on the wild Pennine Way. The spring water makes wonderful tea and the house hums with interest and artistic touches. Comfy old sofas are jollied up with throws, there are homespun rugs and hangings, paintings, plants and a piano. Feed the hens, plonk your boots by the Aga, chat with your lovely leisurely hostess as she turns out a fish pie or a vegetarian treat; food is a passion. Bedrooms are exuberant but cosy, it's great for walkers and there's a hot tub under the stars (bookable by groups in advance). Good value with a lived-in, homely feel.

Price	£55–£60. Singles £30.
Rooms	3: 2 doubles; 1 twin sharing bath.
Meals	Dinner, 3 courses, £16. Packed lunch £5. Pub/restaurant 3 miles.
Closed	Rarely.
Directions	From B6142 for Colne. Pass through Stanbury village, cont. past Old Silent Inn. Access is either via Ponden Mill or Ponden reservoir.

Brenda Taylor
Ponden House,
Stanbury,
Haworth,
Yorkshire BD22 0HR
Tel   01535 644154
Email   brenda.taylor@pondenhouse.co.uk
Web   www.pondenhouse.co.uk

Map 12   Entry 536

Yorkshire

Knowles Lodge

Chris's father built this timber-framed house in 1938 on 18 acres of glorious hillside. It's a comfortable, comforting place to stay. Honey walls and polished floors give the sitting room a light, airy feel, cheerful throws on deep sofas make it cosy, and there are fine views of the River Wharfe and Dales Way through endless windows. Bedrooms are attractive with sprightly fabrics and fresh flowers; draw back the curtains and have your morning cuppa looking at those views. You're superbly well looked after, you can even get married here. Great walking and trout fishing, and the solitude a balm. *Children over eight welcome.*

Price	£80. Singles £50.
Rooms	3: 2 doubles, 1 twin.
Meals	Packed lunch £5. Pubs/restaurants within 3 miles.
Closed	Never.
Directions	From Skipton A59 to Bolton Abbey. At r'bout, B6160 for Burnsall. 3 miles after Devonshire Arms, right immed. after Barden Tower for Appletreewick. Down hill, over bridge, up hill & on for 0.5 miles. Cross bridge; immed. on left.

Pam & Chris Knowles-Fitton
Knowles Lodge,
Appletreewick, Skipton,
Yorkshire BD23 6DQ
Tel   01756 720228
Fax   01756 720381
Email   pam@knowleslodge.com
Web   www.knowleslodge.com

Map 12   Entry 537

Yorkshire

Cundall Lodge Farm

Ancient chestnuts, crunchy drive, sheep grazing, hens free-ranging. This four-square Georgian farmhouse could be straight out of Central Casting. And there's tea and oven-fresh cake to welcome. Homely rooms of damask sofas and pretty wallpaper have views to Sutton Bank's White Horse or the river Swale. Bedrooms are comfy with family furnishings and inviting chairs. This is a working farm with typical farmers' breakfast: free-range eggs, homemade jams and local cured bacon. The garden and river walks guarantee peace. David and Caroline are sociable and generous. *Children over ten welcome.*

Yorkshire

Lawrence House

A classically comfortable house run with faultless precision by John and Harriet – former wine importer and interior decorator respectively. The house is listed, and Georgian, the garden is formal, flagged and herbaceous, the position – by the back gate to Studley Royal, overlooking long meadow and parkland – is supreme. There's a linen-sofa'd drawing room just for guests, and the promise of a very good dinner. Bedrooms and bathrooms are in a private wing: light, well-proportioned, full of special touches. And Fountains Abbey awaits your discovery. *Golf, riding & clay pigeon shooting can be arranged.*

Price	£62-£82.
Rooms	3: 1 double, 1 twin/double; 1 double with separate shower.
Meals	Packed lunch. Pubs/restaurants 2 miles.
Closed	Christmas & January.
Directions	Exit junc. 49 A1(M) onto A168 (Thirsk). Turn off 1st junc. for Cundall. Turn right at the Crab & Lobster. 2 miles on left.

Price	£110. Singles £70.
Rooms	2: 1 twin/double, 1 twin.
Meals	Dinner £28. Pub/restaurant 1 mile.
Closed	Christmas & New Year.
Directions	A1 to Ripon. B6265/Pateley Bridge road for 2 miles. Left into Studley Roger. House last on right.

Caroline Barker
Cundall Lodge Farm,
Cundall, York,
Yorkshire YO61 2RN

Tel 01423 360203
Fax 01423 360805
Email info@lodgefarmbb.co.uk
Web www.lodgefarmbb.co.uk

John & Harriet Highley
Lawrence House,
Studley Roger, Ripon,
Yorkshire HG4 3AY

Tel 01765 600947
Fax 01765 609297
Email john@lawrence-house.co.uk
Web www.lawrence-house.co.uk

Map 12   Entry 538

Map 12   Entry 539

Yorkshire

Mallard Grange

Hens, cats, sheepdogs wander the garden, an ancient apple tree leans against the wall, the boys play cricket on the lawn and guests unwind. Enter the rambling, deep-shuttered 16th-century farmhouse, cosy with well-loved family pieces, and feel at peace with the world. From the white Spode on the tea trays to the generous breakfasts: perfect farmhouse B&B. A winding steep stair leads to big, friendly bedrooms, two cheerful others await in the outhouses and Maggie's enthusiasm for this glorious area is as genuine as her love of doing B&B. *Minimum stay two nights at weekends.*

Price	£70–£90. Singles from £60.
Rooms	4: 1 double, 3 twins/doubles.
Meals	Pubs/restaurants 10-minute drive.
Closed	Christmas & New Year.
Directions	B6265 from Ripon for Pateley Bridge. Past entrance to Fountains Abbey. House on right, 2.5 miles from Ripon.

Maggie Johnson
Mallard Grange,
Aldfield, Ripon,
Yorkshire HG4 3BE
Tel   01765 620242
Mobile   07720 295918
Email   maggie@mallardgrange.co.uk
Web   www.mallardgrange.co.uk

Map 12   Entry 540

Yorkshire

Laverton Hall

Rachel and Christopher have swapped their Fulham B&B for the 'big house' of Laverton with its space, beauty, history (it's 400 years old), three walled gardens and comfort in great measure: feather pillows, thick white towels, all is in apple-pie order. Sumptuous breakfasts are followed by a Cordon Bleu dinner overlooking the garden. The sunny guest sitting room is elegant and charming, the cream and white twin and the snug little single have long views to the river. The area is rich with abbeys and great houses, Harrogate is a half-hour drive and then there are the glorious Dales to be explored.

Price	£90. Singles £50.
Rooms	2: 1 twin/double, 1 single.
Meals	Supper, 3 courses, £20. Pubs/restaurants 1 mile.
Closed	Christmas.
Directions	Leave Ripon on Pateley Bridge Rd. 0.25 miles, right at Garden Centre to Galphay. Through Galphay, 0.5 miles, right at T-junc. to Kirkby Malzeard; 0.5 miles, left to Laverton; 0.5 miles, last house on right.

Rachel Wilson
Laverton Hall,
Laverton,
Ripon,
Yorkshire HG4 3SX
Tel   01765 650274
Email   cwracewear@hotmail.com

Map 12   Entry 541

Yorkshire

The Old Rectory

The house was a rectory first, then the residence of the Bishops of Whitby. Both Turner and Ruskin stayed here and probably enjoyed as much good conversation and comfort as you will. Bedrooms are pretty, traditional and with grand views; the drawing room is classic country house – the sort that foreigners envy – with a fine Venetian window and an enticing window-seat. The elegant, deep pink dining room looks south over a garden of rare old trees. Wander at will to find an orchard, a tennis court and a croquet lawn. Breakfast is generous and thoughtful. *Children over eight welcome.*

Price	From £66. Singles from £40.
Rooms	2: 1 double with separate bath & dressing room; 1 twin with separate bath & shower.
Meals	Pub opposite.
Closed	Rarely.
Directions	Take A168 (Northallerton road) off A19; over r'bout; left into village; house opp. pub, next to church.

Tim & Caroline O'Connor-Fenton
The Old Rectory,
South Kilvington,
Thirsk,
Yorkshire YO7 2NL
Tel   01845 526153
Email   ocfenton@talktalk.net

Map 12   Entry 542

Yorkshire

Lovesome Hill Farm

Who could resist home-reared lamb followed by sticky toffee pudding? This is a working farm and the Pearsons the warmest people imaginable; even in the mayhem of the lambing season they greet you with homemade biscuits and Yorkshire tea. Their farmhouse is as unpretentious as they are: chequered tablecloths, cosy and simple bedrooms (four in the old granary, one in the cottage) with garden and hill views, and a proper Victorian-style sitting room. The A167 traffic hum mingles with the odd sheepdog bark; you are brilliantly placed for the Moors and Dales. Good for walkers, families, business people.

Price	£60. Singles £35-£40. Gate Cottage: £80.
Rooms	5: 1 twin, 1 double, 1 family room, 1 single. Gate Cottage: 1 double.
Meals	Dinner, 2-3 courses, £15-£20. BYO. Packed lunch for walkers. Pub 4 miles.
Closed	December-January.
Directions	From Northallerton, A167 north for Darlington for 4 miles. House on right, signed.

John & Mary Pearson
Lovesome Hill Farm,
Lovesome Hill, Northallerton,
Yorkshire DL6 2PB
Tel   01609 772311
Fax   01609 772311
Email   pearsonlhf@care4free.net
Web   www.lovesomehill.co.uk

Map 12   Entry 543

Yorkshire

Mill Close

Country-house B&B in a tranquil spot among fields and woodland; spacious, luxurious and with your own entrance through a flower-filled conservatory. Beds are large and comfortable, there's a grand four-poster with a spa bath, and candle scones for flickering light. Be spoiled by handmade chocolates, fluffy robes, even your own 'quiet' fridge. A blue and cream sitting room has an open fire – but you are between the National Park and the Dales so walks are a must. Start with one of Patricia's famous breakfasts: bacon and sausages from the farm, smoked haddock or salmon, homemade jams. Bliss.

Price	£80-£90. Singles £45-£50.
Rooms	3: 2 doubles, 1 four-poster.
Meals	Pubs/restaurants 2 miles.
Closed	Christmas & New Year.
Directions	Follow the brown tourist signs from the village of Patrick Brompton on A684. Farm is 1 mile from village.

Patricia Knox
Mill Close,
Patrick Brompton, Bedale,
Yorkshire DL8 1JY
Tel   01677 450257
Fax   01748 813612
Email   pat@millclose.co.uk
Web   www.millclose.co.uk

Map 12   Entry 544

Yorkshire

Rookery Cottage

Before you, the perfect English country village with close-clipped verges; beyond the fruit-treed garden, the glorious Fell. Four 17th-century almshouses have become this sweet retreat run by kind Ursula: a Mrs Tiggy Winkle house in which one low-panelled room leads to another. Waxed oak and shining silver, frilled flounces, a generous bath, Floris soaps, decorative flowers on the basin and loo… it is warm, cottagey, feminine. Breakfast brings homemade jams and marmalades, perhaps kedgeree made from Ronnie's catch of the day. Dine at the old pub opposite, one of the north country's finest.

Price	£70. Singles from £55-£60.
Rooms	2: 1 double, 1 twin, sharing bath.
Meals	Packed lunch £8. Pub 20 yds.
Closed	Rarely.
Directions	From Masham, A6108. Leyburn 8 miles on. House on left, opp. Blue Lion Country Inn.

Mrs Ursula Bussey
Rookery Cottage,
East Witton, Leyburn,
Yorkshire DL8 4SN
Tel   01969 622918
Mobile   07802 712366
Email   ursula@premierecare.co.uk
Web   www.rookerycottage.co.uk

Map 12   Entry 545

Yorkshire

Millgate House

The perfect hideaway, tucked quietly off the main square. One moment you are on a town pavement facing a sober Georgian front; the next, in a lofty room, elegant with Adam fireplace, fine mouldings, period furniture and myriad prints and paintings. Bedrooms and bathrooms are similarly splendid, with wooden shutters, cast-iron baths and dramatic Swale valley views; breakfasts are generous and superb. As if this were not enough, there is the most enchanting walled garden adorned with hostas, clematis, old roses – a feast for the senses in spring and summer. Tim and Austin are engaging hosts.

Yorkshire

Brandymires

The Wensleydale hills lie framed through the windows of the time-warp bedrooms; no TV, no fuss, just calm. In the middle of the National Park, this is a glorious spot for walkers. Gail and Ann bake their own bread and make jams and marmalade, and their delicious, well-priced dinners are prepared with fresh local produce and served at your own table. Two bedrooms, not in their first flush of youth, have four-posters; all have the views. If you're arriving by car, take the 'over-the-top' road from Buckden to Hawes for the most stunning countryside. *Minimum stay two nights. Children over eight welcome.*

Price	£95–£110. Singles £65.
Rooms	3: 1 double, 1 twin; 1 double with separate bath/shower.
Meals	Restaurant 250 yds.
Closed	Never.
Directions	Next door to Halifax Building Society in the centre, opp. Barclays at bottom of Market Place. Green front door with small brass plaque.

Price	£48. Singles £29.
Rooms	3: 1 twin, 2 four-posters, all sharing 2 bath/shower rooms.
Meals	Dinner, 4 courses, £17 (not Thursday). Pubs/restaurant 5-minute walk.
Closed	November-February.
Directions	300 yds off A684, on road north out of Hawes, signed Muker & Hardraw. House on right.

	Austin Lynch & Tim Culkin Millgate House, Richmond, Yorkshire DL10 4JN
Tel	01748 823571
Mobile	07738 298721
Email	oztim@millgatehouse.demon.co.uk
Web	www.millgatehouse.com

	Gail Ainley & Ann Macdonald Brandymires, Muker Road, Hawes, Yorkshire DL8 3PR
Tel	01969 667482

Map 12   Entry 546

Map 12   Entry 547

Yorkshire

Hill Top

Books, magazines, bath essences, biscuits by the bed – and the charming, warm and artistic Christina. Her pretty, listed, limestone farmhouse dates from 1820 and is deceptively big. Ivory walls are a perfect foil for some good furniture and paintings; the sitting room overlooks the charming garden and has a cosy fire. Bedrooms are comfy and conventional; food is fresh, interesting and as homemade as possible. Far-reaching views over rolling countryside in this AONB where waterfalls, moorland and castles beckon. Handy for Scotland or the south.
Babes in arms & children over seven welcome.

Price	£70. Singles £35.
Rooms	2: 1 twin; 1 twin sharing bath (let to same party only).
Meals	Dinner, 2-3 courses, £12.50-£16. Pub/restaurant 1.5 miles.
Closed	Christmas & New Year.
Directions	From Scotch Corner west on A66. Approx. 7 miles on, down hill. Left to Newsham. Through village; 2nd left opp. sign on left for Helwith. House on right, name on gate.

Christina Farmer
Hill Top,
Newsham,
Richmond,
Yorkshire DL11 7QX
Tel   01833 621513
Email   plow67@tiscali.co.uk

Map 12   Entry 548

Yorkshire

Dunsa Manor

Come when there are drifts of snowdrops up the drive. A ha-ha divides the lawns, terraces and paddock from the 600 acres of farmland (arable, dairy, sheep). Built by Ignatius Bonomi in 1841, the listed house has been in the family for 140 years. Spacious reception rooms face south to the hills; equally good-sized bedrooms are furnished with Edwardian and Victorian pieces and 20th-century basins. Outside is a charming new terrace for a fine day with planted pergola and views. Perfect peace and countryside for walking and riding; hire a horse or bring your own, return to an excellent dinner.

Price	£80. Singles £55.
Rooms	2: 1 double with separate bath; 1 family room with separate shower.
Meals	Dinner, 2 courses, £22.50. Pub 3 miles.
Closed	Rarely.
Directions	Off A66 west of Scotch Corner. Left at sign for Dalton, 1.75 miles, into narrow country lane. Approx. 200 yds on left. 1st drive on left.

Shaheen Burnett
Dunsa Manor,
Dalton, Richmond,
Yorkshire DL11 7HE
Tel   01325 718251
Mobile   07817 028237
Email   shaheenburnett@btinternet.com
Web   www.dunsamanor.com

Map 12   Entry 549

Yorkshire

Cliffe Hall

What remains is the Victorian section of an earlier mansion, embellished by Richard's family in 1858. Inside, a beautifully proportioned and charming family home: huge reception rooms, plasterwork ceilings, acres of sofas, family portraits, cases of books. Bedrooms are traditional and uncontrived, bathrooms carpeted, twin beds super-comfy; large windows look onto the glorious grounds (tennis? croquet?) and a lawn that runs down to the Tees where you fish for trout. Soft, timeless grandeur, visiting thesps, a sweet dog and a hostess who is as special as her house.

Price	£80. Singles £40.
Rooms	2 twins, each with separate bath.
Meals	Pub 1 mile.
Closed	10 December–1 January.
Directions	From A1, exit onto B6275. North for 4.2 miles. Into drive (on left before Piercebridge); 1st right fork.

Caroline & Richard Wilson
Cliffe Hall,
Piercebridge,
Darlington,
Yorkshire DL2 3SR

Tel	01325 374322
Fax	01325 374947
Email	petal@cliffehall.co.uk

Map 12   Entry 550

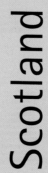

Scotland

Photo: The Berry, entry 606

Aberdeenshire

Old Mayen

Follow narrow lanes crowded by beech trees and hedges, through high rolling hills and fast flowing rivers to this beautiful house perched next to a farm and overlooking the unspoilt valley below. You get classic country-house style in elegant bedrooms, spoiling bathrooms, a book-filled sitting room, cut flowers and a delicious candlelit dinner by a roaring fire. Fran and Jim are infectiously enthusiastic and kind; breakfasts are a moveable feast (outside in good weather) and the garden hums with birds. A fine retreat for tired and jaded souls – and there are castles, distilleries and gardens to visit.

Price	£80. Singles £45.
Rooms	2: 1 double; 1 double with separate shower.
Meals	Dinner £25. Supper £18. Packed lunch £8.
Closed	Rarely.
Directions	From A96, A97 to Banff. After crossing river Deveron (9 miles), left onto B9117; 3 miles, on left behind thick beech hedge.

James & Fran Anderson
Old Mayen,
Rothiemay,
Huntly,
Aberdeenshire AB54 7NL
Tel   01466 711276
Fax   01466 711276
Email   oldmayen@tiscali.co.uk

Map 19   Entry 551

Aberdeenshire

Lynturk Home Farm

The stunning drawing room, with pier-glass mirror, ancestral portraits and enveloping sofas, is reason enough to come, while the food, served in a candlelit, deep-sage dining room, is delicious, with produce from the farm. You're treated very much as friends here and your hosts are delightful. It's peaceful, too, on the Aberdeenshire Castle Trail. The handsome farmhouse has been in the family since 1762 and you can roam the surrounding 300 acres of rolling hills. Inside, good fabrics and paints, hunting prints and some lovely family pieces. "A blissful haven," says a reader. *Fishing, shooting & golf breaks.*

Price	From £70. Singles £45.
Rooms	3: 2 twins/doubles; 1 double with separate bath.
Meals	Dinner, 4 courses, £25. Pub 1 mile.
Closed	Rarely.
Directions	20 miles from Aberdeen on A944 (towards Alford); thro' Tillyfourie, then left for Muir of Fowlis & Tough; after Tough, 2nd farm drive on left, signed.

John & Veronica Evans-Freke
Lynturk Home Farm,
Alford,
Aberdeenshire AB33 8DU
Tel   01975 562504
Fax   01975 563517
Email   lynturk@hotmail.com

Map 19   Entry 552

Aberdeenshire

No. 3 Candacraig Square

If the address suggests a metropolis, note that there is no sign of Nos. 1 or 2 and that the only noise comes from the River Don. Candacraig, the erstwhile laundry for this 1520 estate, is a Highland retreat for those who like to mix style with gentle eccentricity. Mary runs an easy-going ship – breakfast times are negotiated and the art of conversation is practised with an easy flair. There's much comfort, too: claw-foot baths, wall-hangings, old pine dressers, cut-velvet curtains, supper (cock-a-leekie soup, baked brown trout, oatcakes with cheese) by the fire. All this, and Balmoral down the road.

Price	£80. Singles from £47.50.
Rooms	3: 2 doubles; 1 double with separate bath & shower.
Meals	Dinner, 3 courses, £25.
Closed	Rarely.
Directions	East on A944 towards Strathdon. House signed on right through pillared entrance gates.

Mary Williams Edgar
No. 3 Candacraig Square,
Strathdon,
Aberdeenshire AB36 8XT
Tel   01975 651472
Email   no3@candacraig.com
Web   www.candacraig.com

Map 19   Entry 553

Aberdeenshire

Lys-na-Greyne House

Peace, tranquillity and a natural welcome – a superb place. Expect a sweeping stair, sun-streamed rooms, log fires, a warm country-house feel and the most comfortable beds in Scotland. Your room may be huge – two are – and one comes with a dressing room and a balcony. All have family antiques, bathrobes, fine linen and views of river, field, forest and hill where osprey and lapwing glide. Meg picks flowers and organic veg from the garden and her food is delicious; David will happily whisk you off into the hills. Nearby, golf, fishing and castles by the hatful.

Price	£70-£90. Singles from £35.
Rooms	3: 1 twin/double; 2 twins/doubles with separate bath/shower. Extra shower available.
Meals	Supper £20. Dinner £25. Pub/bistro 15-minute walk.
Closed	Rarely.
Directions	From Aboyne, A93 west for Braemar. Just after 50mph sign, left down Rhu-na-Haven Rd. House 400 yds on, 4th gateway on right.

David & Meg White
Lys-na-Greyne House,
Rhu-na-Haven Road, Aboyne,
Aberdeenshire AB34 5JD
Tel   01339 887397
Fax   01339 886441
Email   meg.white@virgin.net

Map 19   Entry 554

Aberdeenshire

Woodend House

Elegant riverside living at a fishing lodge by the river Dee – one of the most magnificent settings in Scotland. Outside, a wild, wonderful garden; inside, beautiful wallpapers and fabrics, rugs and tapestries. The dining hall leads to the kitchen with an Aga, the drawing room has dreamy river views, the large bedrooms ooze comfort and more fabulous views, and the bathrooms have old cast-iron baths and fine toiletries. Breakfast and dinner are local, seasonal and first-class. All this, and a fishing hut and a secure rod room for salmon and sea trout fishing in season. *Minimum stay two nights.*

Price	£100. Singles £65.
Rooms	3: 1 double, 1 twin; 1 twin with separate bath.
Meals	Dinner, 4 courses, £30. Packed lunch £5-£10. Pub 2 miles.
Closed	Christmas, New Year & occasionally.
Directions	About 26 miles west of Aberdeen on A93; Woodend House drive is on left, 4 miles west of Banchory.

Miranda & Julian McHardy
Woodend House,
Trustach, Banchory,
Aberdeenshire AB31 4AY
Tel   01330 822367
Mobile 07812 142728
Email miranda.mchardy@woodend.org
Web   www.woodend.org

Map 19   Entry 555

Angus

Ethie Castle

Amazing. A listed Peel tower that dates to 1300 and which once was home to the Abbot of Arbroath, murdered in St Andrews on Henry VIII's orders. His private chapel remains, as does his secret stair. As for the rest of the house: turret staircases, beautiful bedrooms, a 1500s ceiling in the Great Hall, a Tudor kitchen with a walk-in fireplace that burns night and day. Kirstin and Adrian are experts at breathing new life into old houses and have already started to reclaim the garden. Lunan Bay, one of Scotland's most glorious beaches, is at the end of the road. There's a loch too.

Price	From £95. Singles from £75.
Rooms	3: 1 four-poster; 1 twin/double, 1 double, each with separate bath/shower.
Meals	Dinner, 4 courses with wine, £25. Packed lunch up to £10. Pub/restaurant 3 miles.
Closed	Rarely.
Directions	North from Arbroath on A92; right after Shell garage for Auchmithie; left at T-junc.; on for 2 miles; at BT phone box, private road to Ethie Barns in front.

Adrian & Kirstin de Morgan
Ethie Castle,
Inverkeilor, Arbroath,
Angus DD11 5SP
Tel   01241 830434
Fax   01241 830432
Email kmydemorgan@aol.com
Web   www.ethiecastle.com

Map 16+19   Entry 556

Angus

Newtonmill House

The house and grounds are in apple-pie order; the owners are charming and unobtrusive. This is a little-known part of Scotland, so explore the glens, discover deserted beaches and traditional fishing villages, and play a round or two of golf on one of the many good courses nearby. Return to a cup of tea in an elegant sitting room, then a proper supper of seasonal, local and home-grown produce. Upstairs are crisp sheets, soft blankets, feather pillows, fresh flowers, homemade fruit cake and sparkling, warm bathrooms with thick towels; you are beautifully looked after here.

Price	£80-£96. Singles £50-£58.
Rooms	2: 1 twin; 1 double with separate bath.
Meals	Dinner, 4 courses, £26. Supper £16. Packed lunch £10. Pub 2 miles.
Closed	Christmas.
Directions	Aberdeen-Dundee A90, then B966 towards Edzell. On for 1 mile; driveway marked by pillars and gate lodge; signed.

Mr & Mrs Rickman
Newtonmill House ,
By Brechin,
Angus DD9 7PZ
Tel   01356 622533
Fax   01356 622533
Mobile 07793 169482
Email   rrickman@srickman.co.uk

Map 19   Entry 557

Argyll & Bute

Lochside Cottage

The road runs out in a mile, the hills of Glen Creran cradle you, a private loch laps at the end of the garden. Bedrooms, spotless in 1970s-style, have pretty floral curtains; the spacious drawing room has comfy sofas and a Bluthner Grand piano. Stella and Earle are unrestrained in their pampering: tea when you arrive, maybe in the garden; delicious food beautifully presented; beds turned down and bed lights on, Roberts radios, books, flowers and a mini fridge in one of the rooms. Otters, deer, swans, geese and peace surround you, the walks are stunning and Beinn Sguilard is a three-hour climb.

Price	£60-£72. Singles £30-£36.
Rooms	3: 1 double, 1 twin; 1 twin with separate shower.
Meals	Dinner, 5 courses, £26. BYO.
Closed	Rarely.
Directions	14 miles north of Connel Bridge, 20 miles south of Ballachulish on A828. At north r'bout of new bridge follow Invercreran signs for 2 miles, then straight up glen for 1.5 miles. Cottage on right.

Earle & Stella Broadbent
Lochside Cottage,
Fasnacloich, Appin,
Argyll & Bute PA38 4BJ
Tel   01631 730216
Fax   01631 730216
Email   broadbent@lochsidecottage.fsnet.co.uk
Web   www.lochsidecottage.fsnet.co.uk

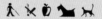

Map 17   Entry 558

Argyll & Bute

Dun Na Mara

Twenty paces from the door, past the standing stone, a sweep of private beach and – on a clear day – dazzling views to Mull. The Arts & Crafts house has been given a minimalist makeover by Mark and Suzanne – ex-architects and friendly, caring, interesting hosts. The result is a luminous interior of low-slung beds, quilted throws, cream bucket chairs, sensual bathrooms, colourful cushions and sea views from three bedrooms. Breakfast on banana and walnut porridge, kedgeree, the full Scottish works; end the day with sherry in the sitting room, magazines, DVDs, beautiful art and books. *Children over 12 welcome.*

Price	£80-£105. Singles £50-£55.
Rooms	7: 5 doubles, 1 twin, 1 single.
Meals	Pubs 3 miles.
Closed	December-January.
Directions	North from Oban on A828; over Connel Bridge; north for two miles; house signed left just after lay-by, before Benderloch village.

Mark McPhillips & Suzanne Pole
Dun Na Mara,
Benderloch,
Oban,
Argyll & Bute PA37 1RT

Tel	01631 720233
Email	stay@dunnamara.com
Web	www.dunnamara.com

Map 17   Entry 559

Argyll & Bute

Sithe Mor House

Terrific views from this lovely house on the shores of Loch Awe; its own bay and jetty below, acres of sky above and a winning pair at the helm. Patsy ensures all runs smoothly and John, a former oarsman of repute and the first man to row each way across Scotland, sweeps you along with joie de vivre. With ornate plasterwork, antlers and oils, lofty domed ceilings in the bedrooms and loch views, this 1880s house combines a baronial feel with massive luxury in bathrooms, beds and fabrics. Stay for dinner, borrow a kilt, marvel at the Oxford and Cambridge boat race memorabilia. *Minimum stay two nights.*

Price	£100-£110. Singles £60-£75.
Rooms	2: 1 double, 1 twin/double.
Meals	Dinner, 4 courses, £35. Restaurants & pub 0.5-3 miles.
Closed	Rarely.
Directions	A82 from Glasgow; A85 from Tyndrum. At Taynuilt, left onto B845 to Kilchrenan village. After 1 mile, single track 'No Through Road' to Taychreggan. House is last on left.

Patsy & John Cugley
Sithe Mor House,
Kilchrenan,
Loch Awe,
Argyll & Bute PA35 1HF

Tel	01866 833234
Email	patsycugley@tiscali.co.uk
Web	www.sithemor.com

Map 17   Entry 560

Argyll & Bute

Glenmore

A pleasing buzz of family life and no need to stand on ceremony. The house was built in 1854 but it's the later 30s additions that set the style: carved doorways, red-pine panelling, Art Deco pieces, oak floors, elaborate cornicing and a curvy stone fireplace. Alasdair's family has been here for 140 years and much family furniture remains. One of the huge doubles is arranged as a suite with a single room and a sofabed; bath and basins are chunky 30s style with chrome plumbing. From the organic garden there are magificent views of Loch Melfort with its bobbing boats; you're free to come and go as you please.

Price	£70-£90. Singles £40.
Rooms	2: 1 family suite; 1 double with separate bath/shower.
Meals	Pubs/restaurants nearby.
Closed	December & January.
Directions	From A816 0.5 miles south of Kilmelford; a private tree lined avenue leads to Glenmore. House signed from both directions. Go past Lodge House at bottom of drive; follow drive for 0.25 miles to big house.

Melissa & Alasdair Oatts
Glenmore,
Kilmelford,
Oban,
Argyll & Bute PA34 4XA

Tel	01852 200314
Email	oatts@glenmore22.fsnet.co.uk
Web	www.glenmorecountryhouse.co.uk

Map 17   Entry 561

Argyll & Bute

Corranmor House

A radiant setting on the Ardfern peninsula. Barbara and Hew are as generous and committed to their guests as they are to the 400-acre farm, where they rear sheep and geese. The drawing room started life as a 16th-century bothy (you'd never guess!), the red dining room sparkles with silver, they enjoy dining with guests and the food is delicious: goose, mutton, lamb, or fish from local landings. Bedrooms are exceptionally private – the double across the courtyard, the suite with the log-fired sitting room. Wander and admire; the eye always comes to rest on the water and boats of Loch Craignish and the Sound of Jura.

Price	£75. Suite £75-£125. Singles £40.
Rooms	2: 1 double & sitting room; 1 family suite & sitting room.
Meals	Lunch from £10. Dinner from £28; with lobster, up to £40. Pubs/restaurants 0.75 miles.
Closed	22 December-3 January; 4th week of August.
Directions	From A816, B8002 to Ardfern, & thro' village; 0.75 miles past church, long white house high on rt. Right by Heron's Cottage, up drive.

Hew & Barbara Service
Corranmor House,
Ardfern,
Lochgilphead, Argyll & Bute
PA31 8QN

Tel	01852 500609
Fax	01852 500609
Email	corranmorhouse@aol.com

Map 14   Entry 562

Argyll & Bute

Melfort House

Enter a wild landscape of hidden glens, ancient oak woods and rivers that tumble to a blue sea. Find a Georgian-style, beautifully renovated house with views straight down the loch, exquisite furniture, designer fabrics, oak flooring and original paintings and prints. Bedrooms are sumptuous, with superb views (especially the Loch room with its Art Deco bathroom in veridian green), soft carpets, warmth and comfort. Yvonne and Matthew (who cooks) are brilliant at looking after you; breakfast on fresh fruit, Stornoway black pudding, homemade tattie scones – even chilli omelettes! Argyll at its finest.

Price	£80–£95. Singles from £60. £10 for sofabed.
Rooms	3: 1 double, 2 twins/doubles.
Meals	Dinner, 3 courses, £24–£26. Packed lunch £7. Pub/restaurant 400 yds.
Closed	Rarely.
Directions	From Oban take A816 south, signed Campbeltown. After 14 miles, go thro' Kilmelford, then right to Melfort. Follow road & bear right after bridge.

Yvonne & Matthew Anderson
Melfort House,
Kilmelford,
By Oban,
Argyll & Bute PA34 4XD
Tel   01852 200326
Email   stay@melforthouse.co.uk
Web   www.melforthouse.co.uk

Map 14   Entry 563

Argyll & Bute

Achamore House

A shop, pub, restaurant, 150 people. No traffic jams here on this island, tucked between the mainland and Islay. Despite its grandeur – turrets, Arts & Crafts doors, plasterwork ceilings – Achamore is homely, with warm wood panelling and light-washed rooms. Bedrooms are huge with shuttered windows, oversize beds, heavy antiques. Owner Don is a coastal skipper – let him speed you over to Jura in his catamaran. You also get the run of the house – billiard room, library, large lounge, TV room (great for kids). With 50 acres of gardens and a quiet beach it's ideal for gatherings. Organic breakfasts, occasional dinners.

Price	£90–£130. Singles from £45.
Rooms	8: 1 double, 1 family room; 2 doubles sharing bath; 2 twins/doubles sharing bath; 2 singles sharing bath.
Meals	Dinner, 4 courses, £32. Pub/restaurant 1 mile.
Closed	Rarely.
Directions	Uphill from ferry landing, turn left at T-junc.; 1 mile, stone gates on right, signed; house at end of drive.

Don Dennis
Achamore House,
Isle of Gigha,
Argyll & Bute PA41 7AD
Tel   01583 505 400
Fax   01583 505 387
Email   gigha@atlas.co.uk
Web   www.achamorehouse.com

Map 14   Entry 564

Ayrshire

Langside Farm

Your hosts' gentle intelligence and humour is reflected in their home – the main part dates back to 1745 – with long views to the east. Inside, a well-proportioned Georgian elegance, fresh contemporary artwork (some Elise's) and a snug Aga kitchen. Deep red sofas, pale striped walls, books and lamps draw you in; pretty bedrooms have a period feel and vary in style. Local (much organic) produce promises fine breakfasts and suppers; water comes from a private spring. There's good walking and golf nearby. Chat in the kitchen, sit by the fire, make yourselves truly at home.

Ayrshire

The Carriage House

An avenue of limes, 250 acres of parkland, rhododendrons, wellingtonia – what a view to wake to! Luke's family have owned the estate and castle for 900 years. Their stylishly converted Carriage House, with its ochre walls, cobbled courtyard and drawing room, is full of light and comfortable good taste; polished floors, handsome antiques, family photographs, contemporary fabrics. Aga-cooked breakfasts are taken in a huge kitchen with hand-crafted fittings. Tennis court, swimming pool, country walks: this is an elegant place to unwind. The Borwicks are confident and keen hosts.

Price	£60-£80. Singles from £35.
Rooms	3: 1 twin/double, 1 twin, 1 four-poster.
Meals	Packed lunch £5.50. Supper £15. Dinner £24.50. Pubs/restaurants 5-10 minute drive.
Closed	November, January & February.
Directions	Langside Farm is 0.7 miles from the Dalry end of the B784. The B784 links the B780 Dalry to Kilbirnie road to the A760 Kilbirnie to Largs road.

Price	£80. Singles £45.
Rooms	3: 2 doubles, 1 twin/double.
Meals	Pubs/restaurants within 3 miles.
Closed	Rarely.
Directions	From Beith enter Dalry on A737. First left (signed Bridgend Industrial Estate); uphill through houses, past farm on right at top of hill. First right into Blair Estate.

	Nick & Elise Quick
	Langside Farm,
	Dalry,
	Ayrshire KA24 5JZ
Tel	01294 834402
Fax	0870 0569380
Email	mail@langsidefarm.co.uk
Web	www.langsidefarm.co.uk

	Luke & Caroline Borwick
	The Carriage House,
	Blair, Dalry,
	Ayrshire KA24 4ER
Tel	01294 833100
Fax	01294 834422
Email	blairenterprises@btconnect.com
Web	www.blairestate.com

Map 14   Entry 565

Map 14   Entry 566

Clackmannanshire

Kennels Cottage

A fresh, stylish gamekeeper's cottage. It's perfect. Step inside to white walls, white sofas, beiges and creams and the odd flash of gold, a buddha in a fireplace, books, paintings and a contemporary lack of clutter. Bedrooms and bathrooms are spotless, bright and designed for comfort; huge towels, gorgeous linen, brand new beds, absolute peace. Tanya and Sandy, fresh from Hong Kong, spoil you with locally sourced breakfasts and eggs from their hens served in a bright white dining room. Explore the garden or take a picnic and wander through what was the Dollarbeg estate, alive with pheasant and deer.

Price	£60-£70. Singles £45.
Rooms	3: 2 doubles, 1 family room.
Meals	Packed lunch £10. Pub 2 miles.
Closed	January & February.
Directions	From Dollar take B913 towards Blairingone. House 2 miles from Dollar just before Blairingone.

Tanya Worsfold & Sandy Stewart
Kennels Cottage,
Dollarbeg, Dollar,
Clackmannanshire FK14 7PA

Tel	01259 742476
Fax	01259 743716
Email	tanya.worsfold@btinternet.com
Web	www.guesthousescotland.co.uk

Map 15   Entry 567

Dumfries & Galloway

Chlenry Farmhouse

A wonderful approach, private and peaceful. Beyond the romantic old buildings in the glen and the rushing burn, the handsome house comes into view. It is a big traditional farmhouse full of old-fashioned comfort and fresh flowers, with charming owners and friendly dogs. In peaceful bedrooms, solid antiques jostle with tasselled lampshades, silk flowers and magazines on country matters; there are proper big bath tubs and suppers for walkers. Meals can be simple or elaborate, often with game or fresh salmon; gardens and golf courses wait to be discovered.

Price	£65. Singles from £40.
Rooms	3: 1 twin with separate bath; 1 double, 1 twin sharing bath.
Meals	Supper, £15. Dinner, 4 courses, £27.50. Packed lunch £6. Pub 1.5 miles.
Closed	Christmas, New Year & occasionally.
Directions	A75 for Stranraer. In Castle Kennedy, right opp. Esso station. Approx. 1.25 miles on, after right bend, signed Chlenry. Down hill, 300 yds on left.

David & Ginny Wolseley Brinton
Chlenry Farmhouse,
Castle Kennedy, Stranraer,
Dumfries & Galloway DG9 8SL

Tel	01776 705316
Mobile	07704 205003
Email	wolseleybrinton@aol.com
Web	www.chlenryfarmhouse.com

Map 14   Entry 568

Dumfries & Galloway

Craigadam

A 1703 house set in 700 acres, where pheasants strut proudly up the drive. The farmhouse becomes a 'country house' inside: a sitting room with three vast sofas and numerous chairs, a dining table that seats 26, seven rooms in the stables, three more in the house, a billiard room and an honesty bar. Delightful, energetic Celia pulls it all together and creates a house-party feel. The food and wines are fabulous and the lamb, venison, partridge and duck come from the family's organic farm. Retire to a themed bedroom (Scottish, African, Chinese), a deep soak and a comfortable bed.

Price	From £84. Singles on request.
Rooms	10 suites.
Meals	Dinner £23. Pub 2 miles.
Closed	Christmas & New Year.
Directions	A75, then north on A712 towards Corsock. After 2 miles, Craigadam signed on right.

Mrs Celia Pickup
Craigadam,
Castle Douglas,
Dumfries & Galloway DG7 3HU
Tel   01556 650100
Fax   01556 650100
Email   inquiry@craigadam.com
Web   www.craigadam.com

Map 15   Entry 569

Dumfries & Galloway

Chipperkyle

Sink into the sofas without worrying about creasing them; this beautiful Scottish-Georgian family home has not a hint of formality, and the sociable Dicksons put you at your ease. Sitting and dining rooms connect through a large arch; there are family pictures, rugs on wooden floors and a log fire. Upstairs: a cast-iron bed dressed in good linen, striped walls, flowered curtains, lots of books and windows with views – this wonderful house just gets better and better. There are 200 acres, dogs, cats, donkeys and hens, and you can walk, play golf, visit gardens, sail or cycle – in magnificent countryside.

Price	£90.
Rooms	2: 1 double; 1 twin with separate bath/shower. Cot available.
Meals	Dinner available for groups. Pub 3 miles.
Closed	Christmas.
Directions	A75 Dumfries ring road for Stranraer. Approx. 12 miles to Springholm & right to Kirkpatrick Durham. Left at x-roads, after 0.8 miles, up drive on right by white lodge.

Willie & Catriona Dickson
Chipperkyle,
Kirkpatrick Durham, Castle Douglas,
Dumfries & Galloway DG7 3EY
Tel   01556 650223
Mobile   07876 014247
Email   special_place@chipperkyle.co.uk
Web   www.chipperkyle.co.uk

Map 11   Entry 570

Dumfries & Galloway

Applegarth House

Here is an old peaceful manse at the top of the hill, right next door to the church, with a 12th-century motte, and the views from the pretty garden stretch for miles around. The house is a good size and airy, with original pine floors, now varnished, and sweeping stairs. Off the large and light landing are three spotless bedrooms with shuttered windows and garden and country views. Jane cooks well: stewed fruits for breakfast and excellent porridge; and, for dinner, guinea fowl with fennel or salmon fishcakes with lemon sauce. After which the tawny owls should lull you to sleep.

Price	£80–£84. Singles from £54.
Rooms	3: 2 twins; 1 double with separate bath.
Meals	Dinner £26. BYO. Hotel restaurant 1.5 miles.
Closed	Rarely.
Directions	M74 junc. 17 to Lockerbie, B7076 for Johnstonebridge. 1st right after 1.5 miles; after 100 yds left over m'way bridge. After 1 mile, right at T-junc., then 2nd left to church. Next to church.

Frank & Jane Pearson
Applegarth House,
Lockerbie,
Dumfries & Galloway DG11 1SX

Tel	01387 810270
Fax	01387 811701
Email	jane@applegarthtown.demon.co.uk

Map 15   Entry 571

Dumfries & Galloway

Knockhill

Fabulous Knockhill: stunning place, stunning position, a country house full of busts and screens, oils and mirrors, chests and clocks, rugs and fires. In the intimate drawing room stuffed with treasures, floor-to-ceiling windows look down the wooded hill. Fine stone stairs lead to country-house bedrooms that are smart yet homely: headboards of carved oak or padded chintz, books and views. Come for a grand farming feel and delicious Scottish meals; the Morgans are the most unpretentious and charming of hosts. Mellow, authentic, welcoming – an enduring favourite.

Price	£80–£84. Singles £54.
Rooms	2: 1 twin; 1 twin with separate bath.
Meals	Dinner £26. Pub 5 miles.
Closed	Rarely.
Directions	From M74 junc. 19, B725 for Dalton for 1.2 miles. Look out for signpost to Hoddam Castle by church in Ecclefechan. Right at next x-roads to Lockerbie, 1 mile on, right at stone lodge. House at top of long drive.

Yda & Rupert Morgan
Knockhill,
Lockerbie,
Dumfries & Galloway DG11 1AW

Tel	01576 300232
Fax	01576 300818
Email	info@morganbellows.co.uk

Map 15   Entry 572

Dumfries & Galloway

Kirklands

Light and airy, the 1800 manse has big classic rooms looking south to England. Friendly Elisabeth runs an immaculate ship, Archie is a gifted gardener. Drawing room windows frame country views; there are log fires, polished floors, charming watercolours, fresh flowers. Generous bedrooms come with crisp linen, patchwork quilts, window seats, maybe a chaise longue; bathrooms are big and old-fashioned. The village is on one side, one of the best trout streams in Scotland is across the lane and a three-mile circular walk starts from the door. *Children over eight welcome.*

Price	£70-£80. Singles £35-£40.
Rooms	3: 1 double, 1 twin; 1 twin/double with separate bath & shower.
Meals	Restaurant 2 miles.
Closed	February.
Directions	M6, junc. 44, then A7 12 miles into Canonbie. Over bridge, signed 'Churchyard', immed. right; immed. left into yard.

Elisabeth & Archie Findlay
Kirklands,
Church Road, Canonbie,
Dumfries & Galloway DG14 0RA
Tel   01387 371769
Fax   01387 371784
Email   archfindlay@fsmail.net

Map 15   Entry 573

Dunbartonshire

Blairbeich Plantation

Past swaying birches to a Swedish wonderland in the woods. It is a beautiful fusion of antique and modern and a mini-loch laps three feet from its walls. There are light stone floors and cathedral ceilings and delightful ground-floor bedrooms that look onto the loch – an enclave of wilderness that universities come to study. Despite all this it is the interior that knocks you flat: Malla – relaxed, friendly, a fine cook – has covered every inch with something spectacular and the sitting room is a private art gallery. Mosaic showers, orchids, woodpeckers… and curling on the loch in winter. Fabulous.

Price	£70-£100. Singles from £60.
Rooms	2 doubles.
Meals	Dinner, 4 courses, £35. Pub/restaurant 1.5 miles.
Closed	Rarely.
Directions	From west, A811 into Gartocharn; 1st right (School Road); 1 mile up to T-junction, then left; house on right, signed.

Malla Macdonald
Blairbeich Plantation,
Gartocharn, Loch Lomond,
Dunbartonshire G83 8RR
Tel   01389 830257
Email   macdonald@blairbeich.com
Web   www.blairbeich.com

Map 14   Entry 574

Edinburgh & the Lothians

Lochmill House

Susan is delightful and kind and spoils you rotten. Her home-baking is wicked (expect a feast for breakfast), her green fingers produce fresh flowers from a pretty, peaceful garden all year round, and she's hot on Scottish history so can help you make the best of your stay. The house is modern and on the edge of town, a mile or so from the M9 and very easy for Edinburgh and Glasgow. Big lovely rooms swim with light, there's a smart multi-windowed sitting room to relax in and spotless country-cosy bedrooms with wicker chairs and crisp linen. *Children over 12 welcome.*

Price	£75. Singles £40.
Rooms	2: 1 twin;
	1 twin with separate bath/shower.
Meals	Occasional supper/dinner.
	Packed lunch £6.
	Pub & restaurants 0.5 miles.
Closed	Christmas & occasionally.
Directions	From west M9, junc 4. From east M9 junc. 3, then A803 into Linlithgow. There, north onto A706 for Bo'ness & 0.2 miles on left. Follow to very end of road.

Mr & Mrs W Denholm
Lochmill House,
3 Lade Court, Linlithgow,
West Lothian EH49 7QF

Tel	01506 846682
Mobile	07759 959414
Email	susanedenholm@hotmail.com

Map 15   Entry 575

Edinburgh & the Lothians

24 Saxe Coburg Place

A ten-minute walk – or an even quicker bus ride – from the centre of Edinburgh, this 1827 house stands in a quiet, no-through road with a communal garden in the centre. There's a garden level entrance to three simple and luxurious bedrooms with extra long beds, good lighting, handsome antiques and spotless bathrooms – one with Paris metro tiling in white and green. Most excitingly you can nip over the street in your bathrobe to the Victorian Baths for a swim, sauna or workout in the gym; all before a delicious continental breakfast in the hall or on the pretty terrace in summer.

Price	£75-£95. Singles £35-£40.
Rooms	3: 1 double, 1 twin/double, 1 single.
Meals	Restaurants/pubs 5-minute walk.
Closed	Rarely.
Directions	From George St, down Frederick St. Over 3 sets of lights, left at bottom of hill. Right up Clarence St; at junction, over to Saxe Coburg St. Saxe Coburg Place is at end.

Diana McMicking
24 Saxe Coburg Place,
Edinburgh EH3 5BP

Tel	0131 315 3263
Email	diana@saxecoburgplace.co.uk
Web	www.saxecoburg.co.uk

Map 15   Entry 576

7 Gloucester Place

A cantilevered staircase, a soaring cupola: the classic Georgian townhouse is five minutes from Princes Street. Rooms are cosy yet immaculate, sprinkled with paintings and decorative things from travels to far-flung places. Bedrooms on the second floor (one shower room is on the first) are comfy, traditional and well-stocked with books and radio (and there are Z-beds for children). Bag the south-facing double with its stunning Art Deco bathroom and garden views. Naomi is pretty relaxed and happy to chat to you or to leave you in peace. An interesting and hospitable place to unwind.

Price	£80–£110. Singles from £50.
Rooms	3: 1 double; 1 double with separate bath; 1 double with separate shower. Extra child beds.
Meals	Pubs/restaurants 300 yds.
Closed	Christmas & rarely.
Directions	From George St (city centre), down Hanover St, across Queen St at lights. Left into Heriot Row, right onto India St, then left.

Naomi Jennings
7 Gloucester Place,
Edinburgh EH3 6EE
Tel 0131 225 2974
Mobile 07803 168106
Email naomijennings@hotmail.com
Web www.stayinginscotland.com

Map 15 Entry 577

21 India Street

Portraits of the Macpherson clan beam down upon you at breakfast, which is served in a sunny and elegant dining room. In this house of great character you are cared for by Zandra, who offers guests the Laird's Room with its half-tester and the Patio Room with its own front entrance. And it's just a hop and a skip up the majestic cobbled streets of New Town to Princes Street and the centre. Zandra plays the Scottish harp, loves to cook, has two beautiful black labs and has written about her life as wife of a clan chieftain living in the wilds at Glentrium – she has some fascinating stories!

Price	£95–£125. Singles £60–£85.
Rooms	2: 1 double, 1 twin.
Meals	Restaurants close by.
Closed	Rarely.
Directions	Down South Queensferry Rd; left at Y-junc; at 2nd Y-junc. left into Craig Leith Rd. Thro' Stockbridge, over lights at bridge; 3rd right into Royal Circus; sharp right thro' Circus Gdns; left into India St.

Mrs Zandra Macpherson of Glentruim
21 India Street,
Edinburgh EH3 6HE
Tel 0131 225 4353
Email zandra@twenty-one.co.uk
Web www.twenty-one.co.uk

Map 15 Entry 578

Edinburgh & the Lothians

7 Danube Street

Impressive architectural features – cantilevered staircase, marble fireplaces, double-barrelled cupola, soaring ceilings – coupled with Fiona's professional interior design talents make for a stunning city base. It is sumptuous: generous curtains, thick bedspreads, fluffy towels and Molton Brown goodies in boutique hotel-style bathrooms. The chandelier has real candles and the beds are four-poster or canopied. Fiona and Colin are lovely, their breakfasts are superb, and you have a fascinating ten-minute stroll through some of Europe's finest classical architecture to the very heart of the city.

Price	£100–£140. Singles £60–£80.
Rooms	3: 1 double, 1 four-poster, 1 single.
Meals	Restaurants 5-minute walk.
Closed	Christmas Day.
Directions	From Edinburgh, Queensferry Rd for Forth Rd Bridge. 3rd right after Dean Bridge into Dean Park Crescent; 2nd right into Danube St.

	Fiona Mitchell-Rose
	7 Danube Street,
	Edinburgh EH4 1NN
Tel	0131 332 2755
Email	seven.danubestreet@virgin.net
Web	www.sevendanubestreet.com

Map 15   Entry 579

Edinburgh & the Lothians

12 Belford Terrace

Leafy trees, a secluded garden, a stone wall and, beyond, a quiet riverside stroll. Hard to believe that Edinburgh's galleries, theatres and restaurants are a few minutes' walk. This Victorian end terrace, beside Leith Water, oozes an easy-going elegance, helped by Carolyn's laid-back but competent manner. Ground-floor bedrooms – she lives at 'garden level' – are big and creamy with stripy fabrics, antiques, sofas and huge windows. (The single has a *Boys Own* charm.) Carolyn spoils with crisp linen, books and biscuits and a delicious, full-works breakfast. After a day in town, relax in the garden.

Price	£60–£100. Singles from £40.
Rooms	3: 1 double, 1 twin/double; 1 single with separate shower.
Meals	Pub/restaurants within a 10-minute walk.
Closed	Christmas.
Directions	From Palmerston Place through 2 sets of lights, downhill on Belford Rd past Menzies Belford Hotel. Immediately left is Belford Terrace.

	Carolyn Crabbie
	12 Belford Terrace,
	Edinburgh EH4 3DQ
Tel	0131 332 2413
Fax	0131 332 0224
Email	carolyncrabbie@blueyonder.co.uk

Map 15   Entry 580

Edinburgh & the Lothians

2 Fingal Place

An elegant house on a Georgian terrace. The leafy 'Meadows' lie opposite (look upwards to Arthur's Seat); theatres, shops, university are a stroll away through the park, yet this is a very quiet house. Your hostess is a Blue Badge Guide and will help plan your trips – or cater for celebrations and graduations with lunch and dinner; it's entirely flexible. Bedrooms are downstairs at garden level and have antique beds, spotless bathrooms and seductive linen; one looks onto a lovely patio garden. Noodle the Llasa Apso and Gillian's cat are equally welcoming. *Parking metered until 6.30pm weekdays.*

Price	£75–£80 (£85–£95 during Festival). Singles from £55.
Rooms	2: 1 twin (with single room attached), 1 twin.
Meals	Pubs/restaurants 100 yds.
Closed	22–27 December.
Directions	From centre of Edinburgh (West End), Lothian Rd to Tollcross (clock) & Melville Drive. At 2nd major lights, right into Argyle Place; immed. left into Fingal Place. Metered parking until 6.30pm on weekdays.

Gillian Charlton-Meyrick
2 Fingal Place,
The Meadows,
Edinburgh EH9 1JX
Tel   0131 667 4436
Email   gcmeyrick@blueyonder.co.uk

Map 15   Entry 581

Edinburgh & the Lothians

20 Blackford Road

From your cushioned window seat you gaze onto a wildlife-filled walled garden – a special spot for breakfast on a warm day. Come for unexpected tranquillity and old-world luxury in the centre of the city. Your quietly friendly, dog and garden-loving hosts give you two comfortable bedrooms, charming with white-painted Victorian shutters. The double, slightly smaller than the twin, has a serene toile de Jouy canopied bed and matching drapes. And there's an elegant drawing room to retire to, private and cosy with cream sofas, soft lights, drinks tray and beautiful books.

Price	£70–£90. Singles £60–£70.
Rooms	2: 1 double/twin, 1 twin, each with separate bath.
Meals	Restaurants 500 yds.
Closed	Rarely.
Directions	A720 city bypass, take Lothianburn exit to city centre. Continue for 2.5 miles on Morningside Rd; right into Newbattle Terrace; 2nd left into Whitehouse Loan. Immed. right into Blackford Road. House at end on left.

John & Tricia Wood
20 Blackford Road,
Edinburgh EH9 2DS
Tel   0131 447 4233
Mobile   07930 452945
Email   jwood@dsl.pipex.com

Map 15   Entry 582

1 Albert Terrace

A warm-hearted home with a lovely garden, an American hostess and two gorgeous Siamese cats. You are 20 minutes by bus from Princes Street yet the guests' snug sitting room overlooks pear trees and clematis and the rolling Pentland Hills. Cosy up in the winter next to the log fire; in summer, take your morning paper onto the terrace above the sunny garden. Books, fresh flowers, interesting art and ceramics and – you are on an old, quiet street – utter, surprising peace. One bedroom has a fine antique American four-poster. Clarissa is arty, easy, generous and loves her guests.

Craigbrae

The Westmacotts are wonderfully easy-going and the stone farmhouse is typically Scottish, with huge windows. In the green and coral drawing room expect family paintings, comfy sofas, loads of books; in the large, prettily decorated bedrooms, thick towels and striped linen. All face west for a sunny afternoon arrival. You are a 12-minute drive from Edinburgh airport but there is farmland and a working cooperage opposite; with luck, you'll be offered a dram! Trains run from Dalmeny village to the city every half hour and Louise can arrange for you to be met at the station.

Price	£65-£85. Singles £35-£42.50.
Rooms	3: 1 double; 1 double, 1 single sharing bath.
Meals	Pubs/restaurants nearby.
Closed	Rarely.
Directions	From centre of Edinburgh, A702 south, for Peebles. Pass Churchill Theatre (on left), to lights. Albert Terrace 1st right after theatre.

Price	£70-£90. Singles from £35.
Rooms	3: 1 double; 2 twins/doubles sharing 2 bath/shower rooms.
Meals	Pubs/restaurants 2 miles.
Closed	Christmas.
Directions	Please ask for directions when booking.

Clarissa Notley
1 Albert Terrace,
Edinburgh EH10 5EA
Tel   0131 447 4491
Email   canotley@aol.com

Louise & Michael Westmacott
Craigbrae,
Kirkliston,
Edinburgh EH29 9EL
Tel   0131 331 1205
Fax   0131 319 1476
Email   louise@craigbrae.com
Web   www.craigbrae.com

Map 15   Entry 583

Map 15   Entry 584

Edinburgh & the Lothians

Inveresk House

All the big villas around here are built on land that once belonged to Inveresk House, hence the enormous trees that shade the house. Alice has chosen to cover every wall with paintings (much is her own vibrant work) and fill every room with ornate antiques, squashy sofas in bright pinks and chintzes, flowers, gilt, mirrors and some seriously gorgeous rugs. Bedrooms and bathrooms are large, comfortable and spotlessly clean with an old-fashioned feel. The house was built on a Roman site and guards a 16th-century secret tunnel; Cromwell plotted his siege of Edinburgh Castle from here.

Price	£90. Singles £65.
Rooms	3: 1 double, 1 twin, 1 family room.
Meals	Pubs/restaurants nearby.
Closed	Rarely.
Directions	From Edinburgh, A199 (A1) to Musselburgh. There, follow signs to Inveresk. At top of Inveresk Brae, sharp right into cul-de-sac. 2nd opening on right, opp. gates with GM on them, bear right past cottages to house.

Alice & John Chute
Inveresk House,
3 Inveresk Village, Musselburgh,
East Lothian EH21 7UA

Tel	0131 665 5855
Fax	0131 665 0578
Email	chute.inveresk@btinternet.com
Web	www.invereskhouse.com

Map 15   Entry 585

Edinburgh & the Lothians

Glebe House

Gwen has lavished a huge amount of time and love on her 1780s manse. The perfect Georgian family house with all the well-proportioned elegance you'd expect, it is resplendent with original features – fireplaces, arched glass, long windows – that have appeared more than once in interiors magazines. Bedrooms are light, airy and hung with generous swathes of fabric. The sea is a stone's throw away and golfers have 21 courses to choose from. There's also a fascinating sea bird centre close by – yet you are 30 minutes from Edinburgh! Regular trains take you to the foot of the castle.

Price	£90. Singles by arrangement.
Rooms	3: 1 double, 1 twin, 1 four-poster.
Meals	Restaurants 2-minute walk.
Closed	Christmas.
Directions	From Edinburgh, A1 for Berwick. Left onto A198, follow signs into North Berwick. Right into Station Rd signed 'The Law', to 1st x-roads; left into town centre; house on left behind wall.

Gwen & Jake Scott
Glebe House,
Law Road, North Berwick,
East Lothian EH39 4PL

Tel	01620 892608
Mobile	07973 965814
Email	gwenscott@glebehouse-nb.co.uk
Web	www.glebehouse-nb.co.uk

Map 16   Entry 586

Eaglescairnie Mains

Wildlife thrives: eight acres of conservation headland have been created and wildflower meadows planted on this 350-acre working farm… you'd never guess Edinburgh is so close. The Georgian farmhouse sits in lovely gardens, its peace interrupted by the odd strutting pheasant. There's a traditional conservatory for summery breakfasts, a perfectly proportioned drawing room (coral walls, rich fabrics, log fire) for wintery nights, and beautiful big bedrooms full of books. Barbara is warm and charming, Michael's commitment to the countryside is wide-ranging, and the atmosphere is gracious and unhurried.

This working farm is used as an example of best practice in combining wildlife and landscape conservation with profitable agriculture and the enhancement of biodiversity – the carbon footprint continues to be reduced through sustainable practices, recycling and waste minimisation. A Finnish Veto 75kw woodchip-eating boiler is fed with coppice from the farm, heating both house and water; 15,000 deciduous trees have been planted along with 2 miles of new hedge, and 2.5 miles of old hedgerows have been restored! There's no stopping these two.

Price	£55–£75. Singles from £35.
Rooms	3: 2 doubles, 1 twin.
Meals	Pub 1 mile.
Closed	Christmas.
Directions	From A1 at Haddington B6368 south for Bolton & Humbie. Right immed. after traffic lights on bridge. 2.5 miles on through Bolton, at top of hill, fork left for Eaglescairnie. Entrance 0.5 miles on left.

Barbara & Michael Williams
Eaglescairnie Mains, Gifford,
Haddington, East Lothian EH41 4HN

Tel	01620 810491
Fax	01620 810491
Email	williams.eagles@btinternet.com
Web	www.eaglescairnie.com

SPECIAL
GREEN ENTRY
see page 17

Map 16 Entry 587

Fife

Blair Adam

If staying in a place with genuine Adam features is special, how much more so in the Adams' family home! They've been in this corner of Fife since 1733: John laid out the walled garden, son William was a prominent politician, Sir Walter Scott used to come and stay... you may be similarly inspired. The house stands in a swathe of parkland and forest overlooking the hills and Loch Leven, with big, friendly, light-flooded rooms filled with intriguing contents. The pretty bedroom is on the ground floor and you eat in the private dining room or with the family in the kitchen – you choose.

Price	From £90. Singles from £50.
Rooms	1 twin & sitting room.
Meals	Dinner, with wine, £20-£25. Restaurants 5 miles.
Closed	Christmas.
Directions	From M90 exit 5, take B996 south for Kelty. Right for Maryburgh, through village, right through pillars onto drive, under motorway via tunnel, then up to house.

	Keith & Elizabeth Adam
	Blair Adam,
	Kelty,
	Fife KY4 0JF
Tel	01383 831221
Mobile	07986 711099
Email	elizabeth@adamofblairadam.co.uk
Web	www.adamofblairadam.co.uk

Map 15   Entry 588

Fife

Ladywell House

Frances Shand Kydd once owned this large stone manse near the (surprisingly) English-looking conservation village of Falkland. Duncan and Camilla are now happily settled here and, apart from Diana's Room, whose décor remains unchanged, they have thrown out the florals and whistled in the new. Bedrooms are smart: cool neutral colours, crisp white linen hugging squishy goose down, shutters opening to wide views and bathrooms that sparkle. Downstairs is easy-going and fun, the atmosphere calm. Duncan cooks a huge, locally sourced breakfast; the village is a ten-minute stroll.

Price	£60-£80. Singles from £45.
Rooms	3: 1 double, 1 twin; 1 twin with separate bath.
Meals	Dinner, with wine, £18-£25. Pub 15-minute walk.
Closed	Christmas & New Year.
Directions	A92 north; 1st exit at 'New Inn' r'bout, signed Falkland. 2.5 miles just before village, farm road on left signed Ladywell House. Then 1st right through black gates.

	Duncan & Camilla Heaton Armstrong
	Ladywell House,
	Falkland, Fife KY15 7DE
Tel	01337 858414
Mobile	07931 304436
Email	duncan@tullochscott.co.uk
Web	www.ladywellhousefife.co.uk

Map 15   Entry 589

Fife

Woodmill

Staying at Woodmill is all about a good day out in the country – and a warm, welcoming return home. Lots of space, deep hot baths, the smell of mellow woodsmoke and fragrant homemade bread, a whisky from the bar, an elegant supper (game in season), a good bottle of wine and a big feather sofa to sink into. Bedrooms are smart with a contemporary twist, bathrooms have big white fluffy towels and there's a countryside view from every window. Guests use a separate staircase so you are assured space and privacy. Golf, fishing and walking nearby. A lovely place to stay.

Price	£85.
Rooms	2: 1 double; 1 double with separate bath.
Meals	Dinner with wine, from £30. Restaurant 6 miles.
Closed	Christmas & New Year.
Directions	On B937 between Lindores and Collessie. 1 mile from Collessie, look for a big white stone at the road end. Turn here then immed. right up drive to house.

	Clare Wade Woodmill, Lindores, Fife KY14 6JA
Tel	01337 810494
Fax	01337 810469
Email	stay@woodmillhouse.co.uk
Web	www.woodmillhouse.co.uk

Map 15+19   Entry 590

Fife

Fincraigs

Immersed in delightful, forgotten countryside, this 18th-century farmhouse, once the factor's house, has an air of great comfort and warmth; Felicity and Tom make you feel instantly at home. There's a sunny drawing room with open fire and old family pieces, and a guest sitting area upstairs. Two pretty bedrooms have lovely linen and fine views over the garden and rolling hills. Fincraigs' ten acres, presided over by ducks and geese, include an orchard and walled garden; expect fabulous home cooking and Tom's delicious wines. Fishing villages, the Tay estuary, Dundee and St Andrews, home of golf, are close by.

Price	From £70. Singles from £40.
Rooms	2: 1 double; 1 twin with separate bath.
Meals	Dinner, 3 courses, from £20. Pubs 3-5 miles.
Closed	Occasionally.
Directions	From A92 heading north, left after Rathillet, at Balmerino Gauldry sign. Fincraigs 1 mile from main road on left.

	Felicity & Tom Gilbey Fincraigs, Kilmany, Cupar, Fife KY15 4QQ
Tel	01382 330256
Fax	01382 330256
Mobile	07971 627813
Email	anyone@fincraigs.freeserve.co.uk

Map 15+19   Entry 591

Fife

18 Queen's Terrace

So peaceful that it's hard to imagine that you're in the heart of St Andrews and a mere ten-minute walk from the Royal & Ancient golf club. Jill's stylish and traditional home shows off her artistic flair; the light, restful drawing room and elegant dining room are full of character, sunlight and flowers. Large bedrooms have especially comfortable beds, crisp linens, whisky and water, and poetry and prose on bedside tables. An enchanting place – and Jill, friendly and generous, is a mine of information on art, gardens and walks; sit on the terrace in summer and admire the water garden. *Children over 12 welcome.*

Price	From £85. Singles £65-£70.
Rooms	4: 3 doubles, 1 twin.
Meals	Dinner, 3 courses with wine, £20-£35.
Closed	Rarely.
Directions	Into St Andrews on A917; pass Old Course Hotel. Right at 2nd mini r'bout, left through arch at 2nd mini r'bout. 250 yds, right into Queens Gardens. Right at T-junc. On left opp. church.

Jill Hardie
18 Queen's Terrace,
St Andrews,
Fife KY16 9QF

Tel	01334 478849
Fax	01334 470283
Email	stay@18queensterrace.com
Web	www.18queensterrace.com

Map 15+19 Entry 592

Fife

Kinkell

An avenue of beech trees patrolled by guinea fowl leads to the house. If the sea views and the salty smack of St Andrews Bay air don't get you, step inside and have your senses tickled. The elegant drawing room has two open fires, a grand piano, fine windows with working shutters upstairs and original pine floor – gorgeous. Bedrooms and bathrooms are spotless, sunny and warm. There's great cooking too, with maybe crab or pheasant served in the dining room; Sandy and Frippy excel in the kitchen. From the front door head down to the beach, walk the wild coast or jump on a quad bike in the back field.

Price	£80. Singles from £50.
Rooms	3 twins/doubles.
Meals	Dinner £25. Restaurants 2-3 miles.
Closed	Rarely.
Directions	From St Andrews, A917 for 2 miles for Crail. Driveway in 1st line of trees on left after St Andrews.

Sandy & Frippy Fyfe
Kinkell,
St Andrews,
Fife KY16 8PN

Tel	01334 472003
Fax	01334 475248
Email	fyfe@kinkell.com
Web	www.kinkell.com

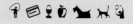

Map 16+19 Entry 593

Fife

Falside Smiddy

Prepare to be enchanted. The old smithy sits snugly on a bend (peaceful at night) somewhere between the home of golf and the fishing village of Crail. Saved from dereliction by Rosie and Keith, it is a home you are invited to share. Expect fresh flowers, maps on walls, books, boots and interesting ephemera – and inpromptu organ recitals from Keith! Small rooms have homemade biscuits and hat stands for clothes, bath and shower sport a hotpotch of towels. All is spotlessly clean. Rosie cooks great casseroles and turns berries into jams, and the wood-burner makes winters cosy. Lovely walks from the door.

Price	£56–£65. Singles £35.
Rooms	2 twins.
Meals	Dinner, 3 courses with wine, £25. Pub 2 miles. St Andrews 4 miles.
Closed	Occasionally.
Directions	From St Andrews, A917 for Crail. After 4 miles, ignore turning for Boarhills, & continue to small river. Over bridge; house 2nd on left.

Rosie & Keith Birkinshaw
Falside Smiddy,
Boarhills,
St Andrews,
Fife KY16 8PT
Tel   01334 880479
Email   rosiebirk@btinternet.com

Map 16+19 Entry 594

Glasgow

Finglen House

The Campsie Hills rise behind (climb them and you can see Loch Lomond), the Fin Burn takes a two-mile tumble down the hill into the garden, and herons and wagtails can be spotted from the breakfast table. All this 40 minutes from Glasgow. Sabrina's designer flair gives an easy, graceful comfort to the whole house: good beds in stylish rooms, proper linen, French touches, eclectic art, cast-iron baths and cream-painted wooden floors. A fresh, elegant drawing room with log fire is yours to share. Douglas, a documentary film maker, knows the Highlands and Islands well; he and Sabrina are fun and good company.

Price	£80. Singles £40.
Rooms	2: 1 double; 1 double with separate bath.
Meals	Pub 5-minute drive.
Closed	Christmas and New Year.
Directions	A81 from Glasgow right on A891 at Strathblane. 3 miles on, in Haughhead, look for a wall & trees on left, & turn in entrance signed Schoenstatt. Immed. left to house.

Sabrina & Douglas Campbell
Finglen House,
Campsie Glen, Glasgow G66 7AZ
Tel   01360 310279
Mobile   07774 820454
Email   sabrina.campbell@btinternet.com
Web   www.finglenhouse.com

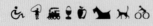

Map 15 Entry 595

Highland

Tanglewood House

Down a steep track through stunning landscape to this modern, curved house on the shore of Loch Broom – and distant views of the old fishing port of Ullapool. The huge drawing room is filled with antique rugs, fine fabrics, original paintings, flowers and a grand piano; sit here and bask in the views from the floor-to-ceiling window. All bedrooms are delightful: bold colours, crisp linen, proper bath tubs with fluffy towels. Anne gives you just-squeezed orange juice and eggs from her hens as well as delicious dinners; explore the wild garden then stroll to the rocky private beach for a swim in the loch. Superb.

Price	£82-£96. Singles £66-£73.
Rooms	3: 1 double, 2 twins.
Meals	Dinner, 4 courses, £33. BYO. Pubs in village 0.5 miles.
Closed	Christmas & New Year.
Directions	On outskirts of Ullapool from Inverness on A835, left immed. after 4th 40mph sign. Take cattle grid on right & left fork down to house.

Anne Holloway
Tanglewood House,
Ullapool,
Ross-shire IV26 2TB
Tel 01854 612059
Email tanglewoodhouse@ecosse.net
Web www.tanglewoodhouse.co.uk

Map 17 Entry 596

Highland

St Callan's Manse

Fun, laughter and conversation flow in this warm, relaxed and happy home. You share it with prints, paintings, antiques, sofas and amazing memorabilia – and three dogs, nine ducks, 14 hens and 1,200 teddy bears of every shape, size and origin. Snug bedrooms have pretty fabrics, old armoires, sheepskin rugs, tartan blankets. Caroline cooks delicious breakfasts and dinners; Robert, a fund of knowledgeable anecdotes, can arrange just about anything. All this in incomparable surroundings: glens, forests, buzzards, deer and the odd golden eagle. A gem. *2.5% credit card charge. Dogs by arrangement.*

Price	£80. Singles £65.
Rooms	2: 1 double with separate bath; 1 double with separate shower.
Meals	Dinner, 2-4 courses, £14.50-£25. BYO. Pub/restaurant in village, 1.5 miles.
Closed	Occasionally.
Directions	From Inverness, A9 north. Cross Dornoch bridge. 14 miles on, A839 to Lairg. Cross small bridge in Rogart; sharp right uphill, for St Callan's church. House 1.5 miles on, on right, next to church.

Robert & Caroline Mills
St Callan's Manse,
Highland,
Rogart, Sutherland IV28 3XE
Tel 01408 641363
Fax 01408 641313
Email email@robertmills.me.uk
Web www.miltonbankcottages.co.uk

Map 21 Entry 597

Highland

Thrumster House

A Victorian's laird's house in 12 acres of sycamore-wooded estate. Drive south a mile to the 5,000-year-old neolithic remains of the Yarrow Archeological Trail for brochs, round houses and long cairns, then back to the big old house, "steamboat gothic" in the words of an American guest. The vaulted hall gives an ecclesiastical feel, with fires burning at both ends and a grand piano on the landing (it gets played wonderfully). Big bedrooms have mahogany dressers, brass beds, floral wallpapers, lots of books. Islay and Catherine look after guests well and conversation flows. There's free trout fishing too.

Price	£80. Singles £45.
Rooms	2: 1 double; 1 twin with separate bath.
Meals	Dinner, 3 courses with wine, £25.
Closed	Rarely.
Directions	A99 north through Ulbster. After 2 miles, pass church & 'Yarrow Archaeological Trail' sign, then 1st left (200 yds) & up drive to house.

Islay MacLeod
Thrumster House,
Thrumster,
Caithness KW1 5TX
Tel   01955 651387
Fax   01955 651733
Email   islay.macleod@btinternet.com
Web   www.thrumster.co.uk

Map 21   Entry 598

Highland

Loch Eye House

A serene place for walkers, golfers, naturalists — and anyone who enjoys sociable dinner at an elegant table where mahogany gleams and wine glasses sparkle. It was Lucinda's dream to live here — she has childhood memories of skating on the loch; now the handsome, sunny house (15th century at the back, 1870 at the front) is exquisitely furnished and filled with fresh flowers. Bedrooms have perfect proportions and harmonious colours, bathrooms are immaculate, one with loch views: spot rare birdlife as you soak. The lawns sweep towards the loch and every view is sublime.

Price	£80. Singles £40.
Rooms	3: 1 double; 1 double, 1 twin, sharing bath.
Meals	Dinner, 3 courses, £30.
Closed	Occasionally.
Directions	A9 for Tain, then B9165 for Fearn. 1st left for Loandhu, then 1.5 miles & on left.

Lucinda Poole
Loch Eye House,
Fearn,
Ross-shire IV20 1RS
Tel   01862 832297
Fax   01862 832914
Email   loofy@ndirect.co.uk

Map 18   Entry 599

Highland

Linsidecroy

Heaven in the Highlands with stunning valley and mountain views. The house, built in 1863 was part of the Duke of Sutherland's estate; Robert, a factor, first set eyes on it 20 years ago and now it is home. A sublime renovation gives you walls of books, valley views and an open fire in the airy drawing room. Super bedrooms come with rugs, crisp linen, books galore and fresh flowers. There are two terraces, one for breakfast, one for pre-dinner drinks; all around you Davina's remarkable garden is taking shape. You can fish and walk, play some golf, or head north to Tongue through Britain's wildest land. Magical.

Price	£80. Singles £50.
Rooms	2: 1 double, 1 twin.
Meals	Hotel 6 miles.
Closed	Christmas, Easter & occasionally.
Directions	A836 west out of Bonar Bridge. After 4 miles, left onto A837. Cross Shin river, then right towards Rosehall & Lochinver, 1.5 miles, double wooden gates on right. House is 150 yds up drive.

Robert & Davina Howden
Linsidecroy,
Lairg,
Sutherland IV27 4EU
Tel   01549 421255
Email   howden@linsidecroy.wanadoo.co.uk

Map 18 Entry 600

Highland

Wemyss House

The setting overlooking the Cromarty Firth is stunning. Take an early morning stroll and spot buzzards, pheasants, rabbits and roe deer; the peace is palpable. The modern house with sweeping maple floors is flooded with light and fabulous views, big bedrooms are warmly decorated with Highland rugs and tweeds, there's Christine's grand piano in the living room and Stuart's handcrafted furniture at every turn. Aga breakfasts include homemade bread, preserves and eggs from a dozen happy hens; dinners sound delicious. Friendly and enthusiastic, Christine and Stuart love welcoming their guests.

Price	£70-£80.
Rooms	3: 2 doubles, 1 twin.
Meals	Supper from £25. Restaurants 15-minute drive.
Closed	Rarely.
Directions	From Inverness, A9 north. At Nigg r'bout, right onto B9175. Through Arabella; left at sign to Hilton/Shandwick; right towards Nigg; past church; 1 mile, right onto private road. House on right.

Christine Asher & Stuart Clifford
Wemyss House,
Bayfield, Tain,
Ross-shire IV19 1QW
Tel   01862 851212
Mobile   07759 484709
Email   stay@wemysshouse.com
Web   www.wemysshouse.com

Map 18 Entry 601

Highland

Craigiewood

The best of both worlds: the remoteness of the Highlands (red kites, wild goats) and Inverness just four miles. The landscape surrounding this elegant cottage exudes a sense of ancient mystery augmented by these six acres – home to woodpeckers, roe deer and glorious roses. Inside, maps, walking sticks, two cats and a lovely, family-home feel – what you'd expect from delightful owners. Bedrooms, old-fashioned and cosy, overlook a garden reclaimed from Black Isle gorse. Gavin runs garden tours and can take you off to Inverewe, Attadale, Cawdor and Dunrobin Castle. Warm, peaceful, special.

Price	£64–£80. Singles £40.
Rooms	2 twins.
Meals	Pub 2 miles.
Closed	Christmas & New Year.
Directions	A9 north over Kessock Bridge. At N. Kessock junc. filter left to r'bout to Kilmuir. After 0.25 miles, right to Kilmuir; follow road uphill, left at top, then straight on. Ignore 'No Through Road' sign, pass Drynie Farm, follow road to right; house 1st left.

Araminta & Gavin Dallmeyer
Craigiewood,
North Kessock, Inverness,
Inverness-shire IV1 3XG
Tel   01463 731628
Mobile   07831 733699
Email   2minty@high-lights.co.uk
Web   www.craigiewood.co.uk

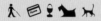

Map 18   Entry 602

Highland

Farr Mains

This much loved home, in epic Highland countryside, has been in the Murray family for three generations. The house is comfortable without being imposing, an 1850 original with later add-ons, now mostly clad in gleaming white wood. Christina is lively, down-to-earth, a warm hostess: wholesome, whole-hearted hospitality is guaranteed – along with home-produced honey and fruit and veg from the garden (pretty, and awash with daffodils in spring). The position is perfect for exploring the Highlands in every direction; return to a cosy drawing room with a peat fire. A llama adds an unexpected, exotic touch.

Price	£60. Singles £40. Suite £70–£90.
Rooms	2: 1 twin, 1 family suite for 2-3.
Meals	Lunch £5. Dinner, 3 courses, £20. Pub/restaurant 10-minute drive.
Closed	Christmas & New Year.
Directions	North of Aviemore for 26 miles, left onto B851 for Fort Augustus. Over bridge, through Inverarnie to Farr. House 2nd or 3rd gate on left, past playground.

James & Christina Murray
Farr Mains,
Farr,
Inverness,
Inverness-shire IV2 6XB
Tel   01808 521205
Fax   01808 521466
Email   farrmains@hotmail.com

Map 18   Entry 603

Highland

The Old Ferryman's House

This former ferryman's house is small, homely and delightful, and just yards from the river Spey with its spectacular mountain views. Explore the countryside or relax in the garden with a tray of tea and homemade treats; there are plants tumbling from whisky barrels and baskets. The sitting room is cosy with a woodburning stove and lots of books (no TV). Generous Elizabeth, a keen traveller who lived in the Sudan, cooks delicious and imaginative meals: wild salmon, herbs from the garden, heathery honeycomb, homemade bread and preserves. An unmatched spot for explorers, and very good value.

Price	£51. Singles £25.50.
Rooms	3: 1 double, 1 twin, 1 single, sharing 1 bath & 2 wcs.
Meals	Dinner, 3 courses, £18.50. BYO. Packed lunch £6.
Closed	Occasionally in winter.
Directions	From A9, follow main road markings through village, pass golf club & cross river. From B970 to Boat of Garten; house on left, just before river.

Elizabeth Matthews
The Old Ferryman's House,
Boat of Garten,
Inverness-shire PH24 3BY

Tel	01479 831370
Fax	01479 831370

Map 18   Entry 604

Highland

Tigh An Dochais

A contemporary, award-winning, 'see-through' house on a narrow strip of land between the road and the rocky shoreline, with stunning views across Broadford bay and the mountains beyond. Full-length windows and a cathedral ceiling allow light to flood in to an oak-floored sitting room with a wood-burner and super modern art. Downstairs are bedrooms with crisp white linen, tartan throws and modern bathrooms with underfloor heating. Neil is passionate about local food; try black pudding from Stornoway at breakfast, good fish and game for supper. Step straight onto the beach here, or stride out for the hills.

Price	£60-£70. Singles £40-£45.
Rooms	3: 2 doubles, 1 twin/double.
Meals	Dinner £10-£20. Packed lunch £5. Pub/restaurant 600 yds.
Closed	Rarely.
Directions	Leave Skye Bridge & follow A87 to Broadford. After 6 miles pass Hebridean Hotel on left, house is 200 yds further up A87 on right.

Neil Hope
Tigh An Dochais,
13 Harrapool,
Isle of Skye IV49 9AQ

Tel	01471 8220022
Email	hopeskye@btinternet.com
Web	www.skyebedbreakfast.co.uk

Map 17   Entry 605

Highland

The Berry

Drive through miles of spectacular landscape then bask in the final approach down a winding single-track road to the hamlet of Allt-Na-Subh — just five houses by the stunning loch. Joan, who paints, is friendly and kind, and her Rayburn-warmed kitchen the hub of this croft-style modern house. Inside is fresh and light with simple bedrooms — one up, one down; the sitting room has open fires and south-facing views. Eat fish straight from the boats, stride the hills and spot golden eagles, red deer and otters. The perfect place for naturalists and artists, or those seeking solace. *Skye is a 20-minute drive.*

Price	£50. Singles from £30.
Rooms	2: 1 double with separate shower; 1 double sharing bath.
Meals	Dinner, 3 courses with wine, £28. Packed lunch £7. Pub 20-minute drive.
Closed	Rarely.
Directions	From A87 at Dornie follow signs for Killilin, Conchra & Salachy. House 2.7 miles on left.

Joan Ashburner
The Berry,
Allt-Na-Subh,
Dornie,
Kyle of Lochalsh,
Highland IV40 8DZ

Tel	01599 588259

Map 17   Entry 606

Highland

The Grange

A Victorian townhouse with its toes in the country: the mountain hovers above, the loch shimmers below and whales have been sighted from the breakfast table. Bedrooms, one in a turret, another with a terrace, are large, luscious, warm and inviting — all crushed velvet, beautiful blankets and immaculate linen. Bathrooms are breathtaking and ooze panache. Expect neutral colours, decanters of sherry, a carved wooden fireplace, a Louis XV bed. Thoughtful breakfasts are served at glass-topped tables with flowers and white china; Joan's warm vivacity and love of B&B makes her a wonderful hostess.

Price	£98-£110. Singles 10% off room rate.
Rooms	3 doubles.
Meals	Restaurants 12-minute walk.
Closed	Mid-November to Easter.
Directions	A82 Glasgow-Fort William; there, right up Ashburn Lane, next to Ashburn guesthouse. On left at top.

Joan & John Campbell
The Grange,
Grange Road, Fort William,
Inverness-shire PH33 6JF

Tel	01397 705516
Fax	01397 701595
Email	info@thegrange-scotland.co.uk
Web	www.thegrange-scotland.co.uk

Map 17   Entry 607

Highland

Invergloy House

A peaceful, no-smoking home run by Margaret, a professional musician and James, a retired chemical engineer. It is a converted coach house with stables in the beautiful Great Glen and sits in 50 wild lochside acres of rhododendron, woodland and wonderful trees – and free fishing. Bedrooms are traditional, warm and welcoming; views of Loch Lochy and the mountains from the big picture window in the guest drawing room are spectacular. Walk to the private shingle beach on the loch, spot the wild roe deer in the grounds, savour the secluded peace and quiet. *Children over eight welcome.*

Price	From £68. Singles £32–£42.
Rooms	2: 1 double, 1 twin.
Meals	Restaurants 2–5 miles.
Closed	Rarely.
Directions	From Spean Bridge north on A82. After 5 miles, house signed on left.

Margaret & James Cairns
Invergloy House,
Spean Bridge,
Inverness-shire PH34 4DY
Tel   01397 712681
Fax   01397 712681
Email cairns@invergloy-house.co.uk
Web   www.invergloy-house.co.uk

Map 18   Entry 608

Moray

Blervie

The Meiklejohn coat of arms flies from the flagpole, an apple's throw from the orchard in which King Malcolm met his death. Blervie is a small 1776 mansion, "a restoration in progress", its finely proportioned rooms crammed with fresh flowers and splendid things to catch the eye. A large dresser swamped in china, a piano in the hall, books everywhere and the sweet smell of burnt beech from grand marble fireplaces. Big bedrooms have comfy old sofas at the feet of four-posters; bathrooms are eccentrically old-fashioned. Fiona and Paddy enjoy country pursuits and looking after their guests.

Price	£70.
Rooms	2: 1 four-poster; 1 four-poster with separate bath. Extra single bed.
Meals	Dinner, 4 courses, £25.
Closed	Christmas & New Year.
Directions	From A96 to Forres. South at clocktower, straight across r'bout onto B9010. Pass hospital; 1 mile on, left at Mains of Blervie sign. Right at farm.

Paddy & Fiona Meiklejohn
Blervie,
Forres,
Moray IV36 2RH
Tel   01309 672358
Email meiklejohn@btinternet.com

Map 18   Entry 609

Moray

Westfield House

This is the grand home of an illustrious family: Macleans have lived here since 1862. The hall is carpeted in clan tartan; the oak stair is hung with oils, standards and the odd ceremonial sword. John farms 500 acres while Veronica cooks sublimely; dinner is served at a long candelabra'd table on a rich red carpet. A winter fire crackles in the guest sitting room, old-fashioned bedrooms are warm and inviting – plump pillows, fine linen, books, lovely views – and the peace is interrupted only by the call of the guinea fowl. Lots of good eating places are nearby.

Price	£80. Singles from £40 .
Rooms	3: 1 twin;
	1 twin with separate bath & shower;
	1 single with separate bath.
Meals	Dinner, 3 courses, £20. Pub 3 miles.
Closed	Rarely.
Directions	From Elgin, A96 west for Forres & Inverness; after 2.5 miles, right onto B9013 for Burghead; after 1 mile, signed right at x-roads. Cont. to 'Westfield House & Office'.

John & Veronica Maclean
Westfield House,
Elgin,
Moray IV30 8XL
Tel   01343 547308
Fax   01343 551340
Email   veronicamaclean@hotmail.com

Map 18   Entry 610

Moray

Balwarren Croft

Thirty acres at the end of a bumpy track, a field of Highland cattle, mixed woodland, ancient dykes, a lochside full of birdlife, a herb garden with over 200 varieties and a burn you may follow down the hill. Hazel and James, warm, friendly, quietly passionate about green issues, came to croft 25 years ago. They licked crumbling walls into shape and the whole place is a delight. A cathedral roof, shiny wooden floors, cashmere blankets, sparkling bathrooms, log fires, delicious breakfasts (home eggs, jams and chutneys) and dinners a treat. A beautiful, uplifting place in an area steeped in mystery – and peace. *Minimum stay two nights.*

Price	£68. Singles £40.
Rooms	2: 1 twin; 1 double.
Meals	Dinner, 3 courses, £22.
	Pub/restaurant 10 miles.
Closed	Rarely.
Directions	North from Aberchirder on B9023. Right at Lootcherbrae (still B9023); 2nd left for Ordiquhill. After 1.7 miles, right at farm track opp. Aulton Farm; last croft up track.

Hazel & James Watt
Balwarren Croft,
Ordiquhill, Cornhill,
Banffshire AB45 2HR
Tel   01466 751688
Fax   01466 751688
Email   balwarren@tiscali.co.uk
Web   www.balwarren.com

Map 19   Entry 611

Perth & Kinross

Grenich Steading

Perched above silvery Loch Tummel is Lindsay's award-winning renovation of a once derelict barn. Inside, blue-and-white Portuguese tiles, seagrass matting and a woodburning stove. You get a kitchen, dining and sitting room so you can self-cater too (minimum one week). Gaze upon mountain-to-loch views, walk in the unspoilt glen or visit the theatre at Pitlochry. Lindsay loves nurturing both garden and guests; her two Scottish deerhounds are welcoming too. The sunsets are fabulous, and there's so much to do you'll barely be inside. *Children over eight welcome. Min. stay two nights weekends May-October.*

Price	£70. Singles £50.
Rooms	2: 1 double; 1 twin sharing bath & sitting room (2nd room let to same party only).
Meals	Dinner by arrangement, Oct to March only, £26 inc. wine. Pub 0.75 miles.
Closed	Christmas & New Year.
Directions	From A9 N of Pitlochry, turn to Killiecrankie. Left onto B8019 for Tummel Bridge & Kinloch Rannoch for 7 miles to Loch Tummel Inn. House, signed, 0.75 miles further on, then up forestry track on right for 0.5 miles.

Lindsay Morison
Grenich Steading,
Strathtummel,
Pitlochry,
Perth & Kinross PH16 5RT
Tel   01882 634332
Mobile   07900 362179

Map 15+18   Entry 612

Perth & Kinross

Beinn Bhracaigh

A door in a wall leads to a secret garden and a handsomely gabled period villa; like the grand house in a fairy tale. Guests have free run of the main rooms – all high ceilings, creamy walls, wooden floors, huge windows – comfortably spread with antiques and period features. Huge, restful bedrooms, with views to hills, are cool in cream and blue. There are power showers and luxury soaps, breakfast is a feast of local produce – with some surprises. After a day's walking, fishing and historical sightseeing, relax with a malt whisky – a choice of dozens – on the veranda. Ann and Alf are great hosts.

Price	£60-£80. Singles from £45.
Rooms	3: 1 double, 2 twins/doubles.
Meals	Dinner, 2-3 courses, £20-£25. Pubs/restaurants within 10-minute walk.
Closed	Rarely.
Directions	From A9, turn for Pitlochry. In town centre, A924 to Moulin & Braemar; 750 yds, then right at brown sign for Hydro Hotel; this leads into Knockard Rd. House near entrance.

Ann & Alf Berry
Beinn Bhracaigh,
Knockard Road, Pitlochry, Perth,
Perth & Kinross PH16 5HJ
Tel   01796 470355
Mobile   07708 668436
Email   info@beinnbhracaigh.com
Web   www.beinnbhracaigh.com

Map 15+18   Entry 613

Perth & Kinross

Craighall Castle

The view from the balcony that circles the drawing room is simply stunning, and the deep gorge provides the fabulous walks where you might glimpse deer, red squirrels and otters. Nicky and Lachie, ever welcoming, battle to keep up with the demands of the impressive home that has been in the family for 500 years. Any mustiness or dustiness can be forgiven, as staying here is a memorable experience. Nothing is contrived, sterile or luxurious, and there's so much drama and intrigue it could be the setting for a film. Breakfast is served in the 18th-century library, and there's a Regency drawing room, too.

Price	£70. Singles £40.
Rooms	2: 1 four-poster; 1 twin (extra single bed) with separate bath.
Meals	Restaurant 3 miles.
Closed	Christmas & New Year.
Directions	From Blairgowrie, A93 for Braemar for 2 miles. Just before end of 30mph limit, sharp right-hand bend, with drive on right. Follow drive for 1 mile.

Nicky & Lachie Rattray
Craighall Castle,
Blairgowrie,
Perth & Kinross PH10 7JB
Tel   01250 874749
Fax   01250 874749
Email   lrattray@craighall.co.uk

Perth & Kinross

Mackeanston House

A 1690 farmhouse full of beautiful pieces: ancient armoires, old pine dressers, creaking floorboards and the biggest beds. Bedrooms have style, floral fabrics and lots of books; one has a bath in which you can lie and look out to views of the hills. Outside, a one-acre walled garden and all-weather tennis court. In a conservatory, overlooking the garden with views to distant Stirling Castle and the Wallace Monument, you dine on salmon from the Teith or game from the hills, and enjoy home-produced fruit, bread and preserves. Colin is a Blue Badge guide. *Local & battlefield tours; wine & whisky weekends.*

Price	£90. Singles £55.
Rooms	2: 1 double, 1 twin/double.
Meals	Dinner £26. Pub 1 mile.
Closed	Christmas.
Directions	From M9, north, junc. 10 onto A84 for Doune. After 5 miles, left on B826 for Thornhill. Drive on left after 2.2 miles, right off farm drive.

Fiona & Colin Graham
Mackeanston House,
Doune, Stirling,
Perth & Kinross FK16 6AX
Tel   01786 850213
Mobile   07921 143018
Email   enquiries@mackeanstonhouse.co.uk
Web   www.mackeanstonhouse.co.uk

Map 15   Entry 615

Perth & Kinross

Old Kippenross

Pink since 1715 (a signal to Jacobites that the house was a safe haven), Old Kippenross rests in a wooden valley overlooking the river Allan – spot herons, dippers and otters. The Georgian part was built above the 500-year-old Tower House, and its rustic white-vaulted basement embraces dining room and sitting room, strewn with soft sofas and Persian rugs. Upstairs there are deeply comfortable sash-windowed bedrooms and warm, well-equipped bathrooms stuffed with towels. Sue and Patrick (who is an expert on birds of prey) are welcoming; breakfast and dinner are delicious. *Children over ten welcome. Dogs by arrangement.*

Price	£88. Singles from £59.
Rooms	2: 1 double, 1 twin.
Meals	Dinner £26. BYO. Pub 1.5 miles.
Closed	Rarely.
Directions	M9 exit 11, B8033 for Dunblane. 500 yds, right over dual c'way, thro' entrance by stone gatehouse. Down drive, 1st fork right after bridge. House along gravelled drive.

Sue & Patrick Stirling-Aird
Old Kippenross,
Dunblane,
Perth & Kinross FK15 0LQ
Tel   01786 824048
Fax   01786 824482
Email   kippenross@hotmail.com

Map 15   Entry 616

Scottish Borders

Skirling House

An intriguing house with 1908 additions, impeccably maintained. The whole lovely place is imbued with the spirit of Scottish Arts & Crafts, and augmented with Italianite flourishes. Mexican blankets embellish chairs, runners soften flagged floors and the carvings, wrought-ironwork and rare Florentine ceiling are sheer delight. Upstairs a more English comfort holds sway: carpets and rugs, window seats and wicker, gentle colours, fruit and flowers. Bob cooks the finest Scottish produce, Isobel shares a love of Scottish contemporary art. Outside, 25,000 newly planted trees and stunning views.

Price	£100. Singles £60.
Rooms	5: 3 doubles, 1 twin, 1 twin/double.
Meals	Dinner £30. Pubs/restaurants 2 miles.
Closed	Christmas & January-February.
Directions	From Biggar, A702 for Edinburgh. Just outside Biggar, right on A72 for Skirling. Big wooden house on right opp. village green.

Bob & Isobel Hunter
Skirling House,
Skirling, Biggar,
Scottish Borders ML12 6HD
Tel   01899 860274
Fax   01899 860255
Email   enquiry@skirlinghouse.com
Web   www.skirlinghouse.com

Map 15   Entry 617

Scottish Borders

Over Langshaw Farm

A peaceful, special place in the rolling hills of the Scottish Borders, with an inspiring commitment to organic food and good husbandry. The energy here goes into Friesians and ewes, family and guests, not fluffy towels and deep sofas! So, a delightful place for families and walkers, with simple bedrooms in farmhouse style and a guest sitting room with a log fire and white shutters. Plus all the nooks and crannies you'd expect from a 1700s house, and a sweet smiling welcome from Sheila. She and Martyn have detailed walking maps and could not be more helpful. Authentic and brilliant value.

Price	£60. Family room £70. Singles £35.
Rooms	2: 1 double; 1 family room with separate bath.
Meals	Dinner from £15. Packed lunch from £4. Pubs/restaurants 4 miles.
Closed	Never.
Directions	North from Galashiels, A7 past Torwoodlea golf course & right to Langshaw. After 2 miles, right at T-junc., then left at Earlston sign in Langshaw. White house, in trees, signed at farm road.

Sheila & Martyn Bergius
Over Langshaw Farm,
Galashiels,
Scottish Borders TD1 2PE
Tel 01896 860244
Fax 01896 860668
Email bergius@boogy.orangehome.co.uk

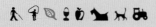

Map 15   Entry 618

Scottish Borders

Fauhope House

Near to Melrose Abbey and the glorious St Cuthberts' Walk, this solid 1890s house is immersed in bucolic bliss. Views soar to the Eildon Hills through wide windows with squashy seats; all is elegant, fire-lit, fresh and serene. Bedrooms are warm with deeply coloured walls, thick chintz, pale tartan blankets and soft carpet; bathrooms are modern and pristine. Breakfast is served with smiles at a flower-laden table and overlooking those purple hills. A short walk through the garden and over a footbridge takes you to the interesting town of Melrose, with shops, restaurants and its own theatre.

Price	From £80. Singles from £55.
Rooms	3 twins/doubles.
Meals	Pub/restaurant 0.5 miles.
Closed	Rarely.
Directions	From A7, through Gattonside; at end of village, at sign on left 'Monkswood', immed. left; right up drive.

Ian & Sheila Robson
Fauhope House,
Gattonside, Melrose,
Scottish Borders TD6 9LY
Tel 01896 823184
Fax 01896 820188
Mobile 07816 346768
Email fauhope@bordernet.co.uk

Map 15   Entry 619

Scottish Borders

Lessudden

A treat to stay in a great and historic tower house in the heart of the Scottish Borders. Your generous hosts give you big cosy bedrooms with private bathrooms and a spacious sitting room with fine old rugs, heaps of books and a log fire. Memorable meals are served at a polished oak refectory table beneath the gaze of Sir Walter Scott's uncle and aunt; they lived here, he was a frequent visitor. The 1680s white-stone stairwell is unique, the décor is traditional and homely, the living is relaxed and Alasdair and Angela care for their guests as open-heartedly as they do their cats, dogs, horses and hens.

Price	From £70. Singles from £50.
Rooms	2: 1 double; 1 twin with separate bathroom.
Meals	Dinner, 3-4 courses, £25. Pub 0.5 miles.
Closed	Rarely.
Directions	North on A68 to St Boswells. Right opp. Buccleuch Arms Hotel, on through village; left up drive immed. beyond turning to golf course.

Alasdair & Angela Douglas-Hamilton
Lessudden,
St Boswells,
Scottish Borders TD6 0BH
Tel 01835 823244
Fax 01835 823244
Email alasdaird@lineone.net
Web www.lessudden.com

Map 16 Entry 620

Scottish Borders

New Belses Farm

Once lost by Lord Lothian in a game of backgammon, this Georgian farmhouse is safe in current hands. Delightful Helen divides her time between cooking – her passion – and caring for sundry pets, fan-tail doves, hens (fox permitting), family, farm and guests. Bedrooms glow in a harmony of old paintings, lush chintzes and beautiful antiques; beds are extra long, towels snowy white. It's like home, only better. Discover great Border towns, stunning abbeys, fishing on the Tweed. Back to a wholesome dinner around the farmhouse table, and coffee on plump sofas by the log fire. Heaven.

Price	£70-£80.
Rooms	2: 1 double, 1 twin.
Meals	Dinner £25. Pubs/restaurants 3.5-5 miles.
Closed	Rarely.
Directions	From Jedburgh, A68 for Edinburgh. Left after 3.5 miles to Ancrum; B6400 Ancrum to Lilliesleaf road; right after 4 miles, down drive (signed).

Peter & Helen Wilson
New Belses Farm,
Ancrum,
Jedburgh,
Scottish Borders TD8 6UR
Tel 01835 870472
Fax 01835 870482
Email wilson699@totalise.co.uk

Map 16 Entry 621

Stirling

The Moss

Rozie loves fishing and Jamie keeps bees; they live in a charming listed house full of lovely things and are great hosts. Outside are 28 acres where deer prune the roses, pheasants roam and a garden seat sits with its toes in the water. Generous, carpeted bedrooms are in a private wing and have big beds with feather pillows, books, flowers and cosy windows that overlook the garden. Expect walking sticks and the bell of HMS Tempest in the porch, rugs in the hall and smart sofas in the log-fired drawing room. Breakfast comes fresh from the Aga and is delivered to a big oak table with lovely long views.

Price	£80. Singles £40.
Rooms	3: 1 twin; 2 doubles sharing bath (2nd room let to same party only).
Meals	Pubs/restaurants within 2 miles.
Closed	Rarely.
Directions	4 miles west of Blanefield. Left off A81 opp. Cairn Conservatories. After 300 yds, over bridge; 1st entrance on left.

	Jamie & Rozie Parker
	The Moss,
	Killearn,
	Stirling G63 9LJ
Tel	01360 550053
Mobile	07787 123599
Email	themoss@freeuk.com

Map 15   Entry 622

Stirling

Blairhullichan

So much to do here in the Loch Lomond and Trossachs National Park, with woodland walks, cycle tracks, your own sandy bay on the edge of Loch Ard for fishing, and a wooded island to wade out to for summery picnics. The house sits high on a slope with fabulous views to the loch from the comfortable drawing room with its large fireplace and stacks of books. Reassuringly old-fashioned bedrooms have new mattresses and crisp linen; bathrooms have good towels and lotions – one has a smart roll top. Bridget gives you a grand breakfast and can point you in the right direction for almost any activity. *Minimum stay two nights.*

Price	£70-£80. Singles £40.
Rooms	3: 1 twin; 2 doubles each with separate bath/shower (one with sitting room).
Meals	Dinner, with wine, £25-£35. Restaurant 10 miles.
Closed	Mid-December-mid-February.
Directions	A81 to Aberfoyle; at Bank of Scotland, onto B829 to Kinlochard; 4.5 miles, pass Macdonald Hotel into village. Left at shop & phone box (road becomes unpaved) pass new wooden house on right. On left, signed.

	Bridget Lewis
	Blairhullichan,
	Kinlochard, Aberfoyle,
	Stirling FK8 3TN
Tel	01877 387341
Fax	01877 387329
Email	jablewis@aol.com
Web	www.blairhullichan.net

Map 15   Entry 623

Stirling

Cardross

Dodge the lazy sheep on the long, slightly bumpy drive to arrive (eventually!) at a sweep of gravel and lovely old (1598) Cardross with its 14th-century tower. Bang on the enormous old door and either Archie or Nicola (plus labradors and Jack Russells) will usher you in. And what a delight it is; light and space, exquisite furniture, wooden shutters, marble fireplaces, fresh flowers, crisp linen, a cast-iron period bath – and that's just the bedroom. It all feels warm, kind and generous, the drawing room is vast, the food is excellent and the lovely Orr Ewings can tell you all the history.

Western Isles

Airdabhaigh

A rare 'undiscovered' corner of Britain… moody hills, lochs and acres of treeless blowy shores are wildly atmospheric. Miles of white sandy beaches too, and vast skies. Flora is inspirational; she's involved in Community Arts and runs dyeing and weaving workshops – a unique island experience. Wood panelling, thick walls, a peat fire, a warm kitchen, the wind whistling outside – and now, just below the house, a restored stone and thatch shieling for writing, reading, painting. Sweet bedrooms are a haven of warmth and simplicity. It's utterly peaceful, 100% authentic, a step back in time. *Ask about creative workshops.*

Price	£90-£100. Singles £50-£55.
Rooms	2: 1 twin; 1 twin with separate bath.
Meals	Occasional dinner. Pubs/restaurants 2.5-6 miles.
Closed	Christmas & New Year.
Directions	A811 Stirling-Dumbarton to Arnprior; then B8034 towards Port of Menteith; 3 miles, then cross the Forth over humpback bridge. Drive with yellow lodge 150 yds from bridge on right.

Price	£40. Singles £22.
Rooms	2: 1 double, 1 twin sharing shower.
Meals	Pub/restaurant within walking distance.
Closed	Rarely.
Directions	From Lochmaddy ferry, left on A867 for 8.6 miles to T-junc. Left on A865 for 2.4 miles (ignore signs to Carinish), then right at church. Up track. House 1st on left.

Sir Archie & Lady Orr Ewing
Cardross,
Port of Menteith, Kippen,
Stirling FK8 3JY

Tel	01877 385223
Fax	01877 385223
Email	adoewing@cardrossestate.demon.co.uk
Web	www.cardrossholidayhomes.com

Flora Macdonald
Airdabhaigh,
Uppertown, Carinish, North Uist,
Western Isles HS6 5HL

Tel	01876 580611
Mobile	07748 935204
Email	floraidh@hebrides.net
Web	www.calanas.co.uk

Map 15   Entry 624

Map 20   Entry 625

Wales

Photo: Quentin Craven

Anglesey

Cleifiog

Liz moved here for the view: you can see why. The creamy Georgian monks' hospice, later an 18th-century customs house, looks across to the wooded coast of Snowdonia; the masts of Beaumaris Bay chink in the wind. As well as being a keen gardener and needlework collector, Liz paints; pursuits that inform the mellow restoration and decoration of this house. Big, bright, elegant rooms, chic yet countrified, are sprinkled with rich tapestries, antique samplers and fresh flowers. Be charmed by the comfort, the welcome, the soft linens, the ample breakfasts and the wonderful soft sea air. *Children over four welcome.*

Price	£65-£85. Singles £40-£55.
Rooms	3: 1 twin/double, 1 twin, 1 suite.
Meals	Pub/restaurant 200 yards.
Closed	Christmas & New Year.
Directions	A55 over Britannia Bridge to Anglesey. A545 to Beaumaris. Past 2 left turns, house is 5th on left facing the sea. Bus stop outside.

	Liz Bradley
	Cleifiog,
	Townsend, Beaumaris,
	Anglesey LL58 8BH
Tel	01248 811507
Email	liz@cleifiogbandb.co.uk
Web	www.cleifiogbandb.co.uk

✕ 🗎 🍷

Map 6 Entry 626

Cardiff

Rock House

Minutes from the pebble beach, the Victorian house with the steeply terraced garden has a warm, inviting feel. Bliss to breakfast outside on fine days and watch the boats on the Bristol Channel; produce is 'fair trade', locally sourced or from the garden. Bedrooms are fresh, light and traditionally furnished with some lovely inherited pieces; beds are comfy, bathrooms carpeted, duvets goose down. Jane and David, easy-going, generous hosts, happily share their home and valuable local knowledge with guests. Wander along the sea front or into town for dinner. Cardiff is a short hop by car or train.

Price	£45-£65. Singles £35-£45.
Rooms	3: 1 double; 2 doubles sharing bath (2nd room let to same party only).
Meals	Packed lunch £4. Restaurants 500 yds.
Closed	Occasionally.
Directions	At r'bout with clock in Penarth centre, straight on; 1st left (Church Rd), 1st right (Bradford Pl) & 1st right onto Beach Lane. Walk down passage & enter thro' back garden.

	Jane & David Maw Cornish
	Rock House,
	9 Beach Road, Penarth,
	Cardiff CF64 1JX
Tel	02920 704314
Fax	02920 704314
Email	rockhouse-penarth@supanet.com
Web	www.rockhouse-penarth.co.uk

✕ 🗎 🍷

Map 2 Entry 627

Carmarthenshire

Sarnau Mansion

Listed and Georgian, the house has its own water supply. Play tennis and revel in 16 acres of beautiful grounds complete with pond and woodland. Bedrooms are simply furnished in heritage colours; bathrooms are big. The oak-floored sitting room with chesterfields has French windows onto the walled garden, the dining room is simpler with separate tables and there's good, fresh home cooking from Cynthia. One mile from the A40, you can hear a slight hum of traffic if the wind is from that direction. You are 15 minutes from the National Botanic Garden of Wales. *Children over five welcome.*

Price	£55-£65. Singles £40-£45.
Rooms	3: 2 doubles, 1 twin.
Meals	Dinner, 3 courses, around £20. BYO. Pub 1 mile.
Closed	Rarely.
Directions	From Carmarthen A40 west for 4 miles. Right for Bancyfelin. After 0.5 miles, right into drive on brow of hill.

Cynthia & David Fernihough
Sarnau Mansion,
Llysonnen Road, Bancyfelin,
Carmarthenshire SA33 5DZ

Tel	01267 211404
Fax	01267 211404
Email	fernihough@so1405.force9.co.uk
Web	www.sarnaumansion.co.uk

Map 6   Entry 628

Carmarthenshire

Mandinam

On a heavenly bluff on the edge of the Beacons, beneath wheeling red kites and moody Welsh skies, lies Mandinam, the 'untouched holy place'. Delightful artistic Marcus and Daniella are its guardians, the farm is now mostly conservation land and they look after you as friends. Be charmed by bold rugs on wooden floors, weathered antiques, lofty ceilings, shutters, fires... and scrumptious meals in a red dining room. The rustic coach house studio, with hillside terrace and woodburner, is for dreamers; the serene four-poster room has underfloor heating. Watch the sun go down before dinner, revel in the peace.

Price	£70-£80. Singles by arrangement.
Rooms	2: 1 studio twin/double, 1 four-poster.
Meals	Lunch or picnic from £7.50. Dinner £25. Pub 2.5 miles.
Closed	Christmas.
Directions	Left at Llangadog village shop; 50 yds; right for Myddfai. Past cemetery, 1st right for Llanddeusant; 1.5 miles, thro' woods on left.

Daniella & Marcus Lampard
Mandinam,
Llangadog,
Carmarthenshire SA19 9LA

Tel	01550 777368
Email	info@mandinam.co.uk
Web	www.mandinam.co.uk

Map 7   Entry 629

Carmarthenshire

Plas Alltyferin

Wisteria-wrapped and delightfully wonky in parts, the Georgian family house comes with 270 secluded acres in the handsome Towy Valley, close to the superb gardens of Aberglasney. The dining room, where you breakfast, has the original panelling; the bedrooms have the charm and patina of guest rooms little-changed for decades. Not the place for you if you like spotlessness and state-of-the-art plumbing, but the views across the ha-ha to the Norman hill fort are timelessly lovely and the welcome is heartfelt. Gerard and Charlotte are the easiest, kindest and dog-friendliest of hosts. *Children over ten welcome.*

Price	£50–£70. Singles £35–£40.
Rooms	2: 1 twin; 1 twin with separate bathroom.
Meals	Pubs/restaurants within 2 miles.
Closed	Rarely.
Directions	From Carmarthen A40 east to Pont-ar-gothi. Left before bridge & follow narrow lane for approx. 2 miles keeping to right-hand hedge. House on right, signed. Call for precise details.

Charlotte & Gerard Dent
Plas Alltyferin,
Pont-ar-gothi, Nantgaredig,
Carmarthenshire SA32 7PF
Tel 01267 290662
Fax 01267 290662
Email dent@alltyferin.co.uk
Web www.alltyferin.co.uk

Map 6   Entry 630

Carmarthenshire

Mount Pleasant Farm

Sheep bleat, red kites fly overhead and the views to the Black Mountain are breathtaking: your bedroom view must be one of the best in this book. Sue and her daughter are delightful and Sue is a brilliant cook. Only the best local lamb and beef will do, the veg is organic and the eggs (bright orange!) are their own; vegetarians are spoiled too. After dinner there's snooker, a log fire, a cosy sofa; then a seriously comfortable bed in a room with a lovely country-house feel. Aberglasney and the National Botanic Garden are nearby, beautiful coastal walks less than an hour away. *Children over 12 welcome. 1.5 hours from Pembroke Dock.*

Price	£60. Singles £30–£35.
Rooms	3: 1 twin/double, 1 single, sharing bath (2nd room let to same party only); 1 twin/double.
Meals	Dinner, 3 courses with wine, £17.50. Packed lunch £7.50.
Closed	Christmas.
Directions	A40 Llandovery-Llandeilo. At Llanwrda, right for Lampeter (A482). Out of village, 1st right after mounted pillar box in lay-by on left. Over bridge & up hill; 1st left. House 1st on right.

Sue, Nick & Alice Thompson
Mount Pleasant Farm,
Llanwrda,
Carmarthenshire SA19 8AN
Tel 01550 777537
Fax 01550 777537
Email rivarevivaluk@aol.com

Map 7   Entry 631

Ceredigion

Broniwan

Carole and Allen have created a model organic farm, and it shows. They are happy, the cows are happy and the kitchen garden is the neatest in Wales. With huge warmth and a tray of Welsh cakes they invite you into their cosy, ivy-clad house of natural browns, reds and the odd vibrant flourish of local art. Another passion is literature; call to arrange a literary weekend. Plentiful birdlife in the wonderful garden with views to the Preseli hills adds an audible welcome from tree-creepers, redstarts and wrens. The National Botanic Garden of Wales and Aberglasney are nearby, the coastal paths a quick drive.

Price	£60-£64. Singles £35.
Rooms	2: 1 double; 1 double with separate bath.
Meals	Dinner £20. BYO.
Closed	Rarely.
Directions	From Aberaeron, A487 for 6 miles for Brynhoffnant. Left at B4334 to Rhydlewis; left at Post Office & shop, 1st lane on right, then 1st track on right.

Carole & Allen Jacobs
Broniwan,
Rhydlewis, Llandysul,
Ceredigion SA44 5PF

Tel	01239 851261
Fax	01239 851261
Email	broniwan@btinternet.com
Web	www.broniwan.com

Map 6   Entry 632

Ceredigion

Fynnon Fendigaid

Arrive through rolling countryside – birdsong and breeze the only sound – to this old farmhouse; within moments you will be sprawled on a leather sofa admiring modern art and wondering how a little bit of Milan arrived here along with Huw and homemade cake. A place to come and pootle, with no rush; you can stay all day to pick gently through the gardens, or opt for hearty walking. Either way your bed is big, the colours are soft, the bathrooms are luxurious and the food is local – try all the Welsh cheeses. Wide beaches are minutes away, red kites and buzzards soar above you. Pulchritudinous.

Price	£60-£70. Singles from £35.
Rooms	2 doubles.
Meals	Dinner, 3 courses, £16. Packed lunch £6. Pub 1 mile.
Closed	Rarely.
Directions	From A487 Cardigan/Aberystwth coast road, take B4334 at Brynhoffnant towards Rhydlewis. 1 mile to junction where road joins from right & lane to house on left.

Huw Davies
Fynnon Fendigaid,
Rhydlewis, Llandysul,
Ceredigion SA44 5SR

Tel	01239 851361
Mobile	07974 135262
Email	ffynnonf@btinternet.com
Web	www.ffynnonf.co.uk

Map 6   Entry 633

Conwy

Rhiw Goch

The 17th-century longhouse overlooks the Lledr valley. Rhiw Goch is a welcoming and secluded home set within 35 hillside acres where wonderful gardens merge seductively into wilder woodland and pasture. Inside are two main living areas, one with a wood-burner and piano you are welcome to play; occasional concerts are held here for charity. Bedrooms have beige carpets, good beds and plenty of space, there are fabulous views from every window and breakfasts are generous. Rhiw Goch is well placed for Snowdonia and all the Lleyn peninsula has to offer. *Minimum stay two nights.*

Price	£70. Singles from £35.
Rooms	2: 1 double, 1 family room, sharing bath.
Meals	Pubs 5-minute drive.
Closed	Christmas & New Year.
Directions	A470 Betws y Coed to Dollgelleau for 3 miles; right, 200 yds after sign for Ponty Pant r'way stn; follow lane to top of hill. Cont. round to right, past green shed to house beyond.

Abigail King
Rhiw Goch,
Pont y Pant,
Dolwyddelan,
Conwy LL25 0PQ
Tel   01690 750231

Map 7   Entry 634

Flintshire

Golden Grove

Huge, Elizabethan and intriguing – Golden Grove was built by Sir Edward Morgan in 1580. The Queen Anne staircase, oak panelling, faded fabrics and fine family pieces are enhanced by jewel-like colour schemes: rose-pink, indigo, aqua. In summer the magnificent dining room is in use; in the winter the sitting room fire counters the draughts. The two Anns are charming and amusing, dinners are delicious and the family foursome tend the garden – beautiful, productive and well-kept. They also find time for a nuttery and a sheep farm as well as their relaxed B&B. Many return to this exceptional place.

Price	£90. Singles £55.
Rooms	3: 1 double; 1 double, 1 twin, each with separate bath.
Meals	Dinner £28.
Closed	November-February.
Directions	Turn off A55 onto A5151 for Prestatyn. At Texaco before Trelawnyd, right. Branch left immed. over 1st x-roads; right at T-junc. Gates 170 yds on left.

Ann & Mervyn and Ann & Nigel
Steele-Mortimer
Golden Grove,
Llanasa, Holywell,
Flintshire CH8 9NA
Tel   01745 854452
Fax   01745 854547
Email   golden.grove@lineone.net

Map 7   Entry 635

Flintshire

Plas Penucha

Polished parquet, tidy beams, a huge Elizabethan panelled lounge with books and open fire – a cosy spot for tea in winter. Plas Penucha – 'the big house on the highest point in the parish' – has been in the family for 500 years. Airy bedrooms have spotless bathrooms and long views across the garden to Offa's Dyke. The L-shaped dining room has a genuine Arts & Crafts interior; outside, rhododendrons and a rock garden flourish and the croquet lawn is smooth. Beyond is Caerwys, birthplace of the National Eisteddfod, and St Asaph, with the smallest medieval cathedral in the country.

Price	From £58. Singles from £29.
Rooms	2: 1 double, 1 twin.
Meals	Dinner £17.50. Packed lunch £4. Pub 3 miles.
Closed	Rarely.
Directions	From Chester, A55, B5122 left for Caerwys. 1st right into High St. Right at end. 0.75 miles to x-roads & left, then straight for 1 mile. House on left, signed.

Mrs Nest Price
Plas Penucha,
Peny Cefn Road,
Caerwys, Mold,
Flintshire CH7 5BH
Tel   01352 720210
Email   nest@plaspenucha.co.uk
Web   www.plaspenucha.co.uk

Map 7   Entry 636

Gwynedd

Lympley Lodge

The solid Victorian exterior belies a surprising interior. Welcoming Patricia, a former restorer, has brought together a gorgeous collection of furniture, while her meticulous paintwork adds light and life to her seaside home. Above is the Little Orme; below, across the main coast road, the sweep of Llandudno Bay. Bedrooms strike the perfect balance between the practical and the exotic; all have crisp linen, rich fabrics, fresh flowers, lovely views. There's an elegant sitting room for guests, a stunning dining room with a Renaissance feel and breakfasts full of local and homemade produce.

Price	£80. Singles £45.
Rooms	3: 1 double, 1 twin; 1 double with separate bath.
Meals	Restaurants/pubs 5-minute drive.
Closed	Mid-December to end of January.
Directions	From Llandudno Promenade, turn right and follow B5115 (Colwyn Bay) up the hill. Pass right turn for Bryn Y Bia. House entrance (board on side of building) on right.

Patricia Richards
Lympley Lodge,
Colwyn Road,
Craigside, Llandudno,
Gwynedd LL30 3AL
Tel   01492 549304
Email   patricia@lympleylodge.co.uk
Web   www.lympleylodge.co.uk

Map 7   Entry 637

Gwynedd

Y Goeden Eirin

An education in Welsh culture, and a stylish spot from which to explore the country. Against the backdrop of wild Snowdonia, surrounded by 20 acres of rough grazing, house and setting have an open seaside feel. Inside presents a cosy picture: Welsh-language and English books share the shelves, paintings by contemporary Welsh artists enliven the walls, an arty 70s décor mingles with sturdy Welsh oak in the bedrooms and bathrooms are chic. Wonderful food is served alongside the Bechstein in the beamed dining room — the welcoming, thoughtful Eluned and John have created an unusually delightful space.

Price	£70-£90. Singles from £35.
Rooms	3: 2 doubles, 1 twin.
Meals	Dinner, 3 courses, £25. Packed lunch £7. Pub/restaurant 1 mile.
Closed	Christmas-New Year.
Directions	From Caernarfon onto Porthmadog & Pwllheli road. A487 thro' Bontnewydd, left at r'bout, signed Dolydd. House 0.5 miles on right, before garage on left.

Dr John & Mrs Eluned Rowlands
Y Goeden Eirin,
Dolydd, Caernarfon,
Gwynedd LL54 7EF
Tel   01286 830942
Mobile   07708 491234
Email   john_rowlands@tiscali.co.uk
Web   www.ygoedeneirin.co.uk

Map 6   Entry 638

Gwynedd

Plas Tan-yr-allt

Who shot Shelley in the drawing room? The poet fled in 1813, the mystery unsolved. The listed house has a colourful history, irresistible to the owners who have just finished a glorious restoration: roll top baths, deep luscious colours, underfloor heating, handsome furniture. *The Daily Telegraph* said Tanny exemplifies "contemporary country-house style"... and there's country-house cooking too. Nik uses local ingredients, and guests eat together at an impressive oak and slate table for dinner – a convivial treat. Wonderful views stretch from the terrace and gardens over the estuary and bay.

Price	£115-£150. Singles £90-£125.
Rooms	6: 3 doubles, 1 twin, 2 four-posters.
Meals	Dinner, 3 courses, £35 (Wed-Sun). Pubs/restaurants 10-minute walk.
Closed	2 weeks in January.
Directions	Leave Tremadog on A498 for Beddgelert. Signed on left after 0.5 miles. House at top of hill.

Michael Bewick & Nick Golding
Plas Tan-yr-allt,
Tremadog,
Porthmadog,
Gwynedd LL49 9RG
Tel   01766 514545
Email   info@tanyrallt.co.uk
Web   www.tanyrallt.co.uk

Map 6   Entry 639

Gwynedd

Abercelyn Country House

The 1729 rectory comes with rhododendron-rich grounds, an immaculate kitchen garden and a mountain stream. The stream has its own history – its waters poisoned Cromwell's horses in the Civil War, enabling the opposition to skedaddle; today Abercelyn is a less battle-scarred retreat. Shutters gleam, logs glow and bedrooms have space, light, smart bathrooms and luscious views. The drawing room overflows with outdoor guides, Ray orchestrates adventure trips to Snowdonia National Park and Lindsay cooks and looks after you beautifully. Bala Lake is a ten-minute stroll. *Guided walks & canoeing.*

Price	£70-£80. Singles £50.
Rooms	3: 2 doubles, 1 twin/double.
Meals	Pub 10-minute drive. Restaurant 15-min walk; free return taxi service.
Closed	Rarely.
Directions	On A494 Bala-Dolgellau road, 1 mile from centre of Bala, opp. Llanycil Church.

Ray & Lindsay Hind
Abercelyn Country House,
Llanycil, Bala,
Gwynedd LL23 7YF
Tel   01678 521109
Fax   01678 520848
Email   info@abercelyn.co.uk
Web   www.abercelyn.co.uk

Map 7   Entry 640

Gwynedd

Dolgadfa

Gasp at the beauty of the road to Dolgadfa, every bend revealing yet another perfect frame of southern Snowdonia – the gentle prelude to the ragged peaks. The youthful Robertsons' slice of this bliss is unexpectedly luxurious. The deep limpid river winds past the listed guest barn where bedrooms – one with stone steps straight onto the riverside garden – are fresh and country-cosy, with gingham curtains and all the trimmings. A bright living room with roaring fire, sofas and Welsh oak floor is yours, and Louise does a fine breakfast. For a couple or a party, a superb place. *Fishing & shooting available.*

Price	£70-£80. Singles £50.
Rooms	3: 1 double, 1 twin; 1 double with separate bath.
Meals	Pub/restaurant in village, 1 mile.
Closed	Christmas.
Directions	B4401; after Llandrillo, 2nd right. Single track road; over bridge; at T-junc. left, on for 1.5 miles; 2nd farmhouse on left. White gate.

Louise Robertson
Dolgadfa,
Llandderfel, Bala,
Gwynedd LL23 7RE
Tel   01678 530469
Mobile   07708 249537
Email   dolgadfa@btinternet.com
Web   www.dolgadfa.co.uk

Map 7   Entry 641

Bryniau Golau

Under clear skies, there are few more soul-lifting views: the long lake and miles of Snowdonia. Each generous room is beautifully furnished – traditional with a contemporary twist, and more glorious views to the garden and lake. Katrina, friendly and adaptable, spoils you with open fires in the sitting room, goose down duvets on the beds, spa baths for all, underfloor heating and scrumptious breakfasts that set you up for the day. Linger on the lawn, perhaps with a drink as the sun sets, and try your hand at fly fishing or rafting. A wonderful place for a house party – and the walking is superb.

Price	£70-£80. Singles £45-£55.
Rooms	3: 2 four-posters, 1 twin/double.
Meals	Supper available. Pubs/restaurants within 1 mile.
Closed	Rarely.
Directions	From Bala B4391; 1 mile, B4403 Llangower. Pass Bala Lake Hotel; look for sign showing left turn; 20 yds after tree, sign on right; left up hill, over cattle grid; 1st on right.

Katrina le Saux
Bryniau Golau,
Llangower,
Bala,
Gwynedd LL23 7BT
Tel   01678 521782
Email   katrinalesaux@hotmail.co.uk
Web   www.bryniau-golau.co.uk

Map 7   Entry 642

The Old Rectory - on the lake

The drive to get here is fantastic and the approach truly beautiful – you see The Old Rectory waiting for you on the other side of the lake. The owners are full of enthusiasm for their fabulous B&B and spoil guests rotten – comfy beds, luxurious baths, WiFi and satellite TV in the rooms, cream teas in the garden and fresh home-cooked meals. Fabulous photos of the lake in its many moods decorate the dining room walls, there's an open fire in the sitting room and binoculars for birdwatching in the bedrooms. Woods and water for walking and fishing, and views from every window over the large, lovely, luminous lake.

Price	From £70.
Rooms	3: 2 doubles; 1 double with sofabed.
Meals	Dinner £20.
Closed	Rarely.
Directions	A470 from Dolgellau. A487 from Cross Foxes Inn, then B4405 (signposted Tywyn). Follow along lakeside; turn right at head of lake and cont. 0.25 miles.

Ricky Francis
The Old Rectory - on the lake,
Talyllyn,
Gwynedd LL36 9AJ
Tel   01654 782225
Mobile   07919 190445
Email   enquiries@rectoryonthelake.co.uk
Web   www.rectoryonthelake.co.uk

Map 7   Entry 643

Monmouthshire

Penpergwm Lodge

On the edge of the Brecon Beacons, a large and lovely Edwardian house. Breakfast round the mahogany table, relax in the warmly inviting sitting room with piano and real fire. The Boyles have been here for years and pour much of their energy into three beautiful acres of parterre and potager, orchard and flowers. Bedrooms are gloriously traditional – ancestral portraits, big windows, good chintz – with garden views; bathrooms are a skip across the landing. A pool and tennis for the sporty, two summer houses for the dreamy, a good pub you can walk to. Splendid, old-fashioned B&B.

Price	£65-£75. Singles £40.
Rooms	2 twins, each with separate bath.
Meals	Pub within walking distance.
Closed	Rarely.
Directions	A40 to Abergavenny; at big r'bout on SE edge of town, B4598 to Usk for 2.5 miles. Left at King of Prussia pub, up small lane; house 200 yds on left.

Catriona Boyle
Penpergwm Lodge,
Abergavenny,
Monmouthshire NP7 9AS

Tel	01873 840208
Fax	01873 840208
Email	boyle@penpergwm.co.uk
Web	www.penplants.com

Map 7   Entry 644

Monmouthshire

The Nurtons

After following the twists and turns of the glorious Wye valley, what a pleasure to be greeted by Adrian and Elsa. The façade of their history-rich home is Victorian, the interior rambling and intriguing, the site ancient. A flagged area conceals a sacred 'healing bath' and, cosily at the back, are two B&B suites with private sitting areas inside *and* out. The two-and-a-half acre plantsman's garden reflects a passion for all things organic, much of which appears, freshly and deliciously, on your plate. Welcoming – and atmospheric. *Pampering breaks also available.*

Price	From £65. Singles from £35.
Rooms	3: 1 double, 1 double & sitting room & child bed, 1 twin & sitting room & sofabed.
Meals	Evening platter £30 for 2 sharing. Packed lunch £5. Pub 0.75 miles.
Closed	Rarely.
Directions	A466 just north of Tintern village, drive to house is opp. the Old Station-Tintern.

Adrian & Elsa Wood
The Nurtons,
Tintern,
Monmouthshire NP16 7NX

Tel	01291 689253
Email	info@thenurtons.co.uk
Web	www.thenurtons.co.uk

Map 7   Entry 645

Monmouthshire

Allt-y-bela

A beautiful and ancient house, built between 1420 and 1599, kicking off an early Renaissance architectural buzz and now perfectly restored for the 21st century. It is reached down a narrow lane and sits in its own private and secluded valley. Here is made-to-measure pampering among soaring beams and period furniture. A log-warmed dining room if you want it with private meals delivered by two clever chefs, and a super kitchen if you want to be more involved. Bedrooms soothe with limewashed walls, fabulous beds, no TV, stunning art, and proper bathrooms that glow in wood. And now the garden is being created...

Price	From £250. Singles from £150.
Rooms	2 doubles.
Meals	Dinner from £35. Kitchen supper £25. Any other meals by arrangement. Pubs/restaurants 3 miles.
Closed	Rarely.
Directions	A449 towards Usk, then B4235 to Chepstow. After 200 yds, unsigned right turn. Follow for 0.5 miles; left into No Through Road, follow for 2 miles.

Louise & Alison Barber
Allt-y-bela,
Llangwm Ucha,
Usk,
Monmouthshire NP15 1EZ
Tel   07892 403103
Email   bb@alltybela.co.uk
Web   www.alltybela.co.uk

Map 7   Entry 646

Monmouthshire

Castle Acre

Between castle and church, the house lies hidden in a walled garden. A low stone and brick building full of light, cleverly converted from stabling and a coach house. Breakfast in the salmon-pink dining room with its glossy antiques, books and garden views. Choose between the terracotta bedroom, overlooking the castle ruins, or the primrose room with adjoining attic – perfect for children – overlooking the church. Bathrooms have tongue and groove panelling; all is cool, pretty and relaxing. Walk Offa's Dyke, the Black Mountains or Three Castles Walk, browse Hay's bookshops, doze in the garden. Sue is warmly efficient.

Price	£80. Singles £40.
Rooms	2: 1 twin/double, 1 double.
Meals	Pub in village.
Closed	Never.
Directions	M4 junc. 24, onto A449. 12 miles; exit Abergavenny. A40 for 9 miles, A465 for Hereford; 6 miles on, right marked Grosmont to T-junc., right to village, right to castle. Drive on right.

Sue Gill
Castle Acre,
Grosmont,
Monmouthshire NP7 8LW
Tel   01981 241078
Mobile   07885 900094
Email   castleacre@aol.com
Web   www.castleacregrosmont.co.uk

Map 7   Entry 647

Pembrokeshire

Bowett Farm

An ancient bluebell wood pulsates with colour in the spring and wild flowers of all kinds bloom in profusion; if you're lucky, you might see a badger. This is a friendly, relaxed house; take tea in the garden or bring wine and Ann will provide the glasses. Relax in the evening in a comfortable sitting room filled with gorgeous Welsh antiques – then to bed. One of the rooms has a fine, restored half-tester bed and a giant bathroom with Victorian washstand. Breakfast on local produce, homemade jams and marmalades, fresh fruit salad and yogurt… the Pembrokeshire coastal path runs nearby.

Price	£65–£70. Singles £40.
Rooms	3: 1 double with separate bath; 1 twin/double with separate shower; 1 single (same party only).
Meals	Packed lunch £5. Pub/restaurant 0.5 miles.
Closed	Mid-October to Easter.
Directions	B4320 from Pembroke for Hundleton. After woods, house 1st on right. Approx. 1 mile from Pembroke centre.

Ann & Bill Morris
Bowett Farm,
Hundleton, Pembroke,
Pembrokeshire SA71 5QS

Tel	01646 683473
Fax	01646 683473
Email	bowett@pembrokeshire.com
Web	www.bowettfarmhouse.co.uk

Map 6   Entry 648

Pembrokeshire

Penfro

This is fun – idiosyncratic and a tad theatrical, rather than conventional and uniformly stylish. The Lappins' home is a tall, impressive Grade II*-listed Georgian affair, formerly a ballet school. Judith's taste – she's also a WW1 expert – is eclectic verging on the wacky and she minds that guests are comfortable and well-fed. You eat communally, and very well, at the big scrubbed table in the flagged, Aga-fired kitchen at garden level… the garden's big and beautiful so enjoy its conversational terrace and hammocks. And discuss which of the three very characterful bedrooms will suit you best, plumbing and all!

Price	£60–£85. Singles from £45.
Rooms	3: 1 double; 1 double, 1 twin both with separate bathroom.
Meals	Packed lunch from £5. Pub 250 yds.
Closed	Rarely.
Directions	A4075 Pembroke; 2 miles to mini r'bout. Straight ahead, down hill, bear right. Right lane past castle; T-junc. on right. Road widens by Chapel Pembroke Antique Centre. House on right.

Judith Lappin
Penfro,
111 Main Street, Pembroke,
Pembrokeshire SA71 4DB

Tel	01646 682753
Mobile	07763 856181
Email	info@penfro.co.uk
Web	www.penfro.co.uk

Map 6   Entry 649

Pembrokeshire

Cresswell House

'Make yourself at home' is Philip's style: easy to do in the old quay master's house with its laid-back clutter and estuary views. The Wights have decorated boldly but with respect for the Georgian interior, and the bedrooms are carpeted and cosy, one with an antique iron four-poster. Bread from a coal-fired oven and suppers delicious and wholesome: perhaps their own wild smoked salmon and home-grown veg. Picnic at the end of the garden amid kingfishers, herons and curlews. It's fun and easy, the setting is wonderful and there's a lively little pub (no food) two minutes away.

Price	£70–£85. Singles £50.
Rooms	3: 1 double, 1 four-poster; 1 twin with separate bath/shower.
Meals	Supper £15. Dinner, 3 courses, £30. Pub 2 miles.
Closed	Occasionally.
Directions	From A477, right onto A4075. Left at brown sign for Cresswell House; on left after 1.4 miles, just before bridge.

	Philip Wight
	Cresswell House,
	Cresswell Quay,
	Pembroke,
	Pembrokeshire SA68 0TE
Tel	01646 651435
Email	phil@cresswellhouse.co.uk
Web	www.cresswellhouse.co.uk

Map 6   Entry 650

Pembrokeshire

Furzehill Farm

Horse experts Val and Paul's new-build farmhouse is a friendly place for families and walkers. The Aga-driven kitchen is the hub and Paul will do you a grand breakfast, and something tasty and local for supper too. There are hunting prints, a modern leather sofa and a brick-surround open fire in the sitting room, and cosy carpeted bedrooms upstairs – one with a shower, two sharing a jazzy jacuzzi. Eco credentials include ground-sourced heating and the young garden promises an above-ground pool. This is a deeply rural spot with a good pub to walk to and the birds of the lovely Cleddau Estuary to admire.

Price	£60–£90. Singles from £30.
Rooms	3: 1 family for 4; 1 double, 1 room with bunkbeds, sharing separate bath.
Meals	Dinner & packed lunch available. Pub/restaurant 3 miles.
Closed	Christmas Day.
Directions	A40 to Canaston Bridge. Right on 4075 (Pembroke & Oakwood). Right at Crosshands; after sharp bend, left (Lawrenny & Cresswell Quay); left again at T-junc (Cresswell Quay). 2nd entrance on left.

	E V Rees
	Furzehill Farm,
	Martletwy, Narberth, Pembrokeshire SA67 8AN
Tel	01834 891480
Mobile	07887 592218
Email	val@furzehillfarm.com
Web	www.furzehillfarm.com

Map 6   Entry 651

Pembrokeshire

Knowles Farm

Two charming owners, great food, sparkling night skies and a quirky pub a short drive. The Cleddau estuary winds its way around this 1,000-acre organic farm – its lush grasses feed the cows that produce milk for the renowned Rachel's Dairy. Your hosts love the area, are passionate about its conservation and let you come and go as you please; picnic in the garden, explore the woods. Gini rustles up scrumptious organic dinners and serves them at a candlelit table that seats 12. Bedrooms are simple and well-maintained, with comfy beds and fresh woodland flowers. Traditional, real-farmhouse B&B.

Price	£54-£64. Singles £27-£35.
Rooms	3: 2 doubles;
	1 twin with separate bath.
Meals	Supper from £12.
	Dinner, 4 courses, £22.
	Packed lunch £6.
	Pub 1.5 miles, restaurant 3 miles.
Closed	Rarely.
Directions	A4075 to Cresselly; turn right.
	Follow signs for Lawrenny to first
	x-roads; straight over; next x-roads
	right; 100 yds on left.

Ms Virginia Lort Phillips
Knowles Farm,
Lawrenny,
Pembrokeshire SA68 0PX
Tel   01834 891221
Fax   01834 891221
Email   ginilp@lawrenny.org.uk
Web   www.lawrenny.org.uk

Map 6   Entry 652

Pembrokeshire

Pentower

Curl up with a cat and watch the ferries coasting to Ireland; porpoises, too, may be spotted! French windows open onto the terrace and a glorious vista stretches out before you. Mary and Tony are easy-going and fun and have done an excellent restoration on the turreted 1898 house, keeping its quarry tiled floors, decorative fireplaces and impressive staircase. Pretty bedrooms are light and airy, with ample wardrobes and huge showers; the Tower Room has the views. There's a tiled dining/sitting room for full English (or Welsh) breakfasts, a 'temple' in the garden for summer and Fishguard is a stroll away.

Price	£65-£70. Singles £40.
Rooms	3: 2 doubles, 1 twin.
Meals	Packed lunch £5.
	Pubs/restaurants 500 yds.
Closed	Rarely.
Directions	A40 to Fishguard town; at r'bout,
	2nd exit onto Main Street. Before
	sharp left bend, right fork onto
	Tower Hill; 200 yds on, through
	house gates.

Tony Jacobs & Mary Geraldine Casey
Pentower,
Tower Hill,
Fishguard,
Pembrokeshire SA65 9LA
Tel   01348 874462
Email   sales@pentower.co.uk
Web   www.pentower.co.uk

Map 6   Entry 653

Powys

Talbontdrain

Way off the beaten track, remote and wild, sits a white-painted stone farmhouse. The Cambrian mountains stretch to the south, the river Dovey lies in the vale below and kind Hilary knows all the walks and can sort special routes for you. She cooks a hearty breakfast too, or a farmhouse supper, and gives you colourful bedrooms – not swish, but with everything you need. There are photographs of garden plants, a pianola, and furniture in such a mix of styles that it all gives a feeling of great informality. The peace is deep – even the cockerel stays quiet until a respectable time – and walkers will adore it.

Price	£52-£60. Singles £26.
Rooms	4: 1 double, 1 family room for 3; 1 twin/double, 1 single sharing shower.
Meals	Dinner, 2 courses & coffee, £16. Packed lunch £6.
Closed	Christmas & Boxing Day.
Directions	Leaving Machynlleth on A489, 1st right signed Forge. In Forge bear right to Uwchygarreg up 'dead end'. 3 miles, pass phone box on left, up steep hill. House on left at top.

Hilary Matthews
Talbontdrain,
Uwchygarreg,
Machynlleth,
Powys SY20 8RR
Tel   01654 702192
Email   hilary@talbontdrain.co.uk
Web   www.talbontdrain.co.uk

Map 8   Entry 654

Powys

The Old Vicarage

Offa's Dyke and the Ridgeway are on the doorstep and Tim and Helen have a passion for food (for years they ran a celebrated pub restaurant). Inside the florid-red Victorian vicarage, light-filled rooms combine period details with modern pizzazz. Traditional wallpapers and cast-iron fireplaces mix with silk-covered headboards and jewel-coloured cushions. Bathrooms are smart with big shower heads; the dining room is all polished tables and gleaming glass. Take breakfast, or an aperitif, in the garden with stunning views. Relaxed indulgence and two generous hosts. *Children over 12 welcome.*

Price	£90-£110. Singles from £60.
Rooms	3: 1 twin/double, 2 doubles.
Meals	Dinner, 4 courses, £30. Packed lunch available.
Closed	Rarely.
Directions	A483, 3.5 miles from Newtown towards Llandrindod Wells, left on sharp right bend, house first on left.

Tim & Helen Withers
The Old Vicarage,
Dolfor, Newtown,
Powys SY16 4BN
Tel   01686 629051
Mobile 07753 760054
Email   tim@theoldvicaragedolfor.co.uk
Web   www.theoldvicaragedolfor.co.uk

Map 7   Entry 655

Powys

Cwmllechwedd Fawr

Wild Wales at its best – drive across the moor where the ponies run free. This is a place for big walks and fresh air – where healthy appetites will be rewarded with wholesome and delicious food, much courtesy of the organic vegetable plot. It's an 1815 house on a working farm, so expect sheep dogs, chickens and cats in the yard. Inside, a breakfast table by a warm Aga, a dining table on worn slate flags, a sitting room cosy with piano and books. Bedrooms have plain wooden furniture and colourful rugs. For summer, a large sheltered terrace with long, lush views. Good people, great value.

Price	£60. Singles £35.
Rooms	2: 1 double, 1 twin/double.
Meals	Dinner, 3 courses, £18. BYO.
Closed	Rarely.
Directions	From A483 to Llanbister on B4356. Follow for 2 miles past chapel on right; across common. Immed. sharp left to Llanbadarn Fynydd; follow hedge on right for 0.3 miles to gate.

John Rath & John Underwood
Cwmllechwedd Fawr,
Llanbister, Llandrindod Wells,
Powys LD1 6UH

Tel	01597 840267
Fax	01597 840267
Email	postmaster@cwmllechwedd.u-net.com
Web	www.cwmllechwedd.u-net.com

Map 7 Entry 656

Powys

The Old Vicarage

For devotees of Victoriana, the house, designed by Sir George Gilbert Scott, is a delight. Your host, charming and fun, ushers you in to a rich confection of colours, dark wood and a lifetime's collecting: you could stay here a dozen times and still see something new. Splendid brass beds, cast-iron radiators, porcelain loos, sumptuous bedspreads and a garden with grotto, waterfall and rill. Dine by candlelight (the food is superb), ring the servants' bell for early morning tea. You are on the English side of Offa's Dyke: look north to the heavenly Radnorshire hills, south to all of Herefordshire.

Price	From £88.
Rooms	3: 2 doubles, 1 twin.
Meals	Dinner, 4 courses, £32.50. Restaurant 10-minute drive.
Closed	Rarely.
Directions	B4355, between Presteigne & Knighton; in village of Norton, immed. north of church.

Paul Gerrard
The Old Vicarage,
Norton, Presteigne,
Radnorshire,
Powys LD8 2EN

Tel	01544 260038
Email	oldvicarage@nortonrads.fsnet.co.uk
Web	www.oldvicarage-nortonrads.co.uk

Map 7 Entry 657

Powys

Trericket Mill Vegetarian Guesthouse

Part guest house, part bunk house, all very informal – all Grade II*-listed. The dining room has been created amid a jumble of corn-milling machinery: B&B guests, campers and bunkers pile in together to fill hungry bellies with Nicky and Alistair's delicious and plentiful veggie food from a chalkboard menu. Stoves throw out the heat in the flagstoned living rooms with their comfy chairs; the bedrooms are simple pine affairs. Set out to explore from here on foot, horseback, bicycle or canoe; lovers of the outdoors looking for good value and a planet-friendly bias will be in heaven.

Price	£58-£69. Singles £39-£47.
Rooms	3: 2 doubles, 1 twin.
Meals	Dinner, 3 courses, £17.50. Simple supper £7.50. Pub/restaurant 2 miles.
Closed	Christmas.
Directions	12 miles north of Brecon on A470. Mill set slightly back from road, on left, between Llyswen & Erwood. Train to Llandrindod Wells; bus to Brecon every 2 hrs will drop at mill on request.

Alistair & Nicky Legge
Trericket Mill Vegetarian Guesthouse,
Erwood, Builth Wells,
Powys LD2 3TQ

Tel	01982 560312
Email	mail@trericket.co.uk
Web	www.trericket.co.uk

Map 7   Entry 658

Powys

Hafod Y Garreg

A unique opportunity to stay in the oldest house in Wales – a 1402 cruck-framed hall house, built for Henry IV as a hunting lodge. Annie and John have filled it with a fascinating mix of Venetian mirrors, Indian rugs, pewter plates, gorgeous fabrics and oak furniture. Dine by candlelight – maybe pheasant pie with chilli jam and hazelnut mash: delicious. Beds have antique patchwork quilts, one bedroom has a dramatic half-tester. You reach the Grade II*-listed house by a bumpy off-road track across gated fields crowded with chickens, cats, goats, birds… a very special, secluded place.

Price	£60. Family room £78. Singles from £50.
Rooms	2: 1 double, 1 family room.
Meals	Dinner, 3 courses, £18.50. BYO. Pubs/restaurants 2.5 miles.
Closed	Christmas.
Directions	From Hay-on-Wye, A479 then A470 to B. Wells. Through Llyswen, past forest on left, down hill. Next left for Trericket Mill, then immed. right & up hill. Straight through gate across track to house.

Annie & John McKay
Hafod Y Garreg,
Erwood, Builth Wells,
Powys LD2 3TQ

Tel	01982 560400
Email	john-annie@hafod-y.wanadoo.co.uk
Web	www.hafodygarreg.co.uk

Map 7   Entry 659

Powys

The Old Post Office

Gleaming oak floors and staircases are proud features of the little guest house that began life as an inn. Bedrooms are large, simple and fresh, beds comfortable, colours earthy. There's a restful sitting room in which exhausted hikers and their dogs can collapse after a recce in the Black Mountains, while bookworms can seek out the second-hand bookshops of Hay-on-Wye. Whatever you do, you'll be captivated by the region. Linda serves sumptuous vegetarian breakfasts in a cosy, cottagey dining room; she and Ed tend to keep to their own part of the house and you come and go as you please.

Price	£70. Singles from £35.
Rooms	3: 1 double, 1 twin/double, 1 double (extra bed).
Meals	Pub 2 miles. Pubs/restaurants in Hay-on-Wye.
Closed	Rarely.
Directions	Hay-on-Wye to Brecon; 0.5 miles, left, signed Llanigon; on for 1 mile, left before school. On right opp. church.

Linda Webb & Ed Moore
The Old Post Office,
Llanigon,
Hay-on-Wye,
Powys HR3 5QA
Tel   01497 820008
Web   www.oldpost-office.co.uk

Map 7   Entry 660

Powys

Tyr Chanter

Warmth, colour, children and activity: this house is fun. Tiggy welcomes you like family; help collect eggs, feed the lambs or the pony, drop your shoes by the fire. The farmhouse and barn are stylishly relaxed; deep sofas, tartan throws, heaps of books, views to the Brecon Beacons and Black Mountains. Bedrooms are soft, simple sanctuaries with Jo Malone bathroom treats. Children's rooms zing with murals; toys, kids' sitting room, sandpit — child heaven. Walk, fish, canoe, book-browse in Hay or stroll the estate. Homemade cakes, whisky to help yourself to: fine hospitality.

Price	£80. Singles £55.
Rooms	4: 1 double; 1 double with separate bath/shower; 2 children's rooms.
Meals	Packed lunch £6. Pub 1 mile.
Closed	Christmas.
Directions	From Crickhowell, A40 towards Brecon. 2 miles left at Gliffaes Hotel sign. 2 miles, past hotel, house is 600 yds on right.

Tiggy Pettifer
Tyr Chanter,
Gliffaes, Crickhowell,
Powys NP8 1RL
Tel   01874 731144
Email   tiggy@tyrchanter.com
Web   www.tyrchanter.com

Map 7   Entry 661

Powys

Llangattock Court

Built in 1690 and mentioned in Pevsner as an 'outstanding example of a country house in this style', this is indeed grand and sits in the middle of the sleepy village, surrounded by a large garden. Both bedrooms are a good size (one has a big French bed and a small shower room) with lovely antiques and a fresh feel; views from one soar across to the Black Mountains. Breakfast in style in the enormous dining room overlooked by framed relatives, stroll through the rose garden, visit a castle or historic house, walk to the local pub for dinner. Morgan is a painter; some of his paintings are on display.

Price	£50-£80. Singles £45.
Rooms	2: 1 double, 1 family suite for 3-4.
Meals	Restaurants/pubs within 1 mile.
Closed	Christmas & New Year; 1-2 weeks October.
Directions	Enter Crickhowell village from B4777. Horseshoe Inn on right; after 60 yds, turn right. Then right 50 yds beyond church. House first on left.

Polly Llewellyn
Llangattock Court,
Llangattock,
Crickhowell, Powys NP8 1PH
Tel 01873 810116
Email morganllewellyn@btinternet.com
Web www.llangattockcourt.co.uk

Map 7 Entry 662

Wrexham

Worthenbury Manor

Homemade bread and Hepplewhite! This is a good, solid house of generous proportions and your hosts live in part of it. Wallow in an antique oak four-poster in a rose-carpeted, chandeliered bedroom full of comfort (books, games and flowers adding a cosy touch) and breakfast on local bacon, sausages and black pudding. Ian, history buff and ex-chef, is gentle, thoughtful and looks after you properly; dinner is quite an occasion. The listed house is close to Chester yet in a quiet, birdsung setting; the original building was enlarged in the 1890s in the William and Mary revival style.

Price	£60-£80. Singles £38-£49.
Rooms	2: 1 four-poster; 1 four-poster with separate bath.
Meals	Dinner, 3 courses, £20. Lunch £12.
Closed	December-February.
Directions	Between A525 Whitchurch-Wrexham & A41 Whitchurch-Chester, on B5069 between Bangor-on-Dee (also called Bangor-is-y-coed) and Malpas. On right before bridge.

Elizabeth & Ian Taylor
Worthenbury Manor,
Worthenbury,
Wrexham LL13 0AW
Tel 01948 770342
Email enquiries@worthenburymanor.co.uk
Web www.worthenburymanor.co.uk

Map 7 Entry 663

By accepting their pledge, we are relying on owners' integrity and honesty to keep to the points listed below. It's not a perfect scheme but the message is right – that it is important to choose food carefully and support local economies. Over 500 owners have signed the pledge. Please understand that those who have not signed the pledge have done so for a variety of reasons and this does not mean they do not provide delicious breakfasts, too.

Fine Breakfast Scheme – Pledge

1. I promise to try and serve breakfasts of the best available ingredients – whether organic or locally sourced.

2. Any certified organic ingredients will be named as such. (Note that the word 'organic' is a legal term. Any uncertified 'organic' ingredients cannot be described as organic.) Where there is a choice of organic certifier I will prefer the Soil Association if possible, recognising that their standards are generally the most demanding.

3. All other ingredients will be, whenever reasonably possible, sourced locally from people/institutions that I know personally or have good reason to believe only provide food of the best quality.

4. Where I have grown food myself I will say so.

5. I will do my best to avoid shopping in supermarkets if good alternatives exist within a reasonable distance.

7. I know that the scheme is an imperfect instrument but accept its principles.

Photo: Dreamstime.com

"My God is the God of Walkers. If you walk hard enough, you probably don't need any other god."
Bruce Chatwin, *In Patagonia*, 1977

It's official. Walking is good for us. Or so the government now tell us, kindly, gently, as if to nincompoops. And why, according to our masters, is it good for us? For our health of course!

Health – the new youth – has thousands of column inches devoted to it every day, entire magazines eager to explain it and suggest a myriad of ways to achieve it, an industry, in fact, keen to make money out of it. Strange how once something becomes official, it can lose its sense of fun.

For walking is about much more than one's physical health and wellbeing. Any real walker will tell you that. There must be, I'm sure, some people who really

don't notice their surroundings as they thunder along, in full Lycra, with an ungainly, power-walk gait; even one or two poor souls who can actually walk a coastal path and think only of how many miles they have under their belt and at what speed they achieved them – but I suspect they are in the minority. I hope they are.

Real walkers know that walking is a joy: anyone can do it, from the age of about one year onwards, while they can still put one foot in front of the other and breathe. It's free and can be done anywhere. You don't need to have a coastal path, although they are spectacular: it can be in town; it doesn't need to be solitary, for some of the most meaningful talks can unravel while walking: you can be pushing a buggy, trying to train a dog, cajoling a toddler, or hoping an elderly person will hurry up. The only real rule is that you need space to keep going if you want, and so it makes sense to do it out of doors. There isn't even any time limit. Walking late at night along city streets can be just as rewarding as a morning stroll along the beach.

Walking puts us in touch with life in a way that driving a car and (I am aware that cyclists may dispute this) riding a bike does not. There is the question of speed, for instance. When we're driving, or cycling full pelt, we do not often stop for a chat with a neighbour, or linger to smell a rose. We couldn't give our dog

Photo: britainonview/ McCormick-McAdam

ten minutes to play with a stranger's dog while we chatted to the stranger about the joys of owning a dog. We would not be able to gaze around us at the trees and flowers, at the landscape. In this way we cut ourselves off from our surroundings as well as from our fellow men.

The Slow Movement has had a lot of press over the last ten years. I would like to go one step further, and introduce the Stop Movement. When we are walking we can stop. If we choose we can make contact with other people, we can examine the slow progress of a beetle crawling up a leaf, we can just sniff the air and watch a bird, we can listen to the grumblings of an old friend, we can feel in touch – even when we are alone with our own thoughts.

In this book you will find places to stay from which you can take wonderful walks. Many of our owners will also provide you with maps, details of good places to stop for a pint or a cup of tea, and they may even be prepared to drop you off somewhere or collect you later. Packed lunches are on offer at over 130 of these special places and you can start many of the walks from the door. And it's not just the obvious areas, like the Lake District or the National Parks, that are good for walking. City walks are often a wonderful way to see architecture from a different perspective, or discover alley ways and parks, docks and cemeteries. Suburbs are a great place for walking, especially if you enjoy gardening, as it

gives you a chance to peek over walls and fences to enjoy other people's plants – in fact, I have one friend who taught her children the names of flowers and trees just from walking around the city they live in and looking at people's gardens.

Expensive kit is not necessary unless you are planning to go high (in which case you may need the warmth of a really good windproof jacket), although in wet weather it is useful to have waterproofs. What is essential is a pair of comfortable shoes or boots, and these should be broken in slowly, perhaps by wearing them around the house or for short walks at first.

We had an email recently from an owner who had been on a family walking holiday to Cornwall and chose not to take the car. The whole family left the house, walked to the station, got the train down to Cornwall and then spent four days walking the coastal path and stopping at B&Bs for the night. Each morning, refreshed after a good sleep and a hearty breakfast, they set off with a packed lunch for the next destination. They declared it the best family holiday ever. And why not? Losing your car and taking to your feet is a wonderfully free feeling, and has the added benefit of restricting the amount of luggage you take – so less washing when you get home!

Many walkers insist there is a spiritual element to walking, and I agree with them. Whether we believe in a higher power or not it is hard to stroll through creation without questioning how it all got there and what our part in it all is. Some religions believe that prayer is asking God for something and meditation is opening ourselves up to receive an answer. When we are walking we are meditating, even if we don't expect to get answers, and in that way we open ourselves up like flowers to the sun.

So, if you want to get a bit fitter, get in touch with your own thoughts – or somebody else's – enjoy better views of countryside, city or suburbs, align yourself with the rhythms of nature and the seasons, see animals in their natural habitat, study birds, possibly open up a bit spiritually – and the list goes on – then you can do no better than get your walking boots on.

Photo: Wales Tourist Board

Wheelchair-accessible

At least one bedroom and bathroom accessible for wheelchair users. Phone for details.

On a budget?

These places have a double room for £70 or under.

Quick reference indices

Quick reference indices

All day
You can stay all day at these places if you wish.

Scotland

Wales

Singles

These places either have a single room or charge no single supplement.

England

Quick reference indices

Quick reference indices

Scotland

Wales

WiFi
Wireless internet access available for guests.

England

Scotland

Wales

National Cycle Network
These Special Places are within two miles of the NCN.

England

Quick reference indices

Quick reference indices

On road section

Traffic-free sections

Proposed routes

Edinburgh

Belfast

Cardiff

London

sus**trans**

JOIN THE MOVEMENT

If you have any comments on entries in this guide, please tell us. If you have a favourite bed & breakfast place or a new discovery, please let us know about it. You can return this form or visit www.sawdays.co.uk.

Existing entry

Property name: _____

Entry number: _____ Date of visit: _____

New recommendation

Property name: _____

Address: _____

_____

Tel: _____

Your comments

What did you like (or dislike) about this place? Were the people friendly? What was the location like? What sort of food did they serve?

_____

_____

_____

_____

_____

Your details

Name: _____

Address: _____

_____

_____ Postcode: _____

Tel: _____ Email: _____

Please send completed form to:
BBB, Sawday's, The Old Farmyard, Yanley Lane, Long Ashton, Bristol BS41 9LR, UK

Have you enjoyed this book? Why not try one of the others in the Special Places to Stay series and get 35% discount on the RRP *

British Bed & Breakfast (Ed 12)	RRP £14.99	Offer price £9.75
British Bed & Breakfast for Garden Lovers (Ed 4)	RRP £14.99	Offer price £9.75
British Hotels & Inns (Ed 9)	RRP £14.99	Offer price £9.75
Pubs & Inns of England & Wales (Ed 4)	RRP £14.99	Offer price £9.75
French Bed & Breakfast (Ed 10)	RRP £15.99	Offer price £10.40
French Holiday Homes (Ed 4)	RRP £14.99	Offer price £9.75
French Hotels (Ed 4)	RRP £14.99	Offer price £9.75
Paris Hotels (Ed 6)	RRP £10.99	Offer price £7.15
Spain (Ed 7)	RRP £14.99	Offer price £9.75
Italy (Ed 4)	RRP £14.99	Offer price £9.75
Portugal (Ed 4)	RRP £11.99	Offer price £7.80
Croatia (Ed 1)	RRP £11.99	Offer price £7.80
Greece (Ed 1)	RRP £11.99	Offer price £7.80
Turkey (Ed 1)	RRP £11.99	Offer price £7.80
Ireland (Ed 6)	RRP £12.99	Offer price £8.45
Morocco (Ed 2)	RRP £11.99	Offer price £7.80
India (Ed 2)	RRP £11.99	Offer price £7.80
Green Places to Stay (Ed 1)	RRP £13.99	Offer price £9.10

*postage and packing is added to each order

To order at the Reader's Discount price simply phone 01275 395431 and quote 'Reader Discount BBB'.

Alastair Sawday's Fragile Earth series

The Little Food Book   £6.99

"This is a really big little book. It is a good read and it will make your hair stand on end"
Jonathan Dimbleby

"...lifts the lid on the food industry to reveal some extraordinary goings-on"
John Humphrys

The Little Money Book   £6.99

"Anecdotal, humorous and enlightening, this book will have you sharing its gems with all your friends"
Permaculture Magazine

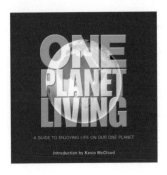

One Planet Living   £4.99

"Small but meaningful principles that will improve the quality of your life."
Country Living

"It is a pleasure to pick up and learn essential facts from."
Organic Life

To order any of the books in the Fragile Earth series call 01275 395431 or visit www.fragile-earth.com

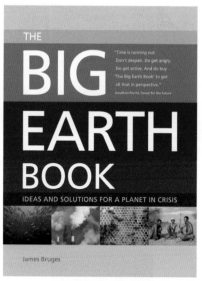

We all know the Earth is in crisis. We should know that it is big enough to sustain us if we can only mobilise politicians and economists to change course now. Expanding on the ideas developed in *The Little Earth Book,* this book explores environmental, economic and social ideas to save our planet. It helps us understand what is happening to the planet today, exposes the actions of corporations and the lack of action of governments, weighs up new technologies, and champions innovative and viable solutions. Tackling a huge range of subjects – it has the potential to become the seminal reference book on the state of the planet – it's the one and only environmental book you really need.

James Bruges's *The Little Earth Book* has sold over 40,000 copies and has been translated into eight languages.

Praise for *The Big Earth Book*:
"Time is running out. Don't despair. Do get angry. Do get active. And do buy *The Big Earth Book* to get all that in perspective." Jonathon Porritt, *Forum for the Future*

"This is a wonderful book – really informative but written in a very clear, easy-to-read way." Patrick Holden, *The Soil Association*

RRP £25.00 To order at the Reader's Discount price of £20 (plus p&tp) call 01275 395431 and quote 'Reader Discount BEB BBB'.

A whole week self-catering in Britain with your friends or family is precious, and you dare not get it wrong. To whom do you turn for advice and who on earth do you trust when the web is awash with advice from strangers? We launched Special Escapes to satisfy an obvious need for impartial and trustworthy help — and that is what it provides. The criteria for inclusion are the same as for our books: we have to like the place and the owners. It has, quite simply, to be 'special'. The site, our first online-only publication, is featured on www.thegoodwebguide.com and is growing fast.

Cosy cottages • Sumptuous castles • Tipis • Hilltop bothies • City apartments and more

www.special-escapes.co.uk

Alastair
Sawday's

Self-catering

As I write, swallows are nesting in our wood-pellet store, the fountain plays in the pond, tall grasses bend before a gentle breeze, and the solar panels heat water too hot to touch – even during a very dull summer. We have, to our delight, created an inspiring and serene place.

The roof was lifted to allow us to fix thick insulation panels beneath the tiles. More panels were fitted between the rafters and as a separate internal wall, and underfloor heating was laid. We are insulated for the Arctic, and almost totally airtight; we open windows for natural ventilation. A very economical Austrian heating boiler sucks in wood-pellets and slowly and cleanly consumes them. Rainwater is channelled to a 6000-litre underground tank and then, filtered, flushes loos and fills basins. Sun-pipes funnel the daylight into dark corners and double-glazed Velux windows pour it into every office. Our electricity consumption is extraordinarily low: we have attractive background lighting, and individual 'task' lights are used only as needed.

We began in the early 90s in a small terraced house in Bristol and then, straining at the seams, decamped to a farm five miles away in the countryside. Beautiful as they were, our new offices leaked heat, flooded whole rooms with light to illuminate one person, and were not ours to alter. We failed our eco-audit in spite of using recycled cooking oil in one car and gas in another, and recycling everything we could.

So we leapt at the chance to buy some old barns closer to Bristol, to create our own eco-offices and start again. Our accountants thought we were mad and there was no time for proper budgeting. The back of every envelope bore the signs of frenzied calculations, and then I shook hands with the farmer and went off on holiday. Two years later we moved in.

We built a green-oak barn between two old barns, and this has become the heart of the offices, warm, light and beautiful. Wood plays a major role: our simple oak desks were made by a local carpenter, my office floor is of oak, and there is oak panelling. Even the carpet tiles tell a story – they are made from the wool of Herdwick sheep from the Lake District. The hill farmers there suffered dreadfully

Photo above: Quentin Craven
Photo right: Tom Germain

during the Foot and Mouth outbreak and the National Trust, landlords to many of them, sought other sources of income for their tenants. The tough wool of the Herdwicks makes great carpet. The choice of other materials, too, was a focus: we used non-toxic paints and finishes and, however difficult they were to apply, they have proved to be gentle and beautiful to live with.

'Events' blew our budget apart, but we have a building of which we are proud and which helped us win two national awards in 2006. Architects and designers are fascinated and we work with a renewed commitment to our environmental policies. Best of all, we are now in a position to encourage our owners and readers to take 'sustainability' more seriously. It has been satisfying to see how much other people enjoy coming to the offices, and it is more and more the case that people applying to us for jobs are doing so because of where and how we work.

I end by answering an obvious question: our office carbon emissions will be reduced by about 75%. Our bills are low and, as time goes by, will be relatively lower – and lower. I am embarrassed to confess that we have not yet completed a new environmental audit, so I cannot report on exact savings. But we subscribe fully to the peak oil theory: that the rate of oil extraction has peaked, or is about to very soon, and we should all be pursuing ways of reducing our dependency on the stuff.

Cynics – and there are still plenty – tell me that there might have been better ways of spending our reserves than by putting them in to an eco-office. But it has been worth every penny and every ounce of effort. Becoming 'green' is a journey and, although we began long before most companies, we still have a long way to go. We would like to be a major influence on our owners, all 5,500 of them, and on our readers and web-users in the reduction of their own ecological footprints.

We need to be as loyal to our convictions as we are to our clients. We are not just a travel publisher. Like every other business, we are part of the community and have a wide responsibility.

Alastair Sawday

① Cumbria

Cumbria

Low Jock Scar

② A good breakfast, a drive off to the high Cumbria hills, the prospect of a slap-up dinner (fresh, local, great value) and a bed in a comfy room. As Low Jock Scar is folded into the leafy valley, so you are wrapped in the warmth of Philip and Alison's welcome. The 70s-built stone house is a homely haven for guests, with its cosy lounge and pretty conservatory for convivial meals. Floral bedrooms, one in the annexe, have garden views – and the gardens, six acres of woodland and burbling beck, are the Midwinters' pride and joy. They are the soul of kindness and run a tight and happy ship.

Middle Reston

A proper Edwardian summer house in the heart of the Lakes (Windermere is the nearest) set high and with mature rhododendrons. Inside is crammed with beautiful dark furniture, Turkish rugs, gorgeous paintings, oak overmantles and fires in every room. Two traditional bedrooms have claret walls and dark carpets; the yellow attic room is more modern; all are a good size and entirely quiet. Make yourselves at home in two huge drawing rooms. Ginny and Simon are great fun and give you a stylish breakfast; then explore the magic outside – especially in spring, with curtseying daffodils and bobbing lambs.

③ Price	£58-£70. Singles from £39.	
④ Rooms	4: 2 doubles, 1 twin; 1 twin/double with separate bath.	
⑤ Meals	Dinner, 5 courses, £23. Packed lunch £4.	
⑥ Closed	November-March.	
⑦ Directions	From Kendal, A6 to Penrith. After 5 miles, Plough Inn on left. After 1 mile turn into lane on left.	

Price	£70-£90.
Rooms	3: 1 double; 2 twins sharing bath.
Meals	Pub 2 miles.
Closed	Christmas & occasionally.
Directions	A591 Kendal-Windermere; 500 yds past 2nd Staveley turning, turn right by small blue bicycle sign, then immediately hard left up drive.

	Alison & Philip Midwinter Low Jock Scar, Selside, Kendal, Cumbria LA8 9LE
Tel	01539 823259
Fax	01539 823259
Email	ljs@avmail.co.uk

	Simon & Ginny Johnson Middle Reston, Staveley, Kendal, Cumbria LA8 9PT
Tel	01539 821246
Fax	01539 821809
Email	simonhj@btinternet.com
Web	www.lake-district-accomodation.com

⑧ 🚶 ✗ 📖 🍷 🐷 🍷 🐕 🐕

🚂 🍷 🐕 🐕

⑨ Map 11   Entry 80

Map 11   Entry 81